D1795505

JUDGMENT AND DECISION MAKING

Neo-Brunswikian and Process-Tracing Approaches

JUDGMENT AND
DECISION MAKING

Neo-Brunswikian and Process-Tracing Approaches

Edited by

Peter Juslin
Uppsala University, Sweden

Henry Montgomery
University of Stockholm, Sweden

1999

LAWRENCE ERLBAUM ASSOCIATES, PUBLISHERS
Mahwah, New Jersey   London

Copyright © 1999 by Lawrence Erlbaum Associates, Inc.
All rights reserved. No part of the book may be reproduced in any form, by photostat, microform, retrieval system, or any other means, without the prior written permission of the publisher.

Lawrence Erlbaum Associates, Inc., Publishers
10 Industrial Avenue
Mahwah, New Jersey 07430

Cover design by Kathryn Houghtaling Lacey

Library of Congress Cataloging-in-Publication Data

Judgment and decision making : neo-Brunswikian and process-tracing approaches / edited by Peter Juslin, Henry Montgomery.
    p. cm.
  Includes bibliographical references and indexes.
  ISBN 0-8058-3254-8 (hardcover : alk paper)
  1. Decision making. 2. Judgment.   I. Juslin, Peter.
  II. Montgomery, Henry.
  BF448.J83 1999
  153.8'3--dc21   99-30900
                                        CIP

Books published by Lawrence Erlbaum Associates are printed on acid-free paper, and their bindings are chosen for strength and durability.

Printed in the United States of America
10   9   8   7   6   5   4   3   2   1

Contributors

Carl Martin Allwood *Department of Psychology, Lund University, Sweden*

Anders Biel *Department of Psychology, Göteborg University, Sweden*

Berndt Brehmer *Department of Operational Studies,   Swedish Defence College*

Baruch Fischhoff *Department of Social and Decision Studies, Carnegie-Mellon University*

Daniel Eek *Department of Psychology, Göteborg University, Sweden*

Pär Anders Granhag *Department of Psychology, Göteborg University, Sweden*

Tommy Gärling *Department of Psychology, Göteborg University, Sweden*

Kenneth R. Hammond *Center for Research on Judgment and Policy, University of Colorado, Boulder, Colorado*

Sven Hemlin *Department of Psychology, Göteborg University, Sweden*

Anders Jansson *Department of Human–Computer Interaction, Uppsala University, Sweden*

Peter Juslin *Department of Psychology, Uppsala University, Sweden*

Niklas Karlsson *Department of Psychology, Göteborg University, Sweden*

Henry Montgomery *Department of Psychology, Stockholm University, Sweden*

Henrik Olsson *Department of Psychology, Uppsala University, Sweden*

Giorgios Rigas *Department of Psychology, Uppsala University, Sweden*

Marcus Selart *Department of Psychology, Göteborg University, Sweden*

Lennart Sjöberg *Center for Risk Research and Department of Economic Psychology, Stockholm School of Economics*

Ola Svenson *Department of Psychology, Stockholm University, Sweden*

Helena Willén *Department of Health Sciences, Skövde University, Sweden*

Anders Winman *Department of Psychology, Uppsala University, Sweden*

To Mats Björkman

Contents

Chapter 1

Introduction and Historical Remarks

Peter Juslin
Uppsala University

Henry Montgomery
Stockholm University

Cognitive psychology is approaching its fortieth anniversary. In this relatively short period, the field has seen immense growth, and specialization into various subdomains like research on memory, problem solving, attention, and language acquisition. Moreover, cognitive psychology is starting to merge with other disciplines, as exemplified by the recent developments referred to as cognitive science and cognitive neuroscience. One of the remarkable features of Swedish work in cognitive psychology is the strong position of judgment and decision making (JDM) research, going back to Mats Björkman's studies of judgment in the sixties (e.g., Björkman, 1965). This observation is made not to de-emphasize the impact of contributions made by Swedes working in other areas, but only to point out that from an international perspective, problems of judgment and decision making have attracted the interest of a surprising number of researchers in Sweden. Their interest is reflected in the chapters of this volume.

Cognitive research on JDM has been greatly influenced by normative models for decision making under uncertainty derived from statistics and economics. The mother of all such normative models originates in Pascal's Wager from 1658 (Hacking, 1975), in which the idea of rational decision making as maximization of expected value is first presented. The modern incarnation of Pascal's idea—the theory of maximization of subjective expected utility (SEU theory)—imposes constraints on a person's decision making that allow the decisions to be interpreted as maximization in terms of a subjective utility function and a subjective probability measure (e.g.,

Savage, 1954). The strong influence of SEU theory on cognitive JDM research has had two important consequences: First, decision making has been conceived of in terms of the two main subcomponents of SEU theory; utility functions and subjective probabilities. Second, research has been guided by a normative/empirical approach, where human decision behavior is compared to the normative yardstick provided by SEU theory. Because SEU theory stresses the subjective nature of utility and probability, it is concerned with the coherence of preferences and beliefs, rather than the correspondence between subjective and environmental states (Hammond, 1996). The research inspired by SEU theory has produced an impressive list of phenomena that seem to demonstrate that human decision behavior violates the coherence requirements of SEU theory—in the popular jargon, that people are victims of cognitive biases (Kahneman, Slovic, & Tversky, 1982).

In view of this dominant influence of SEU theory on JDM research, it is interesting to note that Swedish JDM research has come to depart from this tradition, albeit in two rather different ways. One line of research introduced by Mats Björkman in the 1960s has been influenced by the probabilistic functionalism of Egon Brunswik (Brunswik, 1952; Hammond, 1966); the second line of research was inspired by the work on cognitive processes in other areas of cognitive psychology, primarily problem solving (Newell & Simon, 1972). Both of these traditions in Swedish JDM research are amply illustrated in the chapters of this volume.

NEO-BRUNSWIKIAN RESEARCH ON JUDGMENT AND DECISION MAKING

Chapters 2, 3, and 4 are concerned with dynamic decision making. The research reported in these chapters deviates from traditional JDM research in both of the aspects discussed above. The decision problem is no longer thought of in terms of utilities and probabilities, or maximization of an expected value, but in terms of prolonged interaction with a complex and dynamic system where the decision problem largely takes the form of attaining control of the system. Moreover, the coherence norm is replaced by an evaluation of the correspondence between the intended state of the system and the actual state. Chapter 2 (Brehmer) illustrates how people faced with a dynamic decision task develop simple and efficient heuristics that allow reasonable decision making, despite falling short of rationality as defined by SEU theory. In Chapter 3 (Jansson) research on dynamic decision is applied to the poorly structured problems encountered in everyday life, with a particular concern for the interaction between the goal formulation process and the formation of mental models. In Chapter 4

(Rigas and Brehmer), the puzzling relationship between psychometric intelligence and performance in dynamic decision tasks receives closer scrutiny. The research on dynamic decision making provides one example of a neo-Brunswikian concern with representative design (Brunswik, 1952). The simulation of dynamic systems is an attempt to present the participants in the laboratory with realistic samples of the causal texture of the environment, or at least samples with many properties in common with a real-life decision task.

A second area with a recent re-emergence of Brunswikian ideas is in research on realism or calibration of subjective probabilities (confidence). Subjective probability assessments are well calibrated to the extent that they are realized in terms of the corresponding relative frequencies; that is, in subjective probability category *.xx*, the event should occur with relative frequency *.xx*. The Brunswikian idea of representative design was introduced in the area by the so called ecological models (McClelland & Bolger, 1994), which propose that one important contributor to the overconfidence phenomenon is a violation of representative design. This research is still within the SEU paradigm in the sense of being concerned with subjective probabilities. However, the issue of calibration is approached with models that highlight the correspondence between subjective probabilities and ecological probabilities and thus transcends the traditional coherence norm of SEU theory.

Chapter 5 (Juslin and Olsson) presents theoretical models of calibration of subjective probabilities based on the distinction between Brunswikian and Thurstonian origins of uncertainty in judgment (Juslin & Olsson, 1997). Besides the ecological models, the chapter presents a number of computational models that add stochastic components to the judgment processes of the Brunswik-inspired ecological models (see Erev, Wallsten & Budescu, 1994, on stochastic components). In Chapter 6 (Winman and Juslin), a new model of the hindsight or "knew-it-all-along" phenomenon is presented. This model—the accuracy-assessment model (Winman, Juslin, & Björkman, 1998)—exemplifies the need to carefully understand what the participants are trying to achieve with their judgments, again a basic tenet of Brunswikian psychology. In hindsight experiments the participants may not only be concerned with reproducing the exact answers they selected in foresight (process simulation), but also with producing an overall response pattern that seems appropriate to the accuracy expected in the task. Chapter 6 (Allwood and Björhag) elaborates on how confidence judgments relate to a wider realm of behavior, where the context, social norms, and motivational factors become important. It is proposed that calibration of confidence is determined by multiple factors—reviewed and discussed in the chapter—go beyond what is captured by any current models of confidence in judgment.

PROCESS-TRACING IN HUMAN DECISION MAKING

In the early seventies, Svenson (1974) published a technical report, which subsequently was widely cited in JDM research. Svenson showed that think-aloud data could be used to study the cognitive processes in decision making. This work was continued by Montgomery and Svenson (1976), who proposed that decision making is a sequential process in which different decision rules and information processing strategies can be used at different points in time in order to minimize cognitive effort. This theoretical framework inspired the development of two cognitive process theories of human decision making, namely search for dominance structure (SDS) theory (Montgomery, 1983) and differentiation and consolidation (Diff Con) theory (Svenson, 1992). These theories are presented in Chapters 8 (Montgomery and Willén) and 9 (Svenson), respectively. Both theories stress that decision making is a constructive activity that aims to prepare the individual for efficient action. The theories differ in their view of the role of information structuring and how decision rules are used. SDS theory regards decision making as a search for a good structure (i.e., a structure in which one alternative is dominant). In this search, decision rules play a subordinate role. Diff Con theory views the structuring and the use of decision rules as separate activities, which in conjunction help the decision maker to find sufficient differentiation between the alternatives. Diff Con theory is also concerned with consolidation processes, following after the decision, a topic that is left aside in SDS theory. Chapter 8 also discusses a recent development of SDS theory—the perspective model—that in some respects bridges the gap between SDS theory and Diff Con theory.

The constructive and adaptive nature of JDM is further highlighted in the two chapters that follow. In Chapter 10, Gärling, Karlsson, and Selart investigate how people use mental accounts to control their actions in everyday economic decision making. The idea is that by assigning one's overall wealth into different mental accounts (e.g., current assets, current income, or future income), one will end up with different propensities to consume. Sjöberg criticizes the expectation models of attitude in Chapter 11. In line with SEU theory these models assume that attitudes are formed by combining relatively stable beliefs and values. In contrast, Sjöberg proposes that attitudes as well as values and beliefs are constructed from a common underlying image—the subjective associations connected with the attitude-object.

Chapters 12 through 14 posits JDM in a social context, where outcomes—in one way or another—are determined jointly by the decisions by several individuals. In Chapter 12, Biel, Eek, and Gärling investigate the role of norms as guides to decisions in social dilemmas that complement the evaluation of outcomes. They find that norms matter in social decision making, but in different ways depending on the context of the social dilemma (e.g., what is considered as a fair distribution of outcomes in one context may be perceived as unfair in another). In Chapter 12 Selart and Eek discuss how people who face social decisions (i.e., decision concerning justice) adapt to task and context factors. Finally, in Chapter 14 Hemlin applies JDM research and research on group processes to the peer-review process in science (e.g., at scientific journals and funding agencies). The volume ends with commentaries by Hammond and Fischhoff that serve to place the research presented in the volume into the grander picture of current trends in international JDM research. Hammond provides a penetrating discussion and criticism of the neo-Brunswikian research performed in Sweden, from the perspective of more traditional Brunswikian theory. Fischhoff elaborates on the characteristic features of Swedish JDM research in the process-tracing tradition.

The volume has been subdivided into three main sections. The first section presents chapters that stress the relationship between the laboratory task and the tasks people meet in their natural environments, and in other respects explicitly acknowledge a Brunswikian inheritance. The second section concentrates on JDM as a mental process, and mainly provides work in the tradition of process-tracing studies. The third section highlights the social aspects of JDM. The headings of these three sections are, of course, meant to convey central points of emphasis, and not to be imperative or exhaustive in any sense. Needless to say, "Brunswikians" are interested in mental processes and researchers in the process-tracing tradition acknowledge the importance of considering the natural context of JDM-processes.

The year during which this volume was prepared (1997) is not only the fortieth since the birth of cognitive psychology, but the seventieth since the birth of Mats Björkman—the researcher who pioneered Swedish JDM studies. The contributors to this volume are all colleagues, former doctoral students or "grand" students of Mats Björkman. It is therefore a great pleasure for us to dedicate this volume to him. We also acknowledge the support by the Swedish Council for Research in the Humanities and Social Sciences in the preparation of this volume.

REFERENCES

Björkman, M. (1965). Studies in predictive behavior. Explorations into predictive judgments based on estimation, categorization, and choice. *Scandinavian Journal of Psychology, 6,* 129–156.

Brunswik, E. (1952). *The conceptual framework of psychology.* Chicago: University of Chicago Press.

Erev, I., Wallsten, T. S., & Budescu, D. V. (1994). Simultaneous over- and underconfidence: The role of error in judgment processes. *Psychological Review, 101,* 519–527.

Hacking, I. (1975). *The emergence of probability*. London: Cambridge University Press.

Hammond, K. R. (1966). Probabilistic functionalism: Egon Brunswik's integration of the history, theory, and method of psychology. In K. R. Hammond (Ed.), *The psychology of Egon Brunswik*. New York: Holt, Rinehart, & Winston.

Hammond, K. R. (1996). *Human judgment and social policy: Irreducible uncertainty, inevitable error, unavoidable injustice*. New York: Oxford University Press.

Juslin, P., & Olsson, H. (1997). Thurstonian- and Brunswikian origins of uncertainty in judgment: A sensory sampling model of confidence in sensory discrimination, *Psychological Review, 104*, 344–366.

Kahneman, D., Slovic, P., & Tversky, A. (Eds.). (1982). *Judgment under uncertainty: heuristics-and-biases*. New York: Cambridge University Press.

McClelland, A. G. R., & Bolger, F. (1994). The calibration of subjective probabilities: Theories and models 1980–1993. In G. Wright & P. Ayton (Eds.), *Subjective probability* (pp. 453–482). Chichester: Wiley.

Montgomery, H. (1983). Decision rules and the search for a dominance structure: Towards a process model of decision making. In P. C. Humphreys, O. Svenson, & A. Vari (Eds.), *Analyzing and aiding decision processes* (pp. 343–369). Amsterdam: North-Holland.

Montgomery, H., & Svenson, O. (1976). On decison rules and information processing strategies for choices among multiattribute alternatives. *Scandinavian Journal of Psychology, 17*, 283–291.

Newell, A., & Simon, H. R. (1972). *Human problem solving*. Englewood Cliffs, NJ: Prentice-Hall.

Savage, L. J. (1954). *The foundations of statistics*. New York: Dower.

Svenson, O. (1974). *A note on think-aloud protocols obtained during the choice of a home*. Reports from the Psychological Laboratories, University of Stockholm, No. 421.

Svenson, O. (1992). Differentiation and Consolidation theory of human decision making: A frame of reference for the study of pre- and post-decision processes. *Acta Psychologica, 80*, 143–168.

Winman, A., Juslin, P., & Björkman. (1998). The confidence-hindsight mirror effect in judgment: An accuracy-assessment model for the "knew-it-all-along" phenomenon. *Journal of Experimental Psychology: Learning, Memory and Cognition, 24*, 415–431.

JUDGMENT AND DECISION MAKING IN AN ENVIRONMENTAL CONTEXT

Chapter 2

Reasonable Decision Making in Complex Environments

Berndt Brehmer
Swedish National Defence College

A core element in psychological research on decision making has been comparisons between actual decision behavior and the decision behavior prescribed by normative models. For reasons yet to be discovered by historians, the normative models (usually some form of expected utility theory) acquired the status of standards of rationality, and deviations from what was prescribed by these models was seen as evidence that man was an irrational decision maker. While there is no dearth of examples of less-than-perfect decisions even in high places where experienced decision makers operate, the state of the world nevertheless does not seem to be quite as bad as one would expect from the hypothesis that people are incompetent and irrational decision makers. Nor is there any evidence that the bad decisions that we observe stem from any unwillingness to adhere to the favorite normative theories of psychologists, such as expected utility theory (see von Winterfeldt and Edwards, 1993, for arguments concerning expected utility theory, but see also Einhorn and Hogarth, 1981, for a discussion of the problems involved in applying normative theory in the "real world").

The focus on comparisons between normative theories and actual decision behavior has had two unfortunate consequences. First, it has narrowed psychologists' conception of what a decision is; it has limited the study of decision making to situations that confront the decision maker with a dilemma, and where the decision maker's task is to generate all possible courses of action, evaluate these, and then pick one according to some criterion (usually maximum expected utility). Second, it has turned psychologists' attention away from what should be their special task, that of studying what people do when confronted with decision problems. As a consequence, despite nearly 50 years of decision research, we do not know very much about what people actually do when making decisions. Instead, we have sat in judgment on people as decision makers and arrived at a general characterization of people as decision makers that is probably based on too limited a sample of decision situations and normative theories.[1]

The present chapter takes a different approach. First, it is concerned with decision making in dynamic tasks, a form of decision tasks that is very different from the choice tasks that have been dictated by prevailing normative theories of decision making. Second, it is concerned with what people actually do in these kinds of tasks, rather than with the optimality of their decisions. As we examine their behavior, we shall find that although this behavior may not be optimal, it is at least reasonable in the sense that it "gets the job done." It is argued that such reasonable, but perhaps not optimal, forms of decision making give a more useful conception of how actual decisions are made, and that they explain why the world is not in the sad state that we would expect from the blanket statement than man is an irrational and incompetent decision maker.[2]

DYNAMIC DECISION MAKING

As noted by Edwards (1961), decisions in real life occurs in sequences, and information available for later decisions is likely to be contingent on the nature and consequences of earlier ones. That is, the decisions in real life are likely to be dynamic, rather than static, one-shot affairs. The present chapter follows Edwards's lead, and focuses on dynamic decision making as the kind of task with which we are likely to learn the most about human decision making.

Dynamic decision tasks have three important characteristics (Brehmer & Allard, 1991):

- they require a series of interdependent decisions;
- the state of the task changes, both autonomously and as a consequence of the decision maker's actions;
- the decisions have to be made in real time.

An example will clarify this. Consider the decision problems facing a fire chief charged with extinguishing forest fires. He receives information about fires from a spotter plane, and on the basis of this information he sends out his fire-fighting units. These units then report back to him about their location and activities, and from these reports, the fire chief issues new commands to the units, and this goes on until the fire has been extinguished.

This problem has all of the characteristics of a dynamic problem defined above. Thus, the fire chief has to make a series of decisions sending his fire-fighting units to wherever they are needed. His decisions are interdependent: sending a fire-fighting unit to one location precludes his using it in another location. There is, of course, a positive aspect here too: later decisions can be used to remedy the problems caused by earlier decisions. The state of the fire changes, both autonomously—for example, as a consequence of the weather conditions—and as a consequence of the decision maker's actions—that is, the fire chief's use of his fire-fighting resources. Finally, the decisions have to be made in real time. The fire-fighting units have to be sent to the fire so that they are in place when and where they are needed. If they come too early, they cannot do anything useful, and if they arrive too late, the fire will have grown so large that it may not be possible to extinguish it with the resources sent out. Time is thus of the essence.

NEWFIRE: A MICROWORLD FOR STUDYING DYNAMIC DECISION MAKING

To study these problems, we (Brehmer & Allard, 1991; Løvborg & Brehmer, 1991) have developed a so-called microworld for experiments on dynamic decision making. A microworld (Brehmer & Dörner, 1993) is a computer simulation of a system. It is not designed to be a full-fidelity simulation. Instead, it is related to the system that it simulates in the same way as a woodcut is related to what it represents (Dörner, 1996). That is, it incorporates the main features so that it is possible to recognize what is being simulated, but there is no detail. The latter aspect is important because it means that no special knowledge, for example, about the characteristics of various forms of fire-fighting equipment, is needed to take part in the experiment, and that participants can perform in the simulation with very little training.

The microworld in question is called NEWFIRE (Løvborg & Brehmer, 1991). It is designed to study how people handle spatiotemporal problems, of which fighting forest fires is but one example. Other examples are cleaning up oil spills and engaging in battle. Fig. 2.1 shows how the problem is represented to the participant on the computer screen.

The main part of the screen is taken up by a stylized map of a forest area. Somewhere on the map, we find the base where the fire chief (= the participant) is located. The participant has a number of fire-fighting units at his disposal. He sends out these units by pointing and clicking with the

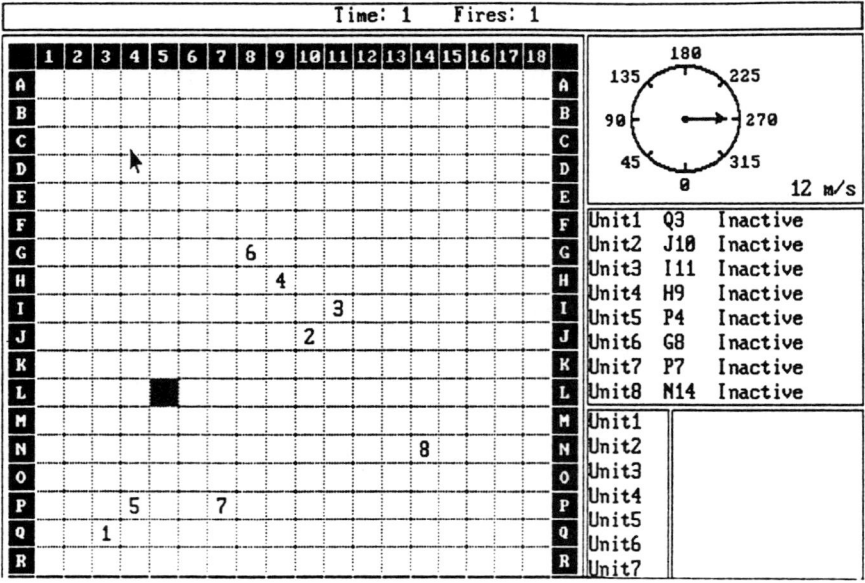

FIG. 2.1. NEWFIRE as seen by the participant on the computer screen.
The numbers show the positions of the fire-fighting units (on the screen
these cells are blue). The solid square indicates the position of the base
(this is brown on the screen). Fire ignition is indicated by a square turning
red; subsequent squares then turn red as the fire spreads. The direction
and speed of the wind is shown in the top panel to the left. The next panel
shows messages from the fire-fighting units, and the bottom panel is where
it is possible to get information about fire fighting units when they are in
the same location.

mouse. The unit then changes color and starts moving, and a message
appears in the lower status table informing the participant that the unit
is on the move. When the unit reaches its destination, and if there is fire
in that destination (or when the fire reaches the square where the unit is
located), it automatically first mobilizes, then fights the fire, and demobi-
lizes. When it has demobilized, it will respond to new commands. This is
signaled by its returning to the original blue color. The participant thus
does not have to be concerned with the specifics of the fire-fighting, but
only with the general spatiotemporal aspects—that is, making sure that
enough fire-fighting units have been sent to the right location at the right
time. In the simulation, the fire model is as close to actual fire models
that we have been able to make it, and it responds to the speed and
direction of the wind and to the nature of the forest (parameters in the
program). It is also possible to vary the characteristics of the fire-fighting

units (the speed at which they move, the time required to extinguish fire, and so on). Finally it is also possible to vary the location of the base and the starting positions of the fire-fighting units. In short, the simulation enables the experimenter to create the scenarios that are required for his or her purposes.

NEWFIRE is a clock-driven simulation: it does not stop and wait for the participant to respond. In experiments with NEWFIRE, participants are given two goals: to protect the base (if the fire reaches the base, the fire chief cannot control his units any more) and to extinguish the fire(s) as quickly as possible. The problem that the participant faces is illustrated in Fig. 2.2. In this time–area diagram, we see how the fire spreads in the simplest case, that of a homogeneous forest with no changes in wind direction or speed. In addition, we see how the area that can be covered by the fire-fighting units changes over time. The slope of the fire function shows the rate at which the fire spreads, and the slope of the fire-fighting function shows the rate at which the fire-fighting units are able to cover area with water (or whatever they are using to extinguish the fire). The intercept of the fire-fighting function is proportional to the number of fire-fighting units (assuming that they are equally efficient). As explained

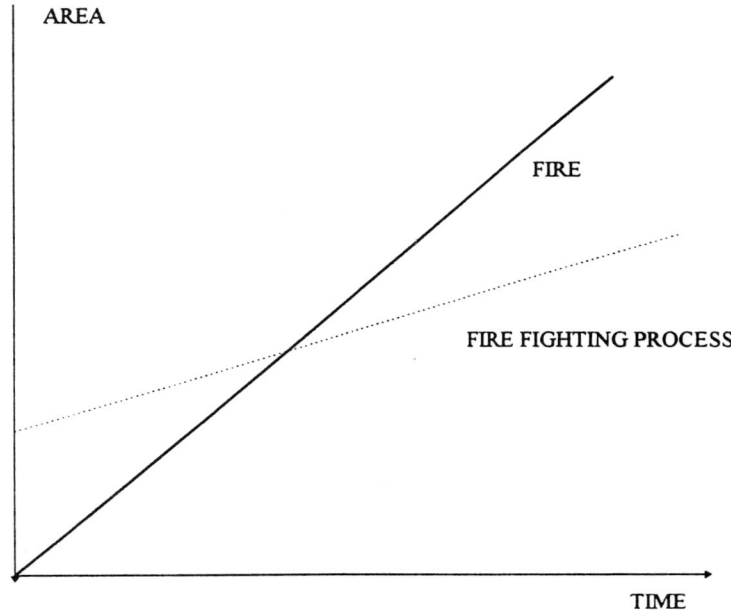

FIG. 2.2. A time–area diagram illustrating the participant's task in NEWFIRE (and spatiotemporal dynamic tasks generally).

in Brehmer (1996), the strategies that are possible depend on the relation between the two functions in the figure. To the left in the figure, before the two functions have crossed, the fire-fighting units can cover more area than the fire. This means that a direct attack on the fire will be successful; it is possible to cover all of the area on fire with the extinguishing agent. After the functions have crossed, this is no longer possible. In this region, the fire spreads faster than the fire chief can cover it. In other words, before the functions have crossed, the fire chief is stronger than the fire, but to the right in the diagram, the fire is stronger than the fire chief. In the latter case, he will have to find means to stop the fire from spreading, and then attack it when it has burned down to a smaller size. At the point where the functions cross, the fire and the fire chief are equally strong, and a direct attack is still possible.

Fig. 2.2 shows an ideal case in that it assumes that the fire-fighting units can be moved in their appropriate positions without delay. In real fire-fighting this is, of course, not possible. In the real world, everything takes time, and the time that things take must be taken into account. The decision maker must compensate for the time that it takes to carry out his decisions. In the case of fire-fighting, the fire chief must thus consider the fact that the fire will spread while the fire-fighting units move from their base to the fire, and he must compensate for this by sending out the number of assets that are required when the assets are in place, not the (lower) number that is required when he makes the decision. This is a form of compensation for the feedback delays in the task, and compensation for such delays lies at the heart of the competence required by dynamic decision tasks (see Brehmer, 1995, for further discussion of this point). In this case, the delay of interest relates to what control engineers call the time constants of the task. Other forms of delay are discussed in Brehmer (1995).

To perform optimally in NEWFIRE (or fire-fighting generally), the participant must learn the actual slopes of the functions in Fig. 2.2 and the time constants. That is, the participant must develop a model of how fires spread under different conditions and of how the fire-fighting process works. In addition, he must be able to predict how long it will take for the fire-fighting units to be in place and be ready to start fighting fire. This is not a simple task, and we use this as our first illustration of reasonable decision making.

ADAPTING TO THE TIME CONSTANTS
OF FIRE FIGHTING

Generally speaking, adapting to the time constants requires the participant to respond quickly and massively to a fire, sending out many more fire-fighting units than would seem to be required by the fire at the point in time when the decision to send out the units was made. There is evidence from a number of experiments (e.g., Brehmer & Allard, 1991) that participants learn to do this.

It is, however, not clear whether this rapid and massive responding is simply a form of open loop responding, or if it is a sign of a well-calibrated feedforward strategy, where the participant has predicted the number of units needed and sent out exactly that number and not just the greatest number of units that he thought that he could afford at the time.

This problem has been investigated in a series of experiments by Brehmer, Løvborg, and Winman (1992) and Magnusson and Brehmer (in preparation). In these experiments, participants were confronted with two kinds of scenarios. In all scenarios, the base was positioned in the middle of the forest, and eight fire-fighting units were placed around it. In all scenarios, the direction of the prevailing wind was from the fire towards the base. In the first kind of scenario, the fire started close to the base, and if the participant reacted as soon as the fire had started, it was possible to extinguish it by sending out one fire-fighting unit to the location of the fire. These scenarios, then, presented fires to the left in the time–area diagram in Fig. 2.2. For second kind of scenario, the fire started at a greater distance from the base. For these scenarios, it was not possible to extinguish the fire directly by sending out a unit to the burning square, for when the unit had reached the fire, it would have spread so that more than one unit was required. Instead, the participant had to stop the spread of the fire by placing three units around it and a fourth directly on the fire. The three units in front of the fire would extinguish the fire as it spread towards the base, while the fourth unit would extinguish the first fire and prevent it from spreading backwards. These scenarios were scenarios to the right in the diagram in Fig. 2.2. These two kinds of scenarios, we thought, would enable us to assess whether the participants used a feedforward strategy. If they did, they would send one unit to the one-unit fires and four units to the four-unit fires, or at least considerably fewer fire-fighting units to the former fires than the latter.

In the experiments reported in Brehmer et al. (1992), the fire did not start immediately but only some time after the start of each scenario. We found that the participants were generally able to extinguish the fires before they reached the base, but we did not obtain any information about whether they used a feedforward strategy or not. Our participants outsmarted us and adopted what, in retrospect, seems a very natural strategy: they simply moved out their fire-fighting units from the base, positioning them some distance from it so that they could fight the two kinds of fires in about the same way. In short, the participants found a way of avoiding taking the time constants into account in any detailed way. As the participants tended to send too many units to the fires, this resulted in fairly expensive fire-fighting, but the participants got the job of extinguishing the fires done.

Magnusson and Brehmer (in preparation) made the obvious counter-move of presenting the same kinds of scenarios to their participants but they did not allow the participants to move their units until the fire had started. They found very little evidence of differentiation between one- and four-unit fires; the participants fought the two kinds of fires in the same manner, sending too many units to the one-unit fires and too few units to the four-unit fires. This suggests that the participants were unable to take the time constants into account when they had to do so. Apparently, the task was too complex.

The lesson to be learned from these experiments is that when given the opportunity, participants find a way of performing a task that they cannot perform in an optimal way in a reasonable way instead. In this case, they did so by devising a strategy that allowed then to perform the task without having to consider the aspects that were problematic—that is, the time constants. This lead to fire-fighting that was more expensive than it might have been had the participants learned the time constants, but it nevertheless got the job done.

Devising a strategy that allows them to bypass excessive cognitive demands is one way in which people can handle complex tasks in a reasonable, but perhaps not optimal way. Another possibility could be to find information that simplifies the task for them. We now turn to a study that investigates this possibility.

USING FREQUENCY INFORMATION
TO SIMPLIFY A COMPLEX TASK

Things do not happen in our environment with uniform frequencies. To stick with the example of fire-fighting, I was informed by representatives from many large fire-fighting departments at a conference on fire-fighting that some 95% of all urban fires are alike and required the same procedures and resources. Such fires require no calculation and no decision making on the part of the fire ground commanders. The remaining 5%, on the other hand, were highly problematic. Perhaps it is difference in frequencies that allowed the urban fire ground commanders studied by Klein, Calder-wood, and Clinton-Cirocco (1986) to rely on recognition and relieved them of decision making on the fire ground.

That people can rely on frequency information to cope with complex tasks was demonstrated by Iosif (1968) in a study of process operators. Iosif found that the operators relied on what they had learned about the relative frequencies of different malfunctions rather than on any actual

understanding of the equipment with which they were working when diagnosing malfunctions. In short, they avoided going into complex forms
of thinking when simpler frequency information was available.

Reason (1993) has pointed to the use of frequency information in the
form of frequency matching as one of defaults to which the cognitive
system reverts when it lacks the information that it needs for deriving a
response in a more informed way. Such form of functioning presumably
becomes possible because frequencies are learned in an automatic and
effortless way (Hasher & Zachs, 1984).

As the example from the urban fire departments discussed above demonstrates, frequency information is relevant to fire-fighting also, and one
might ask whether participants in NEWFIRE would learn to relay on frequency information if such information were available to them instead of
learning the time constants of the fire-fighting task. Elg and Brehmer (in
preparation) tried to answer this question in an experiment using NEW-
FIRE.

Their experiment used a special feature of NEWFIRE that makes it
possible to present a scenario for which the participant decides which
fire-fighting units to send out and where they should be sent. The program
then informs the participant whether he or she made the correct decisions—that is, whether the fire would in fact be extinguished with the
minimum number of fire-fighting units using those that the participant
had selected and positioned. If the participant made the correct decision,
he or she could then ask to see the scenario played out or go on to the
next scenario. If the choice was incorrect, the correct scenario is automatically played out for the participant. The facility is used so that the participant can learn about the correct initial response to a fire without being
misinformed by possible mistakes later in the fire-fighting process.

The experiment by Elg and Brehmer (in preparation) was conducted
in three stages. The first was a frequency learning stage where half of the
participants received 80% scenarios that required two fire-fighting units
and 20% required one unit, while for the other half of the participants,
these conditions were reversed. Then came a test stage that was the same
for all participants with 50% of scenarios requiring one unit and 50%
requiring two units. In this stage, the participants received no feedback.
The third stage was also a test stage where the participants were interviewed
about their strategies.

In the first stage, both groups showed frequency matching in the sense
that their overall use of one or two fire-fighting units followed the relevant
relative frequencies in their task. This is, of course, not particularly infor-
mative, and it tells nothing about whether the participants actually learned
to match frequencies instead of the appropriate rules. Instead, we look at
the second stage and at the conditional probabilities that the participants

would chose the correct number of units—that is, the probability of choosing one unit ($p1$) when one was required ($s1$) and two units ($p2$) when two units were required ($s2$). If the participants frequency match, $p1$ and $p2$ should not vary with the number required but should instead match the frequencies in the task. If, on the other hand, the participants learn the correct rules for the task, they should of course choose two units for all scenarios that require two units, and one unit for all scenarios that require one unit. As can be seen from Table 2.1, the results do not conform to either of these alternatives. For the 80/20 condition, the condition where 80% of the scenarios required two fire-fighting units and 20% required one unit, we find that the participants showed considerable overshooting for the scenarios requiring two units (93% instead of 80%). For the scenarios requiring one unit, the participants' responses are equally divided between one- and two-unit decisions. In the 20/80 condition, that where 20% of the scenarios required two units and 80% one unit, the participants are close to frequency matching for the scenarios requiring one unit (85%) but for the scenarios requiring two units, the participants show the opposite to frequency matching (73% responses involving two units instead of 20% as frequency matching would dictate).

The most striking deviation from frequency matching and from correct responding is that the participants choose to send out two units too often. Thus, the participants who had 80% two-unit scenarios in the first stage send out two units for almost all scenarios requiring two units, and in 50% of the scenarios requiring one unit. The participants who had 80% scenarios requiring one unit in the first stage send out two units in 16% of the scenarios requiring one unit and 73% of the cases requiring two units. One explanation for this is that the participants handle their uncertainty about the actual number of units required by playing it safe: they send

TABLE 2.1
Conditional Probabilities Fire-Fighting problem

Conditional probabilities of sending out one and two fire-fighting units ($p1$ and $p2$, respectively) when one or two fire-fighting units were required to extinguish the fire ($s1$ and $s2$, respectively) for group trained with 80% two-unit fires (the 80/20 group) and that trained with 80% one-unit fires (the 20/80 group) for the second test stage in the Elg and Brehmer experiment.

Conditional Probability	80/20 Group		20/80 Group	
$p2/s2$	.93	(.80)	.73	(.20)
$p2/s1$	.50	(.80)	.16	(.20)
$p1/s2$	.05	(.20)	.27	(.80)
$p1/s1$	.51	(.20)	.85	(.80)

out two units rather than one unit to be reasonably certain that the job of extinguishing the fire actually gets done, even if the resulting cost in terms of the resources used is somewhat higher than it might have been.

In this experiment, then, we do not find the expected frequency matching. Perhaps the task was not difficult enough to force the participant in to the cognitive default of frequency matching. Instead, the participant learn something about the differences between the scenarios that require one unit and those that require two units, and they handle uncertain cases by choosing the safe response of sending out too many rather than too few fire-fighting units.

CONCLUSIONS

A dynamic task such as the fire-fighting task represented by NEWFIRE is a complex task that participants generally are not able to master perfectly (see Brehmer & Allard, 1991). To do so, they would have to develop mental models of fires and how they spread, of how fire-fighting units function, and of the time constants of the process of bringing the units in position. In addition, the participant would have to keep these models active simultaneously so that their outcomes could be compared and an optimal decision derived. Obviously, they do not do this, but develop a more approximate form of processing instead, and find strategies that help make decisions that can be characterized as reasonable rather than optimal. They are reasonable in the sense that they get the job done, even though this is achieved at a higher cost than would have been the case with an optimal strategy. However, compared to what is at stake (the loss of large areas of forest in this case) the price that has to be paid for sending out too many fire-fighting units may nevertheless seem quite low. In many cases, it will not even be possible to detect that the price was too high, for in the absence of a normative model of the task, there is nothing with which to compare the price that was actually paid. The only feedback that is available, therefore, is that the fire was extinguished. This is likely to be the case for most dynamic tasks in the environment, especially those for which correct timing is an important element. Such tasks simply cannot be modeled using current forms of decision theory.

The results presented here might seem trivial in retrospect. What could the participants do except finding a way of placing their fire-fighting units so that the participants did not have to rely on knowledge of the time constants that they obviously did not have, and what could they do except trying to protect themselves against losses of forest than send out too many fire-fighting units when uncertain about how many were required? Perhaps so, but both results were quite unanticipated, and while this may reflect more on the author than on decision theory, nobody warned us before the experiments that the results would be trivial. The experiments were required to discover the participants' strategies in dealing with the decision problems of the kind that a dynamic task such as NEWFIRE poses.

The strategies were discovered because the experiments focused on what the participants actually did, rather than on a comparison between a normative model and actual behavior. Had the focus been on such a comparison, we would have discovered what other experiments on decision making with that focus have discovered: that people do not make optimal decisions. However, by examining the participants' actual behavior, we discovered that although their decisions may not have been optimal, the participants nevertheless made something that could be considered reasonable in that it got the job done, albeit at a higher cost than might have been necessary.

The dynamic character of the task studied here is, of course, an important aspect: it is only by examining the final outcome of a process where the participants are able to adapt and correct earlier mistakes in later decisions that we can discover that the participants actually get the job done. If we had only examined a single decision in the series, we could never have discovered that the participants were able to extinguish the fires.

Fire-fighting is, of course, not the only task to which these considerations apply. Guided by the concept of reasonable decision making, rather than that of optimal decision making, and with a focus on the whole process from initial decision to final outcome, we may well find the explanation for why the world is not in the sorry state that the results from decision research would suggest.

ACKNOWLEDGMENT

This study was supported by a grant from the Swedish Council for Research in the Humanities and Social Sciences.

NOTES

1. This situation is now, at long last, being improved by recent research on "naturalistic decision making" (see Klein, Orasanu, Calderwood, & Zsambok, 1993, for examples).
2. Slovic's (1972) conclusion form a review of studies of decision making under uncertainty that man is a "cognitive cripple" expresses the temper of the times in the seventies and eighties as well as the beginning of the nineties until results form naturalistic decision studies (Klein et al., 1993) and studies of adaptive decision making (Payne, Bettman, & Johnson, 1993) began to change psychologists' attitudes.

REFERENCES

Brehmer, B. (1995). Feedback delays in complex dynamic tasks. In P. A. Frensch & J. Funke (Eds.), *Complex decision making: The European perspective* (pp. 103–130). Hillsdale, NJ: Lawrence Erlbaum Associates.

Brehmer, B. (1996). Man as a stabiliser of systems: From static snapshots of judgement processes to dynamic decision making. *Thinking and Reasoning, 2*, 225–238.

Brehmer, B., & Allard, R. (1991). Dynamic decision making. Effects of complexity and feedback delays. In J. Rasmussen, B. Brehmer, & J. Leplat (Eds.), *Distributed decision making: Cognitive models of cooperative work* (pp. 319–334). Chichester: Wiley.

Brehmer, B., & Dörner, D. (1993). Experiments with computer-simulated microworlds: Escaping both the narrow straits of the laboratory and the deep blue sea of the field study. *Computers in Human Behavior, 9*, 171–184.

Brehmer, B., Løvborg, L., & Winman, A. (1992). Learning the time constants of a dynamic task. In B. Brehmer & J. Leplat (Eds.), *Simulations, evaluations and models* (pp. 88–102). Roskilde: Risø National Laboratory.

Dörner, D. (1996). Über die Verwendung von "Mikrowelten" oder "Computer-Szenarios" in der psychologischen Forschung. In H. Gundlach (Ed.), *Psychologische Forschung und Methoden: Das Versprechen des Experiments* (pp. 53–88). Passau: Passavia Universitätsverlag.

Edwards, W. (1961). Behavioral decision theory. *Annual Review of Psychology, 12*, 473–498.

Einhorn, H. J., & Hogarth, R. M. (1981). Behavioral decision theory: Processes of judgment and choice. *Annual Review of Psychology, 32*, 53–88.

Elg, F., & Brehmer, B. (in preparation). *Frequency matching in a dynamic decision task.* Swedish National Defence College, Stockholm, Sweden.

Hasher, L., & Zachs, R. T. (1984). Automatic processing of fundamental information: The case for frequency of occurrence. *American Psychologist, 39*, 1372–1388.

Iosif, G. (1968). La stratégie dans le surveillance de tableaux de commande. 1. Quelques déterminants de charactère objectif. *Revue Romaine des Sciences sociales et Psychologie, 12*(2), 147–163.

Klein, G. A. (1989). Recognition primed decision making. In W. B. Rouse (Ed.), *Advances in man-machine systems research, vol. 5* (pp. 47–92). New York: JAI.

Klein, G. A., Calderwood, R., & Clinton-Cirocco, A. (1986). Rapid decision making on the fire ground. *Proceedings of the Human Factors Society 30th Annual Meeting, 1*, 576–580.

Klein, G. A., Orasanu, J., Calderwood, R., & Zsambok, C. E. (Eds.). (1993). *Decision making in action: Models and methods.* Norwood, NJ: Ablex.

Løvborg, L., & Brehmer, B. (1991). *NEWFIRE: A flexible system for running simulated fire fighting experiments.* Roskilde: Risø National Laboratory Report M-2953.

Magnusson, S., & Brehmer, B. (in preparation). *How subjects handle the time constants in a dynamic decision task without learning the actual durations involved.* Swedish National Defence College, Stockholm, Sweden.

Payne, J. W., Bettman, J. R., & Johnson, E. J. (1993). *The adaptive decision maker.* Cambridge: Cambridge University Press.

Reason, J. (1993). *Human error.* Cambridge: Cambridge University Press.

Slovic, P. (1972). From Shakespeare to Simon: Speculations—and some evidence—about man's ability to process information. *Oregon Research Institute Bulletin, 12*. (Available from Decision Research, Eugene, Oregon.)

von Winterfeldt, D., & Edwards, W. (1993). *Decision analysis and behavioral research.* Cambridge: Cambridge University Press.

Chapter 3

Goal Achievement and Mental Models in Everyday Decision Making

Anders Jansson
Uppsala University

Within classical decision theory, by which I mean the collection of axiomatic models of uncertainty, risk, and utility (Edwards, 1954; Kahneman & Tversky, 1979; Savage, 1954; von Neumann & Morgenstern, 1947), research on decision making has most often been concerned with well-defined decision problems. In general, however, this is not what decision makers face in everyday and naturalistic decision situations. Instead, they have to deal with unstructured environments with ill-defined problems (Björkman, 1984). One consequence of this mismatch is that the empirical findings reported in scientific journals and books to a large extent have been proven irrelevant or difficult to realize in applied settings. (For an extensive review of the mismatch between classical decision theory and decision making in naturalistic contexts, see Klein, Orasanu, Calderwood & Zsambok, 1993.) One response to this mismatch is to try, not to save the theory, but to look for other ways to model human decision making. This approach started with the work by Simon (1955, 1972). He showed that people do not seek to optimize an outcome of a decision. Rather, they stop analyzing at some more or less implicit level of aspiration, when they feel they have achieved something useful from the problem solving process. The research I will summarize below has been conducted within the paradigm of dynamic decision making. (For a review, see Brehmer, 1992; see also Chapters 2 and 4 of this volume.) It follows one of the fundamental premises of Brunswik's functionalistic framework, the behavior-research isomorphy principle (BRI-Principle; Brunswik, 1952, see also Brehmer, 1984, for a discussion and application to decision research), which states that research must focus where the participant focuses. That is, we can only hope to understand what a participant is doing if we know what he or she is trying to achieve. Let us take two examples from everyday life in Sweden.

In Sweden, new parents have the statutory right to stay home with their newborn child for 360 days in return for a benefit at the rate of compensation for loss of earnings. Moreover, there is an additional 90 days for the parents to utilize at a much lower rate of compensation. When parents are confronted with the possibility to put this right into practice, they will quickly experience that the rules for how this right can be utilized are much more complicated than they first anticipated. For example, between themselves, they must first agree on which of them that shall be staying at home with the child, if one should share the right equally, or if one should sign over the statutory right to the other. After that, they need to decide if they should try to maximize the rate of compensation from the social insurance office and be content with the 360 days, or if they should try to maximize the total number of days that they can stay at home with their child and be content with a lower rate of compensation for a longer time. As if this was not enough, they can also choose to combine the two different rates of compensation, and by this, they can find additional ways to adjust the parental leave according to their own wishes. Finally, they have to decide whether they should plan for a second child to be born within a certain time limit in order to maintain the rate of compensation for loss of earnings that the benefit is based on.

Now imagine another scenario. A 35-year-old usability engineer is deliberately planning to start out on his own in some line of business with which he is well acquainted. He has come to a point where he realizes (as do others) that the conditions are ripe for starting out on his own. He lays down the broad outlines for the enterprise. He knows that he will need financial support to be able to enter the market and he is faced with a number judgments and decisions to make. How can he combine his entrepreneurship with his family's needs and interests? How can he manage the relationship with his present employer in a fruitful cooperation? What scope for the business should he plan for? If or when he decides to enter the market, he will continuously face new problems to solve; these problems will be more or less novel to him, as he has not experienced anything like them before.

These two examples demonstrate the kind of decision problems that people face in their ordinary life. The research I refer to below has taken as its point of departure that human decision making in everyday contexts can be studied as a process where the decision maker's overall purpose is to achieve and maintain control over the situation, whatever it might look like. This suggests that control theory can be useful as a formal framework for the study of human decision making in general, and as such, it is not only relevant for the study of expert problem solving and decision making, but also for the study of decision performance and behavior in novel decision tasks and unfamiliar environments. Control theory as a theory of human behavior has been used with successful results in studies of manual control (see, e.g., Kelley, 1968; Powers, 1971). Psychologists have not found the mathematical framework of control theory very useful, however, and therefore it is useful only as a metaphor (Bainbridge, 1981). This also agrees very much with the ideas of Conant and Ashby (1970). According to them, the very object of decision making can be regarded as that of control. In order to control a situation, however, a person must develop a model of that situation. And, as Brehmer formulated it, "the most general formulation of the problem for research, therefore, is that it is concerned with people's formulation of goals and models as a function of the observability and action possibilities of the system to be controlled" (Brehmer, 1992, p. 218). Observability and action possibilities are properties of the task to be performed, whereas goals and models are properties of the decision maker. In order to carry out experiments according to this general formulation of the research problem, we use computer simulations, or microworlds. (For a description of this methodology, see Brehmer & Dörner, 1993.) We assume that the microworlds we use are ecologically valid operationalizations of everyday decision situations. As simulations, they approximate the structure and character of a sample of undefined real-world decision tasks in an indefinite population of these tasks. It is further assumed that it is not important whether they approximate a certain decision task or not, as long as the behaviors of the microworlds are congruent with the participants' expectations.

The purpose of this chapter is to present a number of studies that investigate human decision behaviors in such computer simulated contexts. First, I will describe the experimental paradigm and review some results from earlier studies using it. In particular, I will focus on the complex relation between mental models and goal achievement. Second, I will present two experiments that investigate if the performance in a complex decision situation can be improved with the help of instructions. Finally, an analysis of individual differences shows that a number of adaptive and maladaptive decision strategies are important determinants in the explanation of decision performance in complex decision situations. Specifically, I will argue that the investigated decision pathologies are consequences of inadequate mental models and deficient goal formulations.

GOALS AND MODELS IN THE STUDY OF DYNAMIC
DECISION MAKING

As the examples above show, a process of goal formulation is often necessary when people have to cope with complex systems because the decision
maker's initial goals are often quite general. This aspect of decision making
in everyday contexts is included in microworld experiments. For example,
in experiments with MORO (Dörner, Stäudel, & Strohschneider, 1986),
the participant's task is to serve as an advisor to a tribe in the southern
Sahara called the Moros. The participant starts with the very general goal
of "improving the conditions of the Moros." Such a goal is quite useless
as a guide to decision making for it implies no specific actions. Therefore,
the initial general goal must be made more precise until the participant
reaches a set of goals with direct action implications. What this level of
precision should be will, of course, depend on the nature of the system
with which the decision maker is working. In MORO, the decision maker
must carry the analysis to a rather low level in the system. Thus, the
participant must first give a more concrete meaning to the general goal
of "improving the conditions of the Moros." One alternative is to provide
more food for the Moros. If the participant chooses to do so, he or she
must decide whether this should be done by increasing the number of
cattle, the amount of millet grown, or both. As the participant has been
told in the instructions that the Moros prefer meat, his or her first choice
is likely to be to increase the number of cattle. This cannot be done
directly, however. To increase the number of cattle, the participant must
first increase the area of grazing land. The participant must therefore first
formulate a new goal relating to the area of grazing land. But this cannot
be achieved directly either. It requires that the participant increases the
water supply, so the participant must now formulate a new lower level goal,
and this must in turn be operationalized in terms of the number of wells
to be bored, whether pumps should be installed, and if pumps are installed,
how much fuel must be ordered for these pumps. It is only at this level
that the goals are precise enough to be implemented in the simulation.
To reach these operational goals, the participant must develop a good
model of the system that makes it possible to decide what lower-level goals
are necessary to reach the general goals given at the start of the experiment.
Fig. 3.1 gives a general overview of the MORO system.

In a complex system such as MORO, it is, however, not sufficient to
think only of the actions and how they relate to the goal. Such "linear
thinking" (Dörner, 1980) is likely to lead to disaster. The participant must
also give some thought to the possible side effects, as well as to the various
future consequences of the line of action that has been chosen. Thus,
when deciding on the number of wells, the participant must also consider

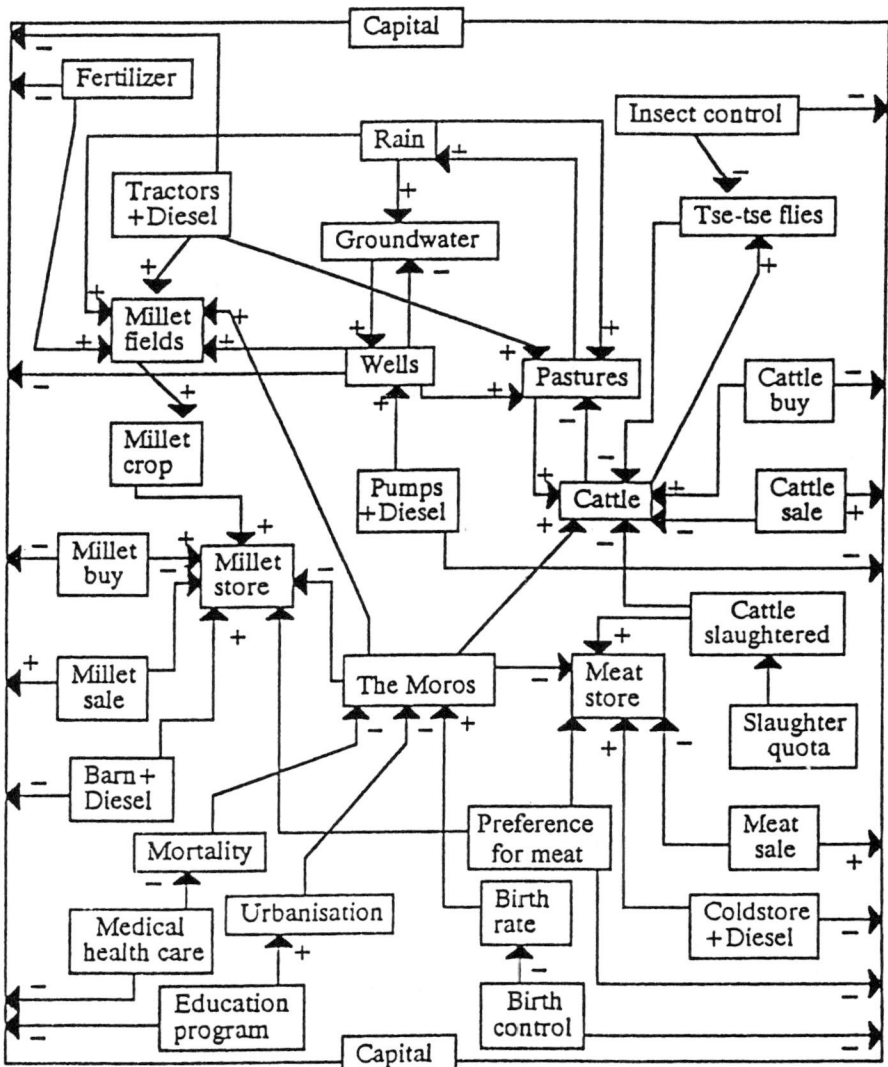

FIG. 3.1. The structure of the MORO system.

what the effect of the wells will be on the amount of groundwater, and
be ready to counteract the exponential growth in the number of cattle
when the area of grazing land increases by increasing the proportion of
cattle that are slaughtered so that overgrazing is avoided. To formulate
adequate goals, the participant must therefore have a good model of the
system, or at least a set of good partial models, that will inform him or

her of both the intended and unintended consequences of a given set of actions. But the participant will not develop any models without having any goals, and the goals that the participant has will determine what models will be developed. There is thus a complex relation between goals and models.

Earlier research with MORO (Schaub & Strohschneider, 1989; Strohschneider, 1986; Stäudel, 1987) has shown that most participants find the system very difficult to control. After some 20 simulated years, they have generally produced exactly the conditions that actually prevail in the southern Sahara: drought, overgrazing, and famine. Indeed, they generally leave the Moros in conditions that are far worse than those prevailing when they started advising them, bad as these were. Specifically, most participants produce catastrophes, the most common being overgrazing. These catastrophes stem from the fact that the participants tend to remove the natural checks on cattle and population by fighting the tsetse flies and diseases without introducing sufficient artificial controls in the form of birth control and slaughter of the cattle, and to increase the area of grazing land at a sufficient rate. As the number of cattle increases exponentially, the participants soon experience overgrazing. When the participants try to cope with this problem by further increasing the grazing land by boring more wells, they deplete the groundwater level with severe water shortages as a consequence. The participants thus try to increase the food supply, an adequate goal in view of the rather problematic conditions of the Moros in this respect at the outset. But the way they go about this, without considering the full set of consequences of their actions, not only prevents them from achieving their overall goal of improving the conditions of the Moros, it also leads to a worsening of those conditions. At the heart of the participants' failure in MORO, then, lies a failure to understand the need to balance the forces that lead to growth in the population and the cattle by introducing new artificial controls and to increase the grazing land at a sufficient rate, and to understand the limits to growth in MORO.

These results suggest that the participants fail to develop an adequate mental model of central aspects of MORO. This is not because MORO requires any special knowledge. MORO does not require any knowledge that the average undergraduate student (who is the typical participant in these experiments) is not likely to have. The problem is not that the participants' mental models are incorrect in any general sense. A generally correct model is not sufficient to succeed in MORO, however. The participant must also develop a concrete form of the model for the MORO simulation. That is, the participant must be able to translate his or her general model into some reasonably precise numerical relations between, say, the current area of grazing land and the likely future number of cattle, between the number of wells and the area of grazing land, and so on. The main cognitive tasks facing the participants in a microworld such as MORO are thus the same as they are in any complex system. They are to recall the models that are in the decision maker's long term memory, and to transform them into a form that is precise enough to enable the decision maker to make the decisions that are needed to control the system.

THE EFFECTS OF PROVIDING SPECIFIC GOALS

The results referred to above suggest that the participants generally find these cognitive tasks quite difficult, in that most participants fail to reach the goal of "improving the conditions of the Moros." Brehmer and Jansson (1993) investigated whether an instruction with specific goals would improve the abilities of the participants to actually reach a higher level of performance. In addition to the general goal of improving the conditions of the Moros, the participants in the experimental group were thus given concrete goals in terms of quantitative target values for seven of the central variables in the system: the area of grazing land, the number of cattle, the groundwater, the capital, the number of Moros, level of medical care, and the size of the millet crop. According to the analysis above, this means that an important part of the participants' cognitive work has been done for them. If they manage to reach these concrete target values, they will both have achieved the goal of improving the conditions of the Moros and they will have produced a set of conditions that will not lead to catastrophes. In short, the participants in the experimental group have been given the general conditions for "sustainable development," to use a popular phrase.

The results of this study showed that the control group performed at about the same level as control groups in earlier experiments with MORO (e.g., Schaub & Strohschneider, 1989; Stäudel, 1987). This conclusion was based upon three different kinds of performance assessments. First, with respect to individual variables, some of the most central of these variables were affected in the same way as in the studies mentioned above. Second, the overall performance with the help of criterion groups showed that the main part of the participants had severe problems with the task of controlling the MORO system in the long run. The criterion groups consist of a taxonomy that makes it possible to classify the participants' performance with respect to the pattern of goal achievement. Finally, the number, as well as the nature, of these catastrophes were rather similar to those obtained in the studies mentioned above. This was interpreted as an independent and successful replication of the earlier studies.

The performance of the experimental group showed that the effects of providing specific goals did not enhance the performance of this group as much as one might have expected. Thus, the main part of the participants in both experimental groups failed to reach a satisfactory level of performance—that is, they ended up with some sort of catastrophe. However, analyses on the behavioral data showed that the participants in the experimental group were affected by the specific goals. Especially, this was obvious on the output side of the system—that is, in the part of the participants' interaction with the system where the participants interrogate the system for more information. In conclusion, it seems as if the participants in the experimental group really tried to accomplish the task of fulfilling the goals in the instruction. They were only partly successful, however.

In the discussion of the results, Jansson (1997) concluded that in a decision task characterized by complexity and opaqueness, it seems to be a good thing to know *what* one wants to achieve in terms of subgoals, and, presumably, the participants in the experimental group developed a better model of the system than did the control group. However, a better model in this sense is a better descriptive model. Further, this better model of the system is probably limited to the parts of the system that were made salient through the different subgoals. Through the instructions, these participants got a hint on which the central variables of the system were. More important, though, is to know *how* to achieve the goals. This amounts to the use of an operative model of the system. The effects of the experimental treatment on the outcome variables was insignificant, suggesting that the specific goals did not provide the majority of participants in this group with a good enough operative model—that is, the participants were not successful in transforming the models they had recalled from their long term memory into a form that was precise enough to enable them to find concrete action alternatives to implement into the simulation.

THE EFFECTS OF TEACHING HEURISTIC
STRATEGIES BY INSTRUCTIONS

How does one manage to develop a good enough operative model of a system like MORO? Apparently, it is not enough to know what one should try to achieve. A number of studies suggest that there may be stable individual differences among people with respect to performance in a microworld like MORO. For example, Schaub and Strohschneider (1989), compared university students with industrial managers in MORO, the same microworld as that used by Brehmer and Jansson (1993). They found that the manager group performed significantly better than the student group. Further, they demonstrated that the difference in performance was due to differences in strategies. Specifically, Schaub and Strohschneider found that the industrial managers spent more time representing the problem in the beginning of the task, made fewer decisions, collected more information, and checked on the results of their decisions to a higher degree than the students. Because the groups did not differ in epistemic knowledge—domain knowledge relevant to the task—Schaub and Strohschneider concluded that the managers had knowledge, helping them to cope with complex, opaque, and dynamic systems of the kind that MORO represents. The students, on the other hand, seemed to lack this kind of knowledge. The managers judged that the demands made by MORO were similar to those made by their ordinary work of running a company, whereas the students did not judge the demands made by MORO as similar to anything they had experienced. Following earlier research by Dörner, Kreuzig, Reither, and Stäudel (1983), and by Stäudel (1987), the ability of the manager group to cope with this task was referred to as heuristic competence: a general competence for coping with complex, dynamic systems. (For a more formal definition of heuristic competence, see Rigas & Brehmer, Chapter 4 of this volume.)

The strategies used by the industrial managers in the study by Schaub and Strohschneider (1989) seem to be highly adaptive in a dynamic task, and it can therefore be argued that these strategies make it possible for the managers to develop more appropriate models of the system. An important research problem is whether it is possible to teach, through instructions, how one can develop the operative mental models that are needed to control a microworld like MORO, and as a consequence, how to achieve goals and subgoals. As part of the now classic Lohhausen study, Dörner et al. (1983) investigated this problem in an experiment where two kinds of instructions were compared. The first one consisted of a general strategic training. This instruction emphasized the importance of general rules for solving complex problems. The second instruction consisted of both this general strategic training and additional training in tactical aspects, stressing the importance of relatively concrete action alternatives. The results showed no significant effect of either of these instructions compared to a control group which did not receive any form of special instruction.

Jansson (1994a), however, investigated the effects of two different experimental instructions, one of them stressing the importance of having a systematic-elaborate strategy and one of having a goal-planning strategy. By applying either one of these strategies, it was assumed that the model enhancement process within the participants could be encouraged. It was assumed that a systematic-elaborate strategy should help the participants in this experimental group to make the MORO system more salient, and, that a goal-planning strategy should help these participants to detect the more important variables of the system. The main difference between the experimental instruction used in Brehmer and Jansson (1993) and the instructions used in Jansson (1994a) is that the latter ones emphasize the importance of having a strategy for how to achieve the general goals, rather than having clearly stated subgoals without requirements for understanding how these goals may relate to each other. The content in the two experimental instructions are described in more detail below.

As reported by Dörner and Schölkopf (1991), an important feature of heuristic competence seems to be the ability of working with a systematic-elaborate strategy—that is, to collect information systematically, to take measures on a regular basis, to check on the measures taken continuously, and so forth. However, for such a strategy to be effective for other participants than those who already utilize it, they must know what to base this strategy upon: a certain minimum level of domain knowledge of the environment they are supposed to perform in. Results in general support of this interpretation were reported by Voss and his colleagues (see Voss, Greene, Post, & Penner, 1983; Voss, Tyler, & Yengo, 1983), who studied expert problem solving in the area of political science. They found that a prerequisite for nonexperts on the former Soviet Union to represent the problem in an appropriate way, and to provide solution processes at the same level of abstraction as experts on this area, is to have both heuristic knowledge and a minimum of domain knowledge. In the systematic-elaborate instruction, the participants got information about the Moros that they would otherwise have had to ask for. All information provided to the participants was taken from the background information that all participants (including the control group) could ask for to inform themselves about the habits and traditions of the Moros. Participants were also instructed to ask for detailed information in all situations and for all aspects of the system. The instructions stressed that they should base their decisions on this kind of information over the simulated years.

Following Dörner and Schölkopf (1991) another aspect of heuristic competence is the ability to work with a goal-planning strategy: to control hypotheses and strategies about the nature of the system, to evaluate one's own actions in the long term, to detect and control developmental trends, and so on. This interpretation stresses the importance of different time scales in a dynamic task, and whether a participant is able to use these scales. A related issue is that of self-reflexion, which is an important aspect of action regulation. Tisdale (1992) concluded that self-reflexion had a positive effect on the quality of problem solving and that this effect was stable and transferable to other problem settings. In the goal-planning instruction, the participants were told to combine an overall perspective (decisions about what to achieve in the long term) with detailed measures (that they should implement their decisions and check their effects carefully). By doing this, they were told that they would enhance their chances of finding a state of balance in the system so that they could feel that they had the situation under control. Further, the great importance of adapting one's thinking and behavior to the demands and circumstances of the situations was stressed. The participants were told that this sometimes mean demands for careful examinations and new decisions, while at other times it may be better to wait and see.

The results were based on two different kinds of performance assessments. First, Table 3.1 below shows the result of the analyses of the individual variables. As a comparison, the values of the corresponding variables in the study by Brehmer and Jansson (1993) are included.

Second, for each participant, the values of the six dependent variables at year 30 in the MORO simulation were used to classify the overall performance of the participants. Following Schaub and Strohschneider (1989), each participant was allocated to a given criterion group. To be allocated to a certain criterion group, a participant must meet the criteria for the six central dependent variables in MORO. Table 3.2 below shows the criteria for each of the six system variables for each criterion group.

Table 3.3 shows the result of the analyses from the overall performance assessments with the help of criterion groups. Again, the corresponding results from the study by Brehmer and Jansson (1993) are included.

TABLE 3.1

The Target Values and the Mean for Each of the Six Dependent Variables at Year 30 in the MORO-Simulation.

Dependent Variables and Target Values in the Simulation	Brehmer & Jansson (1993)		Jansson (1994a)		
	Goal-Specific Instruction	Control Group	Systematic-Elaborate Instruction	Goal-Planning Instruction	Control Group
	n = 20	n = 20	n = 12	n = 12	n = 12
Population ≥ 650	664	348	825	1.330	642
Number of cattle 10.000	2.602	1.311	6.384	6.083	3.707
Millet crops 60 tons	35	24	54	113	42
Grazing land 550 km^2	247	172	437	435	269
Groundwater 100%	94	87	93	94	87
Capital 1.000.000 Rika	860.332	1.339.808	4.585.081	5.231.883	396.125

Note. The only experimental group that received the actual target values in their instructions was the experimental group with the goal-specific instruction in Brehmer and Jansson (1993).

TABLE 3.2
The Criteria for Each of the Six Dependent Variables for Each Criterion Group.

	Criterion Groups					
	1	2	3	4	5	6
Groundwater in %	99%	95%	90%	80%	-	-
Capital in Rika	750.000	0	-100.000	-	-	-
Deaths by hungar	0	0	0	0	0	-
Grazing land in km²	300	300	300	100	10	-
Number of cattle	5.000	5.000	5.000	5.000	-	-
			or	or		
Millet cropt in ton	15.000	15.000	15.000	15.000	-	-

Note. When the participants enter the simulation, with some margin, they all start out in criterion Group 1.

As can be seen from Table 3.3, the overall pattern of goal achievement is quite different compared to the goal achievement for the individual variables, respectively (see Table 3.1 above). For a complex system such as MORO, it is not sufficient to consider performance in terms of individual variables only. A successful participant must balance different goals, and it is not enough to achieve only one or two of the goals. The most important result in Jansson (1994a) is that as many as nine participants out of twelve in both the experimental groups seem to manage to control the system still at year 30 in the simulation.

In order to find out whether the instructions on how to approach the system resulted in enhanced models within participants in the experimental groups, a post-experimental task knowledge questionnaire was used to assess the participants' knowledge of the system. The result of the questionnaire suggests that the reason for the improvements could be explained in terms of better operative mental models of the system within participants in the experimental groups. For example, there was a significant correlation between the overall performance of the participants in the two experimental groups at year 30 in the simulation and on the part of the form where the participants had to judge the outcome of a number of measures on a number of dependent variables in the system. Further, there were significant differences between the experimental groups on the one hand, and the control group on the other hand, on the part of the form where the participants had to decide which were the most appropriate measures if one wanted to affect a certain variable in the system.

Jansson (1994a) showed that, by introducing instructions on how to approach a complex system like MORO, participants can benefit from

TABLE 3.3
Frequency of Participants in Each of the Six Criterion Groups at Year 30 in the Simulation

Criterion Groups		Brehmer & Jansson (1993)			Jansson (1994a)	
		Goal-Specific Instruction	Control Group	Systematic-Elaborate Instruction	Goal-Planning Instruction	Control Group
		$n = 20$	$n = 20$	$n = 12$	$n = 12$	$n = 12$
	1	2	1	6	4	1
	2	1	0	0	0	0
	3	4	1	2	1	0
	4	1	1	1	4	2
Good Performance Total	1-4	8	3	9	9	3
	5	8	12	2	2	4
	6	4	5	1	1	5
Bad Performance Total	5-6	12	17	3	3	9

these instructions and apply strategies that will help them to control the system. Without these instructions, they would have been left with the quite demanding task of developing a strategy for coping with the system, and at the same time, to develop a model of that system. With the instructions in their hands, they could concentrate on the latter task. This leads to the question: Do these participants now possess general heuristic competence? Probably not. It may instead be that the results of this study only demonstrate the effects of using heuristic strategies. That is to say, the participants behaved in accordance with the instructions and as a consequence they appeared to act as if they controlled their behavior better, and by this, in turn increased their ability to control the system. To ascertain what the participants have learned, we need to examine the extent to which the participants' strategies will generalize. MORO is high in opaqueness and complexity but rather low in the dynamic aspects (Brehmer, 1990a). A first attempt to such a generalization is that a systematic-elaborate strategy is possible and needed when people are subjected to systems with severe opaqueness, while a goal-planning strategy is helpful when the system one is about to control is fairly complex.

Apparently, it is possible to catch the more salient features of the adaptive behaviors described by Dörner and Schölkopf (1991), and to teach a group of naive participants these features through instructions on how to

approach the system. It seems as if adaptive decision strategies are necessary, or at least important, for the participants to reach an acceptable level
of performance in microworlds like MORO. An important research question, then, is if the opposite relation holds as well—Does the absence of
adaptive decision strategies lead to bad performance?

THE EFFECTS OF MALADAPTIVE DECISION STRATEGIES

In recent research on dynamic decision making, a number of systematic
maladaptive strategies have been found to accompany the failure of participants in tasks that have a dynamic, complex, and opaque character.
Several studies show that the performance is dependent on strategies inherent in the acting style of the participants (Badke-Schaub, 1989; Dörner,
1980, 1990, 1991, Dörner & Preussler, 1990; Dörner & Schölkopf, 1991;
Schaub, 1991; Tisdale, 1992).

Jansson (1994b) conducted a study on individual differences in the
same sample of participants that were used in the study by Brehmer and
Jansson (1993). This study had two main purposes: 1) to understand
whether these maladaptive strategies are more common among participants with bad performance, as have been suggested by Dörner (1980,
1990, 1991), and 2) to investigate the behavior of the participants before
they have experienced any more dramatic consequences of their decision
making. In this way, it should be possible to decide for all the investigated
maladaptive behaviors whether they should be interpreted as consequences
or precursors of failure.

Seven different maladaptive strategies that previously have been found
to differentiate between good and bad problem solvers were selected
(Dörner, 1980, 1983, 1990, 1991; Dörner & Schölkopf, 1991). These are
described in more detail below.

Acting Directly on Feedback

Depending on the situation, the tendency to act directly on feedback
without any further information can be detrimental for the decision process
of the participants. Dörner (1983, 1990, 1991) points out this salient feature
as one of the behaviors that is present in the repertoire among participants
with bad performance. These participants eliminate obvious errors and
solve the most salient problems by adding new measures or changing the
old ones in a new direction and therefore fail to take into account developments that first become apparent in faint symptoms and vague tendencies (Dörner, 1990). Dörner (1983) suggests that this behavior has its

origin in an insufficient goal formulation process. Instead of trying to get their goals clear in their minds, participants are "muddling through" in a "repair service mode of behavior." According to Brehmer (1990b), this behavior may instead depend on a too-limited model of the system.

Insufficient Systematization

According to Dörner (1990) and Dörner and Schölkopf (1991), one of the tasks in a complex action situation is to gather information. In order to update the model of the system, participants have to explore its current state. At the same time, they have to take new measures. Participants can solve the problem of information gathering activities and decision making actions in two different ways. Some participants might use information and measures in a very mixed pattern. This tendency will create what Dörner calls "insufficient co-ordination of different measures" leading to "collision of measures." Alternatively, participants may instead show a pattern of gathering a solid base of information and then make decisions about all the measures considered.

Insufficient Control of Hypotheses and Strategies

According to Dörner (1990, 1991), unsuccessful participants often fail to check and detect wrong hypotheses and inappropriate strategies. Dörner described this behavior as a tendency to act "ballistically." Participants "fire" their decisions without a plan for checking the effects. Since a complex and opaque system makes it more difficult to ascertain the state of the system, this mistake is a dangerous error. On the one hand, this behavior is seen as a consequence of the participants' difficulties in meeting the demands of a complex action situation. On the other hand, it is seen as a pathology originating in a tendency within the participants of protecting their feeling of competence (Dörner, 1990).

No Self-Reflection

If participants check and detect that the measures taken for a special purpose do not have the supposed effect, the further way of acting can, more or less, take two possible directions. Either the participants can continue with about the same kind of decisions or they can examine their approach to the problem in a self-reflective and critical way and adapt their way of acting to the given circumstances. The failure of not being self-reflective is then primarily a tendency of not adapting to the circumstances but to continue to employ the same kind of decisions. Dörner (1980, 1990) and Dörner and Schölkopf (1991) suggest this behavior to be still another mode of faulty behavior in coping with complex systems. Tisdale (1992) concluded that self-reflection had a positive effect on the quality of problem solving and that this effect was stable and transferable to other problem settings.

Selective Information Gathering

This behavior manifests itself as a tendency to collect information about things that previously have been possible to act on. Information about variables not affected by earlier measures or decisions will not contribute to any feeling of competence and as such they are viewed as irrelevant by participants behaving in this way. "By ignoring and rationalizing information which could refute a hypothesis, it is possible to maintain each hypothesis as long as desired." Thus, it can be seen as a "fortification tendency" (Dörner, 1980). Using the label "dogmatic entrenchment," Dörner (1983) sees this behavior as a deficiency in goal handling. "The individual stops the collection of data or collects only those data that fit into his system of assumptions about reality." Dörner (1990) also uses the term "channeling information collection," which is seen as a tendency to protect the feeling of competence.

Selective Decision Making

Still another pathology is the tendency to concentrate the decisions on measures that apparently lead to changes in accordance with the intentions of the participants. By using only a small part of the decision possibilities, participants enclose themselves into a rather rigid behavior pattern. Again, Dörner (1980) considers this maladaptive behavior as a consequence of participants' attempts to guard their feeling of competence. When confronted with the results of their decision making, some participants have been seen to stick to one subject matter and treat small details carefully, not willing to consider anything else. The areas where these participants enclose themselves are usually the least problematic and therefore unimportant.

"Thematic Vagabonding"

Brehmer (1992) considers this behavior as still another consequence of a deficient goal formulation process. Being unable to make the goals clear in their minds, these participants often try to work on everything in small pieces without any organization. This inability leads to heavy cognitive demands where everything seems to be connected to everything without any structure. By changing the area of pursuit rapidly and jump from theme to theme instead of deciding on a crucial course of action and work on it until completion, participants move from one issue to another. Dörner's (1980, 1983) excellent term for this behavior is "thematic vagabonding" and, as was the case with the two previous behaviors, it is regarded as a mistake originating in the tendency to guard the feeling of competence.

For all the maladaptive strategies, the distribution of participants was made with the help of a judgment procedure involving quantitative and qualitative measures as well as direct impressions from the tape recordings. For each of the investigated behaviors, a number of measures were chosen; for each of these measures, predictions were made according to how these different measures should differentiate between participants exhibiting this behavior and participants who would not exhibit this behavior. The classification of participants with respect to these maladaptive behaviors were then compared to their performance in the MORO simulation that were reviewed earlier in this paper (see the review of the results from Brehmer & Jansson, 1993).

The results from the analyses showed that six out of seven maladaptive strategies were found to be significantly more frequent in participants with bad performance than in participants with better performance. For four of the maladaptive strategies, this difference was very clear. The tendency to act directly on feedback, the inability to systematize the decision making activities, the insufficient control of hypotheses and strategies, and the tendency to make decisions selectively all seem to be important features of a nonoptimal performance in a system such as MORO. The maladaptive strategy of dispensing with self-reflection is a further characteristic of participants with bad performance, even though the difference here is not great. Finally, the maladaptive behavior of "thematic vagabonding," seems to be a pathology exclusively found among participants with bad performance.

Further, the results also showed that all seven behaviors were found before the participants had received any feedback about dramatic consequences of their decision making—that is, the participants exhibited these maladaptive behaviors before they knew that they were going to fail the task to improve conditions for the Moros. Further analyses of the data (Jansson, 1995) showed that those participants who exhibited the maladaptive behaviors had received the same amount and same kind of information as the participants who did not exhibit these behaviors. In contrast to the view that the decision pathologies are consequences of failure, it thus seems clear that the maladaptive strategies can be regarded as precursors of failure in the sense of inadequate mental models and deficient goal formulations within the participants. (However, for a discussion of the results of this study, see Funke, 1995.)

CONCLUSIONS FROM THE EMPIRICAL STUDIES

The majority of the participants in the experimental group in the study by Brehmer and Jansson (1993) failed to reach an acceptable level of performance, despite the fact that they had been given specific target values for several of the central variables in the MORO system. In the discussion of this result, Jansson (1997) assumed that it is not enough to know *what* subgoals to achieve, but more important, to know *how* to achieve them. This means that the participants must establish some sort of proce-dural knowledge in the form of a good enough operative mental model to be able to specify action alternatives on a concrete level. However, an ordinary participant in an experiment with MORO seems unlikely to be able to develop such an operative mental model of the system. Jansson (1994a) showed, however, that if participants are taught adaptive strategies for how to approach a system like MORO, they can benefit from such instructions and perform significantly better than a control group of par-ticipants. The better performances were accompanied by enhanced mental models of the system within these participants. It thus seems as if the complex and opaque nature of MORO demands from the participant a strategy for dealing with such task characteristics in order to be able to develop a good enough operative mental model.

Without such instructions, however, the majority of participants seem to not develop appropriate decision strategies. An important research ques-tion then, is whether the absence of adaptive decision strategies leads to bad performance. The results from Jansson (1994b) suggest that. Six out of seven maladaptive decision strategies were found more often among participants who later ended up with bad performance. More important, all seven behaviors were found before the participants had any indication of any negative consequences, in terms of external feedback cues, to which they could relate their own actions.

In order to understand human decision making in complex, opaque, and dynamic environments, the results from the studies reviewed above suggest that it is not only important to analyse the performance of the participants, but also to analyse the participants' behaviors.

GENERAL CONCLUSIONS

Björkman (1984) concluded that "man's limited cognition in conjunction with technological means of control sometimes may lead to decisions with disastrous consequences in the future" (p. 45). With that conclusion, he not only predicted a number of incidents in real life (for examples of such man–machine failures, see Reason, 1990), but he also predicted the kind of difficulties that participants in microworld experiments would experience only too soon. Unlike the advocates of classical decision theory, however, researchers within the paradigm of dynamic decision making have not interpreted the failure of their participants as "errors" or "biases" according to some arbitrarily chosen norm. Instead, the performance and behavior of the participants in microworld experiments have been evaluated in close connection to the demands that each such microworld has raised. As a consequence, this approach has resulted in two things. First, a number of decision or complex solving behaviors have been examined and described in detail, some of which have been shown to be adaptive decision strategies, whereas others have been interpreted as maladaptive behaviors. Second, the participants' performances have revealed in detail a number of task characteristics with which people have severe problems.

ACKNOWLEDGMENT

The research reported in this chapter was supported by grants from the Swedish Council for Research in the Humanities and Social Sciences.

REFERENCES

Badke-Schaub, P. (1989). How people try to solve the AIDS-problem. Decision making in complex situations: Results of a simulation experiment. *Memorandum 75*, Lehrstuhl Psychologie II, Bamberg University.

Bainbridge, L. (1981). Mathematical equations or processing routines? In J. Rasmussen & W. B. Rouse (Eds.), *Human detection and diagnosis of systems failures*. New York: Plenum.

Björkman, M. (1984). Decision making, risk taking and psychological time: Review of empirical findings and psychological theory. *Scandinavian Journal of Psychology, 25*, 31–49.

Brehmer, B. (1984). Brunswikian psychology for the 1990s. In P. Niemi & K. Lagerspetz (Eds.), *Psychology in the 1990s*. Amsterdam: North-Holland.

Brehmer, B. (1990a). Towards a taxonomy for microworlds. In J. Rasmussen, B. Brehmer, M. De Montmollin, & J. Leplat (Eds.), *Taxonomy for analysis of work domains*. Proceedings of the first MOHAWC workshop, Roskilde, Risö National Laboratory.

Brehmer, B. (1990b). Strategies in real-time, dynamic decision making. In R. Hogarth (Ed.), *Insights in decision making*. Chicago: University of Chicago Press.

Brehmer, B. (1992). Dynamic decision making: Human control of complex systems. *Acta Psychologica, 81*, 211–241.

Brehmer, B., & Dörner, D. (1993). Research with computer simulated microworlds: Escaping the narrow straits of the laboratory as well as the deep blue sea of the field study. *Computers in Human Behavior, 9*, 171–184.

Brehmer, B., & Jansson, A. (1993). Swedes in MORO: I. Effects of goal specificity. Unpublished manuscript, Department of Psychology, Uppsala University.

Brunswik, E. (1952). *Conceptual framework of psychology*. Chicago: University of Chicago Press.

Conant, R. C., & Ashby, W. R. (1970). Every good regulator of a system must be a model of that system. *International Journal of System Science, 1*, 89–97.

Dörner, D. (1980). On the difficulties people have in dealing with complexity. *Simulation and Games, 11,* 87–106.

Dörner, D. (1983). Heuristics and cognition in complex systems. In R. Groner, M. Groner, & W. F. Bischof (Eds.), *Methods of heuristics.* Hillsdale, NJ: Lawrence Erlbaum Associates.

Dörner, D. (1990). The logic of failure. In D. E. Broadbent, J. Reason, & A. Baddeley (Eds.), *Human factors in hazardous situations.* Proceedings of a Royal Society Discussion Meeting. Oxford: Clarendon Press.

Dörner, D. (1991). The investigation of action regulation in uncertain and complex situations. In J. Rasmussen, B. Brehmer, & J. Leplat (Eds.), *Distributed decision making. Cognitive models for cooperative work.* Chichester: Wiley.

Dörner, D., Kreuzig, H. W., Reither, F., & Stäudel, T. (1983). *Lohhausen: Vom Umgang mit Unbestimmtheit und Komplexität.* Bern: Huber.

Dörner, D., & Preussler, W. (1990). Die Kontrolle eines einfachen ökologischen Systems. *Sprache & Kognition, 9,* 205–217.

Dörner, D., & Schölkopf, J. (1991). Controlling complex systems or: Expertise as "Grandmother's Wisdom." In K. A. Ericsson & J. Smith (Eds.), *Toward a general theory of expertise: Prospects and limits.* New York: Cambridge University Press.

Dörner, D., Stäudel, T., & Strohschneider, S. (1986). MORO—Programmdokumentation. *Memorandum 23.* Lehrstuhl Psychologie II, Bamberg University.

Edwards, W. (1954). The theory of decision making. *Psychological Bulletin, 51,* 380–417.

Funke, J. (1995). Some pathologies in the study of pathologies. A comment on Anders Jansson (1994). *Sprache & Kognition, 14,* 91–95.

Jansson, A. (1994a). Strategies in dynamic decision making: Does teaching heuristic strategies by instructions affect performance? In J.-P. Caverni, M. Bar-Hillel, F. H. Barron, & H. Jungermann (Eds.), *Contributions to decision making.* Amsterdam: Elsevier Science Publishers.

Jansson, A. (1994b). Pathologies in dynamic decision making: Consequences or precursors of failure? *Sprache & Kognition, 13,* 160–173.

Jansson, A. (1995). The pathologies *are* precursors of failure—a reply to Funke. *Sprache & Kognition, 14,* 161–169.

Jansson, A. (1997). Strategies and maladaptive behaviors in complex dynamic decision making. Ph.D. dissertation. *Acta Universitatis Upsaliensis: Comprehensive Summaries of Uppsala Dissertations from the Faculty of Social Sciences 65.* Stockholm: Almqvist & Wiksell.

Kahneman, D., & Tversky, A. (1979). Prospect theory: An analysis of decision under risk. *Econometrica, 47,* 263–291.

Kelley, C. R. (1968). *Manual and automatic control: A theory of manual control and its application to manual and automatic control systems.* New York: Wiley.

Klein, G. A., Orasanu, J., Calderwood, R., & Zsambok, C. E. (Eds.). (1993). *Decision making in action: Models and methods.* Norwood, NJ: Ablex.

Powers, W. (1971). *Behavior: The control of perception.* New York: Addison-Wesley.

Reason, J. (1990). *Human error.* Cambridge: Cambridge University Press.

Savage, L. J. (1954). *The foundations of statistics.* New York: Dover.

Schaub, H. (1991). The year of the gardener. Behavior modeling in a complex situation. *Memorandum 9,* Project Group Cognitive Anthropology, Max-Planck-Gesellschaft, Berlin.

Schaub, H., & Strohschneider, S. (1989). Die Rolle heuristischen Wissens beim Umgang mit einem komplexen Problem oder: Können Manager wirklich besser managen? *Memorandum 71,* Lehrstuhl Psychologie II, University of Bamberg.

Simon, H. A. (1955). A behavioral model of rational choice. *Quarterly Journal of Economics, 69,* 99–118.

Simon, H. A. (1972). Theories of bounded rationality. In C. B. Radner & R. Radner (Eds.), *Decision and organisation.* Amsterdam: North-Holland.

Stäudel, T. (1987). *Problemlösen, Emotionen und Kompetenz. Die Überprüfung eines integrative Konstrukts.* Regensburg: Roderer.

Strohschneider, S. (1986). Zur Stabilität und Validität von Handeln in komplexen Realitäts-bereichen. *Sprache & Kognition, 5,* 42–48.

Tisdale, T. (1992). Self-reflection and its part in action regulation. In B. Brehmer & J. Leplat (Eds.), *Simulations, evaluations and models.* Proceedings of the fourth MOHAWC workshop, Roskilde, Risö National Laboratory.

von Neumann, J., & Morgenstern, O. (1947). *Theory of games and economic behavior.* Princeton: Princeton University Press.

Voss, J. F., Greene, T. R., Post, T. A., & Penner, B. C. (1983). Problem-solving skill in the social sciences. In G. Bower (Ed.), *The psychology of learning and motivation* (vol. 17). San Diego: Academic Press.

Voss, J. F., Tyler, S. W., & Yengo, L. A. (1983). Individual differences in the solving of social science problems. In R. F. Dillon & R. R. Schmeck (Eds.), *Individual differences in cognitive processes* (vol. 1). New York: Academic Press.

Chapter 4

Mental Processes in Intelligence Tests and Dynamic Decision Making Tasks

Georgios Rigas
Uppsala University

Berndt Brehmer
Swedish Defence College

There are two reasons why it is important to study the relation between performance in dynamic tasks and test intelligence. First, such studies will contribute to theoretical advances concerning the structure and function of human cognitive abilities, and second, they may also lead to an innovation in the technology of intelligence testing.

Sternberg and Kaufman (1996) claim that intelligence testing has been painfully slow to develop and that it shows the slowest rate of evolution of any major technology. Among the reasons for this situation, they mention the belief that intelligence tests are satisfactory as they are, the costs of developing new tests, the validation of new tests against old ones, and the failure to consider implicit theories of intelligence. Obviously, these reasons are related. Intelligence tests do well in predicting academic success, and it is quite convenient to validate new tests against old ones and various measures of academic performance. However, they are weak predictors of success in nonacademic environments and will remain so for as long as the only developments are computerized versions of old tests or changes in scoring procedures, for instance by using item response theory. What we need are advances in basic psychological theory.

The new field of research on complex problem solving and dynamic decision making using computer-simulated microworlds promises a new view of human cognitive abilities that may provide the basis for new theories. Microworlds are low-fidelity simulations of certain aspects of reality and are characterized by various degrees of dynamic change, complexity, intransparency, and novelty (for reviews see Brehmer & Dörner, 1993; Funke, 1988). There are wide interindividual differences in performance in such microworlds. Yet, intelligence test scores are usually not related to performance in these microworlds (Dörner, Kreuzig, Reither, & Stäudel, 1983; Putz-Osterloh & Lüer, 1981; Stäudel, 1987; Strohschneider, 1991). Such findings are important because they suggest that by using microworlds we may be able to explain different portions of variance than those accounted for by traditional intelligence tests. We do not say that we are there yet, but we claim that adapting the microworlds to the needs of mental testing may lead to the major innovation that Sternberg and Kaufman are calling for.

In brief, in this chapter we argue that the study of the relationship between psychometric intelligence and performance in dynamic decision making tasks is important because it will contribute to theoretical advances about the structure and function of human cognitive abilities and because it may also lead to an innovation in the technology of intelligence testing. We discuss the cognitive demands placed upon the participants by the two different kinds of tasks and the mental processes that may underlie performance. Finally, we present some empirical studies by our research group in Uppsala and discuss their implications.

MENTAL PROCESSES IN INTELLIGENCE TESTS

The specific difficulties that intelligence test takers face depend on the particular test they take, and there exists a great variety of intelligence tests. But intelligence test scores correlate positively, and it is often assumed that the cognitive processes that underlie performance in intelligence tests are similar. Indeed, a positive correlation with established intelligence tests is a sine qua non for a new test.

Theoretical models of mental abilities have been based on correlational studies. Models of the structure of intelligence can be classified as nonhierarchical, in which the factors of intelligence are specified at the same level (Guilford, 1967; Thurstone, 1938), and hierarchical (Burt, 1949; Carroll, 1993; Gustafsson, 1984; Horn & Cattell, 1966; Spearman, 1904; Vernon, 1950). In most hierarchical models a single general ability is placed on the top. One exception is the Gc-Gf theory originally proposed by Cattell (1943). According to this theory, "fluid" intelligence (Gf) reflects basic reasoning abilities and higher mental processes that are able to flow into many kinds of mental activities, while "crystallized" intelligence (Gc) reflects the extent to which an individual was able to profit from experience and education by acquiring skills and knowledge. Gustafsson (1988), using confirmatory factor analytic techniques, concluded that fluid intelligence is equivalent to general intelligence.

A similar (and clearer) picture is obtained when data are analyzed with the radex model, a nonmetric multidimensional scaling technique (Guttman, 1954). The radex model is not mathematically identical to the hierarchical factor model, but the two models are parallel mathematically and empirically (Snow, Kyllonen, & Marshalek, 1984). Factors are usually interpreted as latent traits but they can also be conceptualized as classificatory labels in a continuous space. In the radex method, tests that have a higher average correlation with all other tests in a battery are placed nearer the center in a circular or spherical continuous space. According to Snow et al., (1984) in a perfect radex, the g-factor appears in the center. These authors, in a hypothetical radex map showing their suggested ability and learning simplexes and the content circumplex, placed the Raven test in the center (p. 92). In the simplex arrays of the suggested radex model, tasks are placed according to their complexity. More complex tests are placed nearer the center. Complexity can be conceptualized in terms of the different number of performance components a test requires. The scaling solutions of several data bases reported in Snow et al., (1984) were very similar to the idealized radex map. Complex tests appeared near the center while simpler tests were clustered according to their content—verbal, numerical, or spatial—in separate areas. Raven's progressive matrices, together with some other Gf tests (for example, letter series, necessary arithmetic operations, etc.) occupy the most central regions. These results suggest that the processes underlying performance in the Raven test are not specific to this test. Moreover in a number of factor-analytic studies it has been repeatedly demonstrated that Raven's Advanced Progressive Matrices (APM) is one of the best single measures of g (Jensen, 1987; Raven, Raven, & Court, 1993).

The importance of the complexity continuum is expressed in the following statement by Snow et al., (1984): "We take the complexity continuum of the radex model to be the most important single feature of the correlational evidence on cognitive tasks amassed to date" (p. 93).

Complex tests thus seem to be the best bests tests for estimating g. Hence, we should expect such tests to provide the best predictors of performance in the complex everyday tasks that are simulated by microworlds. The question is, however, whether we are talking about the same kind of complexity in both cases. We need therefore consider the nature of complexity in the context of intelligence testing and in microworlds.

One hypothesis is that complexity in intelligence tests is a function of the number of response components that are required to complete a task successfully. Such components are elementary information processes like encoding, inference, mapping, application, justification, and response (Sternberg, 1979). More complex tasks require all the response components of simpler tasks, plus some additional components. A second hypothesis is that more central components are increasingly involved in more complex tasks. Such components may reflect Spearman's (1927) eduction of relations (inference) or eduction of correlates (application). A third hypothesis is that people differ in the speed with which they process information (Jensen, 1984). In tasks where more components are involved, the reaction time differences for individuals of different mental speeds accumulate. g-scores seem to account for almost the same variance in reaction times as total scores of intelligence tests (Vernon, 1983). Intraindividual variability, measured as the standard deviation of a participants reaction times in a series of trials, has the highest correlation with g-scores (Jensen, 1982). A fourth hypothesis is that:

> more complex tasks may require more involvement of executive assembly and control processes that organize and monitor the operation of response components assembled into a performance program for the task. In particular, complex tasks seem to require adaptation or strategy shifting within and between items as task performance proceeds in a task, and between tasks. (Snow et al., 1984, p. 95)

The ability to adapt that usually requires strategy shifts is probably reflected in the intraindividual variability measures. The two last hypotheses, as well as the first two, regarding the nature of complexity in intelligence test items are compatible, in the sense that any combination of these is possible.

The general suggestions by Snow et al., (1984) about the nature of the processes that underlie performance in intelligence tests were specified and instantiated in APM by Carpenter, Just, and Shell (1990). According to their analysis, which is based on a number of process tracing studies, including eye fixations, verbal protocols, and a series of computer simulations, individual differences in APM scores are due to differences in goal management and abstraction. Since APM has been administered to the participants in our studies, it is important that the processes that seem to underlie performance in this test are considered in some detail. The format of a typical item of APM is illustrated in Fig. 4.1. The participants are instructed to observe the ways the patterns change both horizontally and vertically, in the eight cells of the 3 × 3 matrix in the upper part of the figure, and to use these observations to determine which of the eight alternatives, depicted in the lower part of the figure, is the missing one in the ninth cell.

Carpenter et al., (1990) found that items containing more than one rule are processed incrementally. Each rule is induced in small steps by comparing pairwise the elements in adjoining cells. The verbalization of a rule is followed by a long interval, suggesting that rules are induced one at a time. The patterns of the eye fixations of a group that had to work silently were similar to the group that had to think aloud. The decompo-

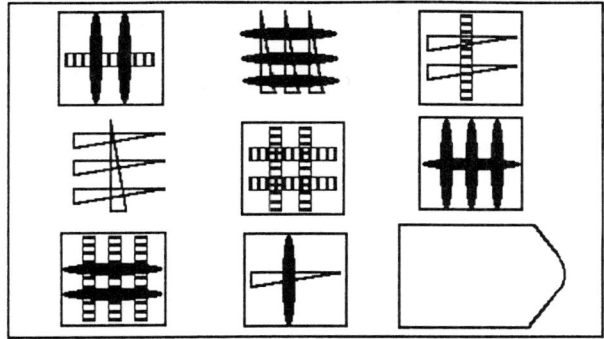

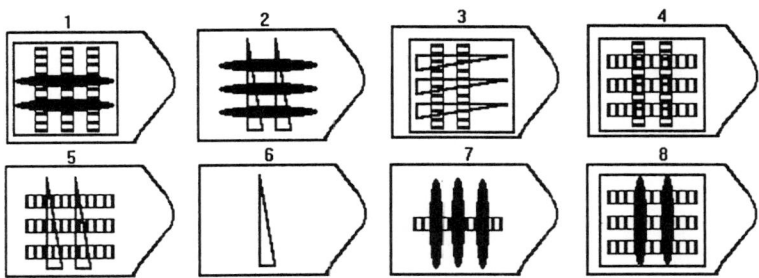

FIG. 4.1. A problem to illustrate the format and the rules of Raven's Advanced Progressive Matrices. The occurrence of the squares can be explained by a distribution of two rule. Orientation, that is, horizontal and vertical elements separately, and two distribution of three values rules, one about the number and one about the kind of figure, are sufficient to explain the variation of the other elements. The correct answer is 5. (This problem is not one of the problems in APM. We use this isomorph in order to protect the security of APM).

sition into subproblems characterizes all participants and seems not to be a source of individual differences. In our own experience with a different method, a computerized version of APM problems (by Rigas, 1995) specially constructed for process tracing studies, the incremental nature of the processing by pairwise comparisons is usually replicated.

Five different types of rules seem to account for the variation of the elements in most of the APM problems.

1. *Constant in a row.* When the same value occurs throughout a row and changes columnwise.
2. *Quantitative pairwise progression.* When an attribute like number or size increases or decreases in adjacent cells.

3. *Addition or subtraction.* When an element is added to or subtracted from another element to produce the third.
4. *Distribution of three values.* When three values from a categorical attribute are distributed through rows and columns.
5. *Distribution of two values.* When two values from a categorical attribute occurs twice in a row or a column and the third value is null.

The rules are listed according to their difficulty. The two most difficult types of rules, distribution of two values and distribution of three values, are exemplified in Fig. 4.1. In order to establish which rules apply to a problem, test takers have to find out which figural elements or attributes are governed by the same rule. This process of correspondence finding (as named by Carpenter et al., 1990) is a source of difficulty because in some of the APM items the cues to the correspondence are ambiguous. The problem depicted in Figure 4.1 is a difficult one because its solution requires:

1. The abandonment of usual correspondence finding heuristics, like the matching names heuristic where elements or figures with the same name are taken to correspond to each other,
2. high abstraction ability in order to consider orientation as the attribute to base the correspondence of the triangles, ellipses and rectangles, and in order to induce the distribution of two rule that determines the squares, and
3. ability to generate appropriate subgoals and to successfully manage the goal hierarchy in working memory.

Kind of figure or number of elements in the cells does not result in any complete set of rules. Orientation—that is, horizontal and vertical elements separately—and two different distribution of three values rules, one about number and one about kind of figure, are sufficient to explain the variation of the other elements when the occurrence of the squares is explained with a distribution of two rule. Let us here consider a possible train of thought after the orientation principle has been adopted:

OK! First row, horizontal elements only.
Rectangle in the first cell, ellipses in the second, and triangles in the third.
Second row. Triangles, rectangles, ellipses.
Third row. Ellipses, triangle, . . . it has to be rectangles!
But how many?
Well! First row. One in the first cell, three in the second, and two in the third.
Second row. Three, two, one.
Third row. Two, one, . . . it must be three!
The horizontal elements must be three rectangles.

In a similar way one can go on to conclude that the missing vertical elements are two triangles. Applying the distribution of two rule to the squares leads to the conclusion that the value of the square in the missing cell must be null. Then it is easy to examine which alternative fits. The correct alternative is 5. This can be verified by considering the variation of the elements columnwise and applying the same rules. It is obvious that in addition to high abstraction ability this problem requires a lot of working memory capacity.

Carpenter et al., (1990) modeled the mental processing in APM of people with high problem solving ability in a computer program they called BETTERAVEN and the mental processing of people with average ability in a program they called FAIRAVEN. In a series of simulations Carpenter et al., (1990) showed how limiting the working memory capacity of the more able model (BETTERAVEN) decreased the number of the Raven problems the model could solve. The main differences between the BETTERAVEN and the FAIRAVEN, which simulates the way APM are processed by participants of intermediate ability, are that FAIRAVEN has no knowledge of the distribution of two rule and no goal monitor. The goal monitor in BETTERAVEN keeps a record of the goals that have been set and can change the current goal to either a parent goal or a subgoal.

DeShon, Chan, and Weissbein (1995) questioned the implicit assumption of Carpenter et al. (1990), that performance in APM requires a homogeneous set of basic cognitive processes. According to Hunt (1974), there are two different strategies that can be used to solve the problems in APM. The first is visual and uses the operations of visual perception, such as continuation and superimposition. The other is analytic, as in the case of Carpernter et al. (1990) that we described in some detail above. Because factor analytic results cannot illuminate this point, DeShon, Chan, and Weissbein (1995) used the verbal overshadowing effect to manipulate experimentally the cognitive processing in APM. This effect occurs when performance in tasks that require spacial operations is impaired by concurrent verbalization. They found that performance in APM problems classified as visual was impaired in the verbalization group. They concluded that "the positive manifold among cognitive ability tests is due to the dependence on overlapping elementary processes such as memorization, response generation, and information representation" (DeShon et al., 1995, p. 150).

In general, we see that both the factor analytic results and the experimental results by Carpenter et al. (1990) and DeShon et al. (1995) are consistent with the view of Snow et al. (1984) that more complex tasks require more involvement of executive assembly and control processes (cited earlier in this chapter).

Intelligence tests, however, have been criticized in a more general way by Neisser (1976) as being appropriate for the assessment of only a subset of the abilities that are required in real-life pursuits (see also Dörner, 1986; Putz-Osterloh, 1993; Rigas, 1997; Wagner & Sternberg, 1985). Unlike most real-life tasks, intelligence test problems are characterized by being formulated by other people, being of little intrinsic interest, having all the needed information given from the beginning, being well-defined, having only one correct answer, and having only one correct solution method. These characteristics make intelligence tests appropriate predictors in many educational settings, at least in those cases where reproduction of knowledge is the primary goal. These same characteristics suggest the reasons why intelligence tests are of limited value in nonacademic environments.

MENTAL PROCESSES IN DYNAMIC DECISION MAKING TASKS

Microworlds have higher face validity with respect to real-life tasks than intelligence tests and seem to demand similar cognitive processes. The problems in microworlds are formulated in general terms that demand elaboration: they are not well defined, only part of the needed information is given at the beginning, they have several possible solutions, and there is more than one correct solution method. Moreover, microworlds differ from intelligence tests with respect to the locus of their complexity. In MORO (Dörner, Stäudel, & Strohscl.neider, 1986; see also Chapter 3 of this volume), a microworld that requires the participant to assume the role of an advisor to a tribe in the southern Sahara, the principal sources of complexity stem from the lack of transparency (the participant must actively interrogate the microworld to find its current state and the relations among the variables) and the number of goals and subgoals that must be pursued. In NEWFIRE (Lövborg & Brehmer, 1991), a microworld in which the participant has to play the role of a fire chief charged with the task of extinguishing forest fires, the main sources of complexity are due to the dynamics and feedback delays in the various processes to be controlled.

A general theoretical model of the processing in microworlds was proposed by Dörner and Wearing (1995). This model is not in the Newell and Simon tradition of problem spaces and goal hierarchies (e.g., Newell & Simon, 1972; Newell, 1990). The focus of this model is on the management of intentions. In brief, knowledge about the structure and state of the reality determine the goals that are the material for the intention generation. The generated intentions are stored in a memory structure called intention memory and their selection is dependent upon the urgency of the situation, the importance of the intention, and the feeling of competence. The actual selected intention is handled by the process of amplification of relevant knowledge structures. The outcome of the process of amplification, which is basically a process of self-questioning, determines whether planning, question-asking, or decision making will come next. A number of phases can be distinguished in the process of action regulation in a complex system. The phases are goal elaboration, hypothesis formation, prediction, planning and decision making, monitoring, and self-reflection. The sequence of the phases is not fixed.

Now, we will consider the different phases of action regulation in the contexts of the MORO simulation (Dörner, Stäudel, & Strohschneider, 1986) as well as that of NEWFIRE (Lövborg & Brehmer, 1991). MORO is a microworld characterized by high complexity, low dynamics, and high degree of intransparency. This computer program simulates the living conditions of a small Sahelian tribe. The participant assumes the role of a development worker. Typically, in our experiments a period of 30 years is simulated. The causal structure of the central variables in the MORO simulation (in most experiments not available to the participants) is shown in Fig. 4.2 (see also Chapter 3 of this volume). NEWFIRE is a real-time dynamic system, highly dynamic and is characterized by low complexity and low intransparency. In this system the participant has to act as a commander of a number of fire-fighting units. The fire-fighting units are well-trained and operate automatically if directed to a burning cell. The participant has to direct particular units to particular cells (see Chapter 2 of this volume).

The goals are often ill-defined and global. This means that the subject has to specify and decompose these goals. The decomposition and integration of (sub)goals requires the processes of dependency analysis (i.e., what influences what), and whole–part analysis. The dynamic management of these two processes is difficult in complex situations with multiple interactions between the goals. In MORO the participants are told that they have to improve the living conditions of the Moros, but they have to decide for themselves what these improvements will be. For one participant significant improvement may be to increase the capital, while for another it is to provide a high standard of health care. These two goals are obviously dependent, because in order to be able to provide the tribe with health care of high standard one needs a lot of capital.

There is a need for a *mental representation* of the structure of the central variables of a microworld. Prior knowledge and collection of information about the system's present state and history are necessary for the construction of a mental representation. To be insensitive to information about aspects of the system not included in one's model of the system has been referred to as channeling error (Dörner & Schaub, 1994) or as myside-bias (Baron, 1993). For instance, some participants in MORO do not seem to understand the important relationship between the pastures and the number of cattles, so when messages about a decrease of the pastures arrive

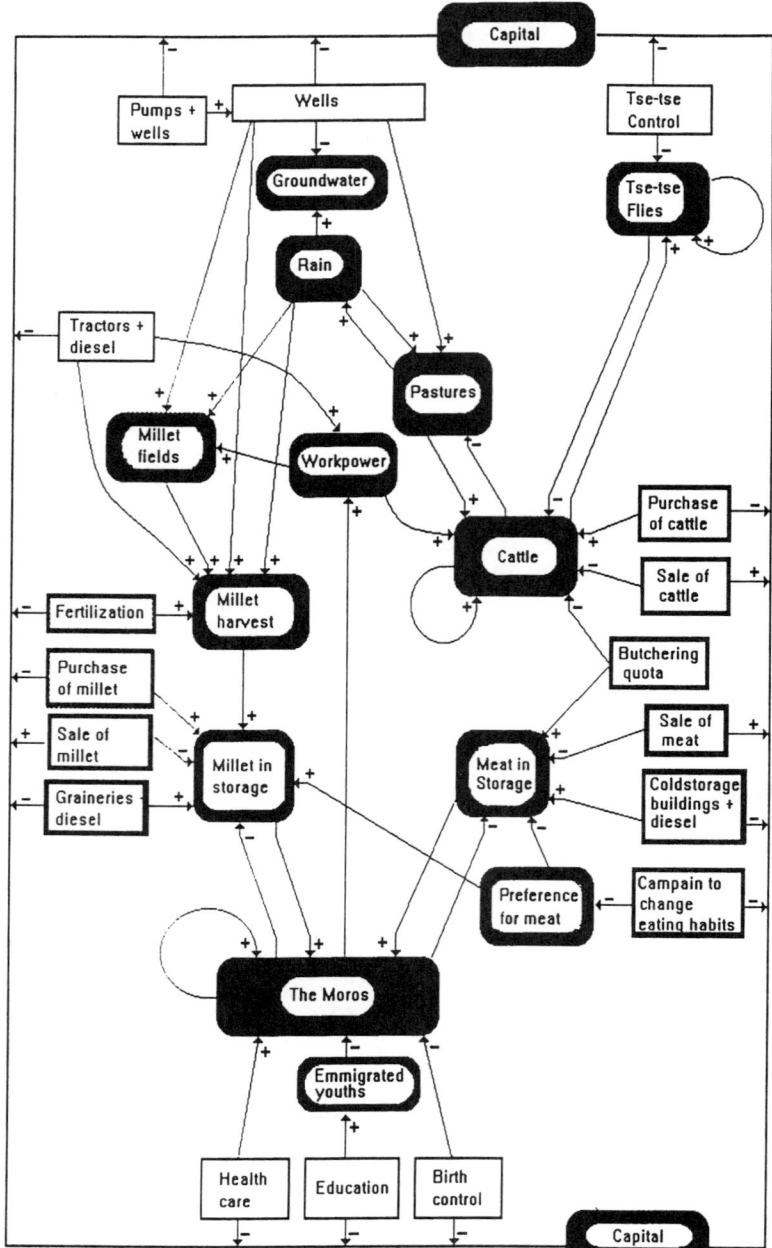

FIG. 4.2. The causal structure of the central variables in the MORO simulation.

they don't seem to care about it. Another error in information collection is encapsulation (i.e., in order to seek comfort from the feeling of uncertainty, participants engage in information collection ad infinitum). Sometimes the situations demand action and under conditions of time pressure a participant may engage in reductive hypothesis formation (i.e., only one or very few variables are supposed to influence everything in the system) or dogmatic entrenchment (i.e., one looks only at those parts of reality that provide noncontradictory information and enhances one's own image of reality).

Prediction of the future state of the system is important, especially in those cases when the desired state will come without any intervention. It is quite common that nonlinear changes are perceived as linear, and oscillating changes are seen as chaotic; both these tendencies are more common when information is received sporadically and at irregular time periods. Feelings or emotional states may also lead to the adoption of an inappropriate prediction model—for example, perceived danger may lead to a gross overestimation of growth, as in the case of the German students that overestimated the development of the AIDS epidemic in West Germany (Badke-Schaub, 1989).

Planning (in the sense of preparing a course of action) and *decision making* can be difficult and time-consuming if one is dealing with a system where actions have a lot of side and long-term effects. The main difficulty here is to balance between the failure to account for important side and long-term effects and the risk of being caught in a vicious cycle of planning. A complex system may cause unpleasant feelings of uncertainty, which can lead to the need to demonstrate one's competence. Actionism or thematic vagabonding (i.e., jumping from one topic to another until a problem is found that can be solved no matter how unimportant the problem might be) are some of the behaviors that have been observed.

Monitoring the effects is problematical in systems with dead times (i.e., delays caused by some process necessary before a decision is effective), time constants (i.e., the time periods required for control actions to change the states of the system), or simply information delays (Brehmer, 1995). In NEWFIRE it will take some time before a fire-fighting unit arrives at the fire (dead time) and before it mobilizes and puts out the fire (time constant). To develop an understanding for the duration of these delays is important for choosing an effective strategy. Generally the evaluation of the appropriateness of one's actions is difficult in systems with time delays.

Self-reflection is often absent or insufficient. The abandonment of self-reflection may be caused by the need to protect the feeling of competence. On the other hand it has been shown (e.g., Hesse, 1982; Reither, 1979; Tisdale, 1992) that induced self-reflection improves the capabilities of problem solving.

Individual differences in the quality of the decisions can be due to differences in the amplification processes, different memory and thinking capacities, or the subjective feeling of competence. The mental representation of a certain environment can be enriched and differentiated by an amplification process. Such a process may involve analysis of the parts, the superordinates, the subordinates, and the context. The process will result in a network of causal relations. The degree of elaboration of the network of causal relations is assumed to be one determinant of performance in microworlds. The ability to construct elaborated causal networks is related to a person's heuristic competence. Heuristic competence is defined as a person's confidence in his or her ability to find any missing operators in order to accomplish a task (Dörner & Wearing, 1995). Heuristic competence is context independent and is a part of a person's actual competence. The context dependent part of actual competence is epistemic competence and is defined as the confidence that one already knows how to fulfill the requirements of a task. According to this theory, the actual competence remains stable in the face of failure only if the heuristic competence of a person is stable. In some of our studies (e.g., Rigas, Brehmer, Brehmer, Elg, & Heikinen, 1997; Rigas & Elg, 1997) the validity coefficients from heuristic competence to performance in MORO were low. The internal consistency coefficients, on the other hand, of various subscales measuring heuristic competence were generally high, so we hypothesized that the problem must be in the respondent nature of these measurements. One possible solution for such problems is to construct operant measures (see Raven, 1988).

In general, we have seen that microworlds have characteristics similar to many real-life domains and demand complex mental processes that seem to be relevant as well in real-life pursuits. The individual differences in behavior and performance in microworlds may be caused by differences in memory and thinking capacity, amplification processes, or heuristic competence.

TESTS AND MICROWORLDS

As should be obvious from the analysis above, although a test such a Raven's Advanced Matrices and a microworld such as MORO are both complex, they are complex in different ways. The description of the processes involved in APM by Carpenter et al. (1990) is at the level of primitive information processes, while the description of the psychological processes involved in work with MORO (Dörner & Wearing, 1995) and above is at the level of quite complex processes. We hypothesize that the individual differences in MORO such as deficiences in mental models or in goal formulations may not be easy to relate to indvidual differences in more primitive information processes. This is because these primitive information processes will be important in all of the complex information processes involved in MORO, and if one of these complex processes fails it is not likely be due to failure of more primitive processes, for the same primitive processes are likely to be involved in both those complex processes that succeed and in those that fail. Therefore, there are no strong reasons for expecting very high correlations between performance in intelligence tests, such as APM, and performance in microworlds, such as MORO. On the other hand, according to the analysis above, the individual differences in behavior and performance in microworlds may be partly determined by differences in memory and thinking capacity, so that stable but low positive correlations should be expected.

In a number of empirical studies the relationship between test intelligence and performance in microworlds has been estimated to be close to zero (e.g., Brehmer & Rigas, 1997; Dörner, Kreuzig, Reither, & Stäudel, 1983; Putz-Osterloh & Lüer, 1981; Rigas, 1997; Stäudel, 1987; Strohschneider, 1991). However, in some other studies a positive relationship between intelligence test scores and performance in microworlds has been found (e.g., Funke, 1983; Hussy, 1989; Süss, Kersting, & Oberauer, 1991; Süss, Kersting, & Oberauer, 1993). These seemingly inconsistent empirical findings (for a review on this topic see Kluwe, Schilde, Fischer, & Oellerer, 1991) have led some researchers (e.g., Beckmann & Guthke, 1995) to argue for the need to consider the influence of potential moderator variables such as naturality, goal definition, semantic embeddedness, transparency, difficulty, and multidimensionality. Although we agree with Beckmann and Guthke (1995) that in order to arrive at a synthesis we have to consider the factorial complexity of both test intelligence and microworld performance by varying systematically individual task components on both sides, we believe that we should also consider the possibility of sampling errors in these studies. If this is the case, then a clearer picture will emerge with a meta-analysis. In addition, we also believe that future studies should be designed in ways that enable the estimation of the predictive validity of both test intelligence and microworld performance in real-life tasks, because this is the main issue from a practical point of view, and not the relationship between test intelligence and microworld performance.

Although the predictive validity that performance measures in microworlds have in real-life tasks has not been studied yet, there exist some studies concerning the concurrent and content validity of behavior and performance in microworlds (Putz-Osterloh, 1987; Putz-Osterloh & Lemme, 1987; Reither, 1981; Schaub & Strohschneider, 1992). In these studies the behavior and performance of an expert group (university professors, company managers, economic aid professionals) is compared to the behavior and performance of a novice group (students). The typical findings in these studies are that experts are more likely to spend more time in the phase of initial orientation and goal elaboration, to think in causal nets and not in causal chains, to consider possible side effects, to acquire more knowledge, to exhibit more concerted decision making behavior, and to achieve higher levels of performance.

EMPIRICAL STUDIES

In the empirical studies that are presented here, the influence of some important factors on the relationship between test-intelligence and performance in dynamic tasks is investigated. These factors are transparency, novelty, and complexity. In general we expect the correlations between test-intelligence and performance in dynamic tasks to increase when the dynamic tasks have some aspects that are similar to intelligence tests (as is for instance the case with NEWFIRE, which does not demand goal elaboration), or are administered in a way that increases the similarity with the intelligence tests (e.g., by increasing transparency).

Studies with MORO

Intransparency (Brehmer & Rigas, 1997). Intransparency has been defined in a number of ways. One of the most inclusive definitions is given by Funke (1991). According to this definition intransparency arises when the number of variables is huge and it is necessary to select the most relevant ones, even if it is in principle possible to assess each one. According to Brehmer and Dörner (1993), intransparency "refers to the fact that not everything is visible, and that some aspects of the system have to be inferred. This means that the subjects have to form hypotheses and test them as a part of the activity" (p. 173). Finally, a somewhat different definition is that given by Putz-Osterloh (1993). According to this definition, a system is not transparent when "the relational network connecting the variables one to another is not shown to the subjects" (p. 291). In this experiment we operationalized transparency in the way proposed by Putz-Osterloh (1993).

Eighty students participated in this study. The design was completely randomized with two conditions, a transparent and an intransparent one. The participants in the transparent condition in addition to the standard instructions had access to a figure similar to Figure 4.2 and a list with all possible types of interventions in the simulation.

The results showed that the performance of the group in the transparent condition was not improved. This may be due to information overload in the transparent group. This result is congruent with the results obtained by

Hussy and Granzow (1987). These researchers found that increasing the richness of the information over a certain level confuses the participants.

From earlier studies (e.g., Hesse, 1982; Putz-Osterloh & Lüer, 1981) it was expected that the correlation between intelligence and performance in MORO would be higher for the group in the transparent condition, because the task of controlling MORO under transparency is more similar to intelligence test taking. One way to evaluate performance in MORO is to count the number of years until the first catastrophe. As expected, the correlation of this dependent variable with intelligence for the transparent group was .43, while for the in-transparent group it was .22. We believe that this result can also be explained by information overload for the participants in the transparent condition. Participants that do well in APM have higher working memory capacity, so they could process the higher amount of information in the transparent condition and keep the system in balance for a longer period.

Learning from Experience (Rigas, 1997). As we stated earlier, efforts to predict performance in dynamic decision making tasks from test-intelligence have not been successful. One hypothesis is that these two different types of tasks place different demands upon the participants that call for different abilities (see also Dörner, 1986). A second hypothesis is that performance scores in microworlds are unreliable (Funke, 1986). A third hypothesis not considered previously in the context of dynamic systems is the task novelty hypothesis—that is, intelligence is most useful in tasks of medium novelty (Raaheim, 1988). These hypotheses, and the extent of learning from experience in a complex dynamic system were investigated in this study. From the theoretical analyses of the difficulties that people have dealing with complex systems (Brehmer, 1995; Dörner, 1996; Sterman, 1989) learning was expected to be limited.

Forty-eight students participated in this experiment. A split-plot factorial design was used. The within-subjects variable was "experience with the system" and it had three levels (participants interacted with MORO three times). The between-subjects variables were (1) same or different starting parameters and (2) experimenter effects (the simulations were led by two different experimenters). In a fourth session Raven's Advanced Progressive Matrices (Raven, 1976) were administered.

Learning by experience in MORO was limited as expected. The participants learned how to earn more money and how to keep more cattle, but performance considering the state of the system as a whole was not improved. In MORO there are four possible types of catastrophes: bankruptcy, groundwater depletion, overgrazing, and starvation. In case of bankruptcy or starvation, participants receive immediate feedback. Regarding these two types of catastrophes, performance improved. For the other two types

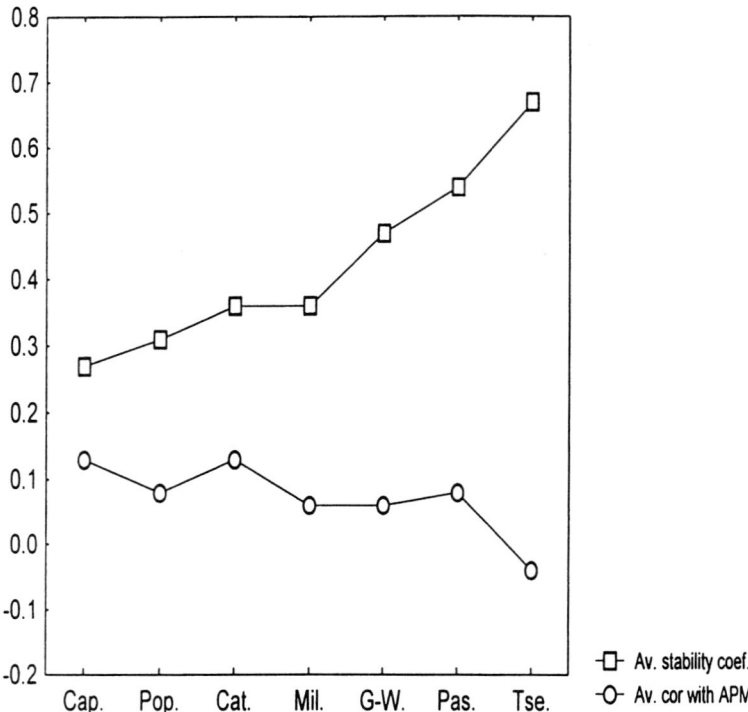

FIG. 4.3. Average stability coefficients of the central variables in the MORO
simulation and average correlations with APM.

of catastrophes there is no information given unless the participant asks
the relevant questions. For these two, performance did not improve.

Intelligence scores did not correlate substantially with performance in
MORO. These results cannot be explained by the task novelty hypothesis.
According to this hypothesis the correlations with APM were expected to
increase. Although from the results of this experiment the explanation
proposed by Funke (1986) cannot be rejected (that is, performance scores
in microworlds are not sufficiently reliable), there are two interesting findings: (1) the correlations with APM scores were not higher for the central
variables that had higher stability coefficients (see Fig. 4.3) and (2) the
correlations of APM with the composite scores of performance, that are
more stable, were also low.

We believe that the main reason for the lack of correlation between
intelligence test scores and performance in MORO is that the different
demands placed upon the participants by the two different types of tasks
call for different mental processes and abilities.

Studies with NEWFIRE

Complexity (Rigas, Carling & Brehmer, 1997). In this study we analyzed behavior in NEWFIRE in terms of strategy components, and examined how the strategy components and performance are related to psychometric intelligence. Time of initial decisions (TID), consideration of wind direction (WDIR), allocation of fire-fighting units (ALLOC), and encircling of the fire (CIRCL) were the strategy components considered here. These strategy components do not demand use of dynamic information (except for ALLOC, which involves a series of decisions). Questions concerning the reliability of performance scores in NEWFIRE were also addressed.

As we said earlier, NEWFIRE is a real-time dynamic system. It is highly dynamic and characterized by low complexity and low intransparency. In this experiment complexity was manipulated by varying the number of fires in a scenario. From the complexity continuum hypothesis (Snow et al., 1984) it was expected that performance in the more complex scenarios would be more dependent on intelligence.

Thirty-six undergraduate students participated in this study. They completed eight scenarios and composite scores were computed. Composite scores were also computed for the less and the more complex scenarios.

The internal consistency was sufficiently high (about .76). The internal consistency of the composite scores of the more complex scenarios was slightly higher than the internal consistency of the less complex scenarios. Contrary to what was expected from the complexity continuum hypothesis intelligence correlated significantly only with the composite scores of the less complex scenarios. These results suggest that the cognitive demands placed upon the participants by dynamic tasks as NEWFIRE, over a certain level of complexity, require abilities not tapped by traditional intelligence tests.

CONCLUDING COMMENTS

The results of the studies reviewed above reveal consistent but low correlations between performance in APM and performance in MORO and NEWFIRE. The question is whether we should expect very high correlations between test performance and microworld performance. Our discussion above suggests that perhaps we should not. At present, we do not have an analysis of performance in microworlds in terms of the primitive information processes that have been used to model performance in APM. One reason for this is that performance in microworlds seem to demand much more complex psychological processes that are very hard to reduce to primitive information processes. Moreover, it seems that all of the more complex processes required to understand what goes on in MORO, for example, seem to require all of the primitive information processes that are required to solve the tasks set by APM. Therefore, we cannot understand the failure of a complex process in MORO in terms of these primitive processes, for if the participant was deficient in one of these primitive processes, all of his or her complex processes should be deficient as well. But this is clearly not the case. In MORO, failures are not the consequence of the failure of all relevant cognitive processes, but the failure only of some of these complex processes.

Intelligence tests such as APM are designed to present tasks that are closely related to primitive processes. Microworlds, on the other hand, are designed so as to require complex processes. Even though in principle it should be possible to reduce complex behavior to the primitive processes tapped by intelligence tests, the fact that participants may succeed with some of complex processes but not with others suggests that an analysis of these complex processes in terms of the more primitive processes measured by intelligence tests cannot succeed. Instead, complex behavior has to be understood at the level of complex behavior, and cannot easily be reduced to primitive processes. If such an analysis were relevant, we should expect massive correlations between intelligence tests and microworld performance. The fact that we do not find such correlations suggests that we need new forms of tests aimed at the more complex processes that we find in the every day tasks that are simulated by microworlds.

ACKNOWLEDGMENT

This study was supported by a grant from the Swedish Council for Research in the Humanities and the Social Sciences.

REFERENCES

Badke-Schaub, P. (1989). *How people try to solve the AIDS problem: Decision making in complex situations: Results of a simulation experiment.* Memorandum No. 23. University of Bamberg: Lehrstuhl für Psychologie II.sa

Baron, J. (1993). Why teach thinking?—An essay. *Journal of Applied Psychology: An International Review, 42,* 191–214.

Beckmann, J. F., & Guthke, J. (1995). Complex problem solving, intelligence, and learning ability. In P. A. Frensch & J. Funke (Ed.), *Complex problem solving: The European perspective* (pp. 103–130). Hillsdale, NJ: Lawrence Erlbaum Associates.

Brehmer, B. (1995). Feedback delays in complex dynamic decision tasks. In P. A. Frensch & J. Funke (Ed.), *Complex problem solving: The European perspective* (pp. 103–130). Hillsdale, NJ: Lawrence Erlbaum Associates.

Brehmer, B., & Dörner, D. (1993). Experiments with computer-simulated microworlds: Escaping both the narrow straits of the laboratory and the deep blue sea of the field study. *Computers in Human Behavior, 9,* 171–184.

Brehmer, B., & Rigas, G. (1997). *Transparency and the relationship between dynamic decision making and intelligence.* Unpublished manuscript.

Burt, C. L. (1949). The structure of the mind: A review of the results of factor analysis. *British Journal of Educational Psychology, 19,* 100–110, 176–199.

Carpenter, P. A., Just, M. A., & Shell, P. (1990). What one intelligence test measures: A theoretical account of the processing in the Raven Progressive Matrices Test. *Psychological Review, 97,* 404–431.

Carroll, J. B. (1993). *Human cognitive abilities: A survey of factor analytic studies.* Cambridge: Cambridge University Press.

Cattell, R. B. (1943). The measurement of adult intelligence. *Psychological Bulletin, 40,* 153–193.

DeShon, R. P., Chan, D., & Weissbein, D. A. (1995). Verbal overshadowing effects on Raven's Advanced Progressive Matrices: Evidence for multidimensional performance determinants. *Intelligence, 21,* 135–155.

Dörner, D. (1986). Diagnostik der operativen Intelligenz [Diagnosis of operative intelligence]. *Diagnostica, 32,* 290–308.

Dörner, D. (1996). *The logic of failure: Why things go wrong and what we can do to make them right.* New York: Holt.

Dörner, D., Kreuzig, H. W., Reither, F., & Stäudel, T. (Eds.). (1983). *Lohhausen. Vom Umgang mit Unbestimmtheit und Komplexität* [Lohhausen. On dealing with uncertainty and complexity]. Bern, Switzerland: Hans Huber.

Dörner, D., & Schaub, H. (1994). Errors in planning and decision-making and the nature of human information processing. *Journal of Applied Psychology: An International Review, 43,* 433–453.

Dörner, D., Stäudel, T., & Strohschneider, S. (1986). *MORO: Programmdokumentation.* Memorandum No. 23. University of Bamberg: Lehrstuhl für Psychologie II.sa

Dörner, D., & Wearing, A. (1995). Complex problem solving: Toward a (computersimulated) theory. In P. A. Frensch & J. Funke (Eds.), *Complex problem solving: The European perspective* (pp. 65–99). Hillsdale, NJ: Lawrence Erlbaum Associates.

Funke, J. (1983). Einige Bemerkungen zu Problemen der Problemlöseforschung oder: Ist Testintelligenz doch ein Prädiktor? [Some remarks on the problems of problem solving research or: Does test intelligence predict control performance?]. *Diagnostica, 29,* 283–302.

Funke, J. (1986). *Komplexes Problemlösen. Bestandsaufnahme und Perspektiven* [Complex problem solving: Overview and perspectives]. Heidelberg, Germany: Springer.

Funke, J. (1988). Using simulation to study complex problem solving: A review of studies in FRG. *Simulation & Games, 19,* 277–303.

Funke, J. (1991). Solving complex problems: Exploration and control of complex systems. In R. J. Sternberg & P. A. Frensch (Eds.), *Complex problem solving: Principles and mechanisms* (pp. 185–222). Hillsdale, NJ: Lawrence Erlbaum Associates.

Guilford, J. P. (1967). *The nature of human intelligence.* New York: McGraw-Hill.

Gustafsson, J.-E. (1984). A unifying model for the structure of intellectual abilities. *Intelligence, 8,* 179–203.

Gustafsson, J.-E. (1988). Hierarchical models of individual differences in cognitive abilities. In R. J. Sternberg (Ed.), *Advances in the psychology of human intelligence,* vol. 4 (pp. 35–71). Hillsdale, NJ: Lawrence Erlbaum Associates.

Guttman, L. (1954). A new approach to factor analysis: The radex. In P. F. Lazerfield (Ed.), *Mathematical thinking in the social sciences.* Glencoe, IL: Free Press.

Hesse, F. W. (1982). Training-induced changes in problem-solving. *Zeitschrift für Psychologie, 190,* 405–423.

Horn, J. L., & Cattell, R. B. (1966). Refinement and test of the theory of fluid and crystalized intelligence. *Journal of Educational Psychology, 57*, 253–270.

Hunt, E. (1974). Quote the Raven? Nevermore! In L. W. Gregg (Ed.), *Knowledge and cognition.* Hillsdale, NJ: Lawrence Erlbaum Associates.

Hussy, W. (1989). Intelligenz und komplexes Problemlösen [Intelligence and complex problem solving]. *Diagnostica, 35*, 1–16.

Hussy, W., & Granzow, S. (1987). Komplexes Problemlösen, Gedächtnis und Verarbitungsstil. *Zeitschrift für Experimentelle und Angewandte Psychologie, 34*, 212–227.

Jensen, A. (1982). The chronometry of intelligence. In R. J. Sternberg (Ed.), *Advances in the psychology of human intelligence,* Vol. 1 (pp. 255–310). Hillsdale, NJ: Lawrence Erlbaum Associates.

Jensen, A. (1984). Test validity: g versus the specificity doctrine. *Journal of Social and Biological Structures, 7*, 93–118.

Jensen, A. (1987). The g beyond factor analysis. In R. R. Ronning, J. A. Glover, J. C. Conoley, & J. C. Witt (Eds.), *The influence of cognitive psychology on testing* (pp. 87–142). Hillsdale, NJ: Lawrence Erlbaum Associates.

Kluwe, R. H., Schilde, A., Fischer, C., & Oellerer, N. (1991). Problemlöseleistungen beim Umgang mit komplexen Systemen und Intelligenz [Problem solving performance when interacting with complex systems and intelligence]. *Diagnostica, 37*, 291–313.

Lövborg, L., & Brehmer, B. (1991). *NEWFIRE—A flexible system for running simulated fire-fighting experiments.* Risö National Laboratory, Roskilde, Denmark.

Neisser, U. (1976). General, academic, and artificial intelligence. In L. Resnick (Ed.), *The nature of intelligence* (pp. 135–144). Hillsdale, NJ: Lawrence Erlbaum Associates.

Newell, A. (1990). *Unified theories of cognition.* Cambridge: Harvard University Press.

Newell, A., & Simon, H. A. (1972). *Human problem solving.* Englewood Cliffs, NJ: Prentice-Hall.

Putz-Osterloh, W. (1987). Gibt es Experten für komplexe Probleme? [Are there experts for complex problems?]. *Zeitschrift für Psychologie, 195*, 63–84.

Putz-Osterloh, W. (1993). Complex problem solving as a diagnostic tool. In H. Schuler, J. L. Farr, & M. Smith (Eds.), *Personnel selection and assessment: Individual and organizational perspectives* (pp. 289–301). Hillsdale, NJ: Lawrence Erlbaum Associates.

Putz-Osterloh, W., & Lemme, M. (1987). Knowledge and its intelligent application to problem solving. *The German Journal of Psychology, 11*, 286–303.

Putz-Osterloh, W., & Lüer, G. (1981). Über die Vorhersagbarkeit komplexer Problemlöseleistungen durch Ergebnisse in einem Intelligenztest [On whether results from a test of intelligence can predict problem solving performance]. *Zeitschrift für Experimentelle und Angewandte Psychologie, 28*, 309–334.

Raaheim, K. (1988). Intelligence and task novelty. In R. J. Sternberg (Ed.), *Advances in the psychology of human intelligence,* Vol. 4 (pp. 73–97). Hillsdale, NJ: Lawrence Erlbaum Associates.

Raven, J. C. (1976). *Advanced Progressive Matrices, Sets I and II.* Oxford, England: Oxford Psychologists Press.

Raven, J. (1988). Toward measures of high-level competencies: A re-examination of McClelland's distinction between needs and values. *Human Relations, 41*, 281–294.

Raven, J., Raven, J. C., & Court, J. H. (1993). *Advanced progressive matrices: Section 1.* Oxford Psychologists Press.

Reither, F. (1979). Über die Selbstreflexion beim Problemlösen [On self-reflection during problem solving]. Unpublished doctoral dissertation, FB 06 Psychologie der Universität Giessen, Germany.

Reither, F. (1981). About thinking and acting of experts in complex situations. *Simulation & Games, 12*, 125–140.

Rigas, G. (1995). *RAVEN-trace* (Computer software). Uppsala University, Department of Psychology.

Rigas, G. (1997). *Intelligence and learning by experience in a dynamic decision making environment.* Paper presented to the 16th Conference on Subjective Probability, Utility, and Decision Making, Leeds, England.

Rigas, G., Brehmer, A., Brehmer, B., Elg, F., & Heikinen, S. (1997). *Reliability and Validity of Heuristic Competence Scales.* Unpublished manuscript.

Rigas, G., Carling, E., & Brehmer, B. (1997). *Does the near zero correlations between test-intelligence and dynamic decision making performance depend on the static character of intelligence tests?* Unpublished manuscript.

Rigas, G., & Elg, F. (1997). *Mental models, confidence, and performance in a complex dynamic decision making environment.* Paper presented to the 15th International System Dynamics Conference, Istanbul, Turkey.

Schaub, H., & Strohschneider, S. (1992). Die Auswirkungen unterschiedlicher Problemlöseerfahrung auf den Umgang mit einem unbekannten komplexen problem [Effects of different experiences with problems on how to deal with with an unknown complex problem]. *Zeitschrift für Arbeits- und Organisationspsychologie, 36,* 117–126.

Snow, R. E., Kyllonen, P. C., & Marshalek, B. (1984). The topography of ability and learning correlations. In R. J. Sternberg (Ed.), *Advances in the psychology of human intelligence,* Vol. 2 (pp. 47–103). Hillsdale, NJ: Lawrence Erlbaum Associates.

Spearman, C. (1904). "General Intelligence": Objectively determined and measured. *American Journal of Psychology, 15,* 201–292.

Spearman, C. (1927). *The abilities of man.* London: Macmillan.

Stäudel, T. (1987). *Problemlösen, Emotionen und Kompetenz* [Problem solving, emotions, and competence]. Regensburg, Germany: Roderer.

Sterman, J. D. (1989). Misperceptions of feedback in dynamic decision making. *Organizational Behavior and Human Decision Processes, 43,* 301–335.

Sternberg, R. J. (1979). The nature of mental abilities. *American Psychologist, 34,* 214–230.

Sternberg, R. J., & Kaufman, J. C. (1996). Innovation and intelligence testing: The curious case of the dog that didn't bark. *European Journal of Psychological Assessment, 12,* 175–182.

Strohschneider, S. (1986). Zur Stabilität und Validität von Handeln in komplexen Realitätsbereichen [On the stability and validity of complex problem solving behavior]. *Sprache & Kognition, 5,* 42–48.

Strohschneider, S. (1991). Problemlösen und Intelligenz: Über die Effekte der Konkretisierung komplexer Probleme [Problem solving and intelligence: The effects of problem concreteness]. *Diagnostica, 37,* 353–371.

Süss, H.-M., Kersting, M., & Oberauer, K. (1991). Intelligenz und Wissen als Prädiktoren für Leistungen bei computersimulierten komplexen Problemen [Intelligence and knowledge as predictors of performance in solving complex computer-simulated problems]. *Diagnostica, 37,* 334–352.

Süss, H.-M., Kersting, M., & Oberauer, K. (1993). Zur Vorhersage von Steuerungsleistungen an computersimulierten Systemen durch Wissen und intelligenz [Predicting control performance in computersimulated systems by means of knowledge and intelligence]. *Zeitschrift für Differentielle und Diagnostische Psychologie, 14,* 189–203.

Thurstone, L. L. (1938). *Primary mental abilities.* Chicago: University of Chicago Press.

Tisdale, T. (1992). Self-reflection and its Part in Action Regulation. In B. Brehmer & J. Leplat (Eds.), *Simulations, Evaluations and Models.* Proceedings of the fourth MOHAWC workshop, Roskilde, Risö National Laboratory.

Vernon, P. E. (1950). *The structure of human abilities.* New York: Wiley.

Vernon, P. E. (1983). Speed of information processing and intelligence. *Intelligence, 7,* 53–70.

Wagner, R. K., & Sternberg, R. J. (1985). Practical intelligence in real-world pursuits: The role of tacit knowledge. *Journal of Personality and Social Psychology, 49,* 436–458.

Chapter 5

Computational Models of Subjective Probability Calibration

Peter Juslin
Henrik Olsson
Uppsala University

Regardless of whether you are about to decide what to have for dinner this evening or if you are faced with the crossing of your personal Rubicon, it is a common experience that you do not always get what you want. The outcomes of your decisions are often uncertain. One consequence of the uncertainty that permeates our lives is the conceptual dissociation between outcome and optimality: even the best of decisions may lead to a poor outcome. Whereas the outcome is often all too easy to ascertain, optimality is a more problematic notion. A common solution involves the weighting of the values of outcomes with their probability, with the recommendation to decide on the option with the highest expected value. The present-day formulation of this idea—subjective expected utility (SEU) theory (e.g., Savage, 1954)—imposes constraints on a person's decision making that allow the decisions to be interpreted as optimization in terms of a subjective utility function and a subjective probability measure. The decision problem is therefore dissected into two subcomponents: values or *utilities* and *subjective probabilities*. Psychological research has accordingly been concerned with people's ability to make subjective probability assessments. One important aspect of subjective probabilities concern their *calibration*, or realism—the extent to which events assigned subjective probability *.xx* tend to occur with relative frequency *.xx*.

In a recent article we introduced a distinction between two origins of error or uncertainty in judgment and decision making (Juslin & Olsson, 1997) named after two of the more well-known probabilists in the history of psychology, Egon Brunswik (Brunswik, 1952; Hammond, 1966) and L. L. Thurstone (e.g., Thurstone, 1927). The Brunswikian origin of error refers to erroneous responses that arise from the optimal use of limited knowledge, as when we use knowledge of an environment to make best guesses in a judgment or prediction task. The Thurstonian origin of error refers to erroneous responses that emanate from the imperfections and stochastic components of the information processing system itself, with one paradigmatic example being when sensory discriminations are perturbed by neural noise. In Juslin and Olsson (1997) we pointed to a number of conceptual and empirical differences between these two origins of error in judgment and decision making.

In this chapter we will illustrate how our understanding of the calibration of subjective probabilities is enlightened by models that explicitly explore the properties and interactions of these two origins of error. In the first section, we discuss the ecological models (Björkman, 1994; Gigerenzer, Hoffrage, & Kleinbölting, 1991; Juslin, 1993b), which model the organism–environment relations that support probabilistic cue-based inference, clearly the heartland of Brunswikian uncertainty. The second section presents the combined error model (Juslin, Olsson, & Björkman, 1997; Juslin, Wennerholm, & Olsson, in press), which adds Thurstonian error to the cognitive processes of the ecological model. In the final section, we briefly present the sensory sampling model (Juslin & Olsson, 1997), a model exclusively concerned with perceptual discrimination tasks dominated by the Thurstonian origin of error (i.e., so called "neural noise").

Before we discuss these models, however, we need to briefly review the main phenomena that need to be accounted for by models of calibration of subjective probabilities.

EMPIRICAL DATA ON CALIBRATION OF CONFIDENCE

Inferential Tasks

1. The Overconfidence Effect. In studies with half-range general knowledge items, the participants select one of two presented answers and assess the probability that the selected answer is correct on a scale from .5 to 1, as illustrated in Example A below:

A. *The Half-Range Format*
   Which country has a population with a higher mean life expectancy?
            a. *Indonesia*   b. *Sudan*

50%	60%	70%	80%	90%	100%
Random					Certain

The most common result in studies with general knowledge items has been overconfidence, where the mean subjective probability of a correct answer $\bar{r}$, exceeds the proportion of correct decisions $\bar{c}$, $\bar{r} - \bar{c}$ is positive. For example, if the participants on average assess the probability that they have chosen the correct answer to be .8 (or 80%), but only have 60% correct, overconfidence is .2. Only recently there have been studies with well-calibrated half-range assessments (e.g., Gigerenzer et al., 1991; Juslin, 1993b, 1994).

In a full-range task the probability that a proposition is true is assessed between 0 and 1. The above Indonesia–Sudan item transformed into full-range format becomes:

B. *The Full-Range Format*
   The population of Indonesia has a higher mean life expectancy than the population
   of Sudan. What is the probability that this statement is true?
   0%   10%   20%   30%   40%   50%   60%   70%   80%   90%   100%
   False   True

With the full-range format, overconfidence is observed when the assessors are too certain that some statements are true and that others are false. The over/underconfidence score is computed by transforming the full-range probabilities into inferred half-range probabilities. One assumes that full-range probabilities above 50% corresponds to a half-range decision in favor of Indonesia and probabilities below 50% as half-range decisions favoring Sudan. In the former case the full-range probability is also the half-range probability, but in the latter case the half-range probability is the complement—1 minus the stated full-range probability. Probabilities of .5 are coded as randomly favoring the truth or falsity of the statements. Mean confidence is then compared to the proportion correct in the manner of half-range data and the resulting score is interpreted in the same way as for the half-range method (Juslin, Olsson, et al., 1997).

With the interval estimation method (a simplified fractile method), the participant is confronted with a statement such as:

C. *Interval Estimation Format*
   Assess the (smallest) interval within which you are 80% certain (probability
   .8) that the mean life expectancy of the population of Indonesia lies:
   Between _____ years and _____ years

With the direct interval estimation method, over/underconfidence scores are computed from the difference between the stated probability interval and the observed event proportion within this interval. Some experts provide well-calibrated judgments with the full-range method, but most of the data suggest overconfidence (Keren, 1991; Lichtenstein, Fischhoff, & Phillips, 1982; Yates, 1990). With interval estimation the common result has been extreme overconfidence (Lichtenstein et al., 1982).

2. The Hard–Easy Effect. With half-range items, over/underconfidence usually covaries with task difficulty, with more overconfidence in more difficult tasks—the so-called hard–easy effect (Lichtenstein & Fischhoff, 1977). The breaking point seems to be around a proportion correct $\bar{c}$ of .75, with overconfidence for item sets with a lower proportion correct and underconfidence for item sets with a higher proportion correct (Juslin, Olsson, et al. 1997; Juslin, Wennerholm, & Olsson, in press; but see also Juslin, Winman, & Olsson, 1998, for a discussion of the methodological problems associated with the hard–easy effect).

3. The Base–Rate Effect. A finding relevant to full-range items is the base–rate effect (e.g., Smith & Ferrell, 1983). When the base–rate of an event is manipulated in the laboratory—for example, by varying the proportion of true statements in a set of items like the one in Example B above—the probability assessors seem unable to accommodate for these base–rate changes, and calibration deteriorates.

4. The Expertise Effect. A common finding is that experts are better calibrated than novices (for reviews see Lichtenstein et al., 1982, Yates, 1990, Keren, 1991), a finding we will refer to as the expertise effect. It is important to note, though, that the calibration of experts is domain specific and differs across areas of expertise (see the review in Chapter 7 of this volume) with poor calibration in some areas (e.g., Yates, McDaniel, & Brown, 1991).

5. Simultaneous Conservatism and Overconfidence. An intriguing result in view of the overconfidence effect, is the conservatism bias in studies of belief revision (Edwards, 1982). In these studies, people seem to revise their beliefs too conservatively in the light of new observations, a finding that—at least on the face of it—seems inconsistent with the result that people provide too extreme subjective probabilities (overconfidence). Only recently, conservatism has been connected to overconfidence in terms of models that stress stochastic components of the judgment process (Erev, Wallsten, & Budescu, 1994).

6. Format Dependence. Preferably, subjective probability assessments should reflect the knowledge state of the assessor, rather than idiosyncrasies in the methods and scales used for the overt response elicitation. Recently, Juslin, Olsson, et al. (1997) and Juslin, Wennerholm, and Olsson (in press) have demonstrated a systematic difference between the half-range and full-range formats. When these methods are applied to the same tasks there can indeed be simultaneous over- and underconfidence, depending on the assessment format—a phenomenon that will be illustrated in a section below.

Sensory Discrimination Tasks

The phenomena summarized above have been observed with tasks that involve probabilistic inference where most errors are explained by unsuccessful inference, the domain of Brunswikian uncertainty. What about tasks dominated by Thurstonian error?

Consider the following two-alternative, half-range tasks:

D. *Which of these two weights is the heavier?*

	a. *Left weight*			b. *Right weight*	
50%	60%	70%	80%	90%	100%
Random					Certain

The participant is presented with two objects that he or she is unable to see. The task is to decide which object is the heavier solely on the basis of haptic information. In this task, the dominating origin of uncertainty is Thurstonian rather than Brunswikian, erroneous decisions arising primarily due to neural noise in the sensory process. This kind of task—which we refer to as sensory discrimination (Juslin & Olsson, 1997)—will be associated with many of the phenomena reviewed above, but there are some significant differences:

1. The Underconfidence Phenomenon. Calibration of confidence in sensory discrimination has been investigated in a number of studies in our laboratory (Björkman, Juslin, & Winman, 1993; Juslin & Olsson, 1997; Olsson & Winman, 1996; Winman & Juslin, 1993, Winman, Juslin, & Björkman, 1998). The results seem to differ from those in cognitive tasks, with a disposition toward underconfidence in sensory tasks (see also Crawford & Stankov, 1997; Peirce & Jastrow, 1884). We performed a "meta-analysis" of 21 sensory discrimination tasks and 44 cognitive, general knowledge tasks collected in our laboratory under comparable circumstances (the analysis and the data are provided in the appendix of Juslin, Olsson, et al., 1998). The results clearly showed that there is more underconfidence bias in sensory discrimination tasks than in cognitive tasks over the entire range of proportion correct.

2. Error-Independence. A second difference between tasks dominated by Brunswikian and Thurstonian error concerns the dependence or correlation of erroneous decisions as evidenced by the solution probabilities in two-alternative decision tasks (i.e., the proportions of participants that selected the correct answer). In sensory discrimination all solution probabilities tend to fall above .5, suggesting error-independence (Juslin & Olsson, 1997). If erroneous decisions reflect Thurstonian error, there is nothing that will make all participants select the wrong alternative; in this sense the errors are independent of each other. Cognitive tasks, on the other hand, are associated with error-dependence because they will often involve cue-based inference, associated with Brunswikian error. If a cue has limited validity and is used consistently by all participants, the inference will more often lead to a correct answer, but for some items it will lead all participants to select the wrong answer. This will imply solution probabilities in the entire interval between 0 and 1, something that is true even if the assessors are well calibrated when presented with a sample of different tasks (Juslin & Olsson, 1997).

COMPUTATIONAL MODELS OF CALIBRATION

Brunswikian Error: The Ecological Model

Most psychological research on probability assessment has been guided by SEU theory, which highlights the importance of coherence—the extent to which the assessments conform with the rules of the probability calculus (Kahneman, Slovic, & Tversky, 1982). While coherence certainly is a desirable property, from a psychological or biological perspective, it seems to be a too weak criterion of adaptive behavior. Survival in a hostile environment will in addition require correspondence between subjective beliefs and environmental states (Hammond, 1996). The correspondence norm has surfaced in research on calibration in terms of the ecological models (Björkman, 1994; Gigerenzer et al., 1991, Juslin, 1993b), which presume that subjective probabilities largely reflect experience with ecological probabilities, a term that refers to the relative frequencies that obtain in a natural environment. Adaptation is thus approached in terms of the correspondence between subjective degrees of belief and corresponding ecological probabilities (or ecological cue validities).

In the original formulations of the ecological models (e.g., Gigerenzer et al., 1991; Juslin, 1993b), decisions and confidence in half-range tasks were assumed to mirror adaptation to a natural environment. It was proposed that people select the answers that are most probably (i.e., frequently) correct in the reference class of situations in their natural environment and confidence or subjective probability is assessed according to the relative frequencies that obtain in this environment. For instance, in regard to Example A above, a participant may recall that Indonesia lies in Asia while Sudan lies in Africa, and use these facts as a probabilistic cue to which country has the higher mean life expectancy. The participant may believe that Asian countries tend to have higher mean life expectancy than African countries and thus that within Asian–African pairs of countries the Asian country most often has the higher mean life expectancy. The continent cue thus suggests that Indonesia probably is the correct answer. This illustrates how limited knowledge of a natural environment can be used to make probabilistic inferences (see Gigerenzer & Goldstein, 1996, for simulations).

The critical implication by the ecological models is that confidence is based on an assessment of the ecological cue validity of the cue used in the choice. In the theory of probabilistic mental models (PMM; Gigerenzer et al., 1991) as well as in other Brunswik-inspired research on calibration (e.g., Björkman, 1994; Juslin, 1993b) the ecological cue validity is defined by the relative frequency of cases in the environment where the cue indicates the correct answer. A cue that always points to the correct answer (high ecological cue validity) elicits high confidence, a cue that is only slightly better than chance (low ecological cue validity) leads to less confidence. For instance, the Asian–African continent cue used by the above participant will select the correct answer in 88% of the cases that may be encountered in the environment. If the participant has a reasonably accurate belief about the ecological cue validity, he or she will express high confidence when confronted with this task, say 90% confidence.

The relative frequencies that support decisions and confidence assessments, the ecological probabilities or ecological cue validities, become part of a person's knowledge in the form of internal probabilities, or internal cue validities (Björkman, 1994; Juslin, 1993b; Juslin, Olsson, et al., 1997). On the assumption of cognitive adjustment—internal probabilities that match the corresponding ecological probabilities—and error-free expression of internal probabilities as overt probability assessments, the confidence assessments should be calibrated to the distribution of situations encountered in a natural environment. If the participant in our example makes a confidence assessment of 90% and is presented with a task sample where the Asian–African cue is allowed to have its ecological cue validity (88%), confidence will be in approximate agreement with the expected proportion correct.

The ecological models naturally highlight the importance of the Brunswikian notion of representative design (Brunswik, 1952). If people are calibrated to a natural environment and if this is to be observable in the laboratory, the task-sample needs to be representative of the statistical structure of the environment. The argument presented by the ecological models is that the overconfidence effect to a large extent has been mediated by a violation of representative design in studies with general knowledge items; the items have been selected in a manner that over-represents those situations where the cue-based inferences fail (Gigerenzer et al., 1991, Juslin, 1993a, 1993b, 1994). Those items where our inferences or "intuitions" lead us to the wrong answer—surprising or misleading items— are more salient and interesting and tend to be over-represented in the item samples presented to participants in calibration studies (see the item-specific analysis in Juslin, 1994). Moreover, the selection strategies relevant to the purpose of discriminating between high and low knowledge on the part of the participants has a similar effect of over-representing those items where the cues lead to the wrong answer. This explanation, of course, contrasts sharply with the received view that overconfidence arise from an information processing bias in human cognition that make us prepro- grammed to overestimate our judgmental and predictive abilities (e.g., Kahneman et al., 1982). The notions of representative and selected item samples are illustrated in Fig. 5.1A.

One example is provided by Juslin (1994), where two samples of two-alternative, general knowledge items were compared: a representative sam- ple where the objects of judgment (world countries) were sampled ran- domly from a natural environment (the countries of the world) and a selected sample intended to be good knowledge-discriminating items. The selected sample was generated by 12 item-selectors naive to the experi- mental hypothesis. Twenty participants responded to both item samples and the calibration curves, where the proportions of correct answers are plotted against confidence, are presented in Fig. 5.1B.

For the representative item sample the proportion correct falls close to the identity line indicating good calibration, but for the selected item set the proportion correct is too low—the overconfidence phenomenon. These results (replicated by Kleitman & Stankov, 1997, Winman, 1997) support the hypothesis that the overconfidence effect may be mediated by a violation of representative design. A number of studies support the hy- pothesis that overconfidence is reduced by selecting objects of judgment randomly from a natural environment (Gigerenzer et al., 1991; Juslin, 1993b, 1995; Juslin et al., 1997; Juslin, Winman, & Persson, 1995). In a quantitative review (Juslin, Winman, & Olsson, 1998), the overconfidence for 95 independent data sets with selected samples was compared to the overconfidence with 35 independent data sets with representative samples (i.e., all data that was published or otherwise available to us at the time, June 1998). The mean overconfidence score across all 95 selected item samples was .10 (95% confidence interval, ± .01), and across all 35 repre- sentative samples the score was .01 (95% confidence interval, ± .01). This difference could not be explained by differences in proportion correct, as has been claimed by Griffin and Tversky (1992). Moreover, when we con- trolled for the end-effects of the probability scale and the linear depend- ency between proportion correct and the over/underconfidence score

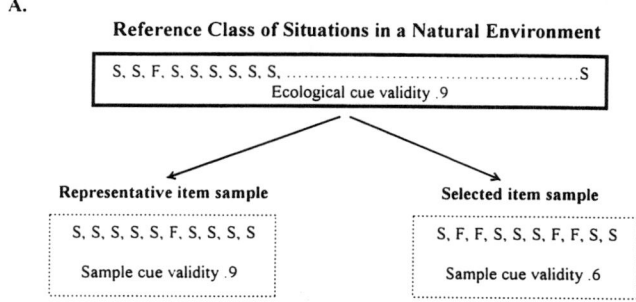

A.

Reference Class of Situations in a Natural Environment

S, S, F, S, S, S, S, S, S, ...S
Ecological cue validity .9

Representative item sample

S, S, S, S, S, F, S, S, S, S

Sample cue validity .9

Selected item sample

S, F, F, S, S, S, F, F, S, S

Sample cue validity .6

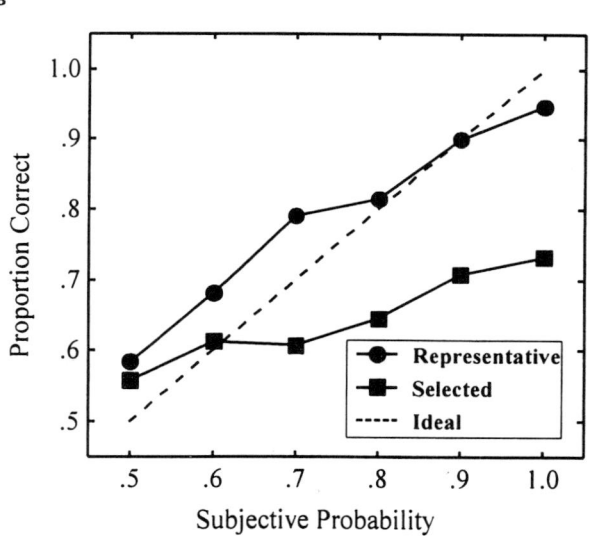

B

FIG. 5.1. Panel A provides a schematic example of representative and selected item sets, where *S* refers to successful applications of a cue and *F* to failures. Depending on how the items are selected the sample cue validity may or may not coincide with the ecological cue validity. Panel B provides the empirical calibration curves for a representative and selected item sample. The dotted line represents perfect calibration. Adapted from "The overconfidence phenomenon as a consequence of informal experimenter-guided selection of almanac items," by P. Juslin (1994), *Organizational behavior and human decision processes, 57*, p. 238. Copyright 1994 by Academic Press Inc. Adapted with permission.

(mean confidence minus proportion correct), the hard–easy effect was close to eliminated for representative item samples (see Juslin, Winman, et al., 1998, for details).

The same basic argument—that confidence assessments reflect knowledge of a natural environment that cannot be accommodated to the idiosyncratic item selections generated in the laboratory—can potentially account also for the hard–easy effect (Gigerenzer et al., 1991; Juslin, 1993a) and the base–rate effect. To illustrate the argument in the context of the base–rate effect, consider Example B above: a full-range item that concerns the relative mean life expectancy of two countries. The ecological model suggests that the probability assessment is based on the ecological probability associated with some probabilistic cue. If the participant relies on the Asian–African continent cue, he or she will assign probability 90% to the statement in Example B. In the laboratory, however, with knowledge of the relevant facts at hand we can assemble samples of Asian–African statements with any proportion (base–rate) of true statements. The participants rely on informed guesses based on their general knowledge of the world and cannot be expected to accommodate to these idiosyncratic manipulations created by the experimenter. This leads to the "insensitivity" to base-rates observed in data (e.g., Smith & Ferrell, 1983).

These examples illustrate that the ecological models capture important aspects of the organism–environment relations that support probabilistic inference. However, there is also evidence that representative design often is not sufficient for the complete elimination of overconfidence and hard–easy effects (Brenner, Koehler, Liberman, & Tversky, 1996; Griffin & Tversky, 1992; Juslin & Olsson, 1997; Soll, 1996). More generally, the ecological models fail to account for the overall pattern of data and provide no explicit mechanisms that can account for the expertise effect, the conservatism/overconfidence effect or the format-dependence effect. Recent research on probability judgment has demonstrated the importance of explicit modeling of stochastic components of the judgment process (Erev et al., 1994). One way to modify the ecological model is to explicitly introduce constraints on the information processing in the form of stochastic components of the judgment process; in short, by introducing Thurstonian error (see also Björkman, 1994; Soll, 1996).

Adding Thurstonian Uncertainty: The Combined Error Model

In contrast to the ecological models which assume error-free cognitive processing,[1] the combined error model introduces two kinds of random error, sampling error in the process where degrees of belief are formed and response error in the process of response elicitation (Juslin, Olsson, et al., 1997). The model is a generalization of the Brunswikian framework as it constitutes a combination of the idea of a fundamentally unbiased information-processing mechanism that relies on probabilistic cues and relative frequencies (the ecological models), with the idea that probability judgments are perturbed by stochastic components of the judgment process (Björkman, 1994; Erev et al., 1994; Pfeifer, 1994; Soll, 1996). The combined error model thus provides a systematic exploration of the hypothesis of an unbiased information processing mechanisms constrained by random processing error. The model is implemented as a computational model that can be fitted to empirical data.

The conceptual scheme of the combined error model is based on the ecological model in the form of PMM theory (Gigerenzer et al., 1991). In the environment there are ecological probabilities (relative frequencies) as conditioned on probabilistic cues. For example, in a task that concerns the subjective probability that the population of an African country exceeds 10 million, the relative frequency of African countries with population larger than 10 million is the ecological probability associated with the cue "African country." Similarly, for a meteorologist, the long run relative frequency of precipitation on days with a specific pattern of meteorological cues defines the ecological probability for this cue pattern. In calibration studies, the internal probabilities—the cognitive representations of the ecological probabilities—are expressed as overt probabilities, which are compared to sample probabilities ascertained for a particular task sample. In a calibration study, the overt probabilities are partitioned into categories (0, .1, . . . 1.0). The mean sample probability is computed in each overt probability category and it defines the calibration curve (see Figure 5.1B), for example, the proportion correct in overt probability category .7 is the mean sample cue validity of the cue-based inferences assigned confidence .7 (or 70%). Representative design requires the sample probabilities to be representative of the ecological probabilities (Gigerenzer et al., 1991; Juslin, 1994). There are three subcomponents of the combined error model, a model of the distribution of ecological probabilities in the environment, a model of the covert probability judgment process, and a model of the response elicitation.

The Environment. For each environment and knowledge state of the probability assessor, there is a distribution of ecological probabilities defined by the cues that can be retrieved by the assessor. In our previous applications (and as a matter of convenience), we have modeled the distribution of ecological probabilities with a Beta-distribution specified by parameters α and β that determine both the mean and the variance of the distribution. If, in addition, we make the simplifying assumption that

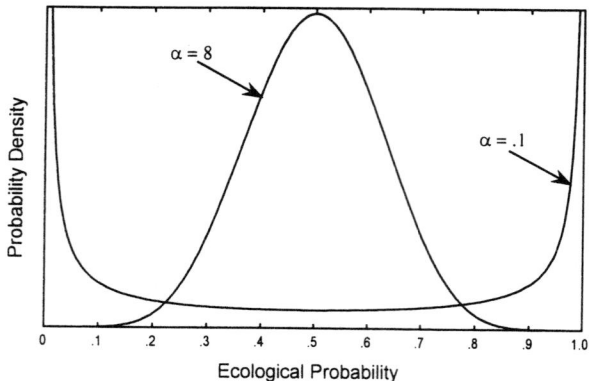

FIG. 5.2. Two distributions of ecological probabilities, as modeled with a
Beta-distribution.

the distribution is symmetric ($\alpha = \beta$), we are left with a single parameter
α that represents the predictability. In Fig. 5.2, two examples of distributions of ecological probabilities are presented.

A high α of, say, 8, represents an environment where most ecological probabilities are close to the to the mean ecological probability, allowing very little predictability over and above the mean ecological probability (base–rate) of the event. When α is low, for example .1, most ecological probabilities are close to either 0 or 1, and the environment allows for high predictability. Note that the predictability parameter will be a function of both the knowledge of the assessor (i.e., the cues known by the assessor) and the inherent predictability of the environment (i.e., the cues afforded by the environment).

Cognitive Processing and Experience.   We assume that PMM theory (Gigerenzer et al., 1991) provides a tentative account for the cognitive processes that form degrees of belief, albeit with the modification that we allow for sampling error in experience and retrieval from memory (see Pfeifer, 1994, and Soll, 1996, for similar approaches). For example, consider a meteorologist who judges the probability of precipitation to be .8. The assessment may arise from observation of 10 previous days with the same cue-pattern, 8 of which were associated with precipitation. Although .8 is a reasonable estimate of the true ecological probability, it may be more or less in error due to the small number of similar days encountered by the meteorologist. Similarly, a participant that responds on the basis of an assessment of the ecological probability that an African country has a more than 10 million inhabitants will only have encountered the population figures of a subset of all the African countries. In other words, when based on limited experience, the process of learning the ecological probabilities is perturbed by sampling error. The assumption of perfect cognitive adjustment is, strictly speaking, the special case of infinite sample size. Note also that sampling error is an unavoidable complication in the process of learning that is relevant to any cognitive algorithm that responds to a sample-input from the environment.

According to the combined error model, internal probabilities p_i are perturbed by a sampling error, naturally represented by the binomial distribution,

$$p_i \approx v_i + e_b(n) \tag{1}$$

where $e_b(n)$ is the binomially distributed sampling error, a function of the parameter for sample size n. At large sample size, corresponding to large experience, sampling error is small and the assessor will have accurate representations of the ecological probabilities; at small sample size, sampling error may be considerable. What is less obvious, perhaps, is that the extent of sampling error is also a function of ecological probability v_i. With the binomial distribution, sampling error variance (i.e., $v_i(1 - v_i)$) is largest around .5, and smallest around the extreme probabilities, 0 and 1. This means that the overall amount of sampling error will be larger in an environment of low predictability (many v_i close to .5), than in a more predictable environment (many v_1 close to 0 and 1). In sum: with more experience, more accurate representations of the ecological probabilities will be formed, but it takes more experience to achieve adaptation to an environment of less predictability.

Response Elicitation. In calibration studies, the participant makes overt responses, either as probabilities in the interval [0, 1] for full-range assessment, or as probabilities in the interval [.5, 1] for half-range assessment. In full-range assessment (as in Example B in the introduction), the overt probabilities are perturbed by a normally distributed response error e_r that arises in the process of overt assessment,

$$r_i \approx p_i + e_r \tag{2}$$

where the extent of response error is determined by the *response error parameter* σ_r^2 (the variance of the normally distributed response error entered in Equation 2). Due to the stochastic components of the response process, from time to time the same internal probability (belief) will receive somewhat different overt probabilities. In Equation 2, the symbol $\approx$ has dual significance: First, it reflects the rounding of the overt probabilities to the response set allowed by the particular scale used (e.g., 0, .1, .2, . . .

1.0). Second, due to the scale boundaries of the full range probability scale, the responses are truncated at the extremes, $p_i + e_r < 0$ is assigned overt probability $r_i = 0$, and $p_i + e_r > 1$ is assigned overt probability $r_i = 1$. This truncation, which corresponds to the fact that response error can never produce overt probabilities outside the interval $[0, 1]$ of the full-range probability scale, leads to end-effects and a "regression" of the calibration curve that appears as miscalibration (illustrated in Fig. 5.3B below).

In half-range (Example A in the introduction), overt assessments r'_i are perturbed by the same normally distributed response error e_r as in full-range assessment,

$$r'_i \approx p'_i + e_r \tag{3}$$

where p'_i is equal to p_i when $p_i > .5$ and p'_i is equal to $1 - p_i$ when $p_i < .5$. This equation models the fact that the assessor decides on the more probable of the two alternatives in a half-range task, where p'_i stands for the internal probability in favor of the chosen answer. For example, when the internal probability of rain is .8, the half-range internal probability of rain is likewise .8. When the internal probability of rain is .2, the half-range internal probability for the event "no rain" is .8. Again, the overt half-range probabilities are rounded to the relevant response set (.5, .6, ... 1.0), and truncated at the extremes of the probability scale, $p'_i + e_r < .5$ is assigned overt half-range probability $r'_i = .5$, and $p'_i + e_r > 1$ is assigned overt half-range probability $r'_i = 1$. This, again, creates end-effects and a "regression" of the calibration curve, but this time within the half-range interval.

To illustrate its predictions, the combined error model has been implemented as a Monte-Carlo simulation. The program simulates a large number of responses generated according to the specified parameters for predictability, sample size (experience), and response error. The simulation starts with a distribution of ecological probabilities. Each level of ecological probability is sampled in proportion to the ecological distribution, and for each sampled ecological probability, an internal probability perturbed by sampling error is generated (Equation 1 above). This internal probability, which can be used to make a decision between alternatives, is, in turn, perturbed by a response error in the translation into an overt probability (Equation 2). When this simulation is repeated many times, the results are distributions of decisions and overt probability assessments which can be analyzed and compared to the corresponding empirical data (see Juslin et al., 1997).

Some of the predictions by the combined error model are summarized in Fig. 5.3, which presents the calibration curves and over/underconfidence scores computed from the responses generated by simulation. Figure 5.3A presents the calibration curves at different sampling error ($n = 5, 10,$

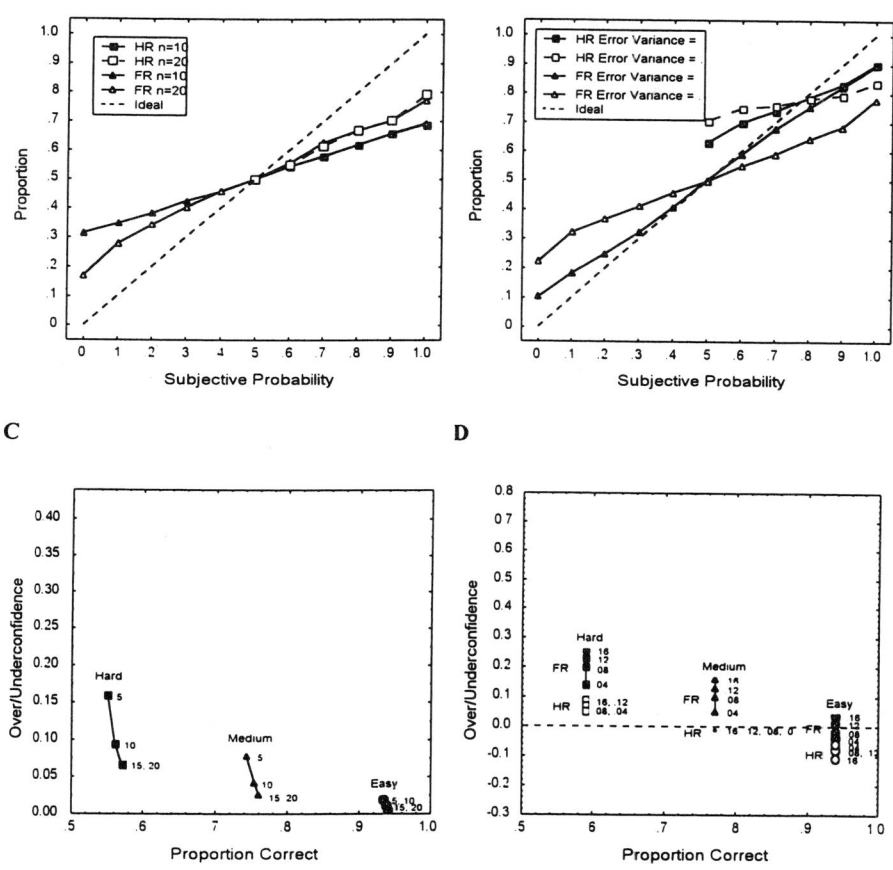

Fig. 5.3. The effects of different levels of sampling error and response error for environments that vary in predictability for half-range assessment (HR) and full-range assessment (FR). Panel A shows the calibration curves for an unpredictable environment ($\alpha = 8$) and two levels of sampling error ($n = 10$ and 20). Panel B shows calibration curves for a moderately predictable environment ($\alpha = 1$) and two levels of response error ($\sigma_r^2 = .04$ and .16). Panel C shows how over/underconfidence varies with environmental predictability ($\alpha = .1$, 1, and 8) and sampling error ($n = 5$, 10, 15, and 20). Panel D shows how under/overconfidence varies with environmental predictability ($\alpha = .1$, 1, and 8) and response error ($\sigma_r^2 = .04$, .08, .12, and .16). Adapted from "Brunswikian and Thurstonian origins of bias in probability assessment: On the interpretation of stochastic components of judgment," by P. Juslin, H. Olsson, & M. Björkman (1997), *Journal of Behavioral Decision Making, 10*, p. 196 and p. 199. Copyright 1997 by John Wiley & Sons, Ltd. Adapted with permission.

15, and 20) in three environments that vary in difficulty ($\alpha = .1$, 1, and 8), where, for illustrative purposes, we assume that response error is zero. Figure 5.3B provides the calibration curves for different response error variance ($\sigma_r^2 = .04$, .08, .12, .16) in the same three environments, with the assumption of no sampling error. The lower panels of Figs. 5.3 present measures of over/underconfidence computed from predicted calibration curves and distributions of overt probabilities, where "FR" refers to full-range and "HR" to half-range. Panel C corresponds to Panel A and is based on sampling error only and Panel D corresponds to Panel B with response error only. All predictions in Fig. 5.3 are based on the assumption of a representative sample of items. For space reasons, the distributions of overt probabilities are not illustrated here (but see Fig. 5.5 below).

Overconfidence and Hard-Easy Effects. Several studies have shown that unbiased random error can result in overconfidence in calibration analysis (Erev et al., 1994; Pfeifer, 1994; Soll, 1996). Because the combined error model involves two such stochastic components, it predicts similar "regression-like" side-effects of random error. More surprising, perhaps, is that these two origins of random error lead to distinct empirical predictions. In Panel A of Fig. 5.3, we see that sampling error introduces a regression of the calibration curve that appears as overconfidence in the calibration analysis. For example, due to sampling error the overt probability category 1.0 will not only contain ecological probabilities of 1.0, but also lower ecological probabilities that happened to produce an observed proportion of 1.0 (leading to internal probability 1.0). Similarly, the overt probability category 0 will also contain ecological probabilities above 0 that happened to generate a sample proportion of 0 merely due to sampling error. This error is entered at the stage where beliefs are formed, prior to response elicitation, and over/underconfidence is thus the same with both the half-range and the full-range methods (i.e., the calibration curves coincide in Fig. 5.3). Panel C of Fig. 5.3 illustrates that sampling error can only produce overconfidence, which is the same in full-range and half-range. The overconfidence effect increases with smaller sample size and is larger in less predictable environments, where both effects contribute to a hard-easy effect with more overconfidence in environments with a lower proportion of correct half-range decisions. As the sample size increases, the calibration curve converges on perfect calibration.

As illustrated in Fig. 5.3B, when we look at full-range assessment, the effects of response error are very similar to those of sampling error: overconfidence bias and a hard-easy effect. With the half-range method, however, response error in the use of the overt probability scale will not introduce systematic overconfidence, but a symmetric hard-easy effect with zero over/underconfidence (roughly) at overt probability .75 (see Fig. 5.3D). Above proportion correct .75 there is underconfidence, while below .75, there is overconfidence. In contrast to sampling error, response error can produce both over- and underconfidence bias.

Calibration and Response Methods. Figure 5.3D also illustrates that the model predicts that over/underconfidence interacts with the assessment scale used for elicitation of subjective probabilities. This phenomenon, referred to as format-dependence, means that when we approach the same tasks with different response methods we may arrive at different or even contradictory conclusions about over/underconfidence. For example, in the predictable environment there is underconfidence when the tasks are investigated with half-range method and simultaneous overconfidence when the same tasks are approached with the full-range method.

The prediction of format-dependence has been tested and confirmed in Juslin, Wennerholm, and Olsson (in press; see also Juslin, Olsson, et al., 1997). To see the point of this demonstration, consider three different ways of eliciting a participant's subjective probability distribution for the value of an unknown quantity, like the population of Bulgaria. With the half-range format the task could be: "The population of Bulgaria exceeds 30 million; (a) True, (b) False." Let us assume that the participant decides on "true" with .9 confidence. Alternatively, with the full-range format we could ask the participant to directly assess the probability from 0 to 1 that the above statement is true. If this assessment is consistent with the previous half-range assessment, the full-range probability will be .9. Finally, one could ask for the .8 probability interval for the participants best estimate of the population of Bulgaria. This amounts to asking for the 10th and the 90th fractile of the subjective probability distribution. If the participant is consistent with the previous responses, the 10th fractile or lower band of the interval will be assessed to 30 million (i.e., because the previous assessments by the participant indicate that he or she believes that the population of Bulgaria exceeds 30 million with probability .9).

From a formal perspective, these three ways of eliciting the subjective probability distribution should lead to the same result, but for practical purposes the choice may merit some thought. The over/underconfidence scores for the three methods when applied to exactly the same judgment tasks are presented in Fig. 5.4 (from Juslin, Wennerholm, & Olsson, in press). While there is underconfidence with the half-range format there is extreme overconfidence with the interval estimation procedure. The stochastic components of the combined error model predict the correct ordering of the response methods, but underpredicts the extreme over-confidence with the interval estimation. One reason for this deviation may

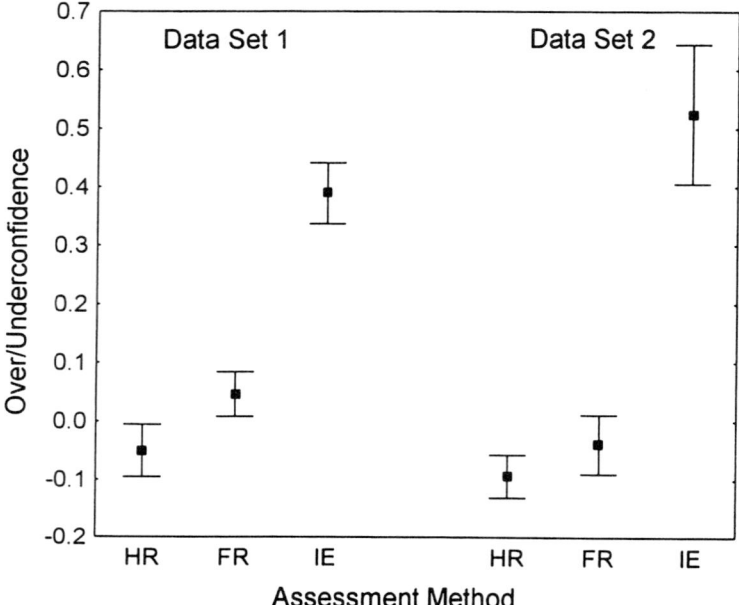

FIG. 5.4. The mean over/underconfidence scores with 95% confidence intervals for three different assessment formats applied to the same judgment tasks for two separate data sets: HR refers to half-range, FR to full-range, IE to interval estimation (simplified fractile assessment). Data from Juslin, Wennerholm, & Olsson (1998).

be that the interval estimation format is particularly susceptible to anchoring-and-adjustment bias (Kahneman et al., 1982). This hypothesis was tested and confirmed in Juslin, Wennerholm, and Olsson (in press) and the reader is referred to this article for further details.

Calibration and Experience. The model provides an explicit mechanism that predicts improved calibration with increased experience. To the extent that overconfidence is a consequence of sampling error, increasing the sample size should decrease overconfidence (see Fig. 5.3C). On the other hand, in an environment of low predictability, overconfidence will persist even in the face of considerable experience. The combined error model thus reproduces the (often) superior calibration of expert probability assessors. The model further suggests that differences in the calibration of experts from different domains may arise primarily from differences in the predictability of their environments, rather than in differences in behavior. The combined error model illustrates that even if the experts behave in the same manner—observing and reporting the sample proportions they observe—their calibration may differ enormously merely due to the properties of the environment.

Base-Rate (Non) Effects and Conservatism/Overconfidence Effects. The model also accounts for the base-rate effect and the conservatism/overconfidence effect. The combined error model suggests two factors that contribute to the base-rate effect:

(a) *Violation of representative design.* The probability assessments reflect knowledge of the ecological probabilities and there is no way in which the assessors can accommodate their assessments to all the base-rates that can be created by the experimenter in the laboratory (i.e., by over- or under-representing the proportion of true statements in the task set, the sample probabilities will deviate from the ecological probabilities). This is the same explanation as afforded by the ecological model.

(b) *A regression effect.* Even if the sample probabilities are representative, if all responses are based on cues with a high ecological probability, the random error will pull towards a lower average overt probability assessment. When all responses emanate from cues with low ecological probabilities, the average overt probability will be higher.

In Erev et al. (1994) it was demonstrated that due to random error the same data may appear both overconfident in calibration analysis and conservative when objective probability is the independent variable, as in the conservatism studies of the 1960s. The combined error model contains stochastic components and will reproduce this effect. Due to the interpretations of the random errors, however, the model provides an additional prediction, the regression when subjective probability is independent variable should be larger than the reverse regression when objective probability is independent variable (i.e., for the same data set, there will be more overconfidence than conservatism). The reason for this asymmetry is that where as response error introduces a regression in both directions, the sampling error will only contribute to the regression when subjective probability is the independent variable, not when objective probability is the independent variable. There are not many data sets around that allow probability assessments to be analyzed in both "directions," alternatively with subjective or objective probability as the independent variable. Those we know of (Erev et al., 1994; Soll, 1996), however, confirm the asymmetry predicted by the combined error model.

Figure 5.5 presents the result of attempting to find parameter values that provide good quantitative fit to empirical data (from Juslin, Olsson, et al., 1997). At present, we have no analytic method to obtain best fitting values and we have to rely on a grid-search procedure (see Juslin, Olsson,

A   B

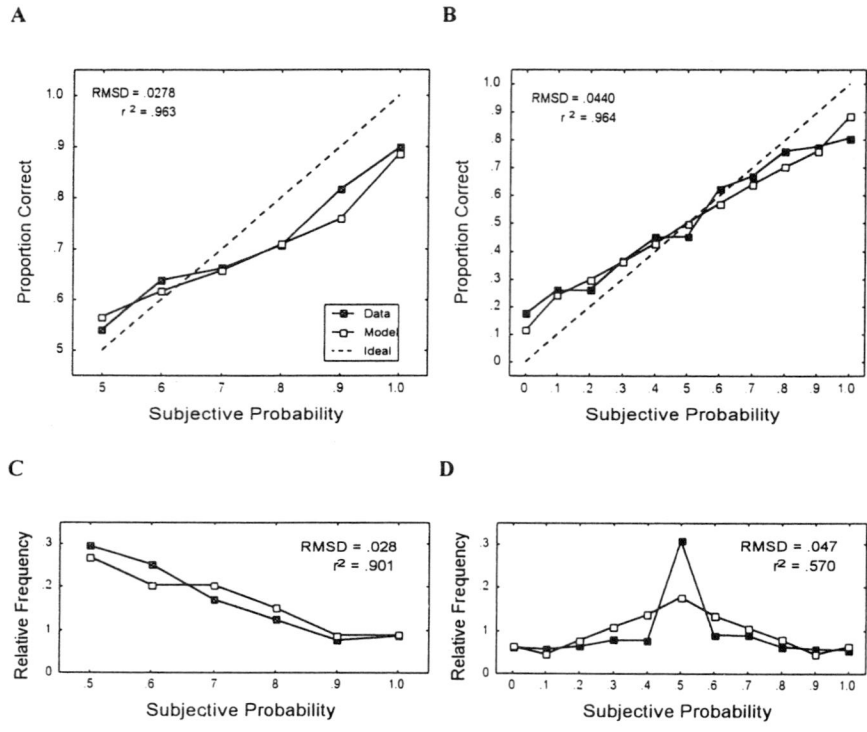

FIG. 5.5. Panel A: Observed (data) and predicted (model) calibration curves for the half-range format. Panel B: Observed and predicted calibration curves for the full-range format. Panel C: Observed and predicted response distributions for the half-range format. Panel D: Observed and predicted response distributions for the full-range format. Adapted from "Brunswikian and Thurstonian origins of bias in probability assessment: On the interpretation of stochastic components of judgment," by P. Juslin, H. Olsson, & M. Björkman (1997), *Journal of Behavioral Decision Making, 10*, p. 205. Copyright 1997 by John Wiley & Sons, Ltd. Adapted with permission.

et al., 1997, for details). There is thus no guarantee that the parameter values we find are optimal according to formal criteria. The results presented in Fig. 5.5 nevertheless suggests that the model can provide a reasonably good quantitative account of the data. The data in Fig. 5.5 are from general knowledge items. The left side of Fig. 5.5 presents data from half-range assessments (Example A in the introduction) and the right side presents data from full-range assessments (Example B). A four-parameter version of the combined error model was fitted to these data. Aside from the parameters discussed above (predictability, sample size, and response error), a fourth parameter was added to account for the fact that not all of the responses were generated by probabilistic cue-based inference. This inference-proportion parameter defines a proportion of responses that are based on noninferential processes, like retrieval of the correct answer from memory which are associated with 100% confidence.

With these four parameters fitted, the 34 data points in Fig. 5.5 were predicted with a Root-Mean-Square-Error (RMSE) of .046, with model predictions that account for 98% of the variance in the empirical data (see Exhibit 6 in Juslin, Olsson, et al., 1997). One interesting observation when the combined error model has been fitted to empirical data is that the best-fitting value of the sample-size parameter is often large (e.g., $n = 60$ in Juslin, Olsson, et al., 1997; but see also Juslin, Wennerholm, & Olsson, in press; Juslin, Winman, & Olsson, 1998), suggesting that the sampling error is often moderate or low even for nonexpert participants.

The points we have tried to illustrate in this section is that the combined error model—wedding a model of the Brunswikian uncertainty involved in probabilistic inference with the idea of Thurstonian uncertainty in the cognitive processes—accounts for the basic phenomena in empirical data, as well as provide a reasonable quantitative account of the data. It therefore remains a challenge for models that postulate an information processing bias to (a) demonstrate that the assumption of a processing bias adds predictive content over and above what is provided by the bias-free combined error model, (b) to specify the nature of this processing bias, and (c) to develop such a conception into a model that can account for the intricate pattern of results reviewed and exemplified in this section.

Thurstonian Uncertainty Alone:
The Sensory Sampling Model

The combined error model captures how Brunswikian and Thurstonian origins of uncertainty interact and affect the calibration associated with a specific task and, indeed, most perceptual and cognitive tasks will be affected by both origins of error. An interesting exception that approaches the extreme of pure Thurstonian uncertainty is pair-comparisons on simple sensory continua—sensory discrimination (Example D in the introduction). What we need is a model that can account for the often observed disposition towards underconfidence, but which also suggests the conditions where this disposition is attenuated or replaced by overconfidence. Our attempt in this respect is the sensory sampling model, a computational model of confidence in sensory discrimination (Juslin & Olsson, 1997).

What cognitive processes underlie decisions, confidence, and response times in a sensory discrimination task like the one in Example D above? In sensory discrimination tasks, we assume that the sensory signal is perturbed by a neural noise—a moment-to-moment variation that creates a pervasive experience of uncertainty when the difference is in the uncertainty zone—modeled as a normally and independently distributed (NID) random variable. Figure 5.6 provides a schematic illustration of the sequential sampling of sensations which, for matters of simplicity, is idealized in the sense of assuming discrete sensations. The deviation from zero in Fig. 5.6 represents the sensation of a difference between the weights, where μ is the error-free perception that would result if neural noise was eliminated. At any moment, the last n sensations are retained in a sensory memory, the size n of which defines the sample size parameter.[2]

The critical assumption is that the decision is based on the participants' overall impression of which weight is the heavier as modeled by the sample mean. So, for example, if the left weight has been perceived to be the heavier on average, the participant decides on the left weight. The confidence assessment reflects the consistency of this overall impression, as modeled by the proportion of sensations that support the decision. If the experience was consistent and held for a proportion 1.0 of the sensations in the memory window, confidence is 1.0 (100%). But if the experience was ambiguous with only 60% of the sensations supporting the decision, confidence is .6. By the

Sequential Sampling of Sensations

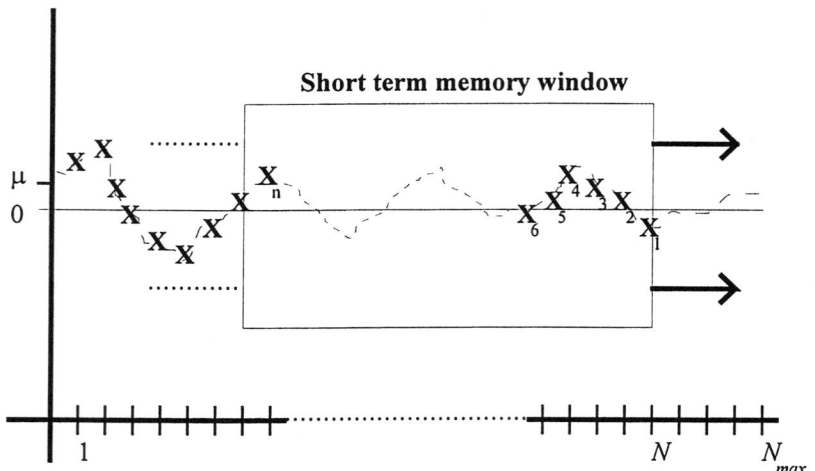

FIG. 5.6. Sequential sampling of sensations and the moving memory window that contains the last n sensations. Adapted from "Thurstonian- and Brunswikian origins of uncertainty in judgment: A sensory sampling model of confidence in sensory discrimination" by P. Juslin & H. Olsson (1997), *Psychological Review, 104*, p. 350. Copyright 1997 by American Psychological Association, Inc. Adapted with permission.

law of large numbers, the decision based on a statistical aggregate (the sample mean) will be more precise and reliable than indicated by the variability of the single sensations (the proportion of which define the subjective experience of confidence). Though at any moment in time each single sensation is transient and variable, the decision that benefits from the overall impression based on a more extended sampling sequence, will be more reliable. This predicts a disposition towards underconfidence.

As with other sequential sampling models (see Luce, 1986 for a review), the number of sampling iterations before a decision is made provides predicted response times. Figure 5.7 provides the predictions for four stimulus units with physical differences that increase from *L1* to *L4*, includ-

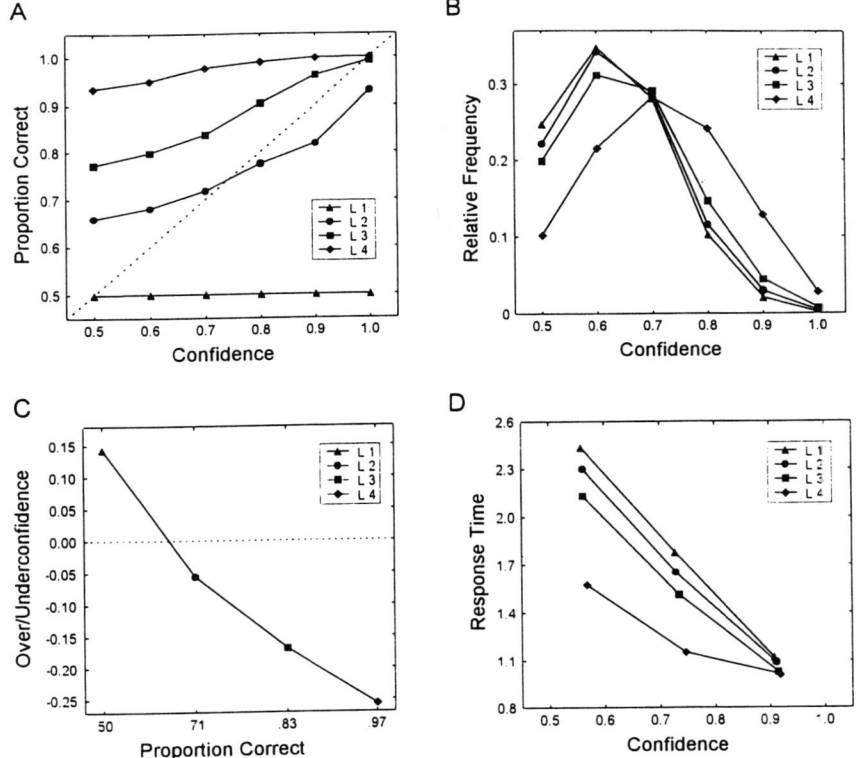

FIG. 5.7. The calibration curves, confidence distributions, over/underconfidence, and response times predicted by the sensory sampling model for four simulated stimulus units. The model has the same three parameter values for all four stimulus units. Adapted from P. Juslin & H. Olsson (1997), "Thurstonian- and Brunswikian origins of uncertainty in judgment: A sensory sampling model of confidence in sensory discrimination," *Psychological Review, 104*, 344–366, with permission from the publishers.

ing one stimulus unit with zero difference (*L1*). Panel A provides predicted calibration curves, Panel B, predicted confidence distributions, Panel C, predicted over/underconfidence for each stimulus unit as a function of proportion correct, and Panel D, the predicted pattern of response times. The empirical data reveal all of these patterns and the quantitative fit is reasonable.

The sensory sampling model predicts circumstances that lead to over-confidence. Three examples will suffice: When the true stimulus difference is zero, the sampling error of the mean introduced by neural noise can only work in one direction, towards an occasional false perception of a stimulus difference (see Fig. 5.7C). These decisions will necessarily be overconfident. Second, when participants are exposed to time pressure, sample size is decreased and the difference between the reliability of mean and single sensations diminishes. This, in turn, leads to a decrease in underconfidence or even to a tendency towards overconfidence (as observed by Baranski & Petrusic, 1994, in conditions with time pressure). Finally, by introducing a perceptual bias parameter in the sensory sampling model that lowers the observed proportion correct, we can account for the overconfidence bias associated with perceptual illusions (see the discussion in Baranski & Petrusic, 1994).

In consideration of some of the claims in the literature, it is worthwhile to stress an important asymmetry: The general claim that there is no difference between cognitive and sensory tasks (Baranski & Petrusic, 1994) is incompatible with the observed difference reported in the meta-analysis in Juslin, Olsson, and Winman (1998)—nor can the decision variable partition model account for these data (Ferrell, 1995). However, the sensory sampling model both accounts for an underlying disposition towards underconfidence in simple, sensory discrimination, and predicts the circumstances where this tendency turns into overconfidence (e.g., time pressure or perceptual illusions). In addition, the sensory sampling model goes beyond previous models by providing a mechanism that connects decisions and confidence with a third dependent variable, response times. With a modified version of the sensory sampling model—*SESAM 2*—Olsson (1998) was able to reproduce entire response time distributions as well as to fit the model to the data reported by Baranski and Petrusic.

A recent application of the model concerns dynamic event perception (Runeson, Juslin, & Olsson, 1998). In experiments on relative mass-discrimination in collisions, the participants' task is to decide which of two colliding objects that has the higher mass. In Runeson et al. (1998), the distinction between Brunswikian and Thurstonian origins of error and the sensory sampling model were used to derive process criteria to distinguish between a cue-heuristic (inferential) and a direct-perceptual mode of processing. According to the cue-heuristic model proposed by Gilden and Proffitt (1989; 1994) performance in the mass-discrimination task is mediated by cue-based inference. This model therefore implies that the data on confidence assessment should have the properties characteristic of the Brunswikian origin of error. In contrast to this model, Runeson et al. formulated a strong version of the direct-perception approach—a perfect-invariant model—that assumes that relative mass-discrimination is based on the pick-up of a single analytically complex invariant that directly specifies the mass-ratio of the colliding objects, where the pick-up is perturbed by a Thurstonian error (i.e., by neural noise as in other simple sensory coding tasks). The structure of the perfect-invariant model thus coincides with the structure modeled by the sensory sampling model. If the participants are operating in a direct-perceptual mode we thus expect the data to present the properties typical of tasks dominated by Thurstonian error. In short, the data should look like the data from simple psychophysical discrimination tasks like line-length discrimination—a task that few would deny the status of direct perception.

The results of independent model fitting indicated that neither model provided a good fit to the prefeedback data, although the general appearance of data suggested some cue-heuristic process (albeit not the one implied by Gilden and Proffitt's [1989; 1994] cue-heuristic model). The postfeedback data, however, was well fitted by the perfect-invariant model. More pertinent, the process criteria discussed above confirmed the model fitting results: In the pretest, there was close to zero overconfidence and error-dependence as is common in tasks that involve Brunswikian error, but in the posttest there was underconfidence and error-independence, the typical pattern in simple sensory coding tasks that are dominated by Thurstonian error. This difference in the pre- and posttest data could not be accounted for in terms of the difference in proportion correct (Runeson et al., 1998). These results exemplify how the distinction between Brunswikian and Thurstonian origins of error—and the sensory sampling model—can be used to diagnose the mode of cognitive processing.

CONCLUDING COMMENTS

In the last years, research on calibration has exploded with models and theories (e.g., Björkman, 1994; Erev et al., 1994, Gigerenzer et al., 1991; Griffin & Tversky, 1992; Juslin & Olsson, 1997; Juslin, Olsson, et al., 1997; May, 1986; Soll, 1996; see McClelland & Bolger, 1994, for a partial review), and calibration research has once again become a central concern to decision researchers. In this chapter, this development has been illustrated by a review of three recent computational models of calibration of subjective probabilities. The ecological model stresses the importance of organism–environment relations and the transfer of knowledge of a natural environment to the laboratory. The combined error model combines the ecological framework in the form of PMM theory with the idea of stochastic components of the judgment process. The sensory sampling model accounts for confidence in sensory discrimination.

Together these theories represent a significant theoretical advance; we now have computational models that can reproduce most of the basic phenomena in the calibration literature. Nevertheless, these models are points of departure rather than a finished research agenda. Still no theories beside the PMM theory (Gigerenzer, 1993; Gigerenzer & Goldstein, 1996; Gigerenzer et al., 1991) and the sensory sampling model (Juslin & Olsson, 1997) provide anything like detailed accounts of the cognitive processes, and even these accounts remain largely untested in their processing details.

A problem with the combined error model is that—even if conjoined with the processing assumptions of PMM theory—the model remains underspecified in its account of the cognitive processes that form degrees of belief (internal probabilities). A second problem is that both the ecological model and its derivative, the combined error model, concentrate only at the processing of frequency information. Although it seems evident that subjective probability is responsive to frequency information, these formulations neglect data suggesting that probability assessment is also affected by similarity, or representativeness (Kahneman et al., 1982). Further developments need to bridge the iron curtain between models that stress frequency and similarity, and connect research on subjective probability and calibration to basic research on memory and categorization.

A working hypothesis in our current research is that the exemplar-based models from categorization (e.g., Medin & Schaffer, 1978; Nosofsky, 1984) can inform research on probability judgment. The exemplar-based models are supported by a large body of data and provide algorithms that respond to both similarity and frequency in a sensible manner. In any event, we hope that the research reviewed in this chapter can serve to stimulate development of more refined and detailed computational models of the cognitive processes that support and underlie the assessment of subjective probabilities.

ACKNOWLEDGMENT

The research reported in this chapter was supported by the Swedish Council for Research in Humanities and the Social Sciences.

NOTES

1. The assumption that there has to be *perfect* cognitive adjustment in the strong sense that even unbiased random error is prohibited in the processes was not always spelled out explicitly in the first presentations of the ecological models (e.g., Gigerenzer et al., 1991;

Juslin, 1993b). Later research has made clear that even unbiased random error will introduce overconfidence (e.g., Erev et al., 1994), and representative selection of items will thus eliminate overconfidence completely only when random error is zero or marginal.

2. It is important to distinguish this sample-size parameter from the parameter with the same name in the combined error model. Sample size in the combined error model refers to the size of the retrieved sample of facts used to make decisions and to assess the probability, whereas the sample size in the sensory sampling model is the size of the memory that holds the transient sensory input used for decisions and confidence.

REFERENCES

Baranski, J. V., & Petrusic, W. M. (1994). The calibration and resolution of confidence in perceptual judgments. *Perception and Psychophysics, 55,* 412–428.

Björkman, M. (1994). Internal cue theory: Calibration and resolution of confidence in general knowledge. *Organizational Behavior and Human Decision Processes, 58,* 386–405.

Björkman, M., Juslin, P., & Winman A. (1993). Realism of confidence in sensory discrimination: The underconfidence phenomenon. *Perception and Psychophysics, 54,* 75–81.

Brenner, L. A., Koehler, D. J., Liberman, V., & Tversky, A. (1996). Overconfidence in probability and frequency judgments: A critical examination. *Organizational Behavior and Human Decision Processes, 65,* 212–219.

Brunswik, E. (1952). *The conceptual framework of psychology.* Chicago: University of Chicago Press.

Crawford, J. D., & Stankov, L. (1996). *Individual differences in the realism of confidence judgments: Overconfidence in measures of fluid and crystallized intelligence.* Unpublished manuscript, University of Technology, Sydney.

Edwards, W. (1982). Conservatism in human information processing. In D. Kahneman, P. Slovic, & A. Tversky (Eds.), *Judgment under uncertainty: Heuristics and biases* (pp. 359–369). New York: Cambridge University Press.

Erev, I., Wallsten, T. S., & Budescu, D. V. (1994). Simultaneous over- and underconfidence: The role of error in judgment processes. *Psychological Review, 101,* 519–527.

Ferrell, W. R. (1995). A model for realism of confidence judgments: Implications for underconfidence in sensory discrimination. *Perception and Psychophysics, 57,* 246–254.

Gigerenzer, G. (1993). The bounded rationality of probabilistic mental models. In K. I. Manktelow & D. E. Over (Eds.), *Rationality: Psychological and philosophical perspectives* (pp. 129–161). London: Routledge.

Gigerenzer, G., & Goldstein, D. G. (1996). Reasoning the fast and frugal way: Models of bounded rationality. *Psychological Review, 103,* 650–669.

Gigerenzer, G., Hoffrage, U., & Kleinbölting, H. (1991). Probabilistic mental models: A Brunswikian theory of confidence. *Psychological Review, 98,* 506–528.

Gilden, D. L., & Proffitt, D. R. (1989). Understanding collision dynamics. *Journal of Experimental Psychology: Human Perception and Performance, 15,* 372–383.

Gilden, D. L., & Proffitt, D. R. (1994). Heuristic judgment of mass ratio in two-body collisions. *Perception and Psychophysics, 56,* 708–720.

Griffin, D., & Tversky, A. (1992). The weighing of evidence and the determinants of confidence. *Cognitive Psychology, 24,* 411–435.

Hammond, K. R. (1966). Probabilistic functionalism: Egon Brunswik's integration of the history, theory, and method of psychology. In K. R. Hammond (Ed.), *The psychology of Egon Brunswik.* New York: Holt, Rinehart, and Winston.

Hammond, K. R. (1996). *Human judgment and social policy: Irreducible uncertainty, inevitable error, unavoidable injustice.* Oxford: Oxford University Press.

Juslin, P. (1993a). An explanation of the hard-easy effect in studies of realism of confidence in one's general knowledge. *European Journal of Cognitive Psychology, 5*, 55–71.

Juslin, P. (1993b). An ecological model of realism of confidence in one's general knowledge. (*Acta Universitatis Upsaliensis: Studia Psychologica Upsaliensia, 14*). Stockholm: Almqvist & Wiksell.

Juslin, P. (1994). The overconfidence phenomenon as a consequence of informal experimenter-guided selection of almanac items. *Organizational Behavior and Human Decision Processes, 57*, 226–246.

Juslin, P. (1995). Well calibrated confidence judgments for general knowledge items, inferential recognition decisions and social predictions. In J.-P. Caverni, M. Bar-Hillel, F. H. Barron, & H. Jungerman (Eds.), *Contributions to decision making—I* (pp. 233–253). Amsterdam: Elsevier Science B. V.

Juslin, P., Hoffrage, U., & Gigerenzer, G. (1997). *Connecting minds to environments: A neo-Brunswikian approach to research on judgment and decision making.* Unpublished manuscript.

Juslin, P., & Olsson, H. (1997). Thurstonian- and Brunswikian origins of uncertainty in judgment: A sensory sampling model of confidence in sensory discrimination. *Psychological Review, 104*, 344–366.

Juslin, P., Olsson, H., & Björkman, M. (1997). Brunswikian and Thurstonian origins of bias in probability assessment: On the interpretation of stochastic components of judgment. *Journal of Behavioral Decision Making, 10*, 189–209.

Juslin, P., Olsson, H., & Winman, A. (1998). The calibration issue: Comments on Suantak, Ferrell and Bolger (1996). *Organizational Behavior and Human Decision Processes, 73*, 3–26.

Juslin, P., Wennerholm, P., & Olsson, H. (in press). Format-dependence in subjective probability calibration. *Journal of Experimental Psychology: Learning, Memory, and Cognition.*

Juslin, P., Winman, A., & Olsson, H. (1998). *The ecological model rides again: On naive empiricism and a priori dogmatism in judgment research.* Unpublished manuscript.

Juslin, P., Winman, A., & Persson, T. (1995). Can overconfidence be used as an indicator of reconstructive rather than retrieval processes? *Cognition, 54*, 99–130.

Kahneman, D., Slovic, P., & Tversky, A. (Eds.) (1982). *Judgment under uncertainty: Heuristics-and-biases.* New York: Cambridge University Press.

Keren, G. (1991). Calibration and probability judgments: Conceptual and methodological issues. *Acta Psychologica, 77*, 217–273.

Kleitman, S., & Stankov, L. (1996). *Ecological and person-oriented aspects of metacognitive processes in test-taking.* Unpublished manuscript, Department of Psychology, University of Sydney.

Lichtenstein, S., & Fischhoff, B. (1977). Do those who know more also know more about how much they know? *Organizational Behavior and Human Performance, 20*, 159–183.

Lichtenstein, S., & Fischhoff, B., & Phillips, L. D. (1982). Calibration of subjective probabilities: The state of the art up to 1980. In D. Kahneman, P. Slovic, & A. Tversky (Eds.), *Judgment under uncertainty: Heuristics and biases* (pp. 306–334). New York: Cambridge University Press.

Luce, R. D. (1986). *Response times.* New York: Oxford University Press.

May, R. S. (1986). Overconfidence as a result of incomplete and wrong knowledge. In R. W. Scolz (Ed.), *Current issues in West German decision research* (pp. 13–30). Frankfurt: Peter Lang.

McClelland, A. G. R., & Bolger, F. (1994). The calibration of subjective probabilities: Theories and models 1980–1993. In G. Wright & P. Ayton (Eds.), *Subjective probability* (pp. 453–482). Chichester, England: Wiley.

Medin, D. L., & Schaffer, M. M. (1978). Context theory of classification learning. *Psychological Review, 85*, 207–238.

Nosofsky, R. M. (1984). Choice, similarity, and the context theory of classification. *Journal of Experimental Psychology: Learning, Memory, and Cognition, 10*, 104–114.

Olsson, H. (1998). *The sensory sampling model revisited: Response time distributions and perceptual bias.* Unpublished manuscript.

Olsson, H., & Juslin, P. (1997). *Realism of confidence in sensory discrimination: Theory and data.* Unpublished manuscript.

Olsson, H., & Winman, A. (1996). Underconfidence in sensory discrimination: The interaction between experimental setting and response strategies. *Perception and Psychophysics, 58,* 374–382.

Peirce, C. S., & Jastrow, J. (1884). On small differences of sensation. *Memoirs of the National Academy of Sciences, 3,* 73–83.

Pfeifer, P. E. (1994). Are we overconfident in the belief that probability forecasters are overconfident? *Organizational Behavior and Human Decision Processes, 58,* 203–213.

Runeson, S., Juslin, P., & Olsson, H. (1998). *Direct visual perception of dynamic properties.* Unpublished manuscript.

Savage, L. J. (1954). *The foundations of statistics.* New York: Dover.

Smith, M., & Ferrell, W. R. (1983). The effects of base rate on calibration of subjective probability for true-false questions: Model and experiment. In P. Humphreys, O. Svenson, & A. Vari (Eds.), *Analyzing and aiding decisions.* Amsterdam: North-Holland.

Soll, J. B. (1996). Determinants of overconfidence and miscalibration: The roles of random error and ecological structure. *Organizational Behavior and Human Decision Processes, 65,* 117–137.

Thurstone, L. L. (1927). A law of comparative judgment. *Psychological Review, 34,* 273–286.

Winman, A. (1997). The importance of item selection in "knew-it-all-along" studies of general knowledge. *Scandinavian Journal of Psychology, 38,* 63–72.

Winman, A., & Juslin, P. (1993). Calibration of sensory and cognitive judgments: Two different accounts. *Scandinavian Journal of Psychology, 34,* 135–148.

Winman, A., Juslin, P., & Björkman, M. (1998). The confidence-hindsight mirror effect in judgment: An accuracy-assessment model for the "knew-it-all-along" phenomenon. *Journal of Experimental Psychology: Learning, Memory, and Cognition, 24,* 415–431.

Yates, J. F. (1990). *Judgment and decision making.* Englewood Cliffs, NJ: Prentice-Hall.

Yates, J. F., McDaniel, L. S., & Brown, E. S. (1991). Probabilistic forecasts of stock prices and earnings: The hazards of nascent expertise. *Organizational Behavior and Human Decision Processes, 49,* 60–79.

Chapter 6

"I Was Well-Calibrated All Along": Assessing Accuracy in Retrospect

Anders Winman
Peter Juslin
Uppsala University

The fact that beliefs tend to come in degrees is clear from the ambiguity, ambivalence, and uncertainty we continually experience in our lives. We may have absolutely no doubt in the proposition that the river Thames flows through London, be quite convinced that Holland is more densely populated than Finland but only have a faint hunch that "Absinthe" is not a precious stone. It should come as no surprise that degrees of belief, confidence, or subjective probabilities play a central role in many normative and descriptive analyses of human behavior. The confidence we have in our convictions is one of the critical components of normative models of rational decision making (e.g., Savage, 1954), but is also receiving increased attention in research on memory performance (Koriat & Goldsmith, 1996), psychophysical discrimination (Baranski & Petrusic, 1994; Juslin & Olsson, 1997; Olsson & Winman, 1996; see also Chapter 5 of the present volume), and applied matters such as eyewitness confidence (Juslin, Olsson, & Winman, 1998; Wells & Murray, 1984). However, two pathologies—or in more appropriate present-day jargon, cognitive biases—haunt much of modern research on confidence assessment: the overconfidence phenomenon and the hindsight or "I-knew-it all-along" phenomenon, both of which may be illustrated by reference to a simple, two-alternative general knowledge question.

In calibration studies that purport to demonstrate the overconfidence phenomenon, the participants are presented with large sets of general knowledge items of the following form—

Which of these two countries has a higher mean life expectancy?
        a) *Egypt,*   b) *Bulgaria.*
        What confidence do you have in your answer?
  50%   60%   70%   80%   90%   100%
  Guessing   Certain
_____

—where the confidence assessments are explicitly interpreted as subjective probabilities (i.e., in the instructions and the analysis). The common result of these studies has been that the mean confidence is higher than the proportion of correct answers—for example, the participants may be 90% certain on average, but only select the correct answer for 60% of the items. These results have traditionally been explained by an information processing bias that make people overestimate the correctness of their knowledge (Kahneman, Slovic, & Tversky, 1982). This interpretation has however been subject to criticism and intense debate in recent years (e.g., Erev, Wallsten, & Budescu, 1994; Gigerenzer, Hoffrage, & Kleinbölting, 1991; Griffin & Tversky, 1992; Juslin, 1993, 1994; Juslin, Olsson, & Björkman, 1997; Juslin, Winman, & Olsson, 1998).

The hindsight bias can be demonstrated with a slightly altered version of the same general knowledge item:

Which of these two countries has a higher mean life expectancy?
        a) *Egypt,*   b) *Bulgaria.*
                  The correct answer is Bulgaria.
Indicate what answer you would have chosen if you had not been told the correct answer, and assess the confidence that you would have had in this answer:
  50%   60%   70%   80%   90%   100%
  Guessing   Certain
_____

In a hindsight task, the participants are shown the correct answer and are told to give the answer they would have chosen, assuming that they had not been presented with the correct answer. The robust finding with this kind of task has been that in retrospect people overestimate how much they knew before they were presented with the facts—they act as if they knew the correct answer all along (see reviews by Christensen-Szalanski & Willham, 1991; Fischhoff, 1975, 1982; Hawkins & Hastie, 1990). For instance, the participants may indicate in retrospect that they would have selected the correct answers for 90% of the items, but when presented with the same items without knowledge of the correct answer they actually select the correct answers for only 60% of the items. Alternatively, the probabilities in a probability assessment task may shift in the direction indicated by the outcome feedback.

In the following, we will use common terminology and refer to the experimental condition where participants respond without knowledge of the correct answer as *foresight*, and to the corresponding condition with knowledge of the correct answer as *hindsight* (the conditions may be either within or between subjects). The hindsight bias has been explained by both motivational factors, such as the ambition to appear knowledgeable to oneself or others, and by cognitive factors (discussed in detail below), with most recent research favoring cognitive over motivational explanations (see Hawkins & Hastie, 1990).

How is Hindsight Bias Related to Overconfidence?

The conceptual relation between overconfidence and hindsight bias has been acknowledged in the literature (e.g., Hawkins & Hastie, 1990; Hoch & Loewenstein, 1989). In general the relation has been interpreted as causal, with hindsight bias causing overconfidence bias (but see Winman, 1997a; 1997b; 1997c). The fact that one in retrospect experiences that one would have got everything right in previous undergoings is assumed to create an inflated feeling of confidence in one's predictive and judgmental abilities. "*I knew all along that this particular horse was destined to win the race, therefore I am confident that I will be able to predict the winner of the next race. . . .*" Both phenomena have been presumed to have a number of detrimental consequences; for example, overconfidence might lead to non-optimal decision making in economic and other circumstances and hindsight bias to an inability to benefit from one's previous experiences.

In this chapter, we will present an alternative model that views both confidence and hindsight responses as emanating from the same process—the judgment of expected accuracy. On this view the two phenomena are not causing one another, but rather are two manifestations of the same underlying factor—a misjudgment of the task difficulty. Central to the notion of our model is that we must distinguish between to qualitatively different strategies that participants may adopt when confronted with a hindsight task. We refer to these separate approaches as *process simulation* and *accuracy assessment* respectively. Whereas process simulation refers to an attempt to simulate the cognitive process that one would have used in foresight to arrive at an answer, accuracy assessment involves an exertion by participants in reproducing their performance—that is, whether or not they would have been correct. Cognitive explanations of hindsight bias have highlighted process simulation issues, while accuracy assessment has been neglected. In order to fully understand what is going on in a hindsight task, we believe that it is necessary to acknowledge that both strategies are being used.

As we shall see, the idea that participants are concerned with accuracy assessment has the power of explaining a variety of observations in the literature, as well as of predicting novel phenomena. The model predicts situations under which the "knew-it-all-along" effect will disappear or even become reversed, phenomena that can not be accounted for by previous explanations of the hindsight phenomenon. Moreover, the model provides quantitative, parameter-free predictions of extent and direction of hindsight bias. Before we introduce the model and confront it with data, however, we need a review of the main alternative explanation of the hindsight phenomenon. We will begin with a description of process simulation and the pitfalls that may be associated with this approach.

PROCESS SIMULATION

Most recent research has supported cognitive over motivational explanations (Hawkins & Hastie, 1990) and we will thus concentrate on the main cognitive accounts of the hindsight bias. A common feature of these explanations is that they implicitly or explicitly presume that the participant responds to the hindsight task by simulating, or reconstructing the cognitive processes that would have been relevant to foresight performance of the task. They might consider what knowledge was available to them before the correct answer was known and try to simulate the inferential or other processes that were likely to have been elicited in this situation. The general idea is that these process simulations, automatically and largely unconsciously, tend to become biased by knowledge of the correct answer (Hawkins & Hastie, 1990).

We describe the information-processing stages discussed by Hawkins and Hastie (1990) in relation to the above example of a general knowledge question. According to the selective recall hypothesis, retrieval of facts from long-term memory becomes biased, or cued, by the stated correct alternative. In hindsight, the participant will retrieve more facts in accordance with the correct answer (e.g., Bulgaria is a European industrial country), and less inconsistent evidence (e.g., Bulgaria used to belong to the Eastern bloc), than he or she would have in absence of feedback, leading to a biased sample of information favoring the correct answer.

The processes of evaluation and integration of evidence provide other sources of bias. In the evidence evaluation process, implications of cues are not always straightforward. Take, for instance, the fact that Bulgaria was a member of the former Eastern bloc. This fact might be taken as evidence for a low mean life expectancy since the Eastern bloc countries often were poor. On the other hand, a highly developed social security system and low crime rates that may indicate a high mean life expectancy also characterized these countries. In such way, a participant may rewrite the story in retrospect so that the indicated correct answer will fit the existing knowledge structures. This might occur as a consequence of implicit processes of "sense-making" or due to outright confirmation bias (Nisbett & Ross, 1980).

In the process of evidence integration all facts are combined to arrive at a response. In this integration, the weights of the different cues may change by receipt of information about the correct alternative. This automatic updating, or rapid learning effect can be described as a shift in the weights $x_1 - x_3$ given to attributes in an integrative procedure such as: life expectancy = x_1 * poverty + x_2 * social security + x_3 * crime rate. Unlike the bias occurring at evidence evaluation, which is described by Hawkins and Hastie (1990) as case-specific, a bias at the integration stage is a learning effect that generalizes to other judgments.

The three explanatory factors discussed here all presuppose that participants engage in process simulation: that they try to reproduce the *exact* answer they would have selected in foresight by "simulating" their foresight cognitive process—for example, by searching for reasons why they would have answered either Bulgaria or Egypt. This research has been exclusively concerned with accounting for ordinary or positive hindsight biases, where the participants overestimate their foresight performance (although these explanations or models are severely underspecified so that definitive claims about the predictions are difficult to make). But, as we shall see, hindsight phenomena need not always involve the overestimation of foresight performance—people may be victims of reversed hindsight biases too.

ACCURACY ASSESSMENT

Without denying the importance of process simulation, we have proposed that in addition participants may be concerned with the probability that they *would have been accurate* (Winman, Juslin, & Björkman, 1998). Instead of asking, "Which answer would I have chosen?," they may ask themselves "In consideration of the task-difficulty, would I have been able to select the correct answer?" This means that the hindsight response may be mediated not only by process simulation but also by more subtle considerations of how difficult this kind of task is known or believed to be: What level of accuracy can be expected? For example, one may be aware that across tasks known to be extremely difficult, one can hardly get every answer correct and this insight may overrule the outcome of a more or less fallible process simulation. The difference between process simulation and accuracy assessment is subtle but important. In terms of the probabilistic functionalism of Egon Brunswik (Brunswik, 1952) one could say that the participants are concerned with the achievement of different target variables.

Expected Accuracy in Foresight

To explain the idea of accuracy assessment, it is useful to introduce some concepts from the literature on calibration of subjective probabilities. In studies with general knowledge items, the participants are typically given a choice between two alternatives and have to indicate their confidence in this choice as a subjective probability in the interval .5 (guessing) and 1.0 (certain). For each participant, confidence ratings are obtained for a large number of items. The participants are said to be calibrated if in the long run the subjective probabilities are matched by the corresponding relative frequencies, that is, they have XX% correct answers in the confidence category with subjective probability .XX. The calibration score C_F is defined by the mean square deviation between confidence r_{Ft} and the corresponding proportion correct $\bar{c}_{Ft}$ (throughout the paper, the subscript F refers to the foresight condition),

$$C_F = \frac{1}{N} \sum_{1}^{T} n_{Ft} (r_{Ft} - \bar{c}_{Ft})^2 \tag{1}$$

where n_{Ft} refers to the number of confidence judgments in confidence category t ($t = 1 \ .. \ T$), N refers to the overall number of confidence judgments, and T to the overall number of confidence categories available (see Lichtenstein, Fischhoff, & Phillips, 1982). When the proportions correct equal the subjective probabilities at each confidence level, the participant is perfectly calibrated with a calibration score of 0. The over/underconfidence bias is measured by the difference between the mean confidence, $\bar{r}_F$ and the overall proportion correct, $\bar{c}_F$, where $\bar{r}_F - \bar{c}_F > 0$ indicates overconfidence and $\bar{r}_F - \bar{c}_F < 0$, underconfidence. For instance, if the mean confidence is .8 but the overall proportion correct is .7, there is overconfidence .1.

The mean probability assigned to the correct answer P_C is

$$P_C = \frac{n_1 \bar{r}_1 + n_0 (1 - \bar{r}_0)}{N} \tag{2}$$

where $\bar{r}_1$ is the mean confidence across the n_1 correct answers, $\bar{r}_0$ is the mean confidence across the n_0 incorrect answers, that is, where the implicit probability assigned to the correct answer was $1 - \bar{r}_0$ on average (see Hoch & Loewenstein, 1989). When Equation 2 is applied to responses made without knowledge of the correct answer, it refers to the foresight mean probability assigned to the correct alternative, P_{CF}. This measure—highly related to measures of discrimination or resolution (e.g., Yaniv, Yates, & Smith, 1991)—indexes the participants ability to assess subjective probabilities that discriminate correct from incorrect answers.

What cognitive processes underlie assessments of confidence, or expected accuracy, in general knowledge items? In the current context, it will be sufficient to make a set of rather weak assumptions about these processes. We assume that the overt confidence response r_{Fi} in foresight reflects a covert assessment of task difficulty x_{Fi}. The covert assessment x_{Fi} is assumed to equal a tacit expectation of a relative frequency of correct decisions in a class of similar items. These assumptions are basically those implied by the instructions in a calibration study (and by the normative analysis). The exact cognitive processes that give rise to feelings of confidence is not our main concern here, but we propose that in a cognitive task confidence often reflects the ecological validity of the probabilistic cues used to select the answers to the items (see Björkman, 1994; Gigerenzer et al., 1991; Juslin, 1993, 1994).

The object of inquiry in calibration studies is the agreement between overt confidence r_{Fi} and an observed relative frequency $\bar{c}_{Fi}$ of correct answers determined from a set of items presented to the participants. If we assume that the potential error in the translation of x_{Fi} into an overt response variable r_{Fi} has zero-expectation, we can distinguish between three possible states in foresight (referred to as states 1, 2 and 3, respectively):

$$r_{Fi} = x_{Fi} = \bar{c}_{Fi} \tag{S1}$$

$$r_{Fi} = x_{Fi} > \bar{c}_{Fi} \tag{S2}$$

$$r_{Fi} = x_{Fi} < \bar{c}_{Fi} \tag{S3}$$

S1 corresponds to good calibration in foresight where overt probabilities (confidence) coincide with proportions correct, S2 to overconfidence where the confidence assessments are systematically higher than the proportions correct, and S3 to underconfidence.

Expected Accuracy in Hindsight

In hindsight too, there will be a covert assessment of x_{Hi} expected accuracy. This covert assessment may be formed by considerations of the quality of the information that would have been available in foresight. In particular, we assume that x_{Hi} is formed by processes and considerations similar to those that gave rise to the covert foresight confidence and thus that both x_{Hi} and x_{Fi} represent beliefs about expected accuracy or task difficulty.

As with the covert foresight confidence x_{Fi}, the hindsight judgment about expected accuracy x_{Hi} is an expectation about a long run relative frequency of correct decisions in a class of tasks with the same difficulty. Across tasks with difficulty $.XX$ (as indicated by a confidence rating of XX), the participants expect about *XX*% of correctly identified answers in foresight. This means that, for example, when the participant is reflecting upon those items for which they were rather confident about their answers—items across which they expected to be correct most of the time in foresight—in the hindsight condition they will likewise expect that they were correct most of the time across these items.

In a two-alternatives, forced-choice hindsight experiment, the participants make retrospective assessments of their foresight decisions and their foresight confidence. When reporting confidence, we can expect that participants simply translate their covert hindsight assessment x_{Ht} of the expected accuracy into the overt hindsight confidence variable r_{Ht}, which represents the assessment of their foresight confidence. According to the accuracy-assessment model, the hindsight assessment x_{Ht} of task difficulty also enters into the participant's assessment of whether or not the correct decision would have been made in foresight. For tasks that are considered to be difficult (low $\bar{x}_{Ht} = r_{Ht}$), the participants will assess a low probability that they would have been correct in foresight, whereas for subjectively easy tasks (high $\bar{x}_{Ht} = r_{Ht}$) participants will grant themselves a higher probability of having been correct. One way to implement this knowledge of the task difficulty is by making sure that the distribution of correct/wrong answers is appropriate to the expected accuracy in the task.

A strong interpretation of the accuracy-assessment strategy is that for each item the participants "randomize" their hindsight decisions, in the sense that they indicate that they would have chosen the correct answer with a probability equal to the task difficulty. This would be a type of behavior similar to the "probability matching" observed in foresight for repetitive categorization and signal detection tasks (Estes et al., 1989; Gluck & Bower, 1988; Healy & Kubovy, 1981), also resembling the general matching law described in animal learning studies (e.g., Herrnstein, 1961; Rachlin, 1976; Williams, 1994). Across the difficult tasks ($\bar{x}_{Ht} = .5$), the participants realize that the probability of being correct is low and for each item they randomize their hindsight indication of the foresight decisions so that in the long run they end up with a hindsight proportion correct $\bar{c}_{Ht}$ equal to .5 across these tasks. Across easier tasks (e.g., $\bar{x}_{Ht} = .9$), on the other hand, the randomization will indicate that they would have got the answers right for most items, $\bar{c}_{Ht} = .9$, and so on for the other levels of difficulty. This idea of a randomization at every item is the strong hypothesis of accuracy assessment.

A second way to implement the accuracy-assessment model—the weak hypothesis of accuracy assessment—is as a high-level monitoring of the hindsight distribution of indicated correct and incorrect decisions that emanate from process simulation. On this hypothesis, the distribution is constrained to yield a pattern of correct/incorrect decisions that is representative of the overall expected accuracy in this kind of task. This allows for process simulation being the primary process that is monitored so as to produce a distribution of correct/false answers that is acceptable in consideration of the expected accuracy. In a task known to be extremely difficult, for instance, it would seem rather silly to indicate that the correct decision would have been made for every item, even if this is suggested by the outcome of process-simulation.

For our current purposes, it will be sufficient to note that participants who are perfectly successful in their implementation of the accuracy-assessment strategy, in its weak or its strong version, will provide hindsight responses that satisfy the following equality:

$$r_{Ht} = x_{Ht} = \bar{c}_{Ht} \tag{A1}$$

This means that across those items where hindsight confidence was assessed to be .XX, participants will have indicated that they would have got $XX\%$ of the items correct, where both responses reflect the same underlying belief about expect accuracy (task difficulty). For example, across tasks believed to be easy—allowing 90% correct decisions—the participants will report a hindsight confidence of .9 and produce a distribution of correct/false answers with a proportion .9 of correct answers. Note that accuracy assessment is a reasonable strategy if participants are aware of the difficulty of ignoring feedback information (and the "knew-it-all-along-effect" is indeed a part of common sense psychology). However, as will be shown below, in some circumstances the strategy leads to systematic errors, appearing as ordinary or *reverse* hindsight biases.

As already hinted in the discussion of the weak hypothesis of accuracy-assessment, we find it unlikely that participants rely exclusively on either process simulation or accuracy assessment. In many tasks there will contributions by both kinds of processes and considerations. We also expect the relative importance of process simulation and accuracy assessment to vary across different tasks (e.g., general knowledge tasks, predictions, sensory discriminations, and so on) depending on, among other things, the degree to which process simulation can be effectively relied on. In Winman et al. (1998), for example, we proposed that the strong version of accuracy assessment is more relevant to sensory discrimination tasks. The transient and variable sensory process with moment-to-moment variation in the subjective experience (Juslin & Olsson, 1997) makes it obvious that the hindsight sensory process is a poor predictor of the foresight decision. In general knowledge tasks, on the other hand, we expect process simulation to be important, since retrieval or reasoning processes can more easily be repeated to simulate earlier foresight performance (although the simulation might be biased by the outcome information, of course). The relative importance of process simulation and accuracy assessment in different tasks is an interesting issue for future research.

In the remaining parts of this chapter we will explore and test the predictions by the accuracy-assessment model. Unfortunately, at present there does not exist any detailed process simulation model to compare (or combine) the accuracy-assessment model with.

Predictions by the Accuracy-Assessment Model

The measures in Equations 1 and 2 above—calibration and probability assigned to the correct answer—can also be applied to hindsight data in order to ascertain hindsight biases. Remember that the null-hypothesis of no hindsight bias implies that retrospective hindsight responses, generated with knowledge of the correct answers, are identical to the foresight responses made without this knowledge (i.e., as required by the instructions for the hindsight condition). The measures computed on foresight and hindsight data should coincide.

When Equation 2 is applied to responses in hindsight, made with knowledge of the correct answer, it describes the hindsight mean probability assigned to correct responses, P_{CH}. A positive "knew-it-all-along-effect" is evidenced either by an indicated higher proportion of correct answers in the hindsight condition than in the foresight condition ($\bar{c}_H > \bar{c}_F$), or by a higher mean probability assigned to the correct answer in hindsight ($P_{CH} > P_{CF}$), or both. The former will be referred to as *decision bias* $\Delta\bar{c}$ and the latter as *probability bias* ΔP_C. Decision bias $\Delta\bar{c}$ is accordingly a measure concerned with decisions, where a positive value means that on a number of trials, participants in retrospect erroneously come to the conclusion that they would have selected the correct answer. For example, a participant that selects the correct answer for 60% of the general knowledge items when presented with them in foresight, but who indicates in hindsight—with the correct answers available—that he or she would have selected the correct answer for 90% of the items, is clearly the victim of a positive decision bias. Probability bias ΔP_C is a function of both decisions and confidence and a positive score means that participants in retrospect overestimate the probability they would have given to the correct alternative— their ability to discriminate true from false answers. A participant that assigns an average probability .95 to the correct answers in hindsight, but who only assigns the correct answer a mean probability .75 in foresight is exhibiting positive probability bias.

These are rather straightforward measures of hindsight or "knew-it-all-along-effects". A more subtle measure of hindsight effects was introduced in Winman et al. (1998) in terms of hindsight calibration. The correspondence between foresight confidence and foresight proportion correct is approached with the notion of calibration (Equation 1). One implication of the accuracy-assessment model is that a similar analysis can be applied to hindsight responses on the basis of the probability ratings r_{Ht} and the proportion of correct decisions $\bar{c}_{Ht}$ obtained in hindsight. Remember that overt hindsight confidence r_{Ht} refers to the participants' assessments of their foresight confidence r_{Ft}, and that $\bar{c}_{Ht}$ is the proportion of retrospectively indicated correct decisions in the same confidence category t (the hindsight equivalent of $\bar{c}_{Ft}$).

If Equation 1 is adapted into an equation for the *hindsight calibration score* C_H we get;

$$C_H = \frac{1}{N} \sum_1^T n_{Ht} (r_{Ht} - \bar{c}_{Ht})^2 \tag{3}$$

where n_{Ht} is the number of hindsight responses in confidence category t ($t = 1 \ldots T$) and N is the total number of responses in hindsight. The hindsight calibration score measures the calibration that participants would have had in foresight, if they had indeed selected the confidence levels and the answers that they indicated in hindsight. If there is no hindsight effect whatsoever and the participants select exactly the same answers and probability estimates in hindsight, the foresight and hindsight calibration scores coincide. If calibration is better in hindsight, this indicates that the participants are victims of an "I was well calibrated all along" effect. We are now in position to formulate Prediction 1:

Prediction 1. The calibration of hindsight responses will be perfect (calibration score 0 in Equation 3) with zero over/underconfidence (follows directly from Assumption 1 and Equation 3).

That is, the indicated proportion correct in hindsight will coincide with the mean confidence rating. This prediction holds when participants are relying exclusively on the accuracy assessment strategy. If we allow for measurement error and the intrusion of other processes, the prediction is relaxed into the expectancy of improved calibration in hindsight, with less over- or underconfidence. The accuracy-assessment model thus implies that across tasks with assessed difficulty $x_{Ht} = .7$ that receive overt hindsight confidence $r_{Ht} = .7$, the hindsight decisions will be distributed so that .7 are correct and .3 are wrong. As this indeed amounts to the subjective long-run expectancy of correct decisions, accuracy assessment can be seen as a matter of striving for a reasonable and coherent response pattern.

In order to derive more specific predictions, a further constraint is needed. In studies where participants have some experience with the foresight task, it will be assumed that the following equality is satisfied—

$$x_{Ht} = x_{Ft} \tag{A2}$$

—which asserts that covert hindsight belief about expected accuracy coincides with the corresponding covert foresight belief about expected accuracy. Assumption 2 implies that the task is familiar to the participants in the sense that they are familiar with the cognitive processes in foresight and with the corresponding (subjective) impressions of foresight task difficulty. In within-subject designs, where participants perform the tasks in foresight before they are confronted with them in hindsight, we expect A2 to be well approximated. For example, a participant who first encounters a task in foresight and experiences a low mean confidence, say $\bar{x}_F = .6$, will recognize that the task is difficult when confronted with it in hindsight ($\bar{x}_H = .6$) and thus expect to be wrong quite often. The assumption will also be satisfied with expert judges that have substantial task experience. Observe that Assumption 2 does not in any way imply that participants have a *correct* belief about the objective task difficulty, only that their belief about difficulty is unchanged from foresight to hindsight.

If we note that by assumption $r_{Ft} = x_{Ft}$ in all three states of over/underconfidence $S1$ to $S3$, apply Assumptions 1 and 2, and compute the arithmetic means, the hindsight proportion c_H of indicated correct decisions can be predicted from the foresight mean confidence $\bar{r}_F$,

$$\bar{c}_H = \bar{r}_F \tag{4}$$

The size of the "knew-it-all-along-effect" in terms of a higher proportion of indicated correct answers in hindsight than the actual proportion of answers in foresight—decision bias $\Delta'\bar{c}$—can thus be predicted from

$$\Delta'\bar{c} = \bar{r}_F - \bar{c}_F \tag{5}$$

where the left hands side of the equation is the predicted decision bias $\Delta'\bar{c}$ and the right hand side is the foresight over/underconfidence. Equation 5 states that the amount of hindsight decision bias is equal to the magnitude of the foresight over/underconfidence bias. Thus, if we know the over/underconfidence in foresight, we can predict the direction and amount of hindsight bias. Let us assume, for example, that the participants assess the foresight confidence to be .9 for a set of tasks, but are overconfident and only have a proportion correct of .8. The same belief about expected accuracy (.9) is used to generate a distribution of correct/false answers equal to .9, leading to a decision bias $\Delta'\bar{c}$ equal .1 (equal to the overconfidence score). By the same logic, underconfidence leads to a reverse hindsight bias. The predicted probability bias $\Delta P'_c$ is defined by

$$\Delta P'_C = P'_{CH} - P_{CF} \tag{6}$$

where P'_{CH} is the predicted probability assigned to the correct answer in hindsight and P_{CF} is the observed probability assigned to the correct answer in foresight. According to Assumption 1 of the accuracy-assessment model, calibration is perfect in hindsight and with this constraint the prediction P'_{CH} is

$$P'_{CH} = 2s_{r_F}^2 + \bar{r}_F^2 + (1 - \bar{r}_F)^2 \tag{7}$$

where $\bar{r}_F$ is the mean and $s_{r_F}^2$ is the variance of confidence in foresight (a proof of Equation 7 is provided in Winman et al., 1998). From Equations 5, 6, and 7 we can predict the extent and direction of hindsight bias from foresight confidence and proportion correct.

The following predictions are corollaries of Prediction 1.

Prediction 2. If participants are well calibrated in the foresight condition of the experiment, there should be no retrospective overestimation of the foresight proportion correct (no decision bias $\Delta\bar{c}$) and no "knew-it-all-along-effect" on probability estimates (no probability bias ΔP_C.) (Follows from S1 and A1 and A2).

Prediction 3. If participants are overconfident in the foresight condition, in hindsight they will overestimate the foresight proportion of correct decisions, and there will be a positive decision bias $\Delta\bar{c}$. The probability bias ΔP_C is computed from Eq. 6 (Follows from S2 and A1 and A2).

The AA model thus captures the intuition that overconfidence and hindsight bias are two different ways of overestimating ones' ability when confronted with a sample of tasks, two manifestations of the same underlying error—a misjudgment of the task-difficulty.

Prediction 4. If participants are underconfident in the foresight condition, in hindsight they will underestimate the foresight proportion of correct decisions, and there will be a negative decision bias $\Delta\bar{c}$. The probability bias ΔP_C is computed from Equation 6 (Follows from S2 and A1 and A2).

Together, Predictions 2 through 4 state that if task difficulty is correctly assessed in foresight, it is likewise correctly assessed in hindsight (Prediction 2) and when it is erroneously assessed in foresight, the same error is manifested in hindsight (Predictions 3 and 4). To the best of our knowledge, Prediction 4 of a reversed hindsight bias is unique to the accuracy-assessment model. Explanations in terms of motivational factors or automatic reconstruction of knowledge structures will have difficulty with accounting for a reversed hindsight bias. If the explanation is that you have a desire to appear competent to yourself and others, or if the outcome knowledge is automatically assimilated in your knowledge structures, you should not underestimate your foresight performance. More generally, Predictions 1 to 4 state a systematic relation between foresight over/underconfidence and extent and direction of hindsight bias; overconfidence is associated with a positive hindsight bias, underconfidence, with a reversed hindsight bias. In the following, we refer to this as the confidence-hindsight mirror effect.

Finally, we derive a slightly different illustration of the confidence-hindsight mirror effect. It has been repeatedly demonstrated (e.g., Gigerenzer et. al., 1991; May, 1987; Sniezek, Paese, & Switzer, 1990) that the overconfidence bias often decreases if one, instead of asking for the confidence of each decision, asks for the overall proportion of correctly solved items after the experiment (i.e., "How many of these *XX* items do you think that you have answered correctly?"). This phenomenon, referred to as the confidence-frequency effect by Gigerenzer et al. (1991), has been explained by the hypothesis that participants activate different reference classes in local and global assessments (i.e., the class of tasks solved with the same probabilistic cue used to make the inference, and the class of previous sets of knowledge-testing questions, respectively). Even if the participants are overconfident in terms of single items, perhaps because they are misguided by "tricky" and difficult questions, they may still be adapted to the fact that sets of general knowledge questions often contain many such tricky items in their global assessments. Therefore, participants are overconfident for single items, but better calibrated for global assessments (see Gigerenzer et al., 1991, on the confidence-frequency effect). If we combine the confidence-frequency effect with the confidence-hindsight mirror effect, we can derive a prediction for global hindsight judgments (i.e., "How many of these *XX* items would you have answered correctly, if you had not been told the correct answers?"):

Prediction 5. When participants are overconfident in local confidence assessments but calibrated in global assessments, as suggested by the confidence-frequency effect, there will be an ordinary hindsight bias in local hindsight judgments, while at the same time no hindsight effect will be observed in global hindsight judgments (follows from the confidence-hindsight mirror effect and the assumption that global foresight assessments and global hindsight assessments reflect a similar judgment of overall expected accuracy).

Again, this prediction seems inconsistent with other explanations of the hindsight bias. Prediction 5 is particularly interesting in consideration of one of the proposed effects of hindsight bias—the inability to appreciate the value of education and training (Fischhoff, 1977). After all, if we feel that everything that was taught to us in a course was something that we already knew all along, we should have little appreciation for the course. If hindsight bias is the result of automatic and unconscious updating and reconstruction of knowledge structures, this indeed seems a plausible prediction, although it has never been tested empirically. The accuracy-assessment model, however, predicts that participants may be victims of a hindsight bias in local item-by-item assessments, while at the same there is no hindsight effect in regard to the assessment of the pre-training level of knowledge. If correct, this would suggest that hindsight bias may have less detrimental effects for education than previously implied.

Fit to Empirical Data

Explaining Previous Results. In a meta-analysis, Christensen-Szalanski and Willham (1991) found that the effect size for the hindsight bias was three times larger for the kind of general knowledge items discussed in this chapter than for medical diagnosis or historical scenarios. Hawkins and Hastie (1990) accounted for this by the proposal that motivational phenomena such as the desire to appear intelligent or cooperative with the experimenter probably play a larger role in almanac studies. However, the explanation of hindsight bias in motivational terms lacks empirical support, and is inconsistent with the reverse hindsight biases that will be reported below.

The accuracy-assessment model provides an explanation of this result, namely that general knowledge studies generally have been associated with more overconfidence in foresight. Juslin (1994) demonstrated how the selection of general knowledge items to test knowledge leads to overconfidence and Winman (1997a) showed that the same selection procedure was associated with a larger "I-knew-it-all-along-effect" as compared to a randomly selected item set. In the selected item set from Winman's (1997a) Experiment 1 where overconfidence was .08, 42% of the items were associated with ordinary hindsight bias, 27% with no hindsight bias, and 31% with a reverse bias. In the representative or random sample of items with marginal underconfidence of −.04, 29% of the items were associated with ordinary hindsight bias, 19% with no hindsight bias, and 52 % with a reverse bias. Hence, in the selected set the modal outcome was an ordinary hindsight bias, but in the random set, a reverse hindsight bias was more common (a similar pattern was observed in Winman's [1997a] Experiment 2). In many hindsight studies, exactly the same items as those utilized for illustrating overconfidence have been used (i.e., Fischhoff, 1977; Hasher, Attig, & Alba, 1981; Wood, 1978). Hindsight bias has also proven to be larger for difficult items known to be associated with more overconfidence (Hoch & Loewenstein, 1989), and for surprising events (Fischhoff, 1975, 1977; Schkade & Kilbourne, 1991). This is exactly the pattern we expect in view of the confidence-hindsight mirror effect because, according to

Prediction 3 above, the extent of foresight overconfidence should be reflected in the amount of retrospective hindsight bias. Experts have often been better calibrated than novices have (Keren, 1987; Murphy & Winkler, 1977; Tomassini, Solomon, Romney, & Krogstad, 1982), although evidence is less than clear-cut. If expertise decreases overconfidence, we should expect experts to show less hindsight bias than novices. Christensen-Szalanski and Willham (1991) did indeed find that studies employing participants more familiar with the task, such as physicians, were associated with a smaller degree of hindsight bias. The correlation corrected for sampling error between task familiarity and effect size was .42.

This serves to illustrate that the accuracy-assessment model can account for the pattern of magnitudes of hindsight bias observed in previous research. However, the merits of a model is also to be measured by its ability to produce novel phenomena and, preferably, phenomena that are difficult to account for with alternative explanations.

The Improvement in Calibration from Foresight to Hindsight and the Confidence-Hindsight Mirror Effect

The predicted tendency for calibration scores to improve from foresight to hindsight is unique to the accuracy-assessment model. Unfortunately, calibration scores have generally not been reported in the literature. The only exception is Hoch and Loewenstein (1989) who reported in their Experiments 2 and 3 that "it appears that outcome feedback . . . leads to improved personal knowledge calibration . . ." (p. 613), a finding that is consistent with expectations of the accuracy-assessment model. Figure 6.1 provides two examples of the empirical finding showing that calibration actually is improved when computed on hindsight rather than foresight data (from Winman et al., 1998). In a calibration curve the proportions correct are plotted against confidence, where the identity line represents perfect calibration. In Panel A, we see data based on general knowledge items associated with overconfidence in foresight; the proportions correct are too low. It is obvious that when the calibration curve is computed from hindsight data, the overconfidence bias disappears and the curve approaches the identity line, as predicted by the accuracy-assessment model. Figure 6.1B presents the calibration curves for a sensory discrimination task with underconfidence in foresight (see Juslin & Olsson, 1997, for an explanation of this phenomenon). In this figure we see that the initial underconfidence (too high proportions correct) disappears in hindsight and the calibration curve again approaches the identity line, this time in conjunction with a reverse hindsight bias.

The examples in Fig. 6.1 could be isolated examples, of course. We have now accumulated data from 16 experimental conditions. All tasks

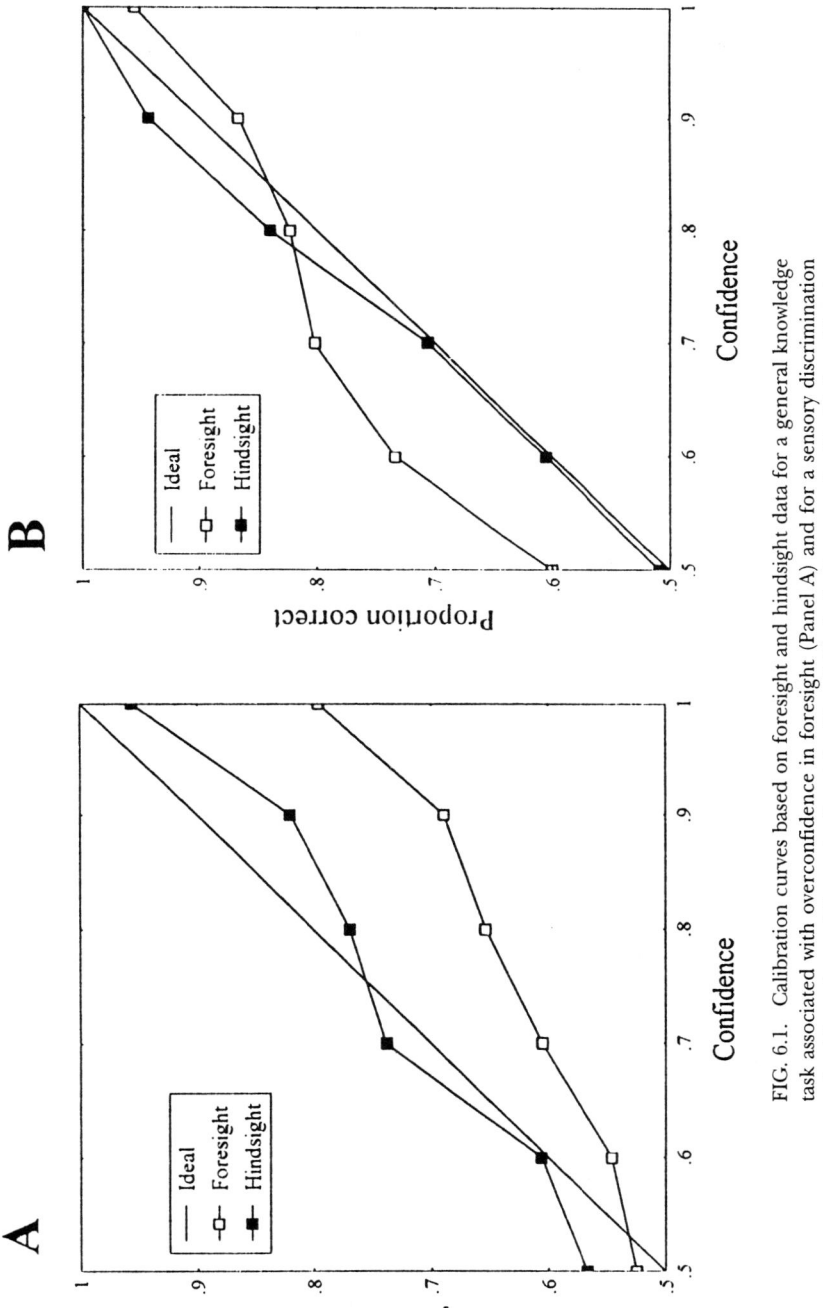

FIG. 6.1. Calibration curves based on foresight and hindsight data for a general knowledge task associated with overconfidence in foresight (Panel A) and for a sensory discrimination task with underconfidence in foresight (Panel B). In both cases, the hindsight calibration curve is closer to the identity line representing perfect calibration.

were two-alternative items of the sort exemplified in the introduction. Two tasks concerned sensory discrimination while the remaining 14 tasks were general knowledge tasks. These data are shown in Fig. 6.2.

The data in Fig. 6.2 are the conditions reported in Winman (1997a, b) and Winman et al. (1998). The black bars indicate calibration for a condition in foresight, and the adjacent white bar the calibration score for the same condition in hindsight. The higher a score is, the worse is calibration. It can be seen that in all 16 conditions, the calibration scores are considerably lower (better) in hindsight than in foresight. We conclude from the data illustrated in Fig. 6.1 that the "I was well calibrated all along" effect appears to be a fairly robust phenomenon.

Figure 6.3 shows predicted and observed bias for the same 16 conditions. Filled squares represent decision bias and empty squares probability bias. Although far from perfect, the fit is reasonable. The correlation between predicted and observed values is .67 for probability bias and .83 for decision bias. Root mean square errors (RMSEs) are .02 (probability bias) and .02 (decision bias). The very low RMSEs suggest that the moderate correlations between predicted and observed bias mainly reflect range restrictions in observed biases (i.e., the observed biases were modest in absolute terms). Furthermore, if we eliminate six conditions in which Assumption 2 of the model—experience with the task in foresight—is likely to be violated the correlations increase to .75 and .90 respectively.

Of particular importance are the conditions where the model predicts reverse hindsight biases, tasks that elicit underconfidence in foresight. In

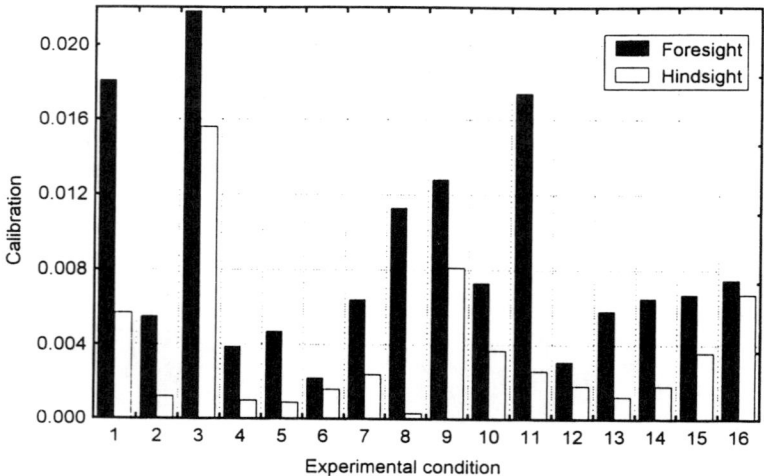

FIG. 6.2. Calibration scores in foresight and hindsight for 16 experimental conditions reported in Winman (1997a, 1997b), and Winman, Juslin, and Björkman (1998).

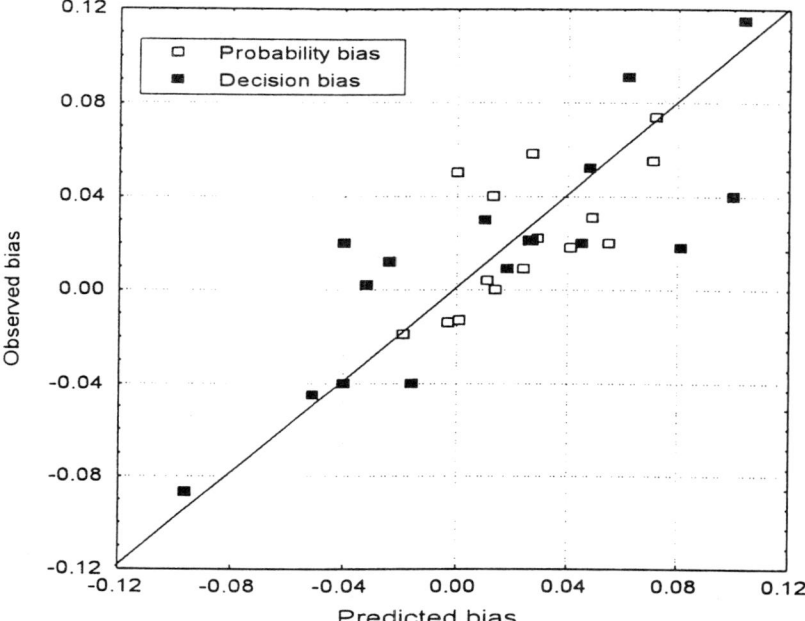

FIG. 6.3. The observed and predicted hindsight biases for the same 16 conditions as in Fig. 6.2 (collected from Winman, 1997a, 1997b, and Winman, Juslin, and Björkman, 1998).

Fig. 6.3 we see that across the eight data points with predicted reverse hindsight bias, only two data points produce slight positive hindsight biases (.01 and .02). Moreover, all data points with a reverse hindsight bias were associated with a foresight over/underconfidence equal to or lower than zero, implying underconfidence. There is evidently support for the confidence-hindsight mirror effect and the reverse hindsight biases predicted by the accuracy assessment model.

THEORETICAL IMPLICATIONS: INFERENCES OR MEMORY PROCESSES?

Aside from the serious practical consequences of hindsight bias alluded to in the introduction, the phenomenon has theoretical importance for our understanding of basic memory issues: How is a semantic knowledge base updated and kept coherent? How is new, and maybe contradictory information integrated with existing memories? Do we store an abstract summary representation of an event, which is affected by, and affects prior representations, or does each event produce a unique trace that coexists with older traces? To what degree is memory influenced by motivational factors? All of these issues are connected to hindsight bias.

The explanation of the phenomenon given by Fischhoff (1975) was that outcome knowledge is immediately assimilated with prior knowledge, leaving no residual information in memory about the original knowledge state. This is similar to the memory mechanisms proposed by Loftus and Loftus (1980) underlying memory inaccuracies after misleading postevent information in research on eyewitness memory (Loftus, 1979a, 1979b). In a typical study of this type, participants view a sequence of slides depicting, for example, a traffic accident. They then receive a narrative account of the event that provides misleading information about what took place. For example, a blue Datsun that occurred in the slides might be described as red. The consistent finding is that misled participants perform more poorly on critical forced-choice test items ("What was the color of the Datsun appearing on the slides?") than do participants who aren't misled. The interpretation by Loftus and Loftus (1980) was that the misleading information "overwrites" the original information, which now is irrevocably lost. This update-and-erase view of human memory suggests that in cases when real-world coexistence of two facts is logically impossible, the later memory trace will substitute the older. This substitution will take place for reasons of cognitive economy: "the most economical procedure may be to dismiss one memory in favor of the other, much as a computer programmer will irrevocably destroy an old program instruction when a new one is created" (Loftus & Loftus, 1980, p. 419).

This is a bold position indeed, suggesting that memory representations are highly mutable, contain major distortions and inaccuracies. We consider this model of human memory as an example of the computer metaphor of the mind taken too far. Further, the update-and-erase view on human memory is in sharp contrast with exemplar- or instance-based models, in which each event to which one attends to gives rise to its own unique memory trace. The exemplar models have proven successful and can account for findings that are problematic for the opposed prototype models (e.g., Hintzman, 1986; Medin & Schaffer, 1978; Nosofsky, 1992).

There is an alternative account of the findings of the misleading postevent information paradigm. McCloskey and Zaragoza (1985) argued convincingly that the procedure introduced by Loftus is inappropriate for assessing effects of misleading information on memory. The authors proposed that participants who remember both the information depicted in the slide (a blue Datsun) and the information in the misleading narrative (a red Datsun) will infer that the experimenter who prepared the narrative must have known what was in the slides (a quite reasonable assumption), and that the Datsun therefore must have been blue. If this account of the misleading postevent information findings is correct it means that the paradigm does not, as purported, investigate "pure" memory processes of encoding and retrieval but rather evidence the operation of inferential processes within participants. In fact, McCloskey and Zaragoza (1985) proposed and showed empirically in six experiments using a modified procedure that misleading postevent information has no effect on memory for the original event.

The account of McCloskey and Zaragoza is similar to the accuracy-assessment model of hindsight bias. In hindsight, the participants are thought to make an inference about whether or not they would have answered the item correctly. The outcome knowledge does neither overwrite any piece of information in the existing knowledge base nor is it assimilated with prior knowledge. In fact, the findings of an elimination or even a reversal of the effect (Winman, 1997a; Winman et al., 1998) are inconsistent with an immediate assimilation account of hindsight bias. The accuracy-assessment model illustrates that a participant's response strategy in solving the task may differ greatly from the psychologist's model of what he or she in fact is doing. The problem of inferring a mental process (i.e., assimilation) from a response pattern (i.e., hindsight bias) is of course central to cognitive psychology in general, and maybe to studies of memory in particular. Egon Brunswik (1952) stated the Behavior-Research Isomorphy principle that holds that research should focus where the organism focuses. If we want to understand what is going on in somebody's mind, we must know what he or she is trying to achieve—for example, is the task solved by inference or retrieval? This principle is still highly relevant today.

REFERENCES

Arkes, H. R. (1988). Comment on the article by Verplanken & Pieters. *Journal of Behavioral Decision Making, 1*, 146.

Baranski, J. V., & Petrusic, W. M. (1994). The calibration and resolution of confidence in perceptual judgments. *Perception and Psychophysics, 55*, 412–428.

Björkman, M. (1994). Internal cue theory: Calibration and resolution of confidence in general knowledge. *Organizational Behavior and Human Decision Processes, 57*, 386–405.

Björkman, M., Juslin, P., & Winman, A. (1993). Realism of confidence in sensory discriminations: The underconfidence phenomenon. *Perception & Psychophysics, 54*, 75–81.

Brunswik, E. (1952). *Conceptual framework of psychology*. Chicago: University of Chicago Press.

Christensen-Szalanski, J. J., & Willham, C. F. (1991). The hindsight bias: A meta-analysis. *Organizational Behavior and Human Decision Processes, 48*, 147–168.

Cohen, J. (1988). *Statistical power analysis for the behavioral sciences* (2nd. ed.). Hillsdale, NJ: Lawrence Erlbaum Associates.

Combs, B., & Slovic, P. (1979). Causes of death: Biased newspaper coverage and biased judgments. *Journalism Quarterly, 56*, 837–843.

118   WINMAN AND JUSLIN

Crawford, J. D., & Stankow, L. (1996). *Individual differences in the realism of confidence judgments: Overconfidence in measures of fluid and crystallized intelligence.* Unpublished manuscript, University of Technology, Sydney.

Erev, I., Wallsten, T. S., & Budescu, D. V. (1994). Simultaneous over- and underconfidence: The role of error in judgment processes. *Psychological Review, 101,* 519–527.

Estes, W. K., Campbell, J. A., Hatsopoulus, N., & Hurwitz, J. B. (1989). Base-rate effects in category learning: A comparison of parallel network and memory storage-retrieval models. *Journal of Experimental Psychology: Learning, Memory, and Cognition, 15,* 556–571.

Fischhoff, B. (1975). Hindsight ≠ Foresight: The effect of outcome knowledge on judgment under uncertainty. *Journal of Experimental Psychology: Human Perception and Performance, 1,* 288–299.

Fischhoff, B. (1977). Perceived informativeness of facts. *Journal of Experimental Psychology: Human Perception and Performance, 3,* 349–358.

Fischhoff, B. (1982). For those condemned to study the past: Heuristics in hindsight In D. Kahneman, P. Slovic, & A. Tversky (Eds.), *Judgment under uncertainty: Heuristics and biases.* New York: Cambridge University Press.

Gigerenzer, G., Hoffrage, U., & Kleinbölting, H. (1991). Probabilistic mental models: A Brunswikian Theory of Confidence. *Psychological Review, 98,* 506–528.

Gigerenzer, G. (1994). Why the distinction between single-event probabilities and frequencies is important for psychology (and vice versa). In G. Wright & P. Ayton (Eds.), *Subjective probability* (pp. 129–161). Chichester, England: Wiley.

Gluck, M. A., & Bower, G. H. (1988). From conditioning to category learning: An adaptive network model. *Journal of Experimental Psychology: General, 117,* 227–247.

Griffin, D., & Tversky, A. (1992). The weighing of evidence and the determinants of confidence. *Cognitive Psychology, 24,* 411–435.

Hasher, L., Attig, M. S., & Alba, J. W. (1987). I knew it all along: Or, did I ? *Journal of Verbal Learning and Verbal Behavior, 20,* 86–96.

Hawkins, S. A., & Hastie, R. (1990). Hindsight: Biased judgments of past events after the outcomes are known. *Psychological Bulletin, 107,* 311–327.

Healy, A., & Kubovy, M. (1981). Probability matching and the formation of conservative decision rules in a numerical analog of signal detection. *Journal of Experimental Psychology: Human Learning and Memory, 7,* 344–354.

Herrnstein, R. J. (1961). Relative and absolute strength of responses as a function of frequency of reinforcement. *Journal of the Experimental Analysis of Behavior, 4,* 267–272.

Hintzman, D. L. (1986). "Schema abstraction" in a multiple-trace memory model. *Psychological Review, 93,* 411–428.

Hoch, S. J., & Loewenstein, G. F. (1989). Outcome feedback: Hindsight and information. *Journal of Experimental Psychology: Learning, Memory, and Cognition, 15,* 605–619.

Juslin, P. (1993). An explanation of the hard-easy effect in studies of realism of confidence in one's general knowledge. *European Journal of Cognitive Psychology, 5,* 55–71.

Juslin, P. (1994). The overconfidence phenomenon as a consequence of informal experimenter-guided selection of almanac items. *Organizational Behavior and Human Decision Processes, 57,* 226–246.

Juslin, P., & Olsson, H. (1997). Thurstonian and Brunswikian origins of uncertainty in judgment: A sampling model of confidence in sensory discrimination. *Psychological Review, 104,* 344–366.

Juslin, P., Olsson, H., & Björkman, M. (1997). Brunswikian and Thurstonian Origins of Bias in Probability Assessment: On the interpretation of Stochastic Components of Judgments. *Journal of Behavioral Decision Making, 10,* 189–209.

Juslin, P., Winman, A., & Olsson., H. (1998). *The ecological model rides again: On naive empiricism and a priori dogmatism in judgment research.* Unpublished manuscript.

Juslin, P., Olsson, H., & Winman, A. (1998). The calibration issue: Theoretical comments on Suantak, Bolger, and Ferrell (1996). *Organizational Behavior and Human Decision Processes, 73*, 3–26.

Kahneman, D., Slovic, P., & Tversky, A. (1982). *Judgment under uncertainty: Heuristics and biases.* Cambridge, England: Cambridge University Press.

Keren, G. (1987). Facing uncertainty in the game of bridge: A calibration study. *Organizational Behavior and Human Decision Processes, 39*, 98–114.

Koriat, A., & Goldsmith, M. (1996). Monitoring and control processes in the strategic regulation of memory accuracy. *Psychological Review, 103*, 490–517.

Lichtenstein, S., Fischhoff, B., & Phillips, L. D. (1982). Calibration of subjective probabilities: The state of the art up to 1980. In D. Kahneman, P. Slovic, & A. Tversky (Eds.), *Judgments under uncertainty: Heuristics and biases* (pp. 306–334). New York: Cambridge University Press.

Loftus, E. F. (1979a). *Eyewitness testimony.* Cambridge: Harvard University Press.

Loftus, E. F. (1979b). The malleability of memory. *American Scientist, 67*, 312–320.

Loftus, E. F., & Loftus, G. R. (1980). On the permanence of stored information in the human brain. *American Psychologist, 35*, 409–420.

Mark, M. M., & Mellor, S. (1994). "We don't expect it happened": On Mazursky and Ofir's (1990) purported reversal of the hindsight bias. *Organizational Behavior and Human Decision Processes, 57*, 247–252.

May, R. S. (1987). *Realismus von subjektiven warscheinklichkeiten: Eine kognitionpsychologische analyse inferentieller prozesse beim overconfidence-phänomen.* [Calibration of subjective probabilities: A cognitive analysis of inference processes in overconfidence]. Frankfurt: Lang.

Mazursky, D., & Ofir, C. (1990). "I could never have expected it to happen": The reversal of the hindsight bias. *Organizational Behavior and Human Decision Processes, 46*, 20–33.

McCloskey, M., & Zaragoza, M. (1985). Misleading postevent information and memory for events: Arguments and evidence against memory impairment hypotheses. *Journal of Experimental Psychology: General, 114*, 1–16.

Medin, D. L., & Schaffer, M. M. (1978). Context theory of classification learning. *Psychological Review, 85*, 207–238.

Murphy, A. H., & Winkler, R. L. (1977). Can weather forecasters formulate reliable probability forecasts of precipitation and temperature? *National Weather Digest, 2*, 2–9.

Nisbett, R. E., & Ross, L. (1980). *Human inference: Strategies and shortcomings of social judgment.* Englewood, Cliffs, NJ: Prentice-Hall.

Nosofsky, R. M. (1992). Exemplars, prototypes, and similarity rules. In A. Healy, S. Kosslyn, & R. Shiffrin (Eds.), *Essays in honor of William K. Estes* (Vol. 1, pp. 149–167). Hillsdale, NJ: Lawrence Erlbaum Associates.

Olsson, H., & Winman, A. (1996). Underconfidence in sensory discrimination: The interaction between experimental setting and response strategies. *Perception & Psychophysics, 58*, 374–382.

Rachlin, H. (1976). *Behavior and learning.* San Francisco: Freeman.

Savage, L. J. (1954). *The Foundations of Statistics* (2nd ed.). New York: Dover.

Schkade, D. A., & Kilbourne, L. M. (1991). Expectation-outcome consistency and hindsight bias. *Organizational Behavior and Human Decision Processes, 49*, 105–123.

Smith, P. L., & Vickers, D. (1989). Modelling evidence accumulation with partial loss in expanded judgments. *Journal of Experimental Psychology: Human Perception and Performance, 15*, 797–815.

Sniezek, J. A., Paese, P. W., & Switzer, F. S., III. (1990). The effect of choosing on confidence in choice. *Organizational Behavior and Human Decision Processes, 46*, 264–282.

Synodinos, N. E. (1986). Hindsight Distortion: "I knew-it-all along and I was sure about it". *Journal of Applied Social Psychology, 16*, 107–117.

Tomassini, L. A., Solomon, I., Romney, M. B., & Krogstad, J. L. (1982). Calibration of auditors' probabilistic judgments: Some empirical evidence. *Organizational Behavior and Human Performance, 30,* 391–406.

Verplanken, B., & Pieters, R. G. (1988). Individual differences in reverse hindsight bias: I never thought something like Chernobyl would happen. Did I? *Journal of Behavioral Decision Making, 1,* 131–147.

Wells, G. L., & Murray, D. M. (1984). Eyewitness confidence. In G. L. Wells & E. F. Loftus (Eds.), *Eyewitness testimony: Psychological perspectives* (pp. 155–170). New York: Cambridge University Press.

Williams, B. A. (1994). Reinforcement and choice. In N. J. Mackintosh (Ed.), *Animal learning and cognition.* San Diego, CA: Academic Press.

Winman, A. (1997a). The importance of item selection in "knew-it-all-along" studies of general knowledge. *Scandinavian Journal of Psychology, 38,* 63–72.

Winman, A. (1997b). *Cognitive processes behind the knew-it-all-along effect.* Unpublished manuscript.

Winman, A. (1997c). *Knowing if you would have known: A model of the hindsight bias.* Acta Universitatis Upsaliensis: Comprehensive summaries of Uppsala dissertations from the faculty of social sciences, *69.*

Winman, A., & Juslin, P. (1993). Calibration of cognitive and sensory judgments: Two different accounts. *Scandinavian Journal of Psychology, 34,* 135–148.

Winman, A., Juslin, P., & Björkman, M. (1998). The confidence-hindsight mirror effect in judgment: An accuracy-assessment model for the "knew-it-all-along" phenomenon. *Journal of Experimental Psychology: Learning, Memory, and Cognition, 24,* 415–431.

Wood, G. (1978). The knew-it-all-along effect. *Journal of Experimental Psychology: Human Perception and Performance, 4,* 345–353.

Yaniv, I., Yates, J. F., & Smith, J. E. K. (1991). Measures of discrimination skill in probabilistic judgment. *Psychological Bulletin, 110,* 611–617.

Part II

JUDGMENT AND DECISION MAKING AS MENTAL PROCESSES

Chapter 7

Feelings of Confidence and the Realism of Confidence Judgments in Everyday Life

Carl Martin Allwood
Lund University

Pär Anders Granhag
Göteborg University

In the last decade, confidence judgments has been a popular research area in psychology (e.g., McClelland & Bolgar 1994). Still, our understanding of such judgments has only improved to a very limited extent. In this chapter we suggest that one way to improve this situation is to more closely attempt to identify the phenomenon under study. By attending more to the complexity of confidence judgments as they actually occur in everyday life, a more realistic understanding of at least some of the issues dealt with in previous research can be achieved. We hope that our characterization of confidence judgments in everyday life will convince the reader that one- or few-factor explanations, such as illustrated by the theories reviewed by McClelland and Bolgar (1994) for general knowledge questions, are unrealistically oversimplified when applied to confidence judgments in everyday life.

In previous research on confidence judgments, it has often not been clear what phenomenon the research is assumed to concern. The tacit assumption has usually been that it is confidence judgments in everyday life that is the object of study, directly or indirectly. However, it is not clear to which extent the phenomenon called *confidence judgment*, researched and presented in the research literature, overlaps with confidence judgments as performed in everyday life.

On a more fundamental level, the criteria used for identifying a phenomenon such as confidence judgments need to be considered. At least two possibilities present themselves. The first is to define the phenomenon in terms of a type of task performed: "a confidence judgment." This involves making an abstract characterization of the phenomenon. In the case of confidence judgments, such a characterization might involve describing confidence judgments as acts of judging the likelihood that a certain task is correctly performed. Given such a characterization, it seems clear that "confidence judgments" could involve processes that might differ radically from instance to instance depending on the circumstances. A problem with this criterion for identifying confidence judgments is, as noted by Cole and Means (1981) in a more general connection, that the concept of *task* is not stable in an everyday context. One reason for this is that task-goals in everyday life are, to a larger extent, negotiable means of reaching higher level goals. This is especially obvious compared to what is commonly the case in the laboratory. Furthermore, the "same task" can actually be very different depending on the constraints and the possibilities in the specific situation, a situation that, in addition, is likely to change over time. Thus, in order to identify the processes of the actual confidence judgment performed, a contextualization of its occurrence seems to be necessary.

A second possibility is to identify the phenomenon by means of the processes involved. This is a difficult way to go for various reasons. For example, further specifications have to be made with respect to how much the processes are allowed to differ before one wants to assume that one has a new phenomenon at hand. Furthermore, one may in the case of confidence judgments, for some reason, feel that one wants to include not just one chain of specific processes under the label "confidence judgments," but two or more. The problem then is that one is utilizing another, unspecified, criterion for delimiting how one defines a confidence judgment. Finally, and this might be the most troublesome point, the processes engaged when confidence judgments are made are not well known. Accordingly, it seems very difficult to identify confidence judgments by way of the processes involved.

In brief, the first criterion of the two discussed above appears to be the more reasonable one to use when identifying confidence judgments. A reason for this suggestion is that the process criterion described above, in similarity to the task criterion, seems to demand that some kind of more abstract notion of confidence judgment be used as a criterion for putting together the mental processes making up a confidence judgment. Thus, the process criterion will not suffice. Given this and given the lack of credible alternatives, it seems reasonable to resort to a task criterion.

If the task criterion is used to identify confidence judgments, then openness is required with respect to the types of processes assumed to be involved. For example, confidence judgments have usually been described in terms of cognitive processes at the level of the individual. Maybe for reasons due to disciplinary tradition in cognitive psychology, intra-individual processes have commonly been assumed to be more fundamental than inter-individual processes. This situation may be gradually changing as an effect of the development of new approaches in cognitive psychology. Examples of such approaches are Situated cognition and Everyday memory, and the development of applied cognitive psychology. In these approaches the individual does not always have priority as the most fundamental unit of analysis. In line with such approaches, processes on the inter-individual level may on occasions naturally be seen as part of the confidence judgment phenomenon. For example, social feedback and expectations of accountability can be expected to influence the realism of confidence judgments (e.g., Allwood & Granhag, 1996a; Arkes, Christensen, Lai, & Blumer, 1987; Luus & Wells, 1994).

On a general level, the mental processes involved when confidence judgments are made are usually characterized as sorting under the "higher mental processes." One of the main conclusions of cognitive psychology in the last century is that such processes are affected by the context in which they occur (e.g., Fodor, 1983). This conclusion supports the suggestion that in order to understand confidence judgments in everyday life, it is important to analyze their contexts.

Below, we will take confidence judgments as they occur in different situations in everyday life, including working life, as the primary phenomenon of interest and we will attempt a characterization of confidence judgments given this assumption. This will first be done on a general level and then more specifically for various professional groups in working life. In the later connection, we discuss how the processes involved in confidence judgments vary as a function of selected features of the situations in which they are made. Finally, in the discussion part of the chapter, we contrast our characterization of confidence judgments in everyday life with typical features of previous research on confidence judgments. Here, we also deal with the questions of explanations of overconfidence and what can be done to improve the realism of confidence judgments in everyday life. As a general preliminary we first briefly describe some features of how confidence judgments have commonly been researched and described in previous research.

CONFIDENCE JUDGMENTS IN PREVIOUS RESEARCH

Commonly, the participants in previous research on confidence judgments have first performed a task: for example, answered a general knowledge question or made a prediction of some future event. Next, they have been instructed to confidence rate their performance. In order to ensure stability in the results, each participant has usually been given a large number of tasks of the same kind. The confidence judgments have been elicited in various forms, the most typical situation being that the participants after having selected one of two given answer alternatives have been asked to confidence rate their choice on a half-range scale. This scale ranges from 50 to 100%, where 50% means "guess" and 100% means "absolutely sure" that the chosen answer is correct.

The next step has been to compute the degree of *realism* of the participant's confidence judgments. In this connection it should be noted that researchers in the field of realism in confidence judgments (calibration studies) are usually very careful to select tasks for which they can be (reasonably) sure of what should count as correct performance. This is done in order to be able to match the participant's answers and confidence judgements (subjective probabilities) to descriptions of states of the world that are socially agreed upon as objective facts. As the present authors experienced in a pilot study aimed at eliciting realistic items to be used as questions in a calibration study, this may be a problem for studies of everyday confidence judgments—for example, for studies in connection with political and environmental debates. A similar problem can also occur in connection with (for example) outcomes related to personal predictions.

The judge's degree of realism is commonly calculated on the basis of her proportion correct answers and her confidence ratings (e.g., Lichtenstein, Fischhoff, & Phillips 1982). When, as is most common, each answer is confidence rated (*item specific* ratings) realism is measured by the degree to which the confidence ratings correspond to the proportion correct. For example, if the participant is correct for 80% of all items confidence rated with 80%, then the person is said to have given *realistic* confidence judgments for these items. Had the person only had 60% of the same items correct she would, in her ratings, have shown a lack of realism called *overconfidence*. Less usual has been to ask the participant to rate her total performance over all questions answered (*frequency* rating). In this connection, lack of realism is measured as the size of the deviance between the actual and the estimated proportion correct answers. Unless otherwise stated, below we will only consider item-specific confidence judgments.

In previous research, confidence judgments have often been described as an instance of metacognition (e.g., Nelson & Narens, 1994). Metacognition is usually defined as involving knowledge (beliefs) about cognition. Applied to confidence judgments this would mean that confidence judgments involve use of knowledge about one's own cognitive properties and/or knowledge about properties of one's cognitive products. Such properties may include beliefs about the relation between the performance judged and some state in the world. This state may either exist now or have existed (as is the case of general knowledge questions) or come to exist in the future (as is the case of predictions).

Nelson and Narens (1994) discussed metacognition in terms of levels of processes and by using the concepts of control and monitoring. They defined metacognition as a situation in which one process level (or several), called the meta-level, controls and monitors another process level (or several), the object-level. Thus, metacognition is characterized by the meta-level processes controlling the processes at the object-level on the basis of information from the controlled object level. The meta-level is assumed to be conscious and reflective.

Conscious processes have commonly been described in the research literature as being more reflective, flexible, possible to plan, and explicitly goal-driven. In contrast, unconscious processes have been described as spontaneous and to a higher degree unfocused (Greenwald, 1992; Lewicki, Hill & Czyzewska, 1992). Although confidence judgments are often assumed to be an example of metacognition it is still worth to consider more closely the extent to which the processes involved in confidence judgments in fact are located on the meta-level, that is the extent to which they are reflective and conscious in kind. This question has not very often been considered in this form in research on confidence judgments. When assumptions have explicitly been made about the types of processes involved, these processes have sometimes been assumed to be conscious and explicit (e.g., Chan, 1992; Berry & Dienes, 1993), but this has not always been the case (e.g., Björkman, 1994; Gigerenzer, Hoffrage, & Kleinbölting, 1991; Juslin & Olsson, 1997; Kelly & Lindsay, 1993).

CONFIDENCE JUDGMENTS IN EVERYDAY LIFE

We next attempt a characterization of confidence judgments as they occur in everyday life. As discussed above, this involves a contextualization of confidence judgments, which includes describing parts of the larger mental and social context in which confidence judgments occur. An intuitively reasonable approach in this connection is to consider the functions and effects of confidence judgments in everyday life. Such an approach, to some extent, contrasts with the more commonly taken approach in research on confidence judgments: to analyze what factors affect such judgments and how. It is commonly accepted that confidence judgments give rise to feelings of confidence (which may or may not be expressed in words or numbers). However, at the same time, it appears to be the case that confidence judgments are often elicited on the basis of feelings of confidence. This will be further discussed below.

Backgrounded and Foregrounded Feelings of Confidence

In order to place confidence judgments into a larger picture we first consider two types of feelings of confidence (see Fig. 7.1). The first type is spontaneous, nonreflective and usually appears as a *background*—rather

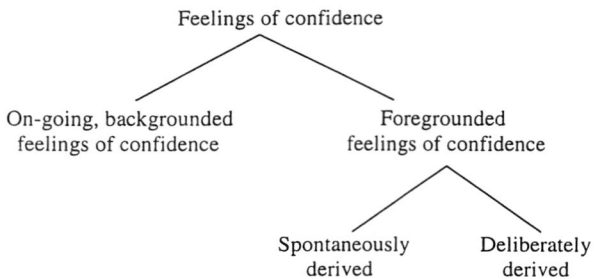

FIG. 7.1. Different types of feelings of confidence.

than as a sharply focused upon—feeling. Maybe due to methodological difficulties, this type of feeling of confidence has not been much researched in cognitive psychology. Phenomenologists such as Schutz (Schutz & Luckmann, 1974) have suggested that most of us live in a world where, most of the time, what appears to be the case is spontaneously taken for granted to be the case. The world, as given, has a quality of self-evidence to it, viz., its presentation in experience co-occurs with a positive feeling of confidence and it is usually not questioned. In line with this, we suggest that the background feeling of confidence for most people, most of the time, is positive in valance. (This is not to say that such an attitude would be defended intellectually by all persons.) Such a background feeling of confidence may be the result of a constantly ongoing monitoring. The fulfillment of projected expectations may contribute to the feeling of self-evidence. When our present experience is compatible with our recent categorizations, the positive background feeling of confidence is supported. (In certain cases fulfillment of expectation may be associated with uncertainty, for example a tricky "puzzle problem" may fulfill my expectations concerning problems of this type and also lead me to be uncertain. However, at such times my feeling of confidence of uncertainty most likely will be foregrounded.) This type of feeling of confidence (background) will not be further discussed below.

The second type of feeling of confidence is *foregrounded* in experience and is often initially experienced as a change in quality. As indicated in Figure 7.1, such feelings may be the result of either spontaneous or deliberate processes. Different types of events may occur that affect the ongoing feeling of confidence. For example, when we experience a mismatch between what we have expected and what actually occurs, a feeling of self-evidence may change into a feeling of uncertainty. This is what phenomenologically inspired writers have called a "break-down." Such mismatches may be due to the occurrence of new information or a new perspective on a belief being taken. An example of relevant information is information telling us that the opening time of the restaurant we intend to visit, has changed or is about to change. Similarly, if someone else takes for granted or as a fact something that I myself have earlier bestowed with low confidence (Kruglanski, 1994), my confidence in the message of this person may be lowered and at the same time foregrounded.

A further type of event which may lead to a lowered feeling of confidence is the activation of knowledge that certain occasions or types of understandings are error prone and extra checks may be called for (compare the "puzzle problem," above). As an illustration: I may know from previous experience that a certain category of persons, such as apprenticeship-learners, are more likely to make errors and that their work needs to be checked. In a situation where I realize that I have employed a person who falls into the apprenticeship category, my feeling of confidence in the quality of her work can decrease and the idea of checking her work may occur to me.

Many (or most?) contexts in which feelings of confidence are foregrounded appear to be contexts in which something is at stake. In such situations we are, for some reason, interested in whether an assumption, an assertion, or a performance is correct or not. An important type of context in which feelings of confidence occur is in connection with decision making and action regulation. An action may be based on the likelihood of some future state of the world but action may also be taken or not as a consequence of some factual state in the world. Possible functions of feelings of confidence in connection with decision making/action are to help decide whether an action should be carried out, if more information should be collected, whether alternative action routes should be planned, or if a plan for an action should be changed with respect to the time, place or how it is carried out.

Some examples of expressions of foregrounded feelings of confidence in everyday life are: "Do I need to go back and check if I locked the door?," "Am I sufficiently sure so that the ice will hold that I dare to walk on it?," "Am I sufficiently sure of the closing time of the restaurant so that I dare state it as a fact to a person asking me?," and "Do I need to collect more information about this company before investing money in it?"

These examples, representative or not, are all directly or indirectly related to the possibility of action on my, or someone else's, part and the consequences of these actions have some importance. Related to this property, it is noteworthy that in all of the examples, one is interested in whether the confidence is above or below a certain level (breaking point). If the confidence level is found to be clearly above or below the level in question further discrimination is not made. If it is approximately at the breaking point, finer grained precision may be attempted (or, if in a social context, at least requested). Whether more fine grained precision is attempted or not may depend on, for example, the consequences of the effects if we are wrong and the cost in time and effort of ensuring a more precise confidence level.

Spontaneously Occurring and Deliberately Elicited
Foregrounded Feelings of Confidence

Foregrounded feelings of confidence may arise as the result of spontaneous, subconscious processes or they may be the result of deliberate
judgments (see Fig. 7.1). It is not entirely obvious that spontaneously
derived feelings of confidence should be called confidence judgments.
However, some authors appear to think so, as witnessed by the following
characterization of confidence judgments made by Narens, Jameson, and
Lee (1994): "confidence judgments correspond to decisions to output
answers during retrieval" (p. 73). The question as to when and how
spontaneously derived feelings of confidence are triggered have, to our
knowledge, not received researchers' attention.

Deliberately elicited confidence judgments are selectively triggered—we
do not make deliberate confidence judgments all the time. Again, to our
knowledge, the question of when, how often, and in what contexts deliberate confidence judgments are triggered in everyday life has not been
the topic of previous research. Instead, as noted above, the typical way of
proceeding in research has been to *instruct* the participants to make confidence judgments—for example, after each performance in a row of performances of a certain type.

Deliberately triggered confidence judgments may be initiated as a consequence of an individual's own deliberations or in interactive or institutionalized social contexts. One example of when initiations of the first type
are likely to occur is when the individual has reason to feel uncertain
about his or her own spontaneous feelings of confidence (i.e., the individual experiences low second-order confidence) and when, at the same
time, these doubts have some important implications for the individual.
Such a situation may be at hand, for example, when the individual plans
to use some limited pool of resources she has access to, as in the case
above of somebody considering the possibility to invest in a company.

In situations where the individual doubts his or her own spontaneous
feelings of confidence, at least three kinds of responses are possible: 1)
Perform an external check (e.g., check that the door is in fact locked), 2)
make a deliberate confidence judgment (how sure am I that I locked the
door), and 3) do nothing. Depending on the cost for making external
checks, this may in many situations be the most effective thing to do. If I
am standing by the door and severely doubt whether I have locked it, I
would check the door rather than perform a deliberate confidence judgment. However, in the same situation, except for being far from home, I
might perform a deliberate confidence judgment in order to scrutinize
how sure I am that I really did not lock the door. Because external checking
in this situation is costly, I want to make sure it is really needed. At the
same time a deliberate confidence judgment may (or may not) in this

situation be cheap. Thus, the result of the comparison between the cost and the judged effectiveness of each of the two options will be decisive for which option of the two is taken. Speaking in favor of checking is that checking, rather than a confidence judgment, will usually appear to be a more direct way to ensure that the goal (locked door) is accomplished.

Although separated above, depending on perspective external checking can be seen as part of making a confidence judgment or not. In an experiential phenomenological perspective external checking may not be experienced as part of a confidence judgment but as part of completing the action (to lock the door). However, in a more abstract task perspective and in analogy with checking the validity of a chain of arguments as part of a deliberate confidence judgment, external checking can be seen as checking the assumptions underlying the feeling of confidence and as bringing the feeling of confidence to an acceptable level. At the same time, the confidence judgment can reasonably be seen as a part of completing the action. This illustrates that confidence judgments in everyday life are often tightly integrated in the flow of other processes.

The second type of initiation of a deliberate confidence judgment occurs in interactive or institutionalized social contexts. An example of an interactive context is when a confidence judgment is made as a response to a request, such as when someone asks me how sure I am that my assertion is correct. The person asking me may do so because she doubts my competence in the knowledge domain in general or because she doubts the specific content of my assertion.

A case of an institutional context for the elicitation of deliberate confidence judgments is at hand when a confidence judgment is made in response to an institutionalized request, for example when confidence judgments are made by weather forecasters. Over time a need for such confidence judgments has been socially recognized and practicing them has been implemented in the work routine of some professional categories. Another example of a professional category making institutionalized confidence judgments is bookmakers who set fixed odds for different gambling events. As will be discussed further below, it should be quite clear to the person giving the confidence judgments in these contexts that his or her professional reputation is at stake. Furthermore, certain mistakes may be more costly than other are (such as underconfidence in a situation where resources are abundant and an attractive investment can be made).

THE REALISM OF CONFIDENCE IN WORKING LIFE

One domain where confidence judgments can be expected to be important is working life. In Table 7.1, we have listed a sample of different professionals that have been studied in calibration research. It can be noted that

TABLE 7.1
A Sample of Professional Groups Studied in Calibration Research

Profession	Task	Result	Type of Confidence Judgment	Temporal Relation (Decision → Outcome)
Auditors (Tomassini, Solomon, Romney, & Krogstad, 1982)	Opinion on a client's financial status	Underconf.	Predictions	long
Bankers (Stael von Holstein, 1972)	Predicting the stock exchange	Overconf.	Predictions	long
Economists (Braun & Yaniv, 1992	Predicting economic downturns	Overconf.	Predictions	long
Bridge players (professional) (Keren, 1987)	Predicting the chances to keep the stated number of contracts	Well-calib.	Predictions	short
Doctors and nurses (Vreugdenhil, 1993)	Diagnosing infections in infants	Overconf.	Predictions	short
Physicians (Christensen-Szalanski & Bushyhead, 1981)	Diagnosing pneumonia	Overconf.	Predictions	short
Psychologists (clinical) (Oskamp, 1965)	Diagnosing and predicting future behavior	Overconf.	Predictions	long
Lawyers (Loftus & Wagenaar, 1988; Malsch, 1989; Goodman-Delahunty, Granhag, & Loftus, 1996)	Predicting the outcome of upcoming court cases	Overconf.	Predictions	long
FBI, CIA, and Secret Service agents (Ekman & O"Sullivan, 1991)	Detecting lies	Overconf.[1]	Retrospective	short
Meteorologists (Murphy & Winkler, 1971)	Weather forecasts	Well-calib.	Predictions	short

[1] However, Secret Service agents were well-calibrated.

a clear majority of the professional groups listed were found to be over-confident in their judgments. Only professional bridge players, meteorologists, and Secret service agents were found to be well calibrated, and one type of expert (auditors) showed a tendency towards underconfidence. All expert groups except one, namely agents asked to detect lies, were asked to state their confidence in predictions. (For this reason and for the sake of brevity, we will below occasionally use the word "prediction" even when it would have been relevant to talk about predictions and assertions). The rightmost column in Table 7.1 is explained in connection with Table 7.2.

Confidence judgments in work life are made in a variety of circumstances that may influence their realism. In the leftmost column in Table 7.2, we have listed a selection of such factors. Next, we explain those factors in Table 7.2 that have not been explained above.

First, whether or not the confidence judgments concern retrospective assertions (e.g., what was the name of the U.S. president in 1970?) or predictions (e.g., who will be the U.S. president in 2003?) may have consequences for the realism of confidence judgments. Whether the confidence judgment is an item specific or a frequency judgment may also be important for the realism of confidence judgments (see Gigerenzer et al., 1991; Granhag, 1997). Although the example of a retrospective task given above refers to semantic knowledge, retrospective assertions can of course also be made in relation to episodic knowledge (are you absolutely sure that this is the woman who attacked you in the alley last night?). The number of possible alternatives can vary between one stated alternative (e.g., how sure are you that this is the right woman?) and several possible alternatives (e.g., out of all these women, who is the one who attacked you last night?). In addition, the alternatives considered can be self-generated or given (see Liberman & Tversky, 1993).

Whether confidence judgments are made individually or by a group obviously can affect the realism in confidence (see Allwood & Granhag, 1996a). This is also the case with respect to whether a person has the chance to affect the outcome (e.g., I'm sure that I will win tomorrow) or not (e.g., it will probably be raining during the race). Realism in confidence can also be affected by factors such as whether or not a person is experienced within the domain s/he is asked about. Furthermore, as discussed above, it can be affected by whether or not the search for relevant information is costly (e.g., to make a realistic confidence judgment about a prediction concerning a possible outburst of a vulcano, you may need to hire a team of experts for a long time, as well as to equip them with expensive instruments) or not (e.g., please, take a few seconds and think about how sure you are that you locked the door).

Two temporal intervals are of importance for the realism in confidence. First, there is the interval between the point in time when the task is first

TABLE 7.2
A Selection of Factors Which May Influence Realism in Confidence

Factor	Example of Possible Values	Lawyers (Goodman-Delahunty et al., 1996)
Type of confidence judgment:	Retrospective judgment vs. predictions; Item-specific judgment vs. frequency	Predictions; Item-specific
Type of knowledge:	Semantic, Episodic, Procedural, Implicit and combined	Combined
Number of possibilities:	One vs. Several	One
Derivation of possibility/ies:	Self-generated vs. Given	Self-generated
Number of confidence judgments:	One vs. many	One
Type of elicitation:	Spontaneous vs. Instructed	Instructed
Number of persons:	Individual vs. Group	Individual
Self-involvement:	Yes vs. No	Yes
Degree of experience:	Low vs. High	Low and High
Cost for search of information:	Low vs. High	(Not investigated)
Temporal relation: (task → decision)	Short vs. Long	Short
Temporal relation: (decision → outcome)	Short vs. Long	Long
Stability of environment:	Low vs. High	(Not investigated)
Feedback:	Yes vs. No	Yes
Type of Feedback:	Clear vs. Ambiguous	Clear
Delivery of Feedback:	Immediate vs. Delayed	(Not investigated)

given and the point in time when it is to be completed (e.g., I want your prediction for the Dow Jones index on my desk tomorrow morning!). The second temporal interval is between the point in time when the prediction is made and when the relevant outcome occurs.

Another factor of relevance for the realism in confidence judgments is the stability of the environment that the topic of the confidence judgment relates to. Brunswikian-influenced researchers have argued that a stable environment allows for the development of valid internal probability cues (i.e., the persons' mental representations mirror the "true" ecological probabilities), and that valid internal cues promote realism in confidence (Björkman, 1994; Gigerenzer et al., 1991; Juslin, 1994).

Finally, we describe three factors in Table 7.2 that have to do with the presence of feedback and the nature of the feedback situation. The first factor concerns whether any feedback is given at all. For feedback given, the second factor concerns whether the feedback is clear or ambiguous. For example, it might be difficult for a clinical psychologist to get clear and straightforward feedback concerning whether or not her diagnosis of a client was correct. In contrast, an economist who predicts changes in a certain index will probably get clear feedback concerning whether s/he was correct or not. Obviously, whether one gets clear feedback or not can vary within a specific professional group, as well as for a specific professional at different occasions.

The third feedback factor in Table 7.2 is whether or not the feedback is immediate or delayed. This factor is often closely related to the temporal interval mentioned above between task decision and information about its "outcome." However, immediate feedback and a short time distance between an assertion and the "outcome" need not overlap. Although the temporal interval is short, the feedback may not be available to the person who made the assertion until a long time after the outcome has occurred.

Each of the studies of the professional groups in Table 7.1 can be characterized in terms of the list of factors given in Table 7.2. As an illustration, lawyers—as Goodman-Delahunty, Granhag, and Loftus (1996) studied them—would end up with the following characteristics based on Table 7.2:

- *Type of confidence judgments*: Item-specific predictions; the lawyers were asked about an upcoming case.
- *Type of knowledge*: Combined; in their prediction the lawyers had to use a combination of different types of knowledge.
- *Number of possibilities*: One; the lawyers stated their confidence in relation to one hypothesis.
- *Derivation of possibilities*: Self-generated; the lawyers generated their own goals.
- *Number of confidence judgments*: One; the lawyers were asked about one single case.
- *Type of elicitation*: Instructed; the lawyers were explicitly instructed to state a certain confidence judgment on a designated scale.
- *Number of persons*: Individual; the lawyers made both the prediction and the confidence judgment individually.

- *Self-involvement*: Yes; it was, at least to a certain extent, possible for the lawyers to affect the outcome of the selected case.
- *Degree of experience*: High and low; lawyers with both high and low experience participated in the study.
- *Cost for the search of information*: Not investigated in the study; the lawyers had to pick a case and make the prediction, as well as the confidence judgment, at the very same occasion.
- *Temporal relation (task → decision)*: Short; see comment on the previous factor.
- *Temporal relation (decision → outcome)*: Long; for the great majority of the cases in the study there was a time period of several months between the date of the prediction and the date of the resolution of the case.
- *Stability of environment*: Not investigated in the study.
- *Feedback*: Yes; the lawyers could use knowledge gained from the outcome of previous cases they had been involved in.
- *Type of Feedback*: Clear; see comment on previous factor.
- *Delivery of feedback*: Delayed; see comment on the temporal relation (decision → outcome) factor, above.

It should be noted that other levels of realism might be found for the various professional groups in Table 7.1 if the values of the factors listed in Table 7.2 are varied. For example, the combination of the values of the factors implemented by Goodman-Delahunty et al. (1996) is just one out of many possible realistic combinations of values one might implement when studying realism in lawyers' confidence judgments. As an illustration, the Goodman-Delahunty et al. study focused on unresolved cases, for which each lawyer individually stated a goal and for which the lawyers themselves, at least to a certain extent, could influence the outcome. Instead, one might study the realism in the lawyers' confidence for retrospective judgments (memory of the registered outcome of their own and/or others cases), or for situations where a team of lawyers, instead of one individual, has to perform confidence ratings of their predictions. One might also design a study where lawyers are instructed to state goals, as well as to make confidence judgments about the chances of reaching them for the cases of other lawyers rather than their own cases. (In such a situation, they would not have the same chance to personally influence the outcome of the cases they were asked to predict).

In brief, the message here is that for a specific professional group, there exists a complex web of values of factors that can be combined in many different ways depending on the situation(s) studied for that particular group of professionals. Thus, without having taken into consideration that different factors interact in different ways depending on the context, it is venturesome to label a certain group of professionals as "well-calibrated" or "overconfident."

Below, we discuss more concretely six factors that all can affect the realism of confidence judgments in various work-contexts: 1) the time interval between the time of the prediction (assertion) and the actual outcome, 2) feedback, 3) social factors, 4) motivational factors, 5) degree of control, and 6) the professionals' degree of experience within the task domain. Some of these factors are selected directly from Table 7.2 and others are somewhat more broadly conceived.

Time Between Prediction and Outcome

Professional groups vary with respect to the time between when the prediction is made and when the outcome of the prediction can be decided. The importance of this temporal distance for realism in confidence has previously been acknowledged by other researchers (see Braun & Yaniv, 1992; Gilovich, Kerr, & Husted Medvec, 1993). Several aspects are relevant here. For example, if the temporal interval between the time of the prediction and the outcome is long (as opposed to short), the chances are greater that new important information will come up during the passage of time. Such information, if available at the time of the prediction, might well have changed the confidence in the stated prediction. Moreover, if the judge believes that she can affect the outcome, she has a long time to do so. This may induce her to give a higher confidence rating. However, several events that lie outside the control of the judge could take place if the time interval is long, compared to short. Such a consideration may lead her to give a more conservative confidence rating.

A short distance between prediction and outcome makes frequent predictions during a limited period of time possible. As an example, it is not uncommon for professional bridge players and meteorologists to make predictions every other day. In contrast, lawyers usually make predictions much more seldom. The consequence is that some professionals get more training than others do to handle probabilities. Both bridge players and meteorologists (groups that normally have a short time interval between prediction and outcome) are professional groups that have proven to be well-calibrated. However, a closer examination of Table 7.1 shows that this does not necessarily imply that a short temporal interval between prediction and outcome equals good calibration. In this connection it can be noted that both doctors and nurses diagnosing infections in infants (Vreugdenhil, 1993), and physicians diagnosing pneumonia (Christensen-Szalanski & Bushyhead, 1981) expressed overconfidence in their predictions. This was the case, although the temporal interval between prediction and outcome was relatively short in both cases. Accordingly, a short temporal interval between prediction and outcome may be an important, but not in itself conclusive, factor in determining whether a certain group of professionals is well-calibrated or not.

Feedback

Professional groups vary between and within themselves with respect to the type of feedback they get on their assertions. Of the different professionals listed in Table 7.1, bridge players will know whether or not they made a correct prediction within minutes after they stated it. In contrast, lawyers who predict the outcome of upcoming court cases might have to wait several months until they will know whether they were right or not. One aspect of the effect of feedback, closely related to the above discussion on temporal interval, is that a short temporal interval between prediction and outcome provides an opportunity for more or less immediate feedback. In contrast, a long temporal distance between prediction and outcome offer no such "on-line" feedback.

Goodman-Delahunty et al. (1996) noted one interesting consequence that may follow from situations where a long time interval exists between prediction and outcome. They found that the lawyers, when reporting the actual outcome of the case, failed to remember their initial goals. More precisely, a bias was noticed in the sense that the lawyers remembered their initial goals as lower than they were. In such a situation a person might argue: I need not adjust (lower) my goals for the future since I have reached the ones I have stated in the past. In short, a long time passage between prediction and outcome may lead to erroneous recall of the initial goal. One consequence of such a situation might be that one becomes insensitive to feedback.

However, the effect of feedback is not only dependent on whether it is immediate or not. One also needs to take into account whether the feedback is ambiguous or clear. For example: it might be a difficult task to decide whether or not a doctor was right in diagnosing an infection in an infant. Compared to physicians and nurses, the feedback that meteorologists and bridge players get is relatively clear and straightforward. This might be one reason why the latter two groups of professionals, in the context researched, have been well-calibrated, while physicians and nurses have not, although the temporal interval between prediction and outcome in all cases, as noted above, is relatively short.

Social Factors

An under-researched group of factors influencing the realism of confidence may be labeled *social factors*. An illustration of this group of factors is that the cost of errors vary and may influence the realism of confidence judgments. For example, as noted above, certain mistakes are more costly than other is (i.e., underconfidence in a situation where resources are plenty and an attractive investment can be made). Moreover, different social contexts may demand and elicit different attitudes towards realism in confidence. For example, an expert might feel the need for a confident appearance, which in turn might lead her to make unrealistic statements about her confidence in her predictions. In this connection, it is important for researchers to distinguish between situations in which, for example, lawyers are expected to *act* highly confident, or even overconfident (e.g., when appearing in front of the court representing a client) and situations in which they are expected to be objective (realistic) (e.g., being consulted by a potential client about the his/her chances of winning a certain case).

Another example of a context where social factors may play an important role for realism in confidence judgments is the situation where an eyewitness is asked to make a statement (e.g., identify a perpetrator from a lineup). Luus and Wells (1994) presented different types of cowitness information to their witnesses after they had identified a perpetrator out of a photo set. The group who was informed that a cowitness had stated that the perpetrator was not present in the array was found to have the lowest confidence score (3.57, on a 10-point scale). The group who was informed that a cowitness had identified the same individual as themselves had the highest confidence score (8.77). In brief, Luus and Wells elegantly showed the malleability of eyewitness confidence by introducing a social factor into the test situation, namely the different types of information communicated about a cowitness' response.

Motivational Factors

Motivational factors are closely related to the social factors discussed above. Several different types of motivational factors come into play in situations where people have to state how confident they are in their own predictions. One important motivational factor, that at least some of the professional groups listed in Table 7.1 may succumb to when making their predictions is "wishful thinking." Babad, Hills, and O'Driscoll (1992) described wishful thinking as a "motivational force reducing objectivity and leading to bias in judgment and prediction" (p. 461). If wishful thinking is seen as a link between preference and prediction, then, for a professional group such as lawyers, a strong preference for a specific outcome of a case may unduly influence their confidence estimate for achieving that specific goal (Goodman-Delahunty et al., 1996). Many motivational factors are tightly intertwined with experienced degree of control, to be discussed next.

Degree of Control

Degree of control concerns whether or not a person who has made a prediction can influence the outcome. Obviously, there is no way a meteorologist can increase the chances that his/her weather forecast will be correct after it's stated. In contrast, a lawyer who puts a lot of energy and time into his/her cases will, at least in the long run, have improved her chances to reach the stated goals.

Research has shown that people have a tendency to overestimate the extent to which some events are controllable. Langer (1975) called this bias "illusion of control." Weinstein (1980, 1982, 1983) has, in several studies, shown that when an event is perceived to be controllable, optimism is likely to occur. However, it should be noted that Budesco and Bruderman (1995) found that the wishful thinking bias *can* exist in the absence of the illusion of control bias.

It is also of relevance that Budesco and Bruderman (1995) found that the illusion of control bias may be a very subtle and sensitive mechanism: When the "chance mechanism is invoked repeatedly and its stochastic characteristics become salient and transparent . . ." (p. 123), there is little room left for the illusion of control bias to operate. This suggests that some professionals (i.e., those who seldom make predictions) are likely to be more exposed to illusion of control than others are (i.e., those who frequently make predictions). Such differences may also exist within a professional group. For example, compare a situation where a lawyer is working with one complex case for 5 years with a situation where a lawyer processes hundreds of divorce cases per year.

Degree of Experience Within a Certain Domain

Obviously, the degree of experience varies between different professionals within an occupational group. Although Goodman-Delahunty et al. (1996) didn't find any differences for realism in confidence between more and less experienced lawyers, such differences cannot be ruled out even for lawyers. It might be that potential differences are hidden because the more experienced professionals have to deal with more difficult predictions. For example, more experienced lawyers are hired for more complex cases. Two, among several other, properties that can be expected to characterize a high degree of experience within a domain are that experts are better at discerning decision-relevant information from less relevant information and that experts are better at processing the selected information effectively. It is likely that such a person will make more realistic confidence judgments compared to a person who lacks these abilities.

DISCUSSION

In the present chapter we have attempted to place confidence judgments in an everyday context, into the larger scene of events of which they are part. Our analysis led us to identify different types of contexts for feelings of confidence and, primarily in everyday working life, to identify a number of different factors that affect confidence judgments.

Our characterization of confidence judgments in everyday life casts doubts on the usefulness of theories that describe such judgments as mostly metacognitive; that is, as mostly involving conscious and reflected processes (e.g., Berry & Dienes, 1993). For example, it appears that the elicitation of confidence judgments and the activation of memory material acting as a base for the feeling of confidence (Allwood & Granhag, 1996b) often occurs on a unconscious and unreflected level.

In this discussion we first consider the implications of all this on issues dealing with the presence and explanation of the overconfidence phenomenon as reported and discussed in previous research. Second, we will discuss implications for attempts to improve the realism of confidence judgments in everyday life.

As pointed out above, most previous research appears to have covered only a small section of the field of different contexts for feelings and judgments of confidence. For example, the elicitation of confidence judgments and the factors that affect such elicitations have not been much studied. However, as will be argued below, such questions are important for the performance of realistic confidence judgments in everyday life. Moreover, in contrast to the typical lab-based calibration study where participants, usually students, are asked to make confidence judgments of retrospective knowledge (general knowledge questions), all professional groups reviewed above (except the different groups of agents detecting lies) were asked to state their confidence in *predictions.* Due to the differences between how most previous research has been carried out and the contexts in which confidence judgments are carried out in working life, it is difficult to know the extent to which results from previous research will generalize to various contexts in working life and in everyday life in general. Future research on confidence judgments should, in a more detailed way, attempt to study the influence of such factors. For example it should attempt to separate and clarify factors that only influence realism in confidence for predictions, only in retrospective tasks and for both predictions and retrospective tasks.

To this date several professional groups have been examined within research on confidence. In contrast to the approach taken in most or all of this research, it should be considered that within every particular expert group a number of different factors can be found that, depending on which other factors are present, may affect the realism in confidence in different ways. The studies reported on professionals so far can, in most cases, only account for a very limited number of all relevant factors that can influence the realism in confidence.

As an illustration, previous research results have shown overconfidence for the professional groups that have been tested on tasks with a long temporal interval between prediction and outcome (e.g., lawyers and economists). Such results might change if one shortens the time interval. For example, a lawyer might be required to predict a client's chances in a future case months, or even years, before it is resolved. In contrast, a lawyer might also be faced with a situation where s/he has to recommend a client either to accept or refuse an out-of-court settlement offer. Such a task-situation is often characterized both by extreme time-pressure and a short time interval between prediction and outcome. In short, for professional groups such as lawyers and economists, both a long and a short temporal interval are of relevance. However, in calibration studies to this date, these two groups have been researched using a long temporal interval only.

Many previous attempts to explain the lack of realism commonly found in confidence studies have concerned confidence judgments of answers to general knowledge questions and have involved a very limited number of factors, usually one or two. For example, in connection with general knowledge questions, Koriat, Lichtenstein, and Fischhoff (1980) explained overconfidence as an effect of a presumed general confirmation bias (these authors also acknowledged the possibility that the translation of feelings of confidence to the verbal description of the feeling is a possible cause of overconfidence), while Gigerenzer et al. (1991) and Juslin (1994) explained overconfidence as an effect of experimenter selected questions. Ferrell and McGoey (1980) explained overconfidence as an effect of the translation of feelings of confidence to the verbal description of the feeling, and Griffin and Tversky (1992) attempted to explain degree of realism as an effect of the balance between an individual's consideration of the weight and the strength of the evidence. In connection with predictions, maybe the most popular explanatory variable has been the presence of feedback (Keren, 1987).

From the description given in this chapter of the various factors, it is hopefully clear that more factors than the ones postulated in these theories affect realism. Furthermore, the factors postulated may not always be detectable (for the case of confirmation bias, see Allwood & Granhag, 1996c, and for the case of experimenter-selected questions, see Griffin & Tversky, 1992). In brief, the moral we believe is plausible to draw from the present chapter is that no few-factor theory will make do on a general level. Moreover, until we have access to a realistic theory dealing with how common various contexts for deliberate confidence judgments are in everyday life (each context with its different constellation of important factors), it is not possible to know if humans, generally, are realistic or not in their everyday confidence judgments.

Much previous research in the area of confidence judgments have attempted to improve the realism of the participants' confidence judgments. These attempts have only been moderately successful. Moreover, it has been found difficult to make the participants give realistic confidence ratings outside of the context in which they were trained (Lichtenstein & Fischhoff, 1980). Fischhoff (1982) argued that such results to a large extent may be due to a deficient analysis of the processes involved in confidence judgments. In connection with improving the realism of confidence judgments in everyday life (including working life) we suggest that such an analysis should take into consideration different important factors (exemplified above) present in the context in which the confidence judgment is made.

In order to improve the realism of confidence judgments in everyday life, we should not only worry about the degree of realism of the confidence judgments actually made. A connected important problem is that a deliberate confidence judgment is often never made at all. The issue of the triggering of confidence judgments is relevant in connection with the realism of confidence judgments, as it is obviously necessary for a confidence judgment to be performed in order for it to have good realism. The person involved may not experience a foregrounded experience of uncertainty at all and for this reason may never even consider making a reflected confidence judgment.

In contrast, a person may initiate a deliberate confidence judgment when she experiences a need to more actively consider the level of her spontaneous confidence feeling. One example of when such a situation may be at hand is when a person experiences uncertainty about her spontaneous confidence feeling (low second-order confidence) and where such doubts have some important implications for the person. One type of uncertainty about one's spontaneous confidence feeling is when a person has reasons to doubt that the feeling is realistic (e.g., the apprenticeship situation and the Christmas problem situation described above). Another type is when the spontaneously experienced confidence feeling is at a "breaking point" level where the person can not use it as a guide to decide whether or not to perform an (internal or external) action. In such a situation the person may experience a need to increase the precision of her confidence feeling further. In spite of the suggestions just made, the conditions in which confidence judgments are elicited are, as noted above, poorly understood. Accordingly, more research is needed on issues such as how persons can be trained to recognize internal or external signals for when there is a need to make deliberate confidence judgments.

The task of improving the realism of confidence judgments in everyday life also demands considering the presence in the situation of factors that may act to decrease realism. Examples of such factors are lack of experience in handling probabilities, presence of illusion of control, wishful thinking, time pressure, and high cost for the search of information.

When a serious attempt is made to increase the realism of confidence judgments in a specific everyday situation, a useful first step to be taken can be to analyze which of the above mentioned factors (and others) are present. A next step could be to attempt to "compensate" the person for the presence or absence of factors that could be expected to influence the realism of the person's confidence judgments. Such compensation could either be made in the person's professional training or in the person's external environment. Furthermore, although (as noted above) confidence judgments are often regarded as metacognitive, the possibility that some or many of the processes occurring when confidence judgments are made are not conscious and reflected should be taken into account when planning training aimed at increasing the realism of confidence judgments. In this connection, we need a better understanding of which of the factors influencing confidence judgments work best on a subconscious level and which work better on a conscious level.

REFERENCES

Allwood, C. M., & Granhag, P. A. (1996a). Realism in confidence judgments as a function of working in dyads or alone. *Organizational Behavior and Human Decision Processes, 66*, 277–289.

Allwood, C. M., & Granhag, P. A. (1996b). Considering the knowledge you have: Effects on realism in confidence judgments. *The European Journal of Cognitive Psychology, 8*, 235–256.

Allwood, C. M., & Granhag, P. A. (1996c). The effects of arguments on realism in confidence judgments. *Acta Psychologica, 91*, 99–119.

Arkes, H. R., Christensen, C., Lai, C., & Blumer, C. (1987). Two methods of reducing overconfidence. *Organizational Behavior and Human Decision Processes, 39*, 133–144.

Babad, E., Hills, M., & O'Driscoll, M. (1992). Factors influencing wishful thinking and predictions of election outcomes. *Basic and Applied Social Psychology, 13*, 461–476.

Berry, D. C., & Dienes, Z. (1993). *Implicit learning.* Hillsdale, NJ: Lawrence Erlbaum Associates.

Björkman, M. (1994). Internal cue theory: Calibration and resolution of confidence in general knowledge. *Organizational Behavior and Human Decision Processes, 57*, 386–405.

Braun, P. A., & Yaniv, I. (1992). A case study of expert judgment: Economists' probabilities versus base-rate model forecasts. *Journal of Behavioral Decision Making, 5*, 217–231.

Budesco, D. V., & Bruderman, M. (1995). The relationship between the illusion of control and the desirability bias. *Journal of Behavioral Decision Making, 8*, 109–125.

Chan, C. (1992). *Implicit cognitive process: Theoretical issues and applications in computer systems design.* Unpublished doctoral dissertation, University of Oxford.

Christensen-Szalanski, J. J., & Bushyhead, J. B. (1981). Physicians' use of probabilistic information in a real clinical setting. *Journal of Experimental Psychology: Human Perception and Performance, 7*, 928–935.

Cole, M., & Means, B. (1981). *Comparative studies of how people think*. Cambridge: Harvard University Press.

Ekman, P., & O'Sullivan, M. (1992). Who can catch a liar? *American Psychologist, 46*, 913–920.

Ferrell, W. R., & McGoey, P. J. (1980). A model of calibration for subjective probabilities. *Organizational Behavior and Human Performance, 26*, 32–53.

Fischhoff, B. (1982). Debiasing. In D. Kahneman, P. Slovic, & A. Tversky (Eds.), *Judgment under uncertainty: Heuristics and biases*. Cambridge: Cambridge University Press.

Fodor, J. (1983). *The modularity of mind*. Cambridge: MIT Press.

Gigerenzer, G., Hoffrage, U., & Kleinbölting, H. (1991). Probabilistic mental models: A Brunswikian theory of confidence. *Psychological Review, 98*, 506–528.

Gilovich, T., Kerr, M., & Husted Medvec, V. (1993). Effect of temporal perspective on subjective confidence. *Journal of Personality and Social Psychology, 64*, 552–560.

Goodman-Delahunty, J., Granhag, P. A., & Loftus, E. F. (1996). *How well can lawyers predict their chances of success?* Unpublished manuscript, Department of Psychology, University of Washington.

Granhag, P. A. (1997). Realism in eyewitness confidence as a function of type of event witnessed and repeated recall. *Journal of Applied Psychology, 82*, 599–613.

Greenwald, A. G. (1992). New look 3 Unconscious cognition reclaimed. *American Psychologist, 47*, 766–779.

Griffin, D., & Tversky, A. (1992). The weighing of evidence and the determinants of confidence. *Cognitive Psychology, 24*, 411–435.

Juslin, P. (1994). The overconfidence phenomenon as a consequence of informal experimenter-guided selection of almanac items. *Organizational Behavior and Human Decision Processes, 57*, 226–246.

Juslin, P., & Olsson, H. (1997). Thurstonian and Brunswikian origins of uncertainty in judgment: A sampling model of confidence in sensory discrimination. *Psychological Review, 104*, 344–366.

Kelley, C. M., & Lindsay, D. S. (1993). Remembering mistaken for knowing: Ease of retrieval as a basis for confidence in answers to general knowledge questions. *Journal of Memory and Language, 32*, 1–24.

Keren, G. (1987). Facing uncertainty in the game of bridge: A calibration study. *Organizational Behaviour and Human Decision Processes, 39*, 98–114.

Koriat, A., Lichtenstein, S., & Fischhoff, B. (1980). Reasons for confidence. *Journal of Experimental Psychology: Human Learning and Memory, 6*, 107–118.

Kruglanski, A. W. (1994). The social cognitive bases of scientific knowledge. In W. R. Shadish & S. Fuller (Eds.), *The social psychology of science*. New York: Guilford.

Langer, E. J. (1975). The illusion of control. *Journal of Personality and Social Psychology, 32*, 311–328.

Lewicki, P., Hill, T., & Czyzewska, M. (1992). Nonconscious acquisition of information. *American Psychologist, 47*, 796–801.

Liberman, D., & Tversky, A. (1993). On the evaluation of probability judgments: Calibration, resolution, and monotonicity. *Psychological Bulletin, 114*, 162–173.

Lichtenstein, S., & Fischhoff, B. (1980). Training for calibration. *Organizational Behaviour and Human Performance, 26*, 149–171.

Lichtenstein, S., Fischhoff, B., & Phillips, L. D. (1982). Calibration of probabilities: The state of the art of 1980. In D. Kahneman, P. Slovic, & A. Tversky (Eds.), *Judgment under uncertainty: Heuristics and biases*. Cambridge: Cambridge University Press.

Loftus, E. F., & Wagenaar, W. A. (1988). Lawyers' predictions of success. *Jurimetrics Journal, 28*, 437–453.

Luus, C. A. E., & Wells, G. L. (1994). The malleability of eyewitness confidence: Co-witness and perseverance effects. *Journal of Applied Psychology, 79*, 714–723.

Malsch, M. (1989). Lawyers' predictions of judicial decisions. A study on calibration of experts. Unpublished doctoral dissertation, Leiden University.

McClelland, A. G. R., & Bolgar, F. (1994). The calibration of subjective probabilities: Theories and models 1980–1994. In G. Wright & P. Ayton (Eds.), *Subjective probability* (pp. 453–482). New York: Wiley.

Murphy, A. H., & Winkler, R. L. (1971). Forecasters and probability forecasts: some current problems. *Bulletin of American Meteorological Society*, 52, 239–247.

Narens, L., Jameson, K. A., & Lee, V. A. (1994). Subthreshold priming and memory monitoring. In J. Metcalfe & A. P. Shimamura (Eds.), *Metacognition knowing about knowing* (pp. 71–92). Cambridge, MA: MIT Press.

Nelson, T. O., & Narens, L. (1994). Why investigate metacognition? In J. Metcalfe & A. P. Shimamura (Eds.), *Metacognition: Knowing about knowing* (pp. 1–25). Cambridge: MIT Press.

Oskamp, S. (1965). Overconfidence in case-study judgments. *Journal of Consulting Psychology*, 29, 261–265.

Schutz, A., & Luckmann, T. (1974). *The structures of the life-world*. London: Heinemann.

Sniezek, J. A., & Buckley, T. (1991). Level of confidence depends on levels of aggregation. *Journal of Behavioral Decision Making*, 4, 263–272.

Stael von Holstein, C. A. (1972). Probabilistic forecasting: An experiment related to the stock market. *Organizational Behavior and Human Performance*, 8, 139–158.

Tomassini, L. A., Solomon, I., Romney, M. B., & Krogstad, J. L. (1982). Calibration of auditors' probabilistic judgments: some empirical evidence. *Organizational Behavior and Human Performance*, 30, 391–406.

Vreugdenhil, H. (1993). *Confidence in knowledge*. Unpublished doctoral dissertation, University of Amsterdam, Department of Psychology.

Weinstein, N. D. (1980). Unrealistic optimism about future life events. *Journal of Personality and Social Psychology*, 39, 806–820.

Weinstein, N. D. (1982). Unrealistic optimism about susceptibility for health problems. *Journal of Behavioral Medicine*, 5, 441–460.

Weinstein, N. D. (1983). Reducing unrealistic optimism about illness susceptibility. *Health Psychology*, 2, 11–20.

Chapter 8

Decision Making and Action: The Search for a Good Structure

Henry Montgomery
Stockholm University

Helena Willén
Skövde University

There is a close link between decision making and action. By making a decision, a person commits him/herself to act in a certain way. However, in behavioral decision research the link between decision making and action is largely neglected. The reason may be that decision making primarily is seen as a question of forming preferences—that is, a question of finding the better or best alternative. However, in contrast to decisions, preferences are not necessarily linked to actions. An individual may prefer alternative *x* to alternative *y* without committing him/herself to any action. That is, the alternatives in preferences need not be action alternatives (e.g., preferences among articles of consumption), which is always true in a decision situation (e.g., in decisions to *buy* an article of consumption).

As a consequence of a large number of empirical findings, the presumed synonymity between preferences and decisions or choices has become problematic. First, it has been found that preferences in a nonchoice context may be inconsistent with people's choices (Lichtenstein & Slovic, 1971; Slovic & Lichtenstein, 1983, Tversky, Sattah, & Slovic, 1988). Second, it has been shown that people's preferences may be practically unrelated to people's actions (Lindberg, Gärling, & Montgomery, 1990; Montgomery, 1993; Rohrman & Borcherding, 1988). That is, people do not necessarily enact an alternative that they prefer. The reason may be that the preference has been formed without making a decision to enact the preferred alternative.

The research findings cited above emphasize the necessity to distinguish between preferences and decisions. Below, a decision making theory—

search for dominance structure (SDS) theory (Montgomery, 1983, 1989)—is presented that highlights this distinction, as well as how predecisonal processes prepare the decision maker for action. The latter feature of the theory contrasts with assumptions in other theories of decision making and action control. After having presented SDS theory, we will review empirical data that bear on the validity of the theory. Thereafter, we will compare SDS theory with other approaches to decision making, which invites a discussion of how SDS theory should be developed or changed. Finally, we will use the literature reviewed in this article as a platform for discussing relationships between decision making and action.

SDS THEORY

Decision Making Phases

SDS theory describes the cognitive process that starts when an individual faces a decision conflict between a number of alternatives and that ends when a decision is made. Each alternative is experienced in terms of its attractiveness on a number of subjectively defined dimensions or attributes. The key idea in the theory is that the decision maker attempts to structure and restructure given information about attributes in such a way that one alternative becomes the self-evident choice. More precisely, the decision maker attempts to find a dominance structure, that is, a cognitive structure in which the to-be-chosen alternative dominates other alternatives on relevant attributes. In a dominance structure the to-be-chosen alternative has at least one clear advantage to other alternatives and all disadvantages, if any, of that alternative are neutralized or de-emphasized.

The search for a dominance structure is assumed to go through four phases: pre-editing, finding a promising alternative, dominance testing, and dominance structuring. Figure 8.1 shows how the process is organized in terms of the four phases.

In the pre-editing phase, which typically occurs early in the decision process, the decision maker attempts to simplify the decision problem by selecting those alternatives and attributes that should be included in the representation of the decision situation.

In the finding a promising alternative phase the decision maker finds a candidate for his or her final choice. An alternative that is more attractive than other alternatives on an important attribute may be selected as a promising alternative. When a promising alternative has been found, the decision maker has formed a preference, albeit a temporary one, for a particular alternative. The question now arises as to whether the decision

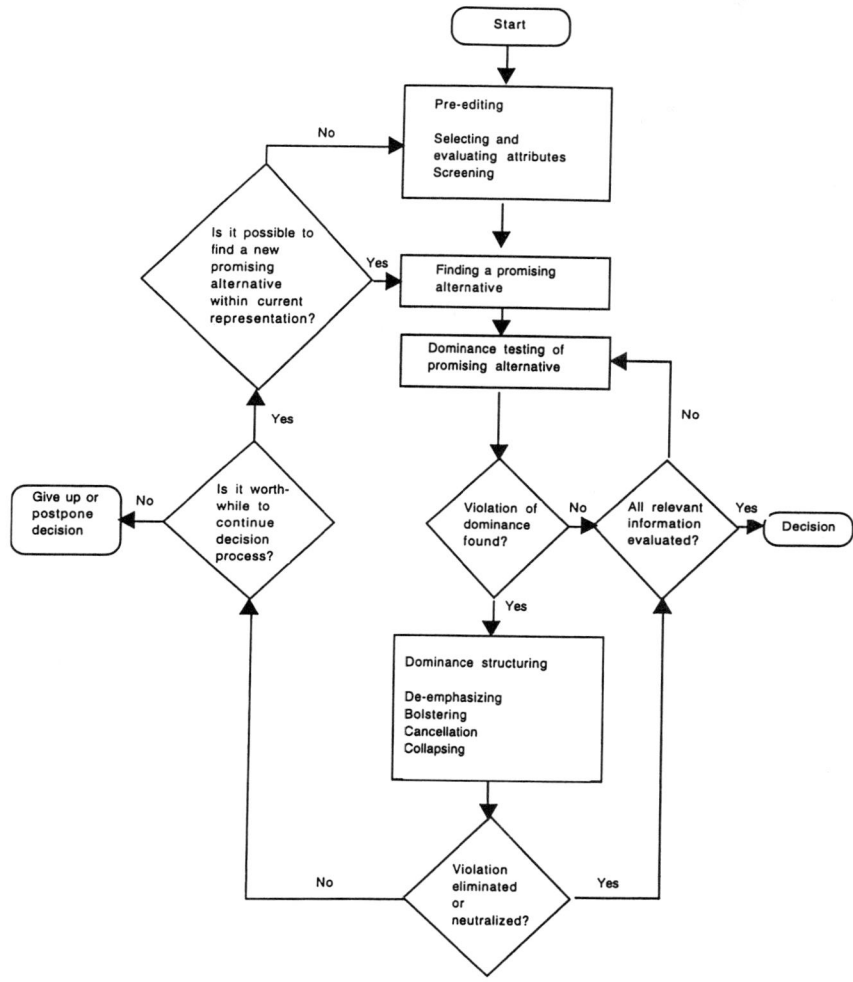

FIG. 8.1. The Search for Dominance Structure (SDS) theory of decision making.

maker can decide to choose this alternative. This question is dealt with in subsequent phases of the decision making process.

The dominance testing phase implies that the decision maker tests whether a promising alternative dominates the other alternatives. These tests could be more or less systematic or exhaustive. If the promising alternative is found to be dominant, it is chosen and the decision process ends.

If, on the other hand, a violation of dominance is found, the decision maker continues to the dominance structuring phase. In this phase the decision maker attempts to neutralize or counterbalance the disadvantage(s) found for the promising alternative. These attempts are based on various operations. The decision maker may de-emphasize a disadvantage by arguing that the probability of the disadvantage is very low and that it could be controlled or avoided in one way or another. Another possibility is to bolster the advantages of the promising alternative and in this way indirectly de-emphasize the disadvantages. In the cancellation operation the decision maker attempts to find dominance by canceling a disadvantage by relating it to an advantage that has some natural connection to the disadvantage in question. Finally, the decision maker may find a dominance structure by collapsing two or more attributes into a new more comprehensive attribute.

If the decision maker fails to find a dominance structure, he or she may go back to a previous phase and make a new start in the search for dominance, or he or she may postpone the decision, if possible.

SDS Theory and Action

To decide is to commit oneself to follow a line of action. The commitment means that the decision maker is ready to defend the decision and stick to it in the face of adverse circumstances. This means that there will be a certain degree of consistency in the decision maker's pattern of behavior. It may be speculated that such a consistency will promote the individual's possibility to reach his or her long-term goals even if the defence of the decision may involve a biased view of the external world.

This view of decision making suggests that it will be important for the individual in his or predecisional processes to build up a basis that may promote postdecisional commitment. In line with this suggestion, Montgomery (1989) assumed that SDS theory portrays the decision making process as a preparation for action. The search for a dominance structure implies that the decision maker prepares him or herself for coping with problems that may arise when implementing a tentatively chosen alternative. In other words, a dominance structure implies that the decision maker has access to counterarguments to any drawbacks of the chosen alternative that have been considered in the decision making process. In this way, the decision maker will have resources to maintain his or her commitment to the chosen line of action.

SDS Theory and Mindsets

SDS theory deviates from other theories that assume that predecisional processes involve a careful and impartial weighing of pros and cons of different choice alternatives (Edwards, 1954; Festinger, 1957; Gollwitzer,

Heckhausen, & Ratajczak, 1990). In a series of recent papers, Gollwitzer and his associates argued that predecisional processes are characterized by a deliberative mindset, which is expected to foster a relatively even-handed and accurate appraisal of evidence (e.g., Gollwitzer et al., 1990; Taylor & Gollwitzer, 1996). These theorists offer a contrasting view of the postdecisional phase, where people plan to implement a chosen alternative. This phase is characterized by an implemental mindset, in which the individual musters motivation, resources, and cognition that favor the achievement of chosen goals.

SDS theory's view of predecisional processes is similar to mindset theory's view of postdecisional processes. Dominance structuring may be seen as an implemental activity. The decision maker "runs" the tentatively chosen alternative and looks for possibilities of solving problems associated with its implementation. However, in contrast to mindset theory the implemental activities in dominance structuring are provisional. Their purpose is not purely implemental but also concerned with testing the feasibility of the tentatively chosen alternative, which occurs in the dominance testing phase. That is, SDS theory states that if the decision maker does not succeed in constructing a dominance structure, he or she abandons the promising alternative. In this way, the search for a dominance structure affords a "window of realism" (Taylor & Gollwitzer, 1996) the size of which is negatively related to the decision maker's motivation to stick to the promising alternative.

The distinction between deliberative and implemental mindsets is strongly supported by empirical data (Gollwitzer, 1990). The same is true for the similar distinction between state and action orientation (Kuhl, 1992). However, the support for the assumption that predecisional processes primarily are deliberative is indirect and meagre. For example, Taylor and Gollwitzer (1996) asked participants to report their recent thoughts related to an unsolved personal problem and found that participants divided their attention about equally between positive and negative consequences of a change decision. Obviously, the request to think of an unsolved problem may have stimulated participants to answer in a way that is consonant with this request—for example, by listing an equal amount of positive and negative consequences. Moreover, participants' sensitivity to the demand characteristics of their task may have been further accentuated by the fact that participants were asked to make retrospective rather than concurrent reports on their thoughts (Ericsson & Simon, 1980). In the following, we will review data that may give a clearer picture of the nature of predecsional processes and their compatibility with SDS theory and, hence, the notion that decision making can be seen as preparation for action.

EMPIRICAL VALIDITY OF SDS THEORY

We will now discuss a body of research findings that all are related to, or compatible with, the key idea of SDS theory: the notion of decision making as a search for a "good" structure that makes one alternative the self-evident choice. Some of this research deals with limited aspects of the decision making process, whereas other findings highlight the decision process as a whole. The research findings also vary with respect to how explicitly they assume that a "good" decision making structure is a dominance structure. The review includes research that clearly supports SDS theory but also data that are less supportive or even appear to be at odds with the theory.

Pre-Editing

There is ample evidence for the hypothesis that decision makers attempt to simplify a given decision problem by focusing on a limited subset of attributes (Svenson, 1979), by rounding off information about attribute levels (Kahneman & Tversky, 1979), and by screening out alternatives that fall short on important attributes (Beach, 1990). However, these research findings belong to those that illustrate a limited aspect of SDS theory, and that also support other decision making models such as prospect theory (Kahneman & Tversky, 1979) and image theory (Beach, 1990).

Finding and Defending a Promising Alternative

Research that has examined decision making as a process across time has shown that before an alternative is definitely chosen, it draws more attention than other alternatives and is judged as more and more attractive as compared with its competing alternatives (Dahlstrand & Montgomery, 1984; Lewicka, 1990; Montgomery & Svenson, 1989; Sedek, Kofta, & Tyszka, 1993). This tendency also holds when the comparison is made between a promising alternative (identified at an early stage of the decision process) and the remaining alternatives (Dahlstrand & Montgomery, 1984). In other words, it appears that initial impressions of the alternatives push the decision maker to widen the gap between a promising alternative and its competitors. The tendency to an increasing attractiveness gap between chosen and nonchosen alternatives as time proceeds has been demonstrated in a number of additional experimental studies (Beckman & Kuhl, 1984; Mann, Janis, & Chaplin, 1969; Tyszka & Wielochovski, 1991). Dahlstrand and Montgomery (1984) showed that the tendency to increase the support for the chosen alternative can be predicted. The same phenomenon has also been found in research on decision making in naturalistic contexts such as career decisions (Soelberg, 1967), various decisions in people's private lives (Blom Kemdal & Montgomery, 1997); residential choices (Lindberg, Gärling, & Montgomery, 1990), and in a case study of a military decision (Montgomery, 1997).

It seems safe to conclude that predecisional processes often deviate from the picture of an impartial decision maker who carefully weighs pros against cons before making his or her decision. On the contrary, we are faced with the picture of a deeply committed decision maker who attempts to prove that a particular alternative definitely is better than its competing alternatives. The validity of this picture is further substantiated in studies of the decision making processes of depressed people (Lewicka, 1990) and persons who have undergone learned helplessness training (Sedek, Kofta, & Tyszka, 1993). In line with the assumption that persons in this precondition lack cognitive resources and/or motivation to build up support for a to-be-chosen alternative, it was found that they examined choice alternatives in a more balanced and impartial manner than was true for nondepressed or non-helpless training control participants (Lewicka, 1990; Sedek, Kofta, & Tyszka, 1993).

Existence of Dominance Structures

The fact that the decision maker manages to increase the support for the chosen alternative does not necessarily mean that the alternative dominates its rivals. Montgomery (1994), however, found strict (or close to strict) dominance for the chosen alternative in a great majority of think-aloud protocols collected in a previous study of housing choices (Montgomery & Svenson, 1989). In the same vein, Lindberg, Gärling, and Montgomery (1989a) found that when information was missing about choice alternatives, participants tended to bolster (enhance) the value of inferred aspects of the finally chosen alternative in such a way more than 90% of the inferences supported or did not speak against the finally chosen alternative. Other studies have identified dominance structures in postdecisional justifications in a political discourse (Axelrod, 1976; Biel & Montgomery, 1986; Gallhofer & Saris, 1989), and in justifications of professorial appointments (Montgomery & Hemlin, 1991).

Dominance Structuring Operations

Many of the process tracing studies that concerned the validity of SDS theory did not examine closely the particular operations that led to the representation supporting the finally chosen alternative. However, the overall pattern in the think-aloud protocols analyzed by Montgomery and Svenson (1989) suggest that participants would rather de-emphasize the value of nonchosen alternatives rather than bolster the value of the chosen alternative. On the other hand, rating data collected in other studies suggest the opposite pattern—that is, more bolstering than de-emphasizing (Lewicka, 1990; Sedek, Kofta, & Tyszka, 1993), as also was true in Lindberg et al.'s study (1989a) of inferences of missing information about choice alternatives. Lindberg et al.'s (1990) naturalistic field study (interviews) of persons looking for a new home evidenced a combined usage of bolstering and de-emphasizing operations. The data suggested that in order to facilitate the choice of a new home, attributes favoring the new dwelling were seen as more important (bolstering) whereas attributes favoring the old dwelling were perceived as less important (de-emphasizing).

In a re-analysis of the think-aloud data previously analyzed by Montgomery and Svenson (1989) on choices between homes, Montgomery (1994) found support for the cancellation operation (canceling disadvantages by relating them to advantages that has some natural connection with the disadvantage). For example, a long traveling time to downtown (disadvantage) was seen as giving an opportunity for relaxation during the journey (advantage). The realism of the collapsing operation (collapsing of two or more attributes to a more comprehensive attribute) is supported by studies showing that housing choices could be predicted from the respondents' beliefs about how the alternatives relate to various general life values such as freedom and security (e.g., Lindberg, Gärling, & Montgomery, 1988, 1989c). We also found that at least 50% of the choice situations were associated with dominance structures on the level of life values (e.g., a chosen alternative is seen as better than or equal to its competitors with respect to freedom, security, family, and so on) whereas on the level of attributes (e.g., size, location, standard) pure dominance structures were rare (Garvill, Gärling, Lindberg, & Montgomery, 1991). The fact that participants' choices appear to have been guided by life values suggest that dominance structures on this level may have facilitated the respondents' choices.

It may be concluded that there exists empirical support for each of the four dominance structuring operations (that is, de-emphasizing, bolstering, cancellation, and collapsing). In addition, recent evidence suggests that dominance structures also may be attained by changing the external situation, with a more direct link to overt action than is assumed in the dominance structuring operations described above. Montgomery (1993) reported data showing that decision makers may not accept negative information about a promising alternative, but instead figure out actions that will improve the alternative. Other studies have shown that the individual may also intervene in the external world before the decision, to increase the support for a promising alternative (Blom Kemdal & Montgomery, 1997; Willén, 1994).

Preferences versus Choices

SDS theory assumes that our preferences should be backed up more by dominance structuring when we anticipate a decision and engage in the search of support for the promising alternative. Hence, SDS theory implies that options should be less differentiated in attractiveness with no requirements to choose as compared to a situation when participants are to make a choice between the same options. This prediction has only been partially validated. It is supported by think-aloud data in terms of an evaluation index, which was calculated for each alternative from the number of positive and negative evaluations of the alternative on specific attributes (Montgomery, Selart, Gärling, & Lindberg, 1994; Selart, Gärling, & Montgomery, 1998), whereas ratings of specific attributes (e.g., size or cost of housing alternatives) and more general values (life values) associated with the options (e.g., health or freedom) gave mixed support (Garvill, Gärling, Lindberg, & Montgomery, 1991; Lindberg, Gärling, & Montgomery, 1989b). Attractiveness on the level of life value is assumed to result from the collapsing operation, because life values are assumed to integrate attractiveness on specific attributes. In line with our prediction, we found a greater mean difference between life value ratings of chosen and nonchosen options than between life value ratings of preferred and nonpreferred options (preference ratings). However, there was no difference between the two tasks with respect to the proportion of cases where the chosen or preferred alternative was dominant on the level of life values (Garvill et al., 1991). On the other hand, approximately 50% of the choice situations included an alternative that was dominant on the level of life values already, before participants were asked to make a choice. Evidently, in these cases there was no need to restructure information in order to attain dominance, but of course there are still 50% of the choice situations which have a nondominant structure.

In a series of studies, SDS theory was used as a point of departure for elucidating the nature of the so-called prominence effect (Montgomery, Gärling, Lindberg, & Selart, 1990; Montgomery, Selart, Gärling, & Lindberg, 1994). This effect concerns the case where a choice has to made between two alternatives that are described on two attributes (e.g., effectiveness and painfulness of two medical treatments). The effect implies that the more important attribute (e.g., effectiveness) looms larger in choice than in a task where participants have matched the two alternatives to be equally attractive. That is, in choices between two options judged as equally attractive, participants tend to choose the option that is superior on the more important attribute (e.g., a treatment that is more effective but also more painful) (Slovic, 1975; Tversky, Sattah, & Slovic, 1988). SDS theory predicts that in the choice situation participants will attempt to restructure the given alternative in such a way that one of the alternatives will be seen as clearly better. In the present case this could mean that participants, in order to attain dominance, emphasize differences between alternatives on the prominent attribute, and de-emphasize differences on the nonprominent attribute. This prediction was indeed confirmed in think-aloud data collected from choices between two alternatives as compared to think-aloud data from preference judgments of the same alternative with no choice requirement (Montgomery et al., 1994). It was also predicted from SDS theory that there would be no prominence effect for preference judgments, because in this task participants would not need to restructure the alternatives in order to be able to make a choice. However, participants in preference judgments also tended to emphasize the prominent attribute more than in the matching task (see also Fischer & Hawkins, 1993; Selart et al., 1994; Selart, 1996). Obviously, SDS theory does not seem able to explain the prominence effect, although the theory itself was supported by the think-aloud data obtained for choices.

Dominance Violations and Dominance Structuring

A straightforward prediction from SDS theory is that if a promising alternative does not dominate a competing alternative, then the decision maker will restructure available information in order to attain dominance. If, on the other hand, the promising alternative is dominant, there is no reason to restructure the information. In Garvill et al.'s (1991) study these predictions were only partially borne out when ratings of levels of life values associated with choice housing alternatives were compared between dominated and nondominated choice sets. In line with the predictions it was found that in the nondominated choice sets participants tended to increase the differentiation between the alternatives when making the choice whereas there was no such tendency in the dominated choice sets. In a recent study of real-life decision processes concerning career choices (Svenson & Hill, 1997), it was found that participants who experienced goal conflicts (that is, dominance violations) tended to reverse the conflict into an advantage favoring the chosen alternative. It can be concluded that decision makers, in line with SDS theory, when encountering a dominance violation may increase the differential support for the alternative to be chosen. However, the resulting cognitive structure may either fall short of strict dominance, or be changed more than is needed to attain dominance.

Other studies have demonstrated that decision making strategies seem to be sensitive to dominance structures or close-to dominance structures in *given* information. That is, when one option dominates another one, participants tend to choose the former rather than a third alternative that is not dominant (Ariely & Wallsten, 1995; Huber, Payne, & Puto, 1982; Tyszka, 1980) and they are less interested in looking for additional options or additional information about the given options (Bockenholt, Albert, Aschenbrenner, & Schmalhofer, 1991; Shafir, Simonson, & Tversky, 1993). Thus, in line with SDS theory it appears that participants do less in order to make a decision when dominance is at hand. Also in line with SDS theory, Ariely and Wallsten (1995) reported data that are compatible with the notion that participants restructure (or categorize) close-to-dominance as being equivalent to dominance. Ariely and Wallsten coined the term *subjective dominance* to denote how decision makers conceive of close-to-dominance.

DEVELOPING AND CONSTRAINING SDS THEORY: A COMPARISON WITH OTHER APPROACHES TO DECISION MAKING

By and large, it appears that SDS theory is congruent with process data on human decision making. In particular, many observations are in line with the key idea in the model that the decision maker attempts to structure and restructure given information about attributes in such a way that one alternative becomes the self-evident choice. Data also support the existence of decision making stages and operations that are largely in line with the model. Apparently, the findings reviewed above are sufficiently encouraging to justify using SDS theory as a platform for further theory development on the nature of human decision making. However, the fact that some predictions from the model have been unsuccessful invites thinking about how the model may be developed or changed. Below, we discuss two approaches to decision making that invite a discussion of how SDS theory may be modified or constrained.

Dominance Structuring or Differentiation?

The concept of dominance is central in the two final stages of SDS theory. In the dominance testing phase the decision maker will react differently depending on whether he or she finds dominance or not. In the dominance structuring phase he or she attempts to attain dominance. However, as noted above, in both contexts empirical data suggest that participants do not make a clear distinction between dominance and what may be interpreted as close to dominance. Moreover, it might be conjectured that in situations when a dominating alternative is only marginally better than its rival, decision makers want to increase the differentiation between the alternatives in order to have a safety margin against preference reversals in the postdecision future (Svenson, 1992). In other words, it may be questioned whether the attainment of a dominance structure is a necessary and sufficient condition for getting to the decision point. Still, dominance as such also seems to be an important decision criterion in cases when one might expect the decision maker to look for more information before making the final decision (Bockenholt et al., 1991; Shafir et al., 1993).

In his differential and consolidation theory of decision making (Diff Con theory), Svenson (1992, 1996, Chapter 9 of this volume) suggested that when a sufficiently high degree of differentiation between a chosen and nonchosen alternatives is at hand, rather than dominance, then the decision maker is ready to make a decision. The rationale for this decision criterion is to choose an alternative that can withstand threats that may appear in the postdecision future. Differentiation may be achieved by three processes: holistic differentiation (which includes matching to previous prototypical decision situations), process differentiation (using decision rules that support the decision), and structural differentiation (which includes changes in the representation of attractiveness, attribute importance, facts, or the decision problem as a whole). Diff Con theory posits that these subprocesses continue after the decision to consolidate the support for the chosen alternative.

Diff Con theory implies that dominance neither is a sufficient nor a necessary decision criterion. The notion of sufficient differentiation offers a more flexible, but also a more loosely defined, decision criterion. However, the problems with validating predictions from SDS theory regarding the role of dominance could be handled, we think, by introducing *subjective* dominance, rather than strict dominance as the decision criterion. Ariely and Wallsten (1995) defines subjective dominance as "a perceived relationship in which a certain difference on some dimension, although noticeable, is considered unimportant and the values on this dimension are considered to be subjectively equal, while simultaneously all other dimensions are clearly perceived as better for one of the items" (p. 224). Subjective dominance differs from strict dominance by *excluding* cases where a strictly dominating alternative is only slightly better than its competitors on favorable attributes. In this situation the decision maker will view the alternatives as being practically the same. Subjective dominance also differs from strict dominance by *including* cases when one alternative has a decisive advantage, although it is not strictly dominant. However, the notion of subjective dominance implies that SDS theory comes closer to Diff Con theory inasmuch as a more vaguely defined decision criterion is introduced. That is, the well defined notion of dominance is replaced by the less well defined notion of subjective dominance.

There are a number of reasons for keeping (subjective) dominance as a decision criterion. First, as discussed above, empirical studies show that decision makers are very sensitive to dominance relations. Second, as also discussed above, people appear to have access to dominance structures in a variety of situations. Third, and most importantly, having access to a dominance structure implies that the decision maker has built up a cognitive basis for acting in line with the decision; that is, to implement the decision. This is because a dominance structure implies that a counterargument is available against any drawback that may be associated with the chosen alternative in the decision maker's representation of the decision problem. Hence, if a drawback that has been taken into account in a dominance structure emerges after the decision is made, the decision maker will be able to defend his or her decision and continue implementing it (Montgomery, 1989). Svenson (1992) himself assumes that an important aim of differentiation is to defend the decision against future threats. Obviously, this goal is facilitated by having access to a dominance structure in the postdecision phase.

Another important difference between SDS theory and Diff Con theory, besides the role of dominance, is that the former model stresses that differentiation is accomplished by a kind of structuring (that is, dominance structuring), whereas Diff Con theory regards structuring as one of several possible ways of attaining differentiation. SDS theory regards the other types of differentiation as subordinate to structuring. By using different decision rules (rule differentiation) the decision maker changes his or her representation of the decision situation (e.g., using the conjunctive rule means that attribute levels are classified as acceptable or not), which in turn is equivalent to or facilitates dominance structuring. Similarly, what Svenson (1992) calls holistic differentiation either leads to a decision or to the finding of a promising alternative (cf. Svenson, 1992, p. 154), which in turn may provide an input to the dominance structuring phase.

Further research is needed to evaluate the validity of the two theories on these discrepant points.

SDS Theory and Naturalistic Decision Making

SDS theory starts out from a general model of human decision making, which for many years has been prevalent in behavioral decision making research. In recent years doubts have been raised about the applicability of this model to decision making in a naturalistic context (e.g., Klein, Orasanu, Calderwood, & Zsambok, 1993). The criticism has concerned the following assumptions: (a) that decision making involves a choice among several options (b) that choice is equivalent to conflict resolution, (c) that decision problems are represented in terms of attributes or dimensions, and (d) that the description of decision making is restricted to mental processes and structures. An alternative picture has emerged in which decision making is seen as (a) typically involving just one option, which has to be accepted or not (Beach & Lipshitz, 1993), (b) as being largely automatic and being based on recognition of prototypical choice situations (Klein, 1993a), (c) as involving attempts to using available information to form coherent stories or scenarios (Beach, 1990; Cohen, Freeman, & Wolf, 1996; Pennington & Hastie, 1993), and (d) as taking place in a dynamic environment with which the decision maker interacts (Brehmer, 1990; Orasanu & Connolly, 1993, Rasmussen, 1993). This picture simultaneously plays down the idea of decision making as conflict resolution between alternative courses of action and the idea that decision making can be studied under well-controlled laboratory conditions.

What are the implications of this picture of naturalistic decision making for SDS theory? Admittedly, in previous research I (Montgomery) have overestimated the role of conflict resolution in decision making. Decisions do not differ from preference judgments in this respect as much as I thought. Our own research (e.g., Garvill et al., 1991; Montgomery, 1994) illustrates that people often have access to ready-made cognitive structures that relieve them from the burden of solving conflicts. On the other hand, SDS theory definitely deals with conflict resolution. However, even if it is true that human decision making very often does not involve conflict resolution, in the sense assumed by researchers in behavioral decision making, these situations still exist and people's decisions in these situations may be of great importance for themselves and for other people. Actually, researchers advocating a naturalistic approach to decision making have reserved a niche for SDS theory in situations involving conflicts between different goals (Cohen, 1993; Klein, 1993b; Lipshitz, 1993).

The holistic and dynamic aspects of human decision making, which could be difficult to study in the laboratory, definitely pose a challenge to SDS theory. However, we regard the SDS theory as having taken a step in that direction inasmuch as (a) dominance structures can be seen as good "gestalts," and (b) the theory's ambition to understand the link between decision making and action may facilitate further modeling on how decision makers interact with the external world.

THE ROLE OF PERSPECTIVE TAKING

A Perspective Model

Another challenge to SDS theory comes from our own research in recent years. SDS theory, as is also true for some other behavioral decision making theories like Diff Con theory, may be seen as models of how the individual attempts to control his or her thinking when confronted with a decision problem. The decision maker avoids certain thoughts and entertains other thoughts in his or her search for a "good gestalt." But what controls the control? To be sure, the individual does not have unlimited freedom to construct any degree of differentiation or any kind of dominance structure. In his perspective model, Montgomery (1994) launched the hypothesis that the decision maker's search for a dominance structure is constrained by the perspective from which the choice alternatives are perceived. In general, it was assumed that a person's evaluation of an object at a given moment is constrained by his/her perspective (evaluative perspective). As is true for perceptual perspectives, an evaluative perspective refers to a relationship between a subject and object. A subject perceives an object from a certain perspective. There are three components in an evaluative perspective: (a) subject identification (that is, identification with role, person, or group of persons that in turn are associated with certain interests), (b) features of the perceived objects, and (c) psychological distance to the objects—that is, the extent to which the object is seen as positively or negatively relevant to the interests associated with the current subject identification. Depending on the congruence between subject identification and object features, there will be more or less strong figure-ground effects, where either positive features of the perceived object form the figure and negative features form the background, or vice versa. The strength of these figure ground effects are assumed to be negatively related to the distance.

The adoption of a subject identification is determined by, on the one hand, the decision maker's value priorities combined with his or her preferred subject identifications, and, on the other hand, by the extent to the interests associated with a given subject identification will be satisfied. The latter factor implies that a decision maker may adopt new subject identifications when changes occur in the (possible) satisfaction interests associated with different subject identifications. For example, a wealthy man who has adopted the subject identification of his heir and, hence, is restrictive with his money, may switch to a beggar identification with ensuing generosity to a particular beggar if he perceives that the beggar needs money much more than the heir does. Basically, perspective changes may occur when the payoff structure of behaviors associated with particular perspectives change. This means that people only to a limited extent have stable value systems that guide their behavior, because they tend to favor values that have a reasonable chance to be satisfied within an available subject identification.

The perspective notion implies that the perceiver is in contact with the external reality. Something is actually seen from a given perspective, although certain sides or aspects of the focused object either are in the foreground whereas other sides or aspects are in the background. A person who is restrictive with money (external reality) thus could be seen as either greedy or economic depending on the adopted perspective, but the person will hardly be seen as generous or extravagant. Hence, according to the perspective model, external reality exerts some degree of control on a decision maker's attempts to structure available information in support of his or her decision. The perspective is also controlled by internal factors—that is, by the subject identification and the distance between the subject identification and the focused object. By switching between different subject identifications the decision maker may emphasize different attributes and aspects of options. Again, the possibilities are restricted, but this time with respect to which subject identifications that are available.

A central tenet in the perspective model is that evaluations have a categorical component. Normally, an object is either viewed from its positive or negative side. The reason is that people need to know how to act in relation to the object. Should it be approached (focus on positive aspects) or avoided (focus on negative aspects)? The wish to approach an object can be interpreted as a wish to include the object in one's self (Gottman, 1994). The inclusion of an object into one's self corresponds to adopting what Montgomery (1994) called an inside perspective. The object becomes integrated with and extends the self and in this sense comes inside the self. The inside perspective implies that subject focuses on positive qualities of the object. Because the object is included in the self, it will be natural to ask how the object may be an asset to the subject. Conversely, when an object is seen as behaving independently of the subject and, and thus seen from an outside perspective, the subject will focus on its negative qualities, that is, on the extent to which the object may threaten the subject's interests. This is assumed to be particularly true when the object's behavior matters very much for the subject, which corresponds to a short psychological distance to the object. From a long distance the subject has a better overview of the object. Both negative and positive qualities can be perceived, but are less intensely experienced. The subject is more indifferent towards the object. However, in order to stabilize the long distance to the object (which may be relevant when a person wants to increase the distance to a rejected alternative), he or she may try to find a viewing position that implies a focus on the object's negative qualities.

Assuming the validity of SDS theory it may now be asked which role perspectives will play in the search for a dominance structure (or for some other kind of differentiation among choice alternatives). Recently, the philosopher Frederic Schick (1997) suggested that a person can make a decision when he or she sees a choice alternative in such a way that it agrees with what he or she wants. For example, if a wealthy man decides to give money to a beggar he may do this because he wants to help poor persons and because he sees the beggar as a very poor person (rather than as, say, an annoying person). Schick stressed that this seeing cannot be reduced to external facts, since it corresponds to one of several possible experiences of the same external fact (e.g., experiencing a beggar as poor rather than as annoying). Apparently, Schick's concept of seeing has links both to the perspective model and to SDS theory. In line with the perspective model, the seeing implies that certain attributes come into the foreground (being poor in our example), whereas other attributes come into the background (being annoying in our example). In the same vein, SDS theory assumes that certain attributes are emphasized or bolstered, which may be equivalent with coming into the foreground, whereas other attributes are deemphasized, which may be equivalent with coming into the background. To conclude, the seeing resulting from perspective taking may help the decision maker to form a dominance structure.

When a decision is of great personal concern the decision maker may want more than just finding a suitable perspective in order to make the decision. He or she may also want that the resulting evaluation is stable across different moments of time. Obviously, the stability increases the more it is supported by features in the environment, which in turn may be affected by behavioral interventions. The stability also increases the more it is supported by different perspectives (which all point to the same action), and the more difficult it is for the individual to change perspectives that support the to-be-chosen alternative. Thus, to a large extent this description of a decision making process is assumed to involve a search for differentiating perspectives, which may be controlled both internally and externally by means of behavioral interventions. Recently, Montgomery (in press) used this framework in a case study of the Swedish general Adam Ludvig Lewenhaupt's decision to surrender the Swedish army in Perevolochna, Ukraine in the year of 1709. Below, the framework will be illustrated in a study of decision making in troubled marital relationships (Willén & Montgomery, 1997).

Empirical Illustration of the Perspective Model: Perspective Shifts in Troubled Marital Relationships as a Way to Structure a Decision Situation

The participants in this study were 12 married or cohabiting couples who were going through a marital crisis. They were recruited through family counseling agencies and through advertisements in a daily paper. The ages varied between 22–65 and the median age was 32. They were all living in Göteborg, Sweden's second largest city. In all couples, at least one of the spouses had seriously considered breaking up the relationship. The data analysis will be focused on the person in each couple who viewed him/herself as the initiator of a possible or actually implemented decision to divorce.

The couples were interviewed in depth with a separate, 1½-hour-long interview with each spouse. The interviews focused on the experience of the partner and his or her behavior in different stages of the relationship. In addition, respondents were asked about their self-image and its changes during the relationship. Another issue concerned decisions made about the relationship in different stages, such as the initial stage, when the couple moved in together, or when a pregnancy occurred.

In addition to dealing with the issues mentioned above, the data analysis focused on identifying perspectives involving identifications with the self, the partner, and a life as a single person in different stages of the relationship. For a given subject identification, we distinguished between inside perspective, and short outside and long outside perspectives. For instance, for subject identification Self we distinguished between self oriented inside perspective on the partner, denoted as S→P (meaning that the partner was seen as fulfilling the respondent's own interests), self oriented short outside perspective on partner, denoted as S(→)P (meaning that the partner was seen as threatening the respondent's goals), and S(→)p meaning that the respondent had distanced him/herself from the partner. In the same vein, P→S stands for partner oriented inside perspective on self (meaning that partner views the respondent as fulfilling his/her interests), and P(→)S for partner oriented short outside perspective on self.

Table 8.1 shows a dramatic finding. In all 12 relationships, the initiator experienced a global perspective shift in his or her view of the partner following the occurrence of a critical event that instigated the respondent to see his or her partner in a new light. As can be seen, in Table 8.1 many perspective shifts could be interpreted as seeing the same trait from a new (negative) side. For instance, Carl's adventurousness evidently was seen as destructiveness experienced after the critical event; Diana's sexiness seems to have been converted to unfaithfulness; Lisa's individualism to egocentricity and as lack of responsibility; and Erik's childishness to being dependent and lazy. (All personal names are fictitious.) In general, before the critical event the partner was seen in a global positive light, whereas an equally global negative light prevailed after the perspective shift. Thus, the respondent had access to a dominance structure favoring the partner before the critical event and an inverse dominance structure that disfavored the partner after the critical event had occurred. It seems reasonable to interpret these re-evaluations as genuine perspective shifts following from the fact the partner was seen as being in conflict with his/her own interests. For instance, sexiness is obviously not seen as something positive when it leads to unfaithfulness. The perspective shifts evidently were not resulting from an active search for a dominance structure, as stressed in SDS theory, but occurred as a natural consequence of a changed perspective.

However, it is also clear from our data that the initiators actively searched for a good structure, which could form the basis for a definite decision. The perspective shift experienced after the critical event was only a first

TABLE 8.1

Experience of Partner Before and After a Perspective Shift Associated With a Critical Event.

Initiator	Before Perspective Shift	Event	After Perspective Shift
Carl	Sporty, healthy, adventurous, beautiful, pessimistic	Gradual process from the beginning	Ill, lazy, frightened, destructive
Diana	Sexy, positive, odd, exciting, interesting	Adultery	Unfaithful, selfish, wants to impose
Lisa	Individualistic, following own rhythm	Baby is born	Egocentric, passive, irresponsible
Erik	Exciting, different, natural, childlike innocence, spontaneous, honest, humorous, wise, sensitive, involved	Second baby is born	Dependent, lazy, irresponsible, depressive undecided, unpredictable, self-centered
Peter	Outgoing, witty, in need of his help	Confession about having a child from partner	Demanding, clinging, helpless
Anders	Kind, mysterious, special, intelligent, having interesting connections	Partner confesses she has never loved him	Needy, helpless, passive, having no interests, no friends
Ulrika	Warm, happy, hard-working, good with the children	Injury leading to partner stop working	Mean, bad tempered, lazy
Tina	Knowledgeable, bohemian, interested, caring, self-confident	Forced to do things she deeply disapproves of	Intruding, odd, incomprehensible, boring, unreliable, inconsiderate, greedy, clumsy uncommitted, brooding over life
Rose-Marie	Handsome, kind calm	A difficult child starting school	Unassertive, submissive, withdrawn, passive
Kerstin	Charming, outgoing, easygoing	Forced to a pregnancy termination	Too interested in other women, drinking too much
Bodil	Purposeful, practical, similar interests, secure	(a)Pregnancy termination, (b)Fearful incident abroad	Uncommunicative, insensitive, selfish, always the same
Sara	Easygoing, happy, positive, warm, caring	A feeling that her love was not reciprocated, followed by an unplanned pregnancy	Submissive, passive, unassertive, uncultivated

165

step to a final decision. In order to reach the decision the individual attempted to find perspectives that gave a stable and clear basis for the decision. Figure 8.2 shows a flowchart depicting different routes to the final decision to divorce or to continue the relationship. The routes can be understood a more or less irregular moves from an initial position close to the partner to a final position in which the initiator had integrated his/herself with an alternative far away from the partner. The moves are accompanied by and resulting from perspective shifts, which in turn are more or less controlled by the individual. The control could be internal (e.g., mental simulation of what it would mean to lead a new life as a single) or external by means of behavioral interventions in the external world. In the latter case, the individual may for instance keep a long distance perspective to the partner by avoiding coming too close to him/her.

Three decision making stages can be discerned in Fig. 8.2. In the *breaking up* stage, the initiator moves away from the partner in the hope of being able to see him from long distance in a self-oriented perspective. If he fails to do so or finds out that he is not prepared for a new life as a divorced person, then he enters into the *vacillation and construal* phase. In that stage, he/she oscillates between moving back to the partner, to find him/herself again being confronted with a short outside perspective, $(S{\rightarrow})P$, and moving to the new life, but still finding it difficult to integrate with oneself, $(S{\rightarrow})A$. In both moves, the individual often tries to adopt a partner-oriented perspective on himself in order to instigate a perspective change. That is, when moving to the partner the individual may accept the partner's critical view of him $(P{\rightarrow})S$, in order to find out how to change one's own behavior in order to attain a situation where both partners have inside perspectives on each other. Typically, these attempts fail and the partner moves to the new life position and attempts to find out what the new life demands of him $(A{\rightarrow})S$. In these oscillations the partner tries to change situation by means of mental activities or overt behavior as exemplified above. Normally, these construal activities favor one of the alternatives implying that the scale finally tips over to a situation where, for example, the individual views it as possible to attain a stable inside perspective on the new life, $S{\rightarrow}A$, and a stable long distance perspective on the partner, $(S{\rightarrow})p$. The individual makes her decision to divorce. But the story is not over here. The individual now faces the problem of implementing his/her decision. In order to do so he enters into *consolidation phase* to make the situation so stable that no return is possible. In this phase the individual often attempts to delegate the responsibility for the divorce decision to the partner or to other external entities. The individual so to speak pushes the environment to make the decision for himself. For example, Carl told his wife Clara: "I will be so rude to you that you can't

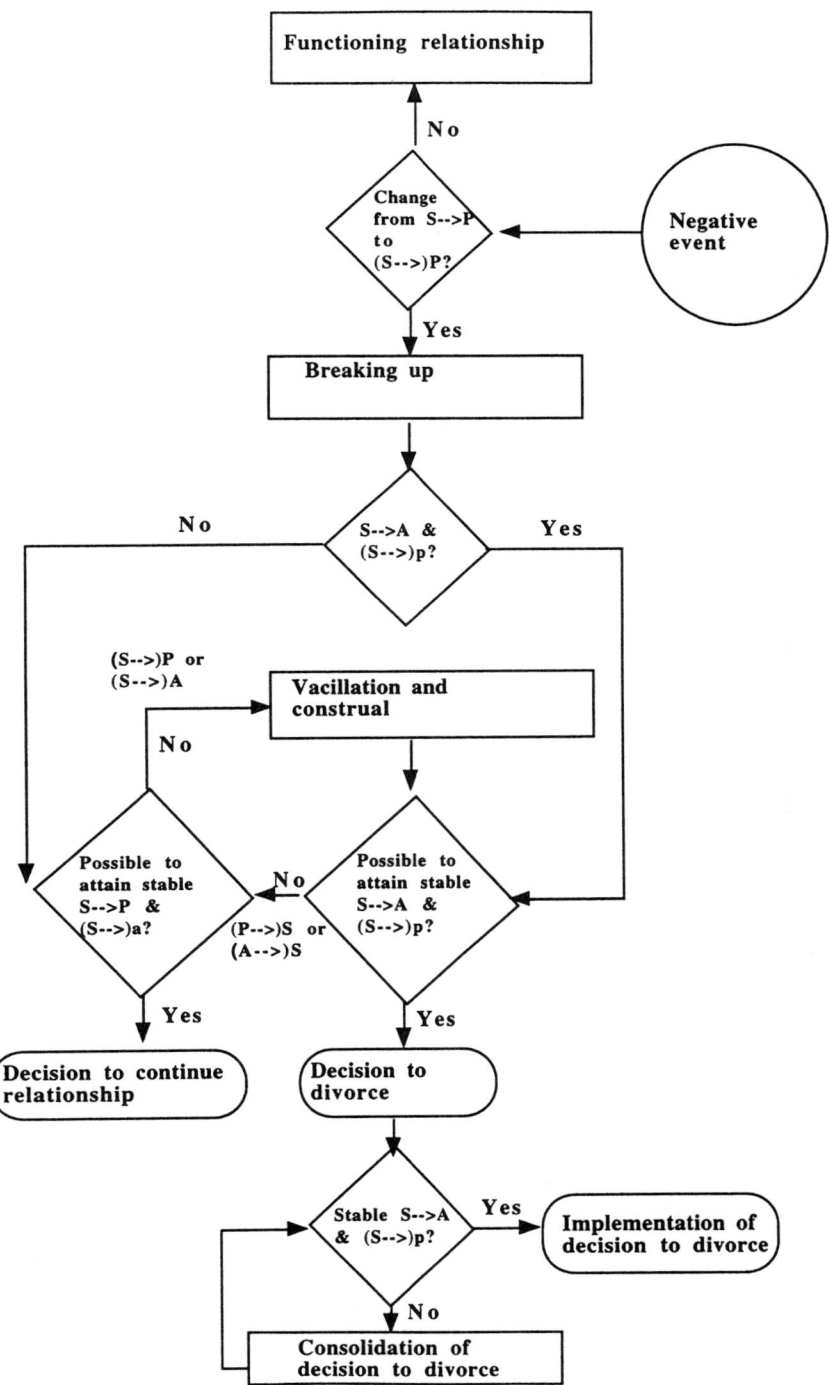

FIG. 8.2.   Flowchart of decision processes in troubled marital relationships.

do anything but leave me." Of course, the participants were not always so aware as Carl about their use of this strategy.

The Meaning of a Good Structure in the Perspective Model

This empirical study shows a painful decision making process that involves one or several perspective shifts, which are more or less deliberately controlled by the individual. The perspective shifts are repeated until the individual attains a stable situation where the adopted perspectives support a certain decision. Obviously, this process involves a search for a good structure. However, it may not be sufficient that one alternative dominates other alternatives in order to make the decision and to implement it. The individual may also feel that his or her present view of the situation is stable, that no perspective shift is possible. In other words, that there is no point of return. This may correspond to Svenson's (1992; Chapter 9 of this volume) proposition in his Diff Con theory that a sufficient degree of differentiation (which may be more than just dominance) in order to make a decision. Hence, in this way the perspective model may bridge over the gap between SDS theory and Diff Con theory.

Obviously, the need for reaching a stable perception of a decision situation is particularly salient when the individual faces decisions of a deep personal significance and when the implementation of the decision is experienced as very painful. In other cases, access to a dominance structure that more or less involves subjective dominance may be sufficient for making the decision.

ACTING AND DECIDING: HOW MAY THEY BE RELATED?

The literature reviewed in the present article shows that the concept of action is prominent in current research on decision making. In this final section, in the light of this literature we will discuss how action may be related to decision making.

Preparation for Action

SDS theory as well as Diff Con theory stresses the link between predecisional processes and the commitment to act in line with the chosen alternative in postdecisional processes. Both theories assume that predecisional processes aim at building up a firm ground for defending the to-be-chosen alternative in a postdecisonal future. The validity of this assumption is backed up by the empirical support for the four phases of SDS theory, as well as for the differentiation assumption in Diff Con theory. It seems clear that people in their decision making processes often manage to increase the cognitive support for the to-be-chosen alternative, which in turn means that later on it will become easier to defend that alternative. That the predecisonal process indeed may be oriented towards facilitating ensuing action is shown by the finding that decision makers may not accept the character of given alternatives, but instead try to figure out how they could improve the alternative to be chosen (Montgomery, 1993).

The perspective model provides further aspects on how the decision maker prepares him/herself for efficient action. The model points to the possibility that a meta-perspective may be necessary for making a decision involving the experience that no change of the present perspective is possible.

Interventions in the External World

The earlier formulations of SDS theory focused on the decision maker's cognitive processes. However, on his or her way to the decision, the individual may also intervene in the external world to increase the support for the alternative to be chosen (Blom Kemdal & Montgomery, 1997; Willén, 1994). Similarly, naturalistic decision theories stress that decision makers interact with a dynamic environment, although the research in this tradition does not seem to be concerned with the support that predecisional action may give to the final decision. The perspective model also concerns how the individual interacts with a dynamic environment, with the purpose of finding and maintaining suitable perspectives.

Thoughts as Actions

The empirical support for dominance structuring is not unequivocal. In general, the support is stronger when think aloud data rather than quantitative ratings were used. Think-aloud data also differentiate more clearly between preferences and choices than is true for rating data. It may be speculated that think-aloud reports reflect an internal argumentation process. In line with the view of thinking advanced in so-called rhetoric psychology (Billig, 1991), dominance structuring may be analogous to arguing with a defender of a competing alternative. Assuming that the argumentation process primarily is expressed in words it follows that verbal data will reflect this process more closely than is the case for ratings.

A stress on the rhetorical and the argumentative character of thinking implies that thinking may be seen as a kind of acting. Just as is the case in conflicts between individuals acting in the external world, the individual decision maker uses his or her thoughts as weapons against an opponent.

In this fight the individual may be more or less successful, which will be manifested in the choice or the rejection of a tentatively chosen alternative.

REFERENCES

Ariely, D., & Wallsten, T. (1995). Seeking subjective dominance in multidimensional space: An explanation of the asymmetric dominance effect. *Organizational Behavior and Human Decision Processes, 63,* 223–232.

Axelrod, P. (Ed.). (1976). *Structure of decision: The cognitive maps of political elites.* Princeton: Princeton University Press.

Beach, L. R. (1990). *Image theory: Decision making in personal and organizational contexts.* Chichester, England: Wiley.

Beach, L. R., & Lipshitz, R. (1993). Why classical decision theory is an appropriate standard for evaluating and aiding most human decision making. In G. A. Klein, J. Orasanu, R. Calderwood, & C. E. Zsambok (Eds.), *Decision making in action: Models and methods* (pp. 21–35). Norwood, NJ: Ablex.

Beckmann, J., & Kuhl, J. (1984). Altering information to gain action control: Functional aspects of human information processing in decision making. *Journal of Research in Personality, 18,* 224–237.

Biel, A., & Montgomery, H. (1986). Scenarios in energy planning. In B. Brehmer, H. Jungermann, P. Lourens, & G. Sevon (Eds.), *New directions in research on decision making* (pp. 205–218). Amsterdam: North-Holland.

Billig, M. (1991). *Ideology and opinions.* London: Sage.

Blom Kemdal, A., & Montgomery, H. (1997). Perspectives and emotions in personal decision making. In R. Ranyard, W. R. Crozier, & Ola Svenson (Eds.), *Cognitive models and explanations* (pp. 72–89). London: Routledge.

Bockenholt, U., Albert, D., Aschenbrenner, M., & Schmalhofer, F. (1991). The effects of attractiveness, dominance, and attribute differences on information acquisition in multiattribute binary choice. *Organizational Behavior and Human Decision Processes, 49,* 258–281.

Brehmer, B. (1990). Strategies in real-time dynamic decision making. In R. Hogarth (Ed.), *Insights in decision making: A tribute to Hillel J. Einhorn* (pp. 262–279). Chicago: University of Chicago Press.

Cohen, M. S. (1993). The naturalistic basis of decision biases. In G. A. Klein, J. Orasanu, R. Calderwood, & C. E. Zsambok (Eds.), *Decision making in action: Models and methods* (pp. 51–99). Norwood, NJ: Ablex.

Cohen, M. S., Freeman, J. P., & Wolf, S. (1996). Metarecognition in time-stressed decision making: Recognizing, critiquing, and correcting. *Human Factors, 38,* 206–219.

Dahlstrand, U., & Montgomery, H. (1984). Information search and evaluative processes in decision making: A computer based process tracing study. *Acta Psychologica, 56,* 113–123.

Edwards, W. (1954). The theory of decision making. *Psychological Bulletin, 51,* 380–417.

Ericsson, K. A., & Simon, H. A. (1984). Verbal reports as data. *Psychological Review, 87,* 215–251.

Festinger, L. (1957). *A theory of cognitive dissonance.* Palo Alto, CA: Stanford University Press.

Fischer, G. W., & Hawkins, S. A. (1993). Strategy compatibility, scale compatibility, and the prominence effect. *Journal of Experimental Psychology: Human Perception and Performance, 19,* 580–597.

Gallhofer, I., & Saris, W. (1989). Decision trees and decision rules in politics: The empirical decision analysis procedure. In H. Montgomery & O. Svenson (Eds.), *Process and structure in human decision making* (pp. 293–311). Chichester, England: Wiley.

Garvill, J., Gärling, T., Lindberg, E., & Montgomery, H. (1991, August). *In search of evidence for dominance structuring in decision making.* Paper presented at the 13th European Research Conference of Subjective Probability, Utility, and Decision Making, Fribourg, Switzerland.

Gollwitzer, P. M. (1990). Action phases and mind-sets. In T. E. Higgins & R. M. Sorrentino (Eds.), *Handbook of motivation and cognition: Foundations of social behavior* (Vol. 2, pp 53–92). New York: Guilford.

Gollwitzer, P. M., Heckhausen, H., Ratajczak, H. (1990). From weighing to willing: Approaching a change decision through pre- or postdecisional mentation. *Organizational Behavior and Human Decision Processes, 45,* 41–65.

Gottman, J. M. (1994). *What predicts divorce? The relationship between marital processes and marital outcome.* Hillsdale, NJ: Lawrence Erlbaum Associates.

Huber, J., Payne, J. W., & Puto, C. (1980). Adding asymmetrically dominated alternatives: Violations of regularity and the similarity hypothesis. *Journal of Consumer Research, 9,* 90–98.

Kahneman, D., & Tversky, A. (1979). Prospect theory. *Psychometrica, 47,* 263–291.

Kant, I. (1959). *Foundations of the metaphysics of morals* (L. W. Beck, Trans.). New York: Bobbs-Merrill. (Original work published 1785).

Klein, G. A. (1993a). A recognition primed decision (RPD) model of rapid decision making. In G. A. Klein, J. Orasanu, R. Calderwood, & C. E. Zsambok (Eds.), *Decision making in action: Models and methods* (pp. 138–147). Norwood, NJ: Ablex.

Klein, G. A. (1993b). Twenty questions: Suggestions for research in naturalistic decision making. In G. A. Klein, J. Orasanu, R. Calderwood, & C. E. Zsambok (Eds.), *Decision making in action: Models and methods* (pp. 389–403). Norwood, NJ: Ablex.

Klein, G. A., Orasanu, J., Calderwood, R., & Zsambok, C. E. (1993). (Eds.). *Decision making in action: Models and methods.* Norwood, NJ: Ablex.

Kuhl, J. (1992). A theory of self-regulation: Action versus state orientation, self-discrimination, and some applications. *Applied Psychology: An International Review, 41,* 97–129.

Lewicka, M. (1990, August). *Mood related differences in predecisional information search strategies.* Paper presented at the 98th Annual Convention of the American Psychological Association, Boston.

Lichtenstein, S., & Slovic, P. (1971). Reversals of preference between bids and choices in gambling decisions. *Journal of Experimental Psychology, 101,* 16–20.

Lindberg, E., Gärling, T., & Montgomery, H. (1988). People's beliefs and values as determinants of housing preferences and simulated choices. *Scandinavian Housing and Planning Research, 5,* 181–197.

Lindberg, E., Gärling, T., & Montgomery, H. (1989a, August). *Decisions with incompletely described alternatives.* Paper presented at the 12th European Research Conference on Subjective Probability, Utility, and Decision Making, Moscow.

Lindberg, E., Gärling, T., & Montgomery, H. (1989b). Differential predictability of preferences and choices. *Journal of Behavioral Decision Making, 2,* 205–219.

Lindberg, E., Gärling, T., & Montgomery, H. (1989c). Subjective belief-value structures as determinants of preferences for and choices among housing alternatives. *Journal of Consumer Policy, 12,* 119–137.

Lindberg, E., Gärling, T., & Montgomery, H. (1990). *Intra-urban residential mobility: Subjective belief-value structures as determinants of residential preferences and choices.* (Umeå Psychological Reports, No. 197). Umeå: Department of Psychology, University of Umeå.

Lipshitz, R. (1993). Converging themes in the study of decision making in realistic settings. In G. A. Klein, J. Orasanu, R. Calderwood, & C. E. Zsambok (Eds.), *Decision making in action: Models and methods* (pp. 103–137). Norwood, NJ: Ablex.

Mann, L., Janis, I., L., & Chaplin, R. (1969). The effects of anticipation of forthcoming information on predecisional processes. *Journal of Personality and Social Psychology, 11,* 10–16.

Montgomery, H. (1983). Decision rules and the search for a dominance structure: Towards a process model of decision making. In P. C. Humphreys, O. Svenson, & A. Vari (Eds.), *Analyzing and aiding decision processes* (pp. 343–369). Amsterdam: North-Holland.

Montgomery, H. (1989). From cognition to action: The search for dominance in decision making. In H. Montgomery & O. Svenson (Eds.), *Process and structure in human decision making* (pp. 23–49). Chichester, England: Wiley.

Montgomery, H. (1993). The choice of a home seen from the inside: Psychological contributions to the study of decision making in housing markets. In T. Gärling & R. G. Golledge (Eds.), *Behavior and environment* (pp. 317–341). Amsterdam: Elsevier.

Montgomery, H. (1994). Towards a perspective theory of decision making and judgment. *Acta Psychologica, 87,* 155–178.

Montgomery, H. (1997). Surrender at Perevolochna: A case study of perspective and action control in decision making under stress. In R. Flin, E. Salas, M. Strub, & L. Martin (Eds.), *Decision making under stress* (pp. 193–204). Aldershot, England: Ashgate.

Montgomery, H., Gärling, T., & Lindberg, E., & Selart, M. (1990). Preference judgments and choice: Is the prominence effect due to information integration or to information evaluation? In K. Borcherding, O. I. Larichev, & D. Messick (Eds.), *Contemporary issues in decision making* (pp. 149–157). Amsterdam: North-Holland.

Montgomery, H., & Hemlin, S. (1991). *Judging scientific quality: A cross-disciplinary investigation of professorial evaluation documents.* (Göteborg Psychological Reports, Vol. 21, No. 4). Göteborg: Department of Psychology, University of Göteborg.

Montgomery, H., Selart, M., Gärling, T., & Lindberg, E. (1994). The judgment-choice discrepancy: Noncompatibility or restructuring? *Journal of Behavioral Decision Making, 7,* 145–155.

Montgomery, H., & Svenson, O. (1989). A think aloud study of dominance structuring in decision processes. In H. Montgomery & O. Svenson (Eds.), *Process and structure in human decision making* (pp. 135–150). Chichester, England: Wiley.

Orasanu, J., & Connolly, T. (1993). The reinvention of decision making. In G. A. Klein, J. Orasanu, R. Calderwood, & C. E. Zsambok (Eds.), *Decision making in action: Models and methods* (pp. 3–20). Norwood, NJ: Ablex.

Pennington, N., & Hastie, R. (1993). Reasoning in explanation-based decision making. *Cognition, 49,* 123–163.

Rasmussen, J. (1993). Deciding and doing: Decision making in natural contexts. In G. A. Klein, J. Orasanu, R. Calderwood, & C. E. Zsambok (Eds.), *Decision making in action: Models and methods* (pp. 158–171). Norwood, NJ: Ablex.

Rohrman, B., & Borcherding, K. (1988, August). *The cognitive structure of residential decisions: A longitudinal field study.* Paper presented at the XXIV International Congress of Psychology, Sydney.

Russo, J. E., Medvec, V. H., & Meloy, M. G. (1996). The distortion of information during decisions. *Organizational Behavior and Human Decision Processes, 66,* 102–110.

Schick, F. (1997). *Making choices. A recasting of decision theory.* Cambridge, England: Cambridge University Press.

Sedek, G., Kofta, M., & Tyszka, T. (1993). Effects of uncontrollability on subsequent decision making: Testing the cognitive exhaustion hypothesis. *Journal of Personality and Social Psychology, 6,* 1270–1281.

Selart, M. (1996). Structure compatibility and restructuring in judgment and choice. *Organizational Behavior and Human Decision Processes, 65,* 106–116.

Selart, M., Gärling, T., & Montgomery, H. (1998). Compatibility and the use of information processing strategies. *Journal of Behavioral Decision Making, 11,* 59–71.

Selart, M., Montgomery, H., Romanus, J., & Gärling, T. (1994). Violations of procedural invariance in preference measurement: Cognitive explanations. *European Journal of Cognitive Psychology, 6,* 417–436.

Shafir, E., Simonson, I., & Tversky, A. (1993). Reason-based choice. *Cognition, 49,* 11–36.

Slovic, P. (1975). Choice between equally valued alternatives. *Journal of Experimental Psychology: Human Perception and Performance, 1,* 280–287.

Slovic, P., & Lichtenstein, S. (1983). Preference reversals: A broader perspective. *The American Economic Review, 73,* 596–605.

Soelberg, P. (1967). Unprogrammed decision making. *Management Review, 3,* 19–29.

Svenson, O. (1979). Process descriptions of decision making. *Organizational Behavior and Human Performance, 23,* 86–112.

Svenson, O. (1992). Differentiation and Consolidation theory of human decision making: A frame of reference for the study of pre- and post-decision processes. *Acta Psychologica, 80,* 143–168.

Svenson, O. (1996). Decision making and the search for fundamental psychological regularities: What can be learned from a process perspective? *Organizational Behavior and Human Decision Processes, 65,* 252–267.

Svenson, O., & Hill, T. (1997). Turning prior disadvantages into advantages: Decision making through the looking glass of differentiation and consolidation theory. In R. Ranyard, W. R. Crozier, & O. Svenson (Eds.), *Decision making: Cognitive models and explanations* (pp. 218–232). London: Routledge.

Taylor, S. E., & Gollwitzer, P. M. (1996). Effects of mindset on positive illusions. *Journal of Personality and Social Psychology, 69,* 213–226.

Tversky, A., Sattah, S., & Slovic, P. (1988). Contingent weighing in judgment and choice. *Psychological Review, 95,* 371–384.

Tyszka, T. (1980). Contextual multiattribute decision rules. In L. Sjöberg, T. Tyszka, & J. Wise (Eds.), *Decision processes and decision analysis.* Lund: Doxa.

Tyszka, T., & Wielochovski, M. (1991). Must boxing verdicts be partial? *Journal of Behavioral Decision Making, 4,* 283–295.

Willén, H. (1994). *How do couples decide about having their first child? An explorative study.* (Göteborg Psychological Reports, 24: No. 1). Göteborg: Göteborg University, Department of Psychology.

Willén, H., & Montgomery, H. (1997, August). *Perspective shifts in troubled marital relationships as a way to structure a decision situation.* Paper presented at the 16th bi-annual conference on Subjective Probability, Utility, and Decision Making, Leeds, UK.

Chapter 9

Differentiation and Consolidation Theory: Decision Making Processes Before and After a Choice

Ola Svenson
Stockholm University

This chapter presents Differentiation and Consolidation (Diff Con) theory. First the concept of levels of decisions will be introduced and exemplified, followed by a brief description of the theory itself. Finally, a set of studies conducted from a Diff Con perspective will be presented with their main findings.

In this chapter, decision making is seen as a creative process in a dynamic environment. This process involves the elicitation of goals, creation of decision alternatives, and comparisons of alternatives with reference to how well they fit the goals. The interest will not be confined to predecision processes only but it will also cover the postdecision phase from a few minutes up to several months.

Naturally, in real life most of these processes have to be well learned quick, automatic, and subconscious to decrease the load on a decision maker's focal thought-processing capacity. In line with this, it is possible to distinguish levels of decision making through reference to the psychological processes needed for different decisions made by the same individual decision maker. To specify, decisions can be classified according to the extent to which the decision maker uses his or her own value system and the information in a decision problem and the complexity of the decision processes. A decision maker's value system is a term used here to summarize all fundamental values, attitudes, motivations, and drives that form the goals in a given situation, and that are of potential importance for a decision. When the value system is mapped onto a decision problem, this creates an attractiveness representation of the problem. Svenson (1990) suggests four different levels of decisions. The higher the level, the more focal thought processes are needed. This includes both the representation of the information about the alternatives and the processing of the information to reach a decision.

For example, the habitual everyday choice of buying milk in the store typically requires no mapping of values, very simple information representation (e.g., color of package), and very simple processing of that information to reach a decision. By way of contrast, a career choice may include the creation and/or identification of alternatives, a careful mapping of values on the alternatives, and a painful processing of conflicting values to reach a final decision. In this case the decision would be classified to belong to a group of higher level decisions needing quite a lot of focal processing capacity. It is important to note that it is the decision maker her- or himself who, in interaction with the decision problem, determines at which level a decision will be made. A simple everyday habitual choice of overtime work may one day be challenged through the death of a close friend due to a heart attack. This event may move the former low-level decision up to a high-level decision, including the creation of new decision alternatives reevaluation of values, the mapping of values, and a more complex processing of the decision problem to stay or leave at five in the afternoon.

In Diff Con theory the alternatives in a decision problem are represented by *aspects* (e.g., in the case of a car alternative: five-passenger station wagon, costing 250,000 Swedish kronor [SEK]) that are ordered on *attributes* (e.g., size represented by five passengers and price represented by SEK 250,000). In most cases there is an attractiveness representation linked to an aspect when a decision is made. For example, paying SEK 210,000 is more attractive than paying SEK 250,000.

It is also assumed that the *importance* of an attribute can be represented on at least a rank order scale. The price of a car may be more important than the size within given ranges of the two attributes. However, exceptions must be assumed—for example, in Level 1 decisions.

In Level 1 decisions there is no assumption of any attractiveness representations at the moment when the decisions are made. For example, Level 1 decisions are often made in quick habitual processes. The decision maker recognizes that a situation is similar to an earlier one, and he chooses the same alternative as last time. This kind of decisions include many quick and largely automatic and unconscious decisions (Shiffrin & Schneider, 1977). Klein (1989) calls such decisions recognition primed; Smith (1992) uses the exemplar model to describe them. Gärling (1992) calls these kinds of choices "decisions according to routines for performance of everyday activities."

Although Level 1 decisions do have relationships to values in the past, an attractiveness representation is not likely to be activated and influence these decisions every time they are made. Instead, other perceptual or cognitive principles (such as similarity by matching) guide Level 1 decisions. However, when the habits or categories were formed in the past, attractiveness and decision rules were the guiding principles and higher-level decisions were made. Thus, Level 1 decisions are seen as the result of an effort-saving principle decreasing focal-processing demands.

In most daily situations, Level 1 decisions are likely to govern most of our behavior. As noted above, the everyday choice of milk is an example of a decision easy to predict. Level 1 decisions may also represent predetermined strategies (e.g., always go by subway, always put on a seat belt, or always drive a little faster than the speed limit). Finally, Level 1 decisions can also function as subprocesses in higher-level decisions and determine a preliminary or reference alternative in a decision process.

In Level 2 decisions, the decision maker refers to attractiveness on one or a few attributes. However, these decisions represent stereotypical and static mappings of the alternatives (e.g., biggest is best). For example, no trade-offs between conflicting attractiveness values are performed. Decisions that are made through direct holistic references to emotions or affects belong to this category as well. Here, there is at least one attractiveness attribute that determines the decision. This contrasts with Level 1 decisions, in which no attractiveness is used at the time of the decision.

In sum, in Level 2 decisions, some decision alternatives are associated with positive or negative emotions that may be sufficient for a decision. To repeat, in contrast with Level 1, Level 2 decisions always refer to an attractiveness (emotional, value, etc.) attribute. This level of decision processes, as well as Level 1 processing, appear in the initial stages of most differentiation processes of a more elaborate nature, but they can also be used later in, for example, comparisons with reference alternatives (which often do not belong to the choice set of alternatives but that are temporarily attended to).

In Level 3 decisions, an easy and mostly automatic correspondence is not assumed between a decision maker's value system and the aspects of the alternatives. Decisions at this level may use trade-offs between the attractiveness of aspects on different attributes and transform attributes into new ones. By way of example, the decision to buy a digital TV set may not be a very familiar decision (in 1998), which probably requires a careful mapping of values on the different aspects characterizing each TV set. Then pros and cons will have to be considered before a final decision can be reached.

As mentioned earlier, decisions at this level are fundamental prerequisites for most decisions at Levels 1 and 2, which at one time were Level

3 (or 4) decisions later transformed into routine decisions. However, the present author does not think he will ever reach those lower levels for decisions between TV sets, but perhaps for TV channels.

In Level 4 decisions, the decision maker encounters or creates a new and unfamiliar problem in which decision alternatives have to be elicited or created. Parts of the decision making processes at this level include problem solving.

Let us exemplify this level with the choice of how to travel from one location to another. Here, the creation of decision alternatives includes making up composite alternatives. That is, an alternative is constructed which contains some part of each of a number of different travel modes. For example, the constructive Level 4 process may generate one (train + taxi) alternative competing with an (air + rental car) alternative. Langer (1994) calls Level 4 decision making "active decision making" and argues that in comparison with the other levels of decision making, active decision making should lead to greater self-esteem, enhanced perceived control and less postdecision regret.

It is interesting to note that almost all judgment and decision research has presented problems that are assumed to be treated on Level 3. For example, a prototypical investigation involves aspects (or cues) on two or more important attributes that (from a normative viewpoint at least) can be combined in a compensatory manner.

All of the decision making levels presented above can be found in Diff Con theory, presented next. However, as in most contemporary decision research, Diff Con theory also tends to focus more on Level 3 decisions than on other kinds of decisions.

DIFFERENTIATION AND CONSOLIDATION THEORY

Differentiation and Consolidation (Diff Con) theory was developed in an effort to both integrate earlier research in behavioral decision theory and to further develop the theoretical foundations for this kind of research (Svenson, 1992).

Diff Con theory deviates from other decision theoretic formulations in some important ways. One is that the goal of a decision process is not just to fulfill one or several decision rules but to find or create, through (1) holistic evaluation, (2) alternative and problem restructuring and (3) application of one or several decision rules, an alternative that is sufficiently superior in comparison to its competitor(s).

The structuring is always performed to reach a goal related to a decision rule (e.g., maximize number of supporting attributes, maximization sum of attractiveness differences supporting an alternative, maximizing similarity to a reference alternative), contingent on the situation and the person in that situation. So, the structuring and information processing according to a decision rule are always contingent and interactive. This process is named *differentiation* and takes place on the hypothetical construct of a differentiation vector related to a differentiation continuum. The process is reflected in, for example, measurable process and structural differentiation processes. In the following sections, some of these processes will be elaborated and explained further.

There are corresponding postdecision processes that work in support of the chosen alternative and against, for example, regret threatening the choice. These processes are called *consolidation* and correspond to predecision differentiation. To exemplify this, repeated reminders of the decision rules used in the decision process may be components of a consolidation process.

The general framework provided by Diff Con can accommodate different existing decision models as subprocesses or special cases (cf. Svenson, 1992). However, note that most contemporary decision theories do not at all consider degree of differentiation or what may be called preference strength, which has been pointed out by Busemeyer and Townsend (1993) in their presentation of *Decision Field Theory*.

As mentioned above, decision alternatives are represented by aspects ordered on attributes. The mapping of goals, values, and other driving forces on decision alternatives results in attractiveness values of the aspects that are essential for all Level 3 and Level 4 decisions as well as for some Level 2 decisions. Attractiveness can be measured in on rank-order order scales or higher metrics and the attractiveness on these scales are not necessarily commensurable across attributes (Svenson, 1979). For example, most people find it hard to apply commensurable attractiveness scales across lives saved and the costs of saving those lives. Explicit trade-offs are often avoided by human decision makers. The importance of different attributes in relation to each other is assumed to be represented on an ordinal or a more advanced scale level. That is, people are assumed to know reasonably well how important the different attributes are to them in a given moment.

Predecision Differentiation

Identifying Decision Alternatives, Goal Elicitation, Screening, and Editing. The initial processing of a decision problem is partly governed by markers, which tell the decision maker where to start. Markers can be perceptual or cognitive and relate to the goal structure and the representation of the decision problem. The nomination of one attribute as most important can be governed by a marker so that the aspects on that attribute are compared first.

A marker can be, for example, the label of an attribute (e.g., costs) or an aspect of an attribute (e.g., SEK 1,000,000). It is assumed that markers are very important and may explain important parts of behavior not otherwise understood. For example, a deviant high price may draw attention to the cost attribute, which is then considered most important attribute. In comparison, in another otherwise very similar decision set, no alternative deviates in price, the price attribute looses in importance. A marker, in the form of a deviant aspect value, does not have to be integrated in itself in the process otherwise than as an initiator of the process. A marker may also, for example, trigger Level 1 decision processes.

Editing or rearranging and grouping the information before a decision is also initiated by markers and essential to reduce the demand of energetic resources (cf. Abelson & Levi, 1985; Coupey, 1994; Kahneman & Tversky, 1979; Ranyard, 1989; Tversky & Kahneman, 1992). Identification of alternatives is important in real-life decisions but it is often trivial in laboratory settings. In many real-life situations, decision problems appear with only one decision alternative at a time which has to be accepted of rejected (cf., Fischhoff, 1996). *Screening* refers to a process in which some alternatives are eliminated from the following decision process (cf. Beach, 1990).

Selection of a Reference and/or Preliminary Choice Alternative. Diff Con theory acknowledges the existence and use of reference decision alternatives. Such alternatives are used as benchmark alternatives: alternatives for which there exists a value mapping. That is, the decision maker knows what he thinks about this alternative. Typically, a reference alternative is not part of the decision set. A reference alternative can be selected in a Level 1 quick process involving a classification without any evaluative component at the time. It may also be derived in more elaborate, conscious, and deliberate processes. The reference alternative can serve in determining aspiration levels (Dembo, 1931) or as an anchor in other respects. To exemplify, many decisions involve the acceptance or rejection of an alternative and then a reference alternative can be used in this process. In applied settings there may often be just one alternative that is considered and the decision therefore concerns a choice between the status quo alternative and one other alternative (cf. Kahneman, Knetsch, & Thaler, 1990; Samuelson & Zeckhauser, 1988; Schweitzer, 1994; Svenson, 1990).

The selection of a preliminary alternative can also involve a quick holistic association as well as more elaborate processes. The preliminary hypothetical choice of one alternative, when it occurs, means that this alternative can be in focus in pairwise comparisons with other alternatives. Montgomery uses the term promising for a preliminary selected alternative (Montgomery, 1983; Montgomery & Svenson, 1989; Chapter 8 of this volume).

Differentiation Leading to a Decision

Early in a decision process there may or may not exist a preliminary choice alternative. If there is such an alternative, this makes the processing and structuring of information more focused as it the centers on the preliminary choice alternative, testing its future as the final choice. If there is no preliminary alternative, or if it has been rejected, the information processing may involve what Beach (1990) calls screening, primarily focused on rejecting alternatives from the choice set.

When a preliminary alternative (or a smaller set of preliminary choice alternatives) has been selected, the differentiation process may be successful or it may fail. If it is successful, the decision maker becomes more certain that the preliminary choice alternative(s) are worth considering further. If it fails, the process has to be reiterated.

According to the theory, the probability of an alternative being chosen is higher if it is first selected as the preliminary choice. This is implied by the fact that differentiation attempts to support the first preliminary choice in a biased way favoring that candidate. Empirical evidence for this can be found in studies outside the Diff Con paradigm (cf. Russo, Medvec, & Meloy, 1996; Shafir, 1993; Shafir & Tversky, 1992) in which more and neutral information is used to increase differentiation supporting the preliminary choice. If the preliminary alternative cannot be sufficiently differentiated, it will be replaced by another candidate, which then becomes the next focus of the differentiation process. Basically, there are three kinds of differentiation processes in Diff Con theory: holistic, process, and structural differentiation.

Holistic Differentiation. Holistic differentiation is quick and may be experienced by the decision maker as something like a classification process (not readily available for conscious control or awareness) leading to the selection of a preferred alternative (Estes, 1994; Klein, 1989). The process can run without any relation to attractiveness at the moment of the decision (but probably when the first decision of this kind was performed).

Emotional or affective factors may also be elicited instantaneously when a decision situation appears and then the holistic differentiation takes place as a Level 2 decision (cf. Zajonc, 1980). Holistic differentiation often leads to a degree of differentiation that is sufficient for a final choice. However, it may also be part of more complex differentiation processes (e.g., in selecting a reference or a preliminary alternative).

Process Differentiation. Process differentiation includes the use of one or more decision rules (e.g., the conjunctive rule, the additive difference rule—cf. Beach, 1990; Svenson, 1979, 1992). Which rule is elicited depends on both the individual, the context, and the structure of the decision problem. The frequently reported initial use of the conjunctive rule in the screening phase to reduce the number of options belongs to this category of differentiation. Changing the acceptance criterion limits on different attributes, in rules using such criteria, is another and related kind of process differentiation.

As an example: when making a decision concerning which car to buy, the car's fuel consumption can be an attribute on which a conjunctive rule is applied. Then, the decision maker starts screening the available alternatives with a preset criterion level: not to accept any alternative that uses more gasoline than 0.65 liters per 10 km on the highway. After having done this, the decision maker finds out that no alternative found at the dealer meets this criterion level. He or she then revises the criterion level up to 0.75 liters, and resumes the screening. Now he or she finds several alternatives. According to Diff Con theory, the decision maker not only makes use of the pass–fail classification, but he or she also notices by how much an alternative exceeds the criterion level: the more the greater the contribution to differentiation.

Thus, the conjunctive rule can be applied with successively stricter criteria of rejection in the early stages of a decision process to reduce the set of possible alternatives. In later stages of the differentiation process, the preliminary choice can be tested against other alternatives in other decision rules, including reference alternatives elicited in the situation. Reference alternatives may correspond to least acceptable levels alternatives (e.g., used in conjunctive rule applications), aspiration level alternatives, and to ideal alternatives.

Diff Con theory requires that a sufficiently superior alternative is chosen. Thus, as mentioned above, a decision rule as used in this context, not only determine which alternative is superior, but also to some extent how much better it is. The use of several decision rules arriving at the same conclusion contribute to the degree of differentiation obtained.

Note, however, that from a normative point of view the rules may be derived from one and the same principle and are therefore logically dependent. In this respect, differentiation may not correspond to rational decision making. A differentiation process may include application first of the additive difference rule, followed by individual evaluations of the two leading alternatives. In the differentiation process, both processes will each support the leading alternative and function as partly independent tests, but in relation to normative theory this process will be regarded as seriously confounded.

Structural Differentiation. Structural differentiation refers to changes in psychological representations of the decision alternatives. All such changes are made in relation to one or several decision rules. Several and different kinds of processes are assumed to take place concurrently and contingent on each other (cf. Svenson, 1992). Structural differentiation processes are of different kinds depending on which components of the structure is the target. The target for restructuring can be the attractiveness of the aspects characterizing the decision alternatives, the importance given to the different attributes and the objective facts behind the aspects.

1. *Attractiveness restructuring* concerns the attractiveness of aspects and, as mentioned above, it is governed by decision rules setting the goals for the process. Restructuring is made possible through uncertainty in the mapping of goals on attractiveness representations, uncertainty in which goals to elicit and the relative importance of the different goals elicited in a particular situation.

To illustrate, a decision maker may be uncertain about how different aspects of a decision relate to his or her goals of, say, independence and security. He or she may also be uncertain as to the relevance of eliciting these particular goals and how to weigh them against each other. These uncertainties are genuine but can also, consciously or unconsciously, be kept fuzzy by the decision maker and used in negotiating the structure with her or himself in structural differentiation before the decision is made. Also, after a decision such uncertainties can be used to support the earlier decision in consolidation processes.

2. *Attribute importance restructuring* refers to changes in the importance of an attribute. As an example, the cost attribute may gradually be given more weight in relation to a quality attribute in a differentiation process. In more formal terms, the differentiation may follow a weighed additive difference rule and be performed through gradually changing the relative importance weights among the two most important attributes.

3. *Fact restructuring* refers to changes in the representation of the reality behind the conceived aspects of the decision alternatives. This is done in relation to a decision rule and to support a hypothetically chosen alternative.

A decision maker citing facts that are biased towards supporting the preliminary choice illustrates fact restructuring. This is also the case when memory retrievals of earlier fact statements are more supportive than they were before the decision or judgment (cf. hindsight effects in Fischhoff, 1975; cognitive dissonance in Festinger, 1964). Fact restructuring parallels attractiveness restructuring and the two are sometimes substitutable.

4. *Problem restructuring* implies using available attributes and/or searching for new facts for alternative ways of representing the decision problem. This may involve new attributes, for example, supporting a preliminary choice or the creation of new alternatives. It may also include new causal structures of available facts.

Problem restructuring includes Level 4 decision processes in which new alternatives can also be created and old ones thoroughly modified. It is very important when it comes to problems such as the type represented by travel mode choices, involving composite or new alternatives. This kind of restructuring may give further support for a preliminary choice alternative but it may also eliminate it from the set of possible alternatives.

General Comments

It is important to emphasize that, although the preliminary choice of an alternative, means that the probability for this alternative to be the finally chosen one is greater than for other equally attractive alternatives, it does not mean that differentiation is always successful for the first preliminary choice. During the differentiation process, different facts and goals typically appear that may affect the status of the preliminary choice considerably. Thus, there are many factors that may lead to the rejection of a preliminary chosen alternative, such as new facts, partly different goals elicited during the process, and mappings of these goals changing during the decision process. If the preliminary choice alternative cannot remain the leading one, a new preliminary alternative or set of alternatives will have to be selected to move the decision process ahead.

Attractiveness restructuring may depend on the pattern of aspects in a decision problem. If, for example, the preliminary chosen alternative is initially far better on the most important attribute (e.g., costs), there is less of a need to consolidate on that attribute than if it is just barely superior. If the second most important attribute (e.g., comfort) also supports the chosen alternative then there is less of a need to consolidate than if it conflicts with the chosen option. If the attractiveness difference is already sufficient on the most important attribute (e.g., chosen alternative sufficiently cheaper) then there is room for attention to and consolidation of the second most important attribute (comfort).

The different decision rules included in Diff Con theory have not been listed in this chapter. This does not mean that they are not sufficient for reaching a decision, but that for reasons of brevity, the interested reader is referred to earlier presentations of the theory (Svenson, 1992), and earlier presentations of different decision rules (e.g., Svenson, 1979).

Waiting for the Environment to Decide

Hitherto the dynamics in Diff Con theory have concerned the application of decision rules and other processes, which, to at least some extent, have been driven by the decision maker her or himself. However, in most applied contexts decisions are made and implemented in dynamic environments.

This means that, over time, the decision problem changes due to ongoing systems dynamics including the effects of the implementation of a decision.

For example, the choice between bus and taxi may be postponed while the decision maker waits for the next bus. If the bus does not appear in time, the taxi alternative will become sufficiently differentiated by the dynamics of the environment (the attributes of arrival in time and comfort becoming sufficiently superior for the taxi alternative to balance out costs).

In fact, decision makers may avoid the responsibility and pain of differentiating alternatives that are rather similar in attractiveness through just waiting. In many cases there is a chance that facts appear and that a situation changes so that differentiation will be easier. In addition, waiting means that psychological processes may work towards further differentiation more or less by themselves, or through more or less conscious thinking about the postponed decision. Therefore, time gives an opportunity of both externally and internally driven differentiation.

The Role of Uncertainty in Diff Con Theory

Uncertainty or subjective probability concerning events and outcomes has been modeled as part of the attractiveness uncertainty (Svenson, 1992) or as an independent attribute in Diff Con theory (Svenson & Malmsten, 1996). However, uncertainty has not in itself been given such a prominent role as in expected value theories of decision making. Differentiation of this attribute in Diff Con theory can be related to, for example, wishful thinking (Cyert, Dill, & March, 1958; Slovic, 1966) and consolidation of the subjective probability attribute to the hindsight phenomenon (Fischhoff, 1975).

Uncertainty concerning future goals and attractiveness mappings are modeled in Diff Con theory as a component in differentiation and consolidation, beyond the point where one alternative is better that its closest competitor. To exemplify, Fischhoff, Slovic, and Lichtenstein (1980), Jungermann (1983), and Kahneman and Snell (1992) have treated the uncertainty of goals, present and future utilities in a decision theoretic framework, which relates to the use of attractiveness uncertainty in Diff Con theory.

Postdecision Consolidation

Following a decision, internal subjective processes continue to work on the prior decision. Thinking about an earlier decision involves feelings of regret, which may be related to factors such as the loss of a decision opportunity, loss of the good things of the rejected alternative, and a perhaps disturbing awareness of the bad things that were after all associated

with the chosen alternative but kept under control during the differentiation phase. The implementation of the decision may or may not be associated with negative consequences, so also the external environment may
lead to feelings of regret or contribute to consolidation. Subjective consolidation processes are active as responses to the above factors and to
create cognitively clear representations of the decision alternatives.

Postdecision consolidation processes can be classified according to the
following: (1) structural and rule postdecision consolidation, (2) implementation of decision, (3) post-implementation consolidation (structural and
rule) and monitoring of decision, (4) outcome of decision, and (5) post-out-
come consolidation (structural and rule) and monitoring of decision.

Postdecision consolidation is performed in processes similar to those in
the predecision phase. To repeat, after a decision the decision maker has
now lost the opportunity of choice, the unique good aspects of the rejected
alternative(s) are gone and she or he is stuck with the bad aspects of the
chosen alternative. This can create postdecision dissonance (cf. Festinger,
1964) or regret (Loomes & Sugden, 1982) that has to be managed psychologically and/or in the implementation phase.

As mentioned above, partly in response to these challenging threats,
predecision differentiation can be continued in what is now called postdecision consolidation. In some cases, in particular when decisions have
been quick and perhaps immature, postdecision consolidation supporting
the decision may be a late substitute for predecision processes (cf. Svenson,
1992). In addition, consolidation can be supported by (external) monitoring during the implementation stage and later.

Monitoring means that the decision maker acts to change the situation
so that he or she receives increased support for his or her prior decision.
In fact, this may imply a series of supporting decisions of the kind studied
in dynamic decision paradigms (Brehmer, 1992; Chapters 2, 3, and 4 of
the present volume).The same kinds of differentiation processes (holistic,
process, and structural) as presented in the predecision phase appear in
the postdecision consolidation phase also. However, some decision rules
such as the conjunctive rule may be less frequent after the decision than
before because of its predecisional screening character. Postdecision consolidation is important in strengthening a decision, forming it into a habit
and to develop a general strategy. Postdecision consolidation may be seen
as one important factor for explaining conservatism in people's behavior
such as food choices, travel mode choices, and other repeated decisions.

What Drives Differentiation and Consolidation Processes?

Differentiation processes are primarily driven by the need of reaching a
decision. But why should this decision process produce one alternative
that is sufficiently superior through application of the different ways of

differentiation presented above? Generally speaking, differentiation and consolidation can be seen as driven by at least two partly independent sets of component forces.

The first of these relates to the organization of psychological representations so that they conform with or approach earlier known or other simple cognitive structures or "gestalts." This set of components has been treated by different theorists, some of whom will be mentioned soon. The other set of component forces is related to a safety or stability motive and refers more clearly to the postdecision phase.

The first of the above-mentioned sets of driving factors is more related to a decision and how it is perceived at the moment. One way of looking at this is to relate any changes of the representation of decision alternatives to an initial representation, which is arousal driving and leads to dissonance reduction (Festinger, 1957). Empirical studies starting with Zanna and Cooper (1974) have shown that dissonant cognitions give rise to negative emotional arousal (cf. Eagly & Chaiken, 1993).

One way of reducing this negative emotional arousal is to restructure a decision problem so that the cognitive dissonance is eliminated (through applying a decision rule or restructuring the problem). Cooper and Fazio (1984) stated that dissonance was driven by negative consequences instead of inconsistency of cognitions. Harmon-Jones, Brehm, Greenberg, Simon, and Nelson (1996) showed that this is not necessary. According to Diff Con theory there is no need of negative consequences for differentiation and consolidation to take place.

Factors in the second group of driving factors are related to the safety and stability motives. The role of these factors is to avoid unnecessary effort to be spent on decision reversals and changes of implementation plans following a decision. As mentioned earlier, incentives to change a decision can originate in, for example, feelings of regret and unpredicted outcomes. Predecision differentiation positions the chosen alternative in as strong a position as needed or possible and consolidation processes defend the achieved degree of superiority of the chosen alternative after the decision.

Other factors in this set of driving factors can be related to more cognitive explanations (Bem, 1965, 1967) and to attribution theory (Kelley, 1967) and self-serving biases (Greenwald, 1980). Verplanken and Svenson (1997) have elaborated the possible effects of different kinds of involvement in a decision on differentiation and consolidation, thereby adding to the classification of motives behind differentiation and consolidation.

It is important to note that most of the research, including for example dissonance, which relates to Diff Con has been focused on restructuring. However, it must be pointed out that Diff Con also stresses the inevitable use of decision rules (associated with different kinds of information gathering patterns) as necessary means for reaching a decision and sufficient degrees of differentiation and consolidation. Thus, Diff Con theory is not a theory of restructuring only. Instead it is equally much a theory about rules, structures, and restructuring. In this way and some others it differs from dissonance theory.

Diff Con Theory and Cognitive Dissonance Theory

In the past, postdecision processes have most often been treated within the framework of Cognitive Dissonance theory (Festinger, 1957, 1964). Diff Con theory relates to the classic cognitive dissonance approach, but differs from it in several ways.

As mentioned above, Diff Con stresses the existence of different decision rules more than dissonance theory. One of the differences is that Diff Con represents decision alternatives by aspects on attributes. Classical dissonance theory used holistic evaluations (Festinger, 1964) or information about pros and cons of a chosen alternative (Frey, 1986). The importance or weight of each attribute has been shown to be an essential element of Diff Con theory, and this has no correspondence in most cognitive dissonance approaches.

The goal of a decision process is, through decision rules and if necessary restructuring, to create a sufficiently superior alternative in Diff Con. In the cognitive dissonance approach it is to create cognitive consistency. Diff Con originated from a decision theoretic approach and tends to treat predecision processes to a greater extent than cognitive dissonance research which originates from social psychology.

EMPIRICAL FINDINGS RELATING TO DIFF CON THEORY

The Paradigm and Some Key Studies

The following describes empirical work that concerns structural differentiation and consolidation only. Thus, the very interesting and important issue of which decision rules are active in this process will not be addressed other than in an indirect way. Other researchers, such as Beach (1990), have described decision making as consisting of different phases in which different types of identifiable rules are applied in the same way as asserted in Diff Con theory. Most of the studies of differentiation and consolidation peformed so far concern postdecision processes. However, some of the most important studies cover both pre- and postdecision processes.

In a prototypical experiment testing structural differentiation and consolidation, each alternative is characterized by aspects on attributes. The attributes may be selected by the decision maker him or her self as in Fig. 9.1, which gives the attributes characterizing two career alternatives (personnel organization and general psychology) according to a decision maker. Here, the aspects on the attributes are marked on evaluative scales from poor to good, used as measures of attractiveness. In order to follow the differentiation and consolidation processes in terms of restructuring, participants are asked to repeat the ratings on the scales at different points in time before and after the decision.

In an early study by Svenson and Benthorn (1992), participants were asked to make choices among alternatives, which belonged to areas of great interest to the participants (children aged 11 and 12 years). Diff Con theory predicts differentiation and consolidation of decisions that are important to the decision maker. The alternatives (e.g., computer games for the boys) were described by marks on scales for four attributes like those in Figure 9.1. An hour or a week later the participants were again confronted with their prior decisions, but now with empty attribute scales. They were asked to mark the attractiveness of the alternatives on the scales again, just as they were previously.

The results showed that for the average participant, the attractiveness values were changed so that on the most important attributes the support was greater for the chosen alternative in retrospect than it was at the time of decision. However, one week had to elapse before these effects became significant (Fig. 9.2). This experiment showed that, in order to detect an effect, interindividual differences had to be accounted for by sorting the attributes for each participant into a rank order of importance for the decision. Then all data from the most important attribute were first aggregated across participants and then for the second most important attribute, and so on.

If the data were analyzed according to labels (quality of picture, etc.), no results could be found. This was because each individual's decision

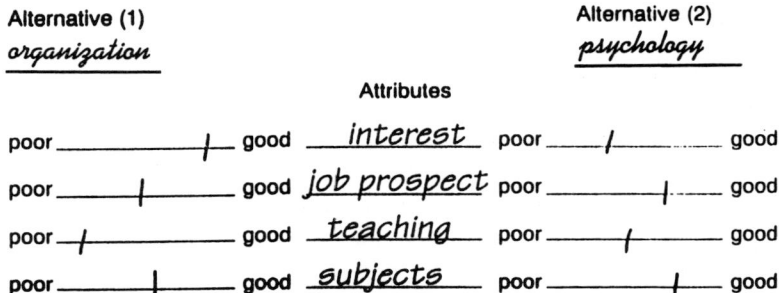

FIG. 9.1. An example of attractiveness representation.

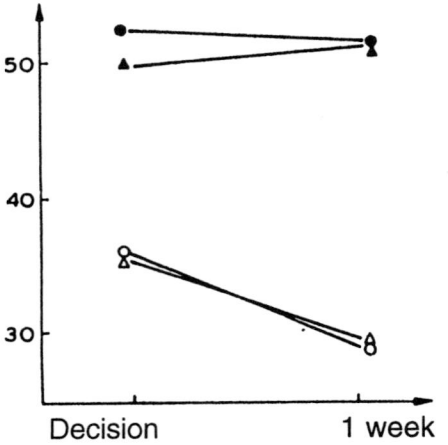

FIG. 9.2. Mean attractiveness ratings of chosen (filled symbols) and non-chosen (open symbols) alternatives on most attractive (circles) and second most important attractive (triangles) attributes. From Svenson and Benthorn (1992).

process was guided by order of importance of the attributes, but the order of importance differed across participants making the analysis of attributes according to their labels meaningless. This was elaborated further by Svenson (1996).

Diff Con theory predicts that increased involvement (for example, induced by a need of later justifying a decision) should increase differentiation and/or consolidation. This effect of increased involvement was assumed to be reflected in increased structural consolidation. Svenson, Ortega Rayo, Andersen, Sandberg, and Svahlin (1994) investigated this hypothesis. However, their experiments showed that an instruction to later justify a decision instead decreased postdecision consolidation. It seemed as if the decision makers were more cautious to remember the aspect values if they knew that they would later be asked to justify their prior decision. There was no test of process consolidation in terms of the decision rules applied, but in terms of structural consolidation the Diff Con prediction was clearly falsified. It was interesting to note that if participants were asked just to remember which alternative they had chosen, structural consolidation could be found.

So far, the studies only treated imagined choice alternatives involving memory reproduction. Diff Con theory predicts that involvement induced by real decision alternatives should induce differentiation and consolidation. It also predicts that the outcome of a decision should affect the consolidation processes following the outcome.

In a study by Svenson and Malmsten (1996), real decision alternatives (audiotape headset players) were used. Depending on the participants' decisions, headsets were also given to participants. Participants were children aged 11 and 12; they started the experiment by investigating the headsets. One of the headsets (blue) was cheaper and the other (red) was more expensive and of a higher quality. The decision was between which of two lotteries to go for, the lottery with the blue or the red headset as a prize. After having decided which lottery to go for the participants threw a dice. For the red lottery there was a 2 in 6 chance of getting a ticket and for the blue lottery a 3 in 6 chance of getting a ticket. So, participants who preferred the blue lottery took a smaller risk of not getting a ticket at all than those selecting the red lottery. For those who got a ticket in either lottery, the chance of winning a headset was the same for the red and the blue lotteries.

The results from this experiment are illustrative. Among those who went for the blue lottery, half of the participants won a lottery ticket and half lost. Figure 9.3 shows the results for the ticket-winning and ticket-losing groups respectively. It is clear that participants who won tickets for the blue headset restructured their attractiveness evaluations of the chosen (blue) headset in relation to the nonchosen one (red), after the outcome of the dice through (post in Fig. 9.3). For the winners, the blue headset that they had the chance of getting became superior to the more expensive red headset in the post measurements. For those who lost, the changes were not significant. So the results indicated that the preference order between two alternatives on the two most important attributes could be reversed depending on the outcome of a decision.

It was a surprise that the restructuring processes were so strong that they reversed the preference order among alternatives on the most important attributes in that experiment. However, it may be argued, the attributes were given to the participants and they only marked the attractiveness of

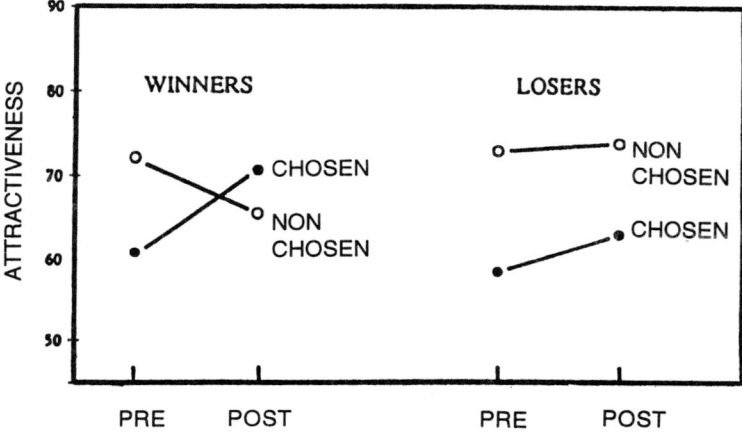

FIG. 9.3. Mean attractiveness ratings across two most important attributes of chosen (filled symbols) and non-chosen alternative (open symbols). From Svenson and Malmsten (1996).

aspects on those particular attributes. Therefore, it was decided to investigate attractiveness restructuring in a field experiment with real and involving decision alternatives that should be chosen by each individual participant him or herself. Of course, this would generate a great range of different attributes. This would imply great difficulties in the data analyses if they were planned to follow the labels signifying the meaning of an attribute. Fortunately, earlier research and Diff Con theory implies that the importance of an attribute is a more fruitful classification than the label. Therefore, the analyses in the following study were always conducted according to attribute importance.

Svenson and Hill (1997) followed adult students making decisions concerning which course to follow during the next academic year. The decisions were very important to the students as they gave competence for future careers. The decision makers were followed over a period of several months from before the decision and up to the time when the students started their course work. In this way both structural differentiation and consolidation could be studied.

The results showed that not all students differentiated and consolidated through restructuring of their attractiveness representations. However, participants who exposed a value conflict on one of their two most important attributes used attractiveness differentiation and consolidation. A value conflict was present when the chosen alternative was inferior on an important attribute. To exemplify, a student may chose an alternative that he finds less interesting than another alternative, but that has a greater chance of leading to a job. When the data were aggregated for the conflict attribute, the results showed that, not only was the conflict eliminated over time; the prior disadvantage on that attribute was turned into a sufficient advantage (Fig. 9.4).

Again, it is important to point out that only attractiveness restructuring was investigated. We know little or nothing from these experiments about process differentiation, decision rules used in differentiation and consolidation, and so forth. But it seems clear that for participants without a decision conflict, the restructuring differentiation and consolidation processes are not as strong as for participants with value conflicts. However, these processes should not be considered nonexistent. Svenson and Benthorn (1992) found that even dominating decision alternatives were consolidated after a decision increasing their superiority over the dominated alternative over time.

Summarizing Some of the Findings

The results from postdecision attractiveness restructuring consolidation processes have shown that (1) postdecision structural consolidation occurs regularly (Svenson & Benthorn, 1992; Svenson & Hill, 1997; Svenson et

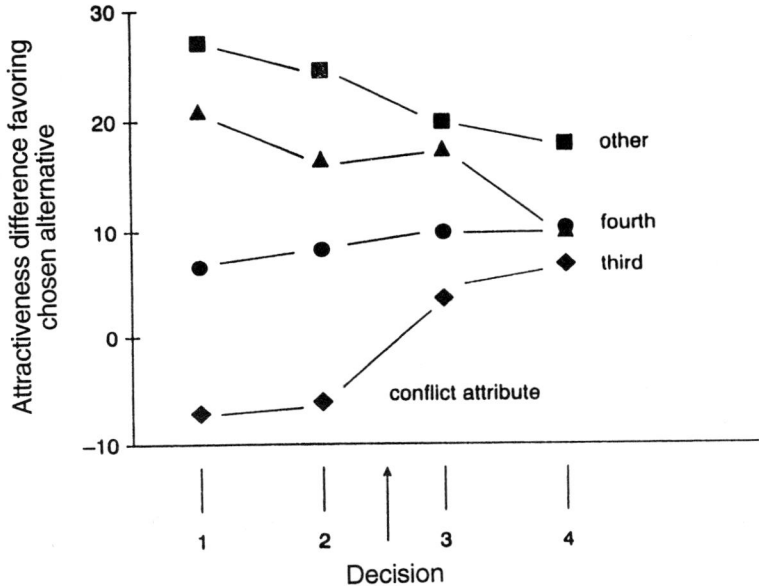

FIG. 9.4. Attractiveness advantage (difference) for chosen over non-chosen alternative over time. From Svenson and Hill (1997).

al., 1994); (2) participants differ in degree of importance ascribed to different attributes and that this difference must be used in the data analyses (Benthorn, 1994; Svenson, 1996); (3) aspects on the one and/or second most important attributes are predominantly used in postdecision consolidation; (4) uninteresting and noninvolving decision problems may not lead to postdecision consolidation, while interesting and more involving problems can (Benthorn, 1994; Svenson et al., 1994); (5) an increase in consolidation did not follow a need of postdecision justification (Svenson et al., 1994); (6) aspect attractiveness restructuring was much stronger than attribute importance restructuring (Malmsten, 1996; Svenson & Shamoun, 1997); and (7) decision outcome feedback speeds up postdecision consolidation processes and that the outcome affects the degree of consolidation (Svenson & Malmsten, 1996).

The results from experiments on differentiation structuring within the Diff Con paradigm have shown that (1) predecision differentiation occurs in particular when goal conflicts are reflected in the most important attributes; (2) analyses on the group level indicate that differentiation was performed through increasing the advantage on the conflict attribute and at the same time decreasing the advantage on an important already superior attribute; (3) the predecision differentiation processes were continued beyond the point of decision into the postdecision period; and (4) attractiveness restructuring was more prevalent than importance restructuring during the predecision period. Other studies in other contexts have illustrated predecision differentiation in terms of early rejection of several alternatives. This has been followed by selection of one preliminary choice alternative and processes, which can also be interpreted as reflecting differentiation (e.g., Bettman, Johnson, & Payne, 1991; Montgomery & Svenson, 1989; Russo et al., 1996; Svenson, 1974, 1979).

CONCLUDING COMMENTS

The preceding presentation has assumed that decision alternatives are represented in alternatives times attribute matrices. However, there are other competing ways of representing decision alternatives. One of these is a scenario-type script version (Beach, 1990). This means that participants use their imagination to run scenarios into the future representing different alternatives. This way of representing alternatives does not conflict with an alternative times attribute representation, but it may provide a better foundation for a model of decision processes in some cases.

The alternative times attribute representation seems to imply that, in principle, decision makers use each attribute for the evaluation of at least two alternatives. However, it is also possible to assume that some attributes are used for only one alternative and others for another alternative forcing compensatory thinking across attributes. To exemplify, a decision process between the alternatives of a divorce and of continuing a marriage may use the attributes of security and habit supporting the no-divorce alternative weighed against the aspects on the attributes of variety in life and pleasure supporting the divorce alternative. Again, this can be modeled straightforward in an alternative times attribute representation, but perhaps another representation could be intuitively more appealing for modeling the psychological processes taking place. It would be interesting to explore how Diff Con could be adopted to alternative representations of decision alternatives such as those exemplified above. However, as shown in this chapter, there is still a need for a great deal of research within the existing Diff Con representation of decision problems, such as explorations of decision rules in process differentiation and consolidation, using the alternative times attribute representation relied on in the present chapter.

ACKNOWLEDGMENT

This study was supported by grants from the Swedish Council for Research in the Humanities and Social Sciences and Royal Netherlands Academy of Arts and Sciences through a NIAS scholarship.

REFERENCES

Abelson, R. P., & Levi, A. (1985). Decision making and decision theory. In G. Lindzey & E. Aronson (Eds.), *Handbook of social psychology* (3rd ed, pp. 231–309). New York: Random House.

Beach, L. R. (1990). *Image theory: Decision making in personal and organizational contexts.* Chichester, England: Wiley.

Bem, D. J. (1965). An experimental analysis of self-persuation. *Journal of Experimental Social Psychology, 1,* 199–218.

Bem, D. J. (1967). Self perception: An alternative interpretation of cognitive dissonance phenomena. *Psychological Review, 74,* 183–200.

Benthorn, L. J. (1994). *On post-decision processes.* Doctoral dissertation, Published by Lund University, Lund, Sweden.

Bettman, J. R., Johnson, E. J., & Payne, J. W. (1991). Consumer decision making. In T. S. Robertson & H. H. Kassarjian (Eds.), *Handbook of consumer behavior.* Englewood Cliffs, NJ: Prentice-Hall.

Brehmer, B. (1992). Dynamic decision making: Human control of complex systems. *Acta Psychologica, 81,* 211–241.

Busemeyer, J. R., & Townsend, J. T. (1993). Decision Field theory: A dynamic-cognitive approach to decision making in uncertain environment. *Psychological Review, 100,* 432–459.

Cooper, J., & Fazio, R. H. (1984). A new look at dissonance theory. In L. Berkowitz (Ed.), *Advances in experimental social psychology* (Vol. 17, pp. 229–264). New York: Academic Press.

Coupey, E. (1994). Restructuring: Constructive processing of information displays in consumer choice. *Journal of Consumer Research, 21,* 83–99.

Cyert, R. M., Dill, W. T., & March, J. G. (1958). The role of expectations in business decision making. *Administrative Science Quarterly, 3,* 307–340.

Dembo, T. (1931). Der Ärger als dynamisches Problem. *Psychologische Forschung, 15,* 1–144.

Eagly, A. H., & Chaiken, S. (1993). *The psychology of attitudes.* New York: Harcourt Brace Jovanovich.

Estes, W. K. (1994). *Classification and cognition.* New York: Oxford University Press.

Festinger, L. (1957). *A theory of cognitive dissonance.* Stanford, CA: Stanford University Press.

Festinger, L. (1964). *Conflicts, decision and dissonance.* Stanford, CA: Stanford University Press.

Fischhoff, B. (1975). Hindsight is not equal to foresight: The effect of outcome knowledge on judgment under uncertainty. *Journal of Experimental Psychology: Human Perception and Performance, 1,* 288–299.

Fischhoff, B. (1996). The real world: What good is it? *Organizational Behavior and Human Decision Processes, 65,* 232–248.

Fischhoff, B., Slovic, P., & Lichtenstein, S. (1980). Knowing what you want: Measuring labile values. In T. Wallsten (Ed.), *Cognitive processes in choice and decision behavior* (pp. 64–85). Hillsdale, NJ: Lawrence Erlbaum Associates.

Frey, D. (1986). Recent research on selective exposure to information. In L. Berkowitz (Ed.), *Advances in experimental social psychology.* Vol. 19. New York: Academic Press.

Gärling, T. (1992). The importance of routines for the performance of everyday activities. *Scandinavian Journal of Psychology, 33,* 170–177.

Greenwald, A. G. (1980). The totalitarian ego: Fabrication and revision of personal history. *American Psychologist, 35,* 603–618.

Harmon-Jones, E., Brehm, J. W., Greenberg, J., Simon, L., & Nelson, D. E. (1996). Evidence that the production of aversive consequences is not necessary to create cognitive dissonance. *Journal of Personality and Social Psychology, 70,* 5–16.

Jungermann, H. (1983). The two camps on rationality. In R. W. Scholz (Ed.), *Decision making under uncertainty.* Amsterdam: North-Holland.

Kahneman, D., Knetsch, J. L., & Thaler, R. H. (1990). Experimental tests of the endowment effect and the Coase theorem. *Journal of Political Economy, 98,* 1325–1348.

Kahneman, D., & Snell, J. (1992). Predicting a changing taste: Do people know what they will like? *Journal of Behavioral Decision Making, 5,* 187–200.

Kahneman, D., & Tversky, A. (1979). Prospect theory: an analysis of decisions under risk. *Econometrica, 47,* 263–291.

Kelley, H. H. (1967). Attribution Theory in social psychology. In D. Levine (Ed.), *Nebraska Symposium on Motivation* (Vol. 15, 192–238). Lincoln: University of Nebraska Press.

Klein, G. A. (1989). Recognition—primed decisions. In W. B. Rouse (Ed.), *Advances in man—machine system research* (Vol. 5, pp. 47–92). Greenwich, CT: JAI.

Langer, E. (1994). The illusion of calculated decisions. In R. C. Schank & E. Langer (Eds.), *Beliefs, reasoning and decision making: Psycho-logic in honor of Bob Abelson.* Hillsdale, NJ: Lawrence Erlbaum Associates.

Loomes, G., & Sugden, R. (1982). Regret theory: An alternative theory of rational choice under

Malmsten, N. (1996). *Studies of post-decision processes.* Doctoral dissertation, Published by Stockholm University, Stockholm, Sweden.

Montgomery, H. (1983). Decision rules and the search for a dominance structure: Towards a process model of decision making. In P. C. Humphreys, O. Svenson, & A. Vari (Eds.), *Analyzing and aiding decision processes* (pp. 343–369). Amsterdam: North-Holland.

Montgomery, H., & Svenson, O. (1989). A think aloud study of dominance structuring in decision processes. In H. Montgomery & O. Svenson (Eds.), *Process and structure in human decision making.* Chichester, England: Wiley.

Ranyard, R. (1989). Structuring and evaluating simple monetary risks. In H. Montgomery & O. Svenson (Eds.), *Process and structure in human decision making.* Chichester, England: Wiley.

Russo, J. E., Medvec, V. H., & Meloy, M. G. (1996). The distortion of information during decisions. *Organizational Behavior and Human Decision Processes, 66,* 102–110.

Samuelson, W., & Zeckhauser, R. (1988). Status quo bias in decision making. *Journal of Risk and Uncertainty, 1,* 7–59.

Schweitzer, M. (1994). Distentangling status quo and omission effects: An experimental analysis. *Organizational Behavior and Human Decision Processes, 58,* 457–476.

Shafir, E. (1993). Choosing versus rejecting: Why some options are both better and worse than others. *Memory & Cognition, 21,* 546–556.

Shafir, E., & Tversky, A. (1992). Thinking through uncertainty: Nonconsequential reasoning and choice. *Cognitive Psychology, 24,* 449–474.

Shiffrin, R. M., & Schneider, W. (1977). Controlled and automatic human information processing: II. Perceptual learning, automatic attending, and a general theory. *Psychological Review, 84,* 127–190.

Slovic, P. (1966). Value as a determiner of subjective probability. *IEEE Transactions on Human Factors in Electronics,* vol. HFE-7 (pp. 22–28).

Smith, E. R. (1992). The role of exemplars in social judgment. In L. L. Martin & . Tesser (Eds.), *The construction of social judgments.* Hillsdale, NJ: Lawrence Erlbaum Associates.

Svenson, O. (1974). A note on think aloud protocols obtained during the choice of a home. *Reports from the Psychological Laboratories.* Stockholm University No. 421, Stockholm, Sweden.

Svenson, O. (1979). Process descriptions of decision making. *Organizational Behavior and Human performance, 23,* 86–112.

Svenson, O. (1990). Some propositions for the classification of decision situations. In K. Borcherding, O. I. Larichev, & D. M. Messich (Eds.), *Contemporary issues in decision making.* Amsterdam: Elsevier.

Svenson, O. (1992). Differentiation and consolidation theory of human decision making: A frame of reference for the study of pre- and post decision processes. *Acta Psychologica, 80,* 143–168.

Svenson, O. (1996). Decision making and the search for psychological regularities: What can be learned from a process perspective? *Organizational Behavior and Human Decision Processes, 65,* 252–267.

Svenson, O., & Benthorn, L. J. (1992). Consolidation processes in decision making: Post-decision changes in attractiveness of alternatives. *Journal of Economic Psychology, 13,* 315–327.

Svenson, O., & Hill, T. (1997). Turning prior disadvantages into advantages: Differentiation and consolidation in real-life decision making. In R. Ranyard, W. R. Crozier, & O. Svenson, *Decision making: Cognitive models and explanations* (pp. 218–232). London: Routledge.

Svenson, O., & Malmsten, N. (1996). Post-decision consolidation overtime as a function of gain or loss of an alternative. *Scandinavian Journal of Psychology, 37,* 302–311.

Svenson, O., & Ortega Rayo, A., Andersen, M., Sandberg, A., & Svahlin, L. (1994). Post-decision consolidation as a function of instruction to the decision maker and decision problem. *Acta Psychologica, 87,* 181–197.

Svenson, O., & Shamoun, S. (1997). Predecision conflict and different patterns of postdecision attractiveness restructuring: empirical illustrations from an important real-life decision. *Scandinavian Journal of Psychology, 38,* 243–251.

Tversky, A., & Kahneman, D. (1992). Advances in prospect theory: Cumulative representation of uncertainty. *Journal of Risk and Uncertainty, 5,* 297–323.

Verplanken, B., & Svenson, O. (1997). Personal involvement in human decision making: Conceptualisations and effects on decision processes. In R. Ranyard, W. R. Crozier, & O. Svenson (Eds.), *Decision making: Cognitive models and explanations* (pp. 40–57). London: Routledge.

Zajonc, R. B. (1980). Feelings and thinking: Preferences need no inferences. *American Psychologist, 35,* 151–175.

Zanna, M. P., & Cooper, J. (1974). Dissonance and the pill: An attribution approach to studying the arousal properties of dissonance. *Journal of Personality and Social Psychology, 29,* 703–709.

Chapter 10

The Role of Mental Accounting in Everyday Economic Decision Making

Tommy Gärling
Niklas Karlsson
Marcus Selart
Göteborg University

How people make economic decisions with the aim of managing scarce resources, primarily of money but also of time and effort, is an ecologically valid topic that has been a focus of economic psychology (Wärneryd, 1988), although largely neglected in psychological research on judgment and decision making. In fact, almost every day people face economic decisions concerning earning, spending, and saving money. A ubiquitous aspect of such decisions is that they entail choices between immediate and deferred consumption. Examples are ample: Should I spend money on a nice evening at a restaurant now, or should I save the money for my vacation next summer? Because I have the opportunity to buy an attractive CD player, should I buy it now even though it is likely that I will need the money in the future for repairing my aging washing machine? Apparently, choosing an immediate attractive outcome may be a threat to future well-being, or, to put it differently, not choosing an immediate outcome is a sacrifice that will pay off later.

When making choices between outcomes occurring at different points in time such as between immediate and deferred consumption, people must perform value comparisons taking into account at which time in the future the outcomes occur. Such comparisons are difficult, because people's cognitive capacity in evaluating future events may be limited. In a major conceptual analysis of decision making, risk taking, and psychological time, Björkman (1984) notes that although the concept of "expected utility" (implying a time interval between the choice of an alternative and the outcome of the choice) has been central in decision making research, the time dimension has somewhat paradoxically not been extensively investigated.

Choices between outcomes at different points in time have often been referred to as intertemporal in the literature. A closely related issue is how people exert self-control. Exerting self-control may be necessary to overcome the benefits of an immediate outcome in favor of more farsighted preferences. Shefrin and Thaler (1988, 1992) proposed that the use of mental accounts is a strategy of self-control, applicable to choices between immediate and deferred consumption.

In this chapter we first briefly review previous research on intertemporal choice and self-control. Second, we introduce the concept of mental accounting and show how it may constitute a strategy of self-control. Third, we report an attempt to replicate the study by Shefrin and Thaler (1988) aimed at demonstrating how the process of decomposing wealth in mental accounts affects expected future consumption. Fourth, we outline how mental accounting theory and alternative theories may explain how temporary income changes influence specific buying decisions. Such decisions between immediate and deferred consumption highlights the role of mental accounting as a self-control strategy. Finally, we present the results of a study that tests predictions from the different theories.

INTERTEMPORAL CHOICE AND SELF-CONTROL

In most decisions, consequences or outcomes are not immediate but occur in the future. Therefore, decision makers frequently need to choose between alternatives with outcomes occurring at different points in time, thereby engaging themselves in intertemporal choice. In the middle of the last century economists like Rae, Senior, and Jevons addressed the question of why people discount the future, in order to understand relations between surplus product, capital, and interest (Loewenstein, 1992). In their analyses these early economists saw emotional factors as contributing to the discounting of the future: Rae and Senior mainly in terms of psychological discomfort of deferring consumption, and Jevons in terms of hedonic influence of the thought of future consumption diminishing with time. At the turn of the century, Böhm-Bawerk and Fischer conceptualized intertemporal choice in more motivational and cognitive terms. Thus, as Björkman (1984) did, they attributed discounting to people's lack of willingness and ability to imagine the future.

In the discounted utility model proposed by Samuelson (1937) and Koopmans (1960) psychological content disappeared or was disguised. The model has been the dominating account in economics of how intertemporal choices are made. According to this model, people compare present values of future outcomes by applying fixed discount rates. A basic assumption is that preferences for two alternatives only depend on the absolute time interval separating them (Koopmans, 1960; Loewenstein & Prelec, 1992), a property that is labeled stationarity. However, as first noted by Strotz (1956), people are often inconsistent and may reverse their preferences, although the absolute time difference between the occurrences of two outcomes are constant while both outcomes are postponed. For example, a person may prefer one apple today to two apples tomorrow but at the same time prefer two apples after 10 days to one apple after 9 days. Prelec and Loewenstein (1991) labeled this violation of the stationarity property the common difference effect. The effect has been demonstrated in several studies on human participants (Benzion, Rapoport, & Yagil, 1989; Thaler, 1981) as well as in animal studies (Ainslie, 1975).

Ainslie (1975) argued that assuming a reversal of preference is necessary to understand why people (and animals) may be both impulsive and exert impulse control. If not, people would be consistent in their preference for either the immediate or the distant outcome, and they would not need to exert self-control to overcome a preference for an immediate outcome. Ainslie (1975; Ainslie & Haslam, 1992a) and others (Chung & Herrnstein, 1967; Herrnstein, 1961; Loewenstein & Prelec, 1992) proposed a hyperbolic discount function to replace the exponential function in the discounted utility model. Such a more deeply curved function appears to account for a large body of empirical data in animal and human time-discounting. A suggested interpretation of the common difference effect is that a larger risk is associated with a larger delay (Benzion et al., 1989; Keren & Roelofsma, 1995). The risk and uncertainty associated with delayed outcomes is assumed to be an important factor determining the shape of the discount function. However, others (e.g., Rachlin & Siegel, 1994) have argued that discounting is the elementary process that underlies uncertainty. What may be concluded is that evidence suggests that time delay and uncertainty are related.

A different perspective on why people have time-inconsistent preferences is offered by Loewenstein (1996). He argues that the immediate experience of visceral factors, such as drive states, moods or emotions, and physical pain have disproportionately large effects on behavior and tend to dominate the importance of more farsighted goals or preferences. Moreover, people appear to be unable to anticipate the impact of visceral factors on future behavior.

In recent research on intertemporal choice, there are a number of findings in addition to the common difference effect that are inconsistent with the discounted utility model (Prelec & Loewenstein, 1991; Loewenstein & Prelec, 1992). Such reported inconsistencies are: less proportional discounting for large than for small dollar amounts (Thaler, 1980); asymmetric preferences between delaying and speeding up rewards (or consumption) (Loewenstein, 1988; Loewenstein & Prelec, 1992); and asymmetries between the discounting of gains and losses (Benzion et al., 1989; Prelec & Loewenstein, 1991; Shelly, 1993, 1994; Thaler, 1980).

A vast majority of studies of intertemporal choice have investigated how single future outcomes are discounted. More recently the question has been raised concerning whether or not multiple outcomes are also subject to time discounting. In fact, a reported finding is that sequences of outcomes occurring in the future are not discounted (Loewenstein & Prelec, 1993; Stevenson, 1993). According to Loewenstein and Prelec (1993), people tend to prefer sequences of outcomes that improve over time and are also motivated by a desire to spread consumption evenly over time. An unresolved intriguing question that arises from the differences in discounting of single and sequences of outcomes is, When is an outcome considered to be single or included as part of a sequence?

A general conclusion is that in intertemporal choice people have time-inconsistent preferences. Such inconsistencies are not something that people necessarily are unaware of. Quite to the contrary, people often adopt different self-control strategies in order to counteract inconsistent preferences. Self-control typically involves efforts to resist temporary or shorter-term preferences in order to achieve longer-term preferences. Mischel and collaborators (Mischel, Cantor, & Feldman, 1997; Mischel, Shoda, & Rodriguez, 1992) have investigated individual differences and underlying psychological processes in delay of gratification in children. In a large number of studies in which children would receive a superior reward if they were able to wait, it was found that factors like attention to the reward, distractions, and cognitive representations of the reward (e.g., thinking of a chocolate-bar reward in terms of a good-tasting snack or a "brown rectangular box") affected the children's ability to delay gratification.

Ainslie and Haslam (1992b) distinguished between four basic ways of exercising self-control: extrapsychic mechanisms, control of attention, preparation of emotion, and formulating personal rules. Hoch and Loewenstein (1991) modeled self-control as a struggle between two psychological forces: desire and willpower. A shorter-term preference may by its proximity in time increase the desire relative to a longer-term preference. However, increased willpower works in the opposite direction by attempting to overcome such temporarily increased desires for a shorter-term preference. Two general classes of self-control strategies were proposed by Hoch and Loewenstein (1991): those that reduce desire and those that overcome desire through willpower. Examples of desire-reducing self-control strategies are avoidance of situations that are likely to increase desire, postponement of choice until some future date, and distraction (e.g., thinking about something else), which may both reduce desire for a shorter-term preference and decrease frustration of waiting for a longer-term preference. Examples of self-control strategies induced by willpower are precommitments—for instance, imposing constraints on future behavior either through external means or internal means such as personal rules or economic cost assessment that make obvious the advantage of a longer-term preference. The classification of self-control strategies by Ainslie and Haslam (1992b) bears a close resemblance to the classification by Hoch and Loewenstein (1991). Control of attention and preparation of emotion may be subsumed under desire-reduction strategies, whereas extrapsychic mechanisms and personal rules may be subsumed under willpower strategies.

The evidence thus suggest that people have time-inconsistent preferences, and that they are both driven by the temptation to achieve immediate preferences and to exert self-control with the goal of achieving longer-term preferences. Both desire-reduction and willpower as strategies for self-control aim at overcoming the temptation of immediate consumption of a specific object or in a specific situation. The decomposition of wealth and the constraining of consumption through the use of mental accounts (Shefrin & Thaler, 1988, 1992) however, may serve as a self-control strategy at a more general level, as it is not formed in relation to a specific situation or object. Mental accounting may therefore be of particular interest to investigate.

MENTAL ACCOUNTING

How people cognitively describe decision outcomes is the focus of much judgment and decision-making research (Gärling, Karlsson, Romanus, & Selart, 1997). In this context mental accounting refers to a process of categorizing outcomes (Henderson & Peterson, 1992; Tversky & Kahneman, 1981). The concept of the mental account was introduced by Thaler (1980, 1985) and Tversky and Kahneman (1981; Kahneman & Tversky, 1984). Tversky and Kahneman (1981, p. 456) defined a mental account as "an outcome frame which specifies (i) the set of elementary outcomes that are evaluated jointly and the manner in which they are combined, and (ii) a reference outcome that is considered neutral or normal." As an empirical example, in presenting different scenarios to participants Tversky and Kahneman (1981) found that a larger percentage of participants would buy a new theater ticket if they had lost the equivalent amount of money as compared to the percentage of participants that would replace a lost theater ticket. As an explanation of these results, they suggested that participants evaluated the loss of the ticket and the price of a new ticket in the same mental account while the loss of money and the price of a ticket were evaluated separately.

In Tversky and Kahneman (1981) the coding of outcomes in mental accounts is specific to the decision to be made. It should be contrasted to the mental accounts referred to by Shefrin and Thaler (1988, 1992) in their behavioral life-cycle theory, which instead are a priori held mental accounts that are part of people's financial knowledge and therefore presumably higher-order, more stable cognitive structures (Ranyard, 1995). Specifically, Shefrin and Thaler (1988, 1992) used mental accounting as a description of how people categorize and impose restrictions on monetary assets. According to this theory, people categorize monetary assets in three mental accounts: current income, current assets, and future income. Shefrin and Thaler did not argue that these three accounts are exhaustive, but that they are the most basic and general ones. The current asset account may, for instance, be divided into subaccounts, and different households may use different subaccounts. Such subaccounts may for instance be to have assets for special goals, as holiday money or money for clothings. In a study of Japanese housewives, Kojima and Hama (1982) found evidence for the decomposition of wealth in nine different mental accounts (or "psychological purses" as they were labeled).

The behavioral life-cycle theory was proposed as a psychologically more plausible alternative to Modigliani and Brumberg's Nobel-prizewinning life-cycle theory of saving behavior (1954) and the related permanent income hypothesis (Friedman, 1957). According to the life-cycle theory, people strive toward uniform consumption during the life cycle, which implies that they take loans when their income is low and expected to be higher in the future, and that they save when their income is higher than expected. Empirical observations have however indicated that current income may be a more important factor than the theory predicts, and that middle-age households have a higher degree of consumption than younger and older households (Courant, Gramlich, & Laitner, 1986).

Since current assets, current income, and future income in the behavioral life-cycle theory correspond to actual accounts, one may question what is gained by labeling them *mental* accounts. An important reason is the implication that mental accounts psychologically induce constraints on the use of money. Thus it is implied that mental accounts are self-control devices. Above we noted that desire-reduction and increasing willpower aim at overcoming the temptation of immediate consumption of a specific object or in a specific situation. The use of mental accounts (Shefrin & Thaler, 1988, 1992) is assumed to serve as a self-control strategy at a more general level by imposing constraints on money. Because it is not formed in relation to a specific situation or object, the use of mental accounts is particularly well suited to explain findings concerning patterns of consumption and saving across the life cycle.

Shefrin and Thaler (1988) referred to the internal conflict, within an individual, between short-term and long-term preferences as a conflict between a planner and a doer. The planner is assumed to be farsighted and to strive toward maximization of life-long utility, while the coexisting doer is assumed to be myopic and impulsive, striving towards maximization of immediate utility. In order to satisfy long-term preferences, it is necessary to adopt self-control. Because pure willpower is seen as very costly, people are assumed to seek other strategies to achieve self-control. The decomposition of wealth in mental accounts may be one such strategy that work in the direction of achieving also long-term preferences. The marginal propensity to consume from the three different mental accounts is assumed to decrease from current income to current assets and from the latter to future income. That is, the temptation to spend money on consumption is expected to be greatest from the current income account, next greatest from the current assets account, and least from the future income account. It should be noted that this is in sharp contrast to the life-cycle theory (Modigliani & Brumberg, 1954), which assumes that money from different accounts (or in different asset positions) is completely exchangeable (termed the principle of fungibility of money). In fact, existing data (Courant, Gramlich, & Laitner, 1986) are more consistent with the alternative theory in showing that consumption is more dependent on current income than expected. Furthermore, there is a greater than expected resistance to spread out consumption evenly over the life cycle by borrowing and using savings. Both these observations are clearly predicted from the use of mental accounts.

The behavioral life-cycle theory and the concept of mental accounts bring new light on how people make intertemporal choices. It does not primarily explain why people show time-inconsistent preferences but highlights that they often do this in relation to how they view their economic situation. In the following we will empirically explore the assumption that people vary in how tempted they are to consume immediately rather than deferring consumption depending on in which mental account money is available.

FUTURE CONSUMPTION EXPECTATIONS: A PARTIAL REPLICATION

In lack of any direct test of the hypothesis that the propensity to consume differs across the three mental accounts current income, current assets, and future income, Shefrin and Thaler (1988) conducted a survey with MBA students as participants. All participants were asked to estimate how much they expected that their consumption would increase during the following year if they received a windfall of $2400. The questions differed with regard to when the windfall was received and how it was split. Shefrin and Thaler obtained support for their hypothesis in that the expectation to consume was greater when the windfall came in increments of $200 per month (current income) than when it came immediately as a lump sum (current assets), and in that the expectation to consume was smallest when the windfall came as a lump sum in the future (future income). The median amounts participants expected to consume were $1200, $785, and $0, respectively. Recently, Selart, Karlsson, and Gärling (1997) attempted to replicate these results. Another objective of the study was to extend the findings to expected consumption in response to temporary income *decreases.*

As discussed above, a central assumption in the study of intertemporal choice is that when an outcome occurs is important for the decision. In the study by Shefrin and Thaler (1988), participants were asked to indicate changes in their expected future consumption during a year—that is, consumption spread out over a period of time. Furthermore, when receiving a windfall as increments per month or as a future lump sum, participants were asked to imagine and evaluate outcomes that occur in the future. Hence, drawing on empirical results on intertemporal choice (e.g., Loewenstein & Prelec, 1992), different predictions than those made by Shefrin and Thaler are possible to make. If people discount future benefits, they may expect to increase consumption more when an increase in income is received immediately as a lump sum than when it is received as increments per month. Likewise, they may expect to increase consumption more when receiving an income increase as increments per month than when receiving a lump sum in the more distant future.

A new feature of the Selart et al. (1997) study was that the questions asked by Shefrin and Thaler (1988) were repeated for income decreases. It is not clear which predictions the behavioral life-cycle theory would make in this case. However, in accordance with the results concerning how future outcomes are discounted (Loewenstein & Prelec, 1992), it was predicted that the expectation to cut down on consumption when facing an income decrease (monetary loss) should be less when it came in decrements per month than when it came immediately in a lump sum. Expected consumption was also predicted to be less when the monetary loss came as a future lump sum than when it came in decrements per month. Thus, participants were expected to adjust the least to future outcomes.

According to prospect theory (Kahneman & Tversky, 1979; Tversky & Kahneman, 1991), a general characteristic of how people evaluate outcomes is loss aversion; that is, losses loom larger than gains. It was therefore expected that people to a larger extent would adjust consumption to income decreases than to income increases. Several studies of intertemporal choice have reported asymmetries between the discounting of gains and losses (Benzion et al., 1989; Prelec & Loewenstein, 1991; Shelly, 1993, 1994; Thaler, 1980). However, because both heavier discounting of gains than losses and heavier discounting of losses than gains have been documented in different studies, it was difficult to make unambiguous predictions based on asymmetries between the discounting of losses and gains.

In summary, we wanted to further test the validity of the hypothesis that people, because they categorize wealth in mental accounts, expect to consume more after a wealth increase that come as increments per month than an increase that come immediately as a lump sum, and that they expect to consume less if the increase come as a lump sum in the future (Selart et al., 1997). Because outcomes occur at different points in time, alternative predictions are however possible to make based on the notion of discounting of future outcomes. These predictions are applicable to both wealth increases and decreases. It is predicted that people expect to adjust their consumption more if a wealth change come immediately as a lump sum than if it come as increments or decrements per month, and that they expect to adjust the least if it come in the more distant future.

Using the same question format as the survey of Shefrin and Thaler (1988), respondents were asked to estimate how much they expected to change their consumption if they received a temporary income change. In three account-specific versions of the question, the income change was framed as coming immediately as a lump sum, as increments (or decrements) per month during a year, or as a lump sum with interest in 12 months. For one group of participants the income change was framed as an income increase and for another group as an income decrease. The income increases (in Swedish krona) were either 12000 ($1700) or 6000 ($850), the income decreases either 6000 ($850) or 3000 ($425).

The data sets consisted of usable responses from 996 participants in a Swedish nationwide random sample (response rate close to 50%) and 277 participants (response rate 58%) in a random sample of students at Göteborg University. In particular in the nationwide sample, a large proportion of participants reported that they did not expect to change their consumption. Of those participants who did, without exceptions those asked to imagine that they had received income increases expected to increase consumption whereas those asked to imagine that they had received income decreases expected to decrease consumption. Because the distributions of the estimates were positively and negatively skewed respectively, the estimates were recoded as adjustments (increases or decreases) of consumption. The mean proportions are given in Table 10.1 for each income change condition and sample. As may be seen, in both samples the participants expected to make most adjustment when an income increase came immediately as a lump sum (current assets) and not in increments per month (current income). Furthermore, participants expected to make the least adjustments when the income increase came in a future lump sum (future income). These results are in line with the alternative predictions based on previous research on discounting of future outcomes. Thus, the results obtained by Shefrin and Thaler (1988) were not replicated. However, they were replicated for the median estimates made by

TABLE 10.1
Mean Proportions of Adjustment to Income Changes in the Nationwide and Student Sample Related
to Income Change and Mental Account

	Income Increase						Income Decrease					
	$1,700/year			$850/year			$850/year			$425/year		
Sample	I	A	F	I	A	F	I	A	F	I	A	F
Nationwide	.46	.55	.13	.40	.53	.10	.64	.77	.72	.42	.68	.57
Student	.84	.82	.20	.61	.79	.15	.61	.76	.71	.63	.80	.75

Note. I denotes an income change coded as current income; A an income change coded as current assets; and F an income coded as future income

the student sample (note that Shefrin and Thaler only reported median estimates and collected data for students). The results were different for income decreases. In both samples participants expected to adjust consumption less when the income decrease came as decrements per month than when it came as an immediate and a future lump sum. These results are partially accounted for by the notion of discounting of future outcomes. As expected, in line with loss aversion, adjustments of consumption were larger for an income decrease than an income increase.

In conclusion, the results of our study failed to replicate the results of Shefrin and Thaler (1988). Additionally, we found that respondents had different expectations about future consumption when the questions were asked for income decreases. The questions in our study as well as in Shefrin and Thaler referred to outcomes occurring at different times in the future. A plausible reason for the lack of support for the use of mental accounts may therefore be that the willingness to consume from different mental accounts were confounded with the motivation to discount future outcomes. Supporting this, the results were in some respects better accounted for by theories of intertemporal choice (Loewenstein & Prelec, 1992).

EFFECTS OF INCOME CHANGES
ON BUYING DECISIONS

Although ongoing mental accounts have attracted research interest (Heath, 1995; Hirst, Joyce, & Schadewald, 1994; Selart et al., 1997; Shefrin & Thaler, 1988, 1992; Thaler, 1990; Winett & Lewis, 1995), the impact they are predicted to have on specific economic decisions such as buying rather than on general consumption expectations has not been investigated. Yet the decomposition of wealth by means of use of mental accounts should have such an impact. The use of mental accounts in specific buying decisions rather than in general expectations of future consumption may in fact make mental accounting more apparent as a strategy of self-control. That is, the internal conflict between immediate or deferred consumption may be more salient in a buying decision. The choice of immediate consumption may therefore be more likely when using current income after having experienced a temporary income increase than when having to use current assets after a temporary income decrease, although total assets are equal in the two cases. In this way the categorization of wealth in mental accounts may serve as an explanation of how and why temporary income changes influence buying decisions. There are however also other suggested explanations of how and why a prior outcome (such as an income change) may influence choices.

Despite that most research on decision making has focused on isolated decisions, there are several occasions in everyday life in which decisions or outcomes depend on each other. Such interrelated decisions may be labeled sequential. A number of findings have been reported on this topic, including effects of prior outcomes on subsequent choices, escalation, and sunk cost effects (see, e.g., Gärling et al., 1997, for a review).

An assumption made in prospect theory (Kahneman & Tversky, 1979; Tversky & Kahneman, 1991, 1992) is that prospects or options are edited, that is, they are organized and reformulated in order to simplify evaluation and choice. Such editing operations include integration or segregation of prior outcomes.

Thaler and Johnson (1990) proposed a hedonic editing model to account for and specify when outcomes are integrated or segregated. The basic assumption in this model is that people edit outcomes so as to maximize the quality of their hedonic experiences (i.e., to maximize value). The hedonic editing model is thus a normative theory and Thaler and Johnson (1990) note that it is therefore likely to fail since it does not consider cognitive constraints. They argue, however, that it provides a point of comparison for other models. Two events or outcomes (x and y) are said to be integrated if they are combined before being subjectively evaluated (i.e., $v(x, y) = v(x + y)$) and to be segregated if they are evaluated separately (i.e., $v(x, y) = v(x) + v(y)$) (Thaler, 1985). If we assume that outcomes are evaluated in accordance with prospect theory (Kahneman & Tversky, 1979), integration or segregation matters because different evaluations will result. Because the value function in prospect theory is nonlinear and steeper for losses than for gains, it will be generally true that $v(x + y) \neq v(x) + v(y)$. Given the value function in prospect theory, people who maximize value are assumed to segregate gains, integrate losses, integrate smaller losses with larger gains, and segregate smaller gains from larger losses. In empirically testing the model by, for instance, asking participants how much a loss would hurt after that they had incurred another loss, Thaler and Johnson only found partial support for their predictions. In disagreement with the prediction, it was however shown that people preferred to segregate rather than integrate losses.

Linville and Fischer (1991) offered the renewable resources model as an alternative account of integration or segregation of outcomes. In addition to assuming that outcomes are evaluated in accordance with the value function in prospect theory, people are assumed to possess limited but renewable resources to cope with both positive and negative outcomes. According to the model, people are therefore expected to segregate two positive outcomes, segregate two negative outcomes, and integrate one positive and one negative outcome. By asking participants whether they preferred two emotionally significant events to occur on the same day (integration) or on different days (segregation), Linville and Fisher (1991) obtained support for their model. The same general pattern of results (segregation of two positive events and of two negative events, integration of one positive and one negative event) were found within three different domains: academic (successes or failures on exams), financial (monetary losses or gains), and social (positive or negative encounters with people).

Both the hedonic editing and the renewable resources model assume that people are integrating or segregating outcomes with the goal of maximizing value. A decision maker may, however, often be more concerned about avoiding negative outcomes than to attain positive ones (Larrick, 1993). It has also been found that anticipated negative events receive larger attention and are processed more comprehensively than positive ones (Peeters & Czapinski, 1990; Taylor, 1991). Drawing on these generalizations, Gärling and Romanus (1997) proposed an alternative account of when and why outcomes are integrated or segregated, called the loss-sensitivity principle. Assuming, as in the hedonic editing model and renewable resources model, that outcomes are evaluated in accordance with prospect theory, the main difference from these models stems from the notion of avoiding negative outcomes rather than attaining positive ones. This notion of motivational shift implies, according to the loss-sensitivity principle, that prior outcomes are only integrated with expected losses. In a series of experiments (Gärling & Romanus, 1997; Gärling, Romanus, & Selart, 1994; Romanus, Hassing, & Gärling, 1996; Romanus, Karlsson, & Gärling, 1997), the loss-sensitivity principle was tested by asking participants to indicate their satisfaction with the possible outcomes of a gamble after having experienced a prior loss, a prior gain, or no prior outcome. In line with the hypothesis, prior outcomes only influenced satisfaction with an expected loss, with increased satisfaction after a gain and decreased satisfaction after a loss compared to after no outcome.

CONFIRMING EVIDENCE

The primary aim of an experiment we have conducted was to investigate how temporary income increases and decreases affect choices between immediate and deferred consumption. Unless such temporary income changes modify wealth or total assets, it should not influence choice according to normative decision theory (von Neuman & Morgenstern, 1947; Savage, 1954). Although we failed to replicate the support Shefrin and Thaler (1988) obtained for the use of mental accounts in people's expectations of future consumption, the use of mental accounts may still be a valid component in their everyday economic decisions such as decisions to buy. A possible reason for the lack of support in the study of people's expectations of future consumption is that the money were available in the mental accounts at different points in time. Hence, the willingness to consume from different mental accounts were confounded with the discounting of future outcomes. This is not the case in specific buying decisions. In the experiment we therefore aimed at investigating the validity of the behavioral life-cycle theory (Shefrin & Thaler, 1988) as an explanation of how and why temporary income changes influence specific buying decisions. Predictions from the behavioral life-cycle theory were contrasted to predictions from the renewable resources model (Linville & Fischer, 1991) and the loss-sensitivity principle (Gärling & Romanus, 1997). In the two latter theories it is assumed that the buying decision depends on the context of the buying situation (i.e., whether buying is perceived as positive or negative).

According to Shefrin and Thaler (1988, 1992) people decompose wealth into different mental accounts (i.e., current income, current assets, and future income) for which the propensity to consume differs. A temporary income change may result in that money for consumption has to be taken from different mental accounts, and thus should have an influence on a buying decision. It is expected that the propensity to consume is greater from current income than from current assets. An income increase is therefore predicted to increase the likelihood of choosing to buy. The reverse is expected for an income decrease if it implies that saved money must be used. Whether buying is positive or negative should have no effect.

Unlike the prediction from the behavioral life-cycle theory, the buying situation is expected to be a determining factor in the renewable resources model. Buying may psychologically constitute a positive or negative event. For instance, buying a new attractive model of a consumer product may be perceived to be positive, whereas replacing a broken product may be perceived to be negative or at least less positive than buying a new model. As noted above, Linville and Fisher (1991) received empirical support for the renewable resources model in showing that participants segregated two positive events (gain savoring), segregated two negative events (multiple loss aversion), and integrated a positive and a negative event (loss buffering). Hence, whether buying is perceived as positive or negative will, according to the renewable resources model, result in different effects of a temporary income increase (assumed to be positive) and a temporary income decrease (assumed to be negative) on the propensity to consume. If buying is perceived as positive, the renewable resources model predicts that participants will be more likely to defer consumption when receiving an income increase due to their preference to segregate two positive events. In contrast, participants are expected to be more likely to buy immediately when faced with an income decrease due to their preference to integrate a positive and a negative event. If buying is viewed as negative, the renewable resources model predicts the reverse: participants will be more likely to buy immediately when they receive an income increase and to defer consumption when faced with an income decrease.

An alternative explanation of integration and segregation of prior outcomes is the loss-sensitivity principle proposed by Gärling and Romanus (1997). According to this principle, a prior outcome is only integrated with expected losses. Hence, an income change will only be integrated and affect the choice to buy when buying is perceived as negative (i.e., as a loss). It is therefore expected that when buying is perceived to be negative it is more likely after an income increase and less likely after an income decrease. Income change is not expected to have an effect when buying is perceived as positive.

Forty-eight undergraduates at Göteborg University participated in the experiment. They were offered hypothetical choices between buying a durable good immediately or deferring consumption after having experienced a temporary income increase or decrease. Because participants in the income-decrease condition were asked to imagine that they had saved money, this condition was equivalent to the income-increase condition with respect to total assets.

Different groups of participants were asked to imagine positive or negative buying events. In the positive buying events, they were told that they owned a product that they had wanted for a long time and now considered replacing with a new and better model. In the negative buying event, they were told that a product they owned had broken down and that they considered replacing it.

For each hypothetical situation participants were first asked to make a choice to buy the product (either a CD player, a bookcase, a Walkman, or a writing table) or deferring to buy it. Then they rated how likely they were to choose the way they did on a continuous scale from 0 to 100, where 0 was defined as not especially likely (i.e., that one is almost equally likely to choose the other alternative), 50 as rather likely, and 100 as very likely. Table 10.2 shows the means of the ratings of likelihood that were given a positive sign if participants chose to buy and a negative sign if they chose to wait (thus ranging from −100 to 100). Statistical analyses showed that the only reliable effect was obtained of income change (whether an increase or decrease). Although not statistically significant, the likelihood to buy was rated less for the positive than for the negative buying event. Thus, the framing of buying as positive and negative appeared to have been successful. Nevertheless, any interaction between consumption event and income change was absent.

Because participants in the income-decrease condition were more unwilling to use the money they had saved (current assets) as compared to participants in the income-increase condition where the equivalent amount of money was coded as current income, the results were clearly in line with the prediction from the behavioral life-cycle theory (Shefrin & Thaler, 1988, 1992) of how mental accounts are used. The decomposition of wealth in mental accounts violates the principle of fungibility in the life-cycle theory of saving behavior (Modigliani & Brumberg, 1954). It is also a violation of expected utility theory (von Neuman & Morgenstern, 1947; Savage, 1954) in which decisions are assumed to be made in relation to total assets or wealth. Hence, the use of mental accounts have important implications for how people make decisions.

The absence of an interaction between the framing of buying as positive or negative and temporary income change discredited the renewable resources model and the loss-sensitivity principle as explanations of the results. The question therefore arises why these explanations do not seem to be valid, although they accurately predicted the results in previous studies (Linville & Fischer, 1991; Thaler & Johnson, 1990; Gärling & Romanus, 1997; Gärling et al. 1994; Romanus et al., 1996; Romanus et al., 1997). In the studies supporting the loss-sensitivity principle, participants integrated a prior outcome only with a potential loss. The rationale is that they are concerned

TABLE 10.2
Means of Ratings of Likelihood to Consume for Different Consumption Events and Income-Change Conditions

Consumption Event	Income Decrease	Income Increase
Negative	-33.9	11.2
Positive	-54.6	-9.2

about negative outcomes. The results obtained by Linville and Fisher (1991) in support for the renewable resources model concerned preferences for emotional impactful events occurring on the same or on different days. Both the loss-sensitivity principle and the renewable resources model highlight affective control. However, because in the present experiment the choices were between immediate or deferred consumption, it is possible that issues about self-control, entailed in the use of mental accounts, is regarded as more important than affective control.

SUMMARY AND CONCLUSIONS

People are facing a variety of economic decisions every day. Several of these decisions are intertemporal choices in which outcomes that occur at different points in time have to be evaluated. Because future outcomes generally are discounted, it may sometimes be necessary to adopt strategies of self-control in order to overcome the temptation of obtaining immediate outcomes in favor of longer-term preferences. The categorization of wealth in mental accounts suggested by Shefrin and Thaler (1988, 1992) in their behavioral life-cycle theory may serve as a self-control strategy. In contrast to other strategies of self-control (Ainslie & Haslam, 1992b; Hoch & Loewenstein, 1991), the use of mental accounts is likely to work at a more general level, as it is not formed in relation to a specific situation or object.

In a questionnaire study of the effect of mental accounts on expectations of future consumption (Selart et al., 1997), we were however unable to replicate the results of Shefrin and Thaler (1988). It was suggested that, because the questions to participants included outcomes occurring at different points in time, the use of mental accounts may have been concealed by the motivation to discount future outcomes. In support of this interpretation, the results were instead better accounted for by theories of intertemporal choice (e.g., Loewenstein & Prelec, 1992).

Yet in another experiment we conducted, support was obtained for the use of mental accounts, predicted by the behavioral life-cycle theory, as an explanation of how a temporary income change influences specific buying decisions involving choices between immediate and deferred consumption. The renewable resources model (Linville & Fischer, 1991) and the loss-sensitivity principle (Gärling & Romanus, 1997) were discredited as explanations, because no interaction was found between whether the income change was a decrease or increase and whether buying was positive or negative.

The decomposition of wealth in mental accounts violates the principle of fungibility in the life-cycle theory of saving behavior (Modigliani & Brumberg, 1954) as well as expected utility theory (von Neuman & Morgenstern, 1947; Savage, 1954) in which decisions are assumed to be made taking total assets or wealth into account. Hence, the use of mental accounts have important implications for how people make decisions. It has also implications for the understanding of saving behavior, suggesting that current income may be a more important factor than predicted from the life-cycle theory (Modigliani & Brumberg, 1954).

One may ask to what extent the results from fictitious buying situations are possible to extend to real-life situations? On the one hand, one may expect participants to be more rational, in the sense of behaving in line with normative theory, when responding in situations with real outcomes. On the other hand, one may expect that people in real-life situations are influenced by other factors such as temptation and impulsiveness. Such factors could therefore decrease the effectiveness of mental accounts as a self-control device. Hence, the incentive to use mental accounts should be greater in real life but at the same time be less effective. It is reasonable to think that the pronounced use of mental accounts in the present studies also to some degree extend to real-life situations. Nevertheless, the important role of visceral factors (Loewenstein, 1996) may be downplayed. An important task for future research is therefore to investigate how mental accounts and visceral factors interact in self-control strategies.

ACKNOWLEDGMENTS

The authors' own research reported in this chapter was financially supported by grant #94-0086:2C from the Swedish Council for Social Research. We thank Peter Juslin and Henry Montgomery for valuable comments on a previous version.

REFERENCES

Ainslie, G. (1975). Specious reward: A behavioral theory of impulsiveness and impulse control. *Psychological Bulletin, 82,* 463–509.

Ainslie, G., & Haslam, N. (1992a). Hyperbolic discounting. In G. Loewenstein & J. Elster (Eds.), *Choice over time* (pp. 57–92). New York: Russel Sage Foundation.

Ainslie, G., & Haslam, N. (1992b). Self-control. In G. Loewenstein & J. Elster (Eds.), *Choice over time* (pp. 177–212). New York: Russel Sage Foundation.

Benzion, U., Rapoport, A., & Yagil, J. (1989). Discount rates inferred from decisions: An experimental study. *Management Science, 35,* 270–284.

Björkman, M. (1984). Decision making, risk taking and psychological time: Review of empirical findings and psychological theory. *Scandinavian Journal of Psychology, 25,* 31–49.

Chung, S., & Herrnstein, R. J. (1967). Choice and delay of reinforcement. *Journal of the Experimental Analysis of Behavior, 10,* 67–74.

Courant, P., Gramlich, E., & Laitner, J. (1986). A dynamic micro estimate of the life cycle model. In H. G. Aaron & G. Burtless (Eds.), *Retirement and Economic Behavior*. Washington, DC: Brookings Institute.

Friedman, M. (1957). *A theory of the consumption function*. Princeton: Princeton University Press.

Gärling, T., Karlsson, N., Romanus, J., & Selart, M. (1997). Influences of the past on choices of the future. In R. Ranyard, R. Crozier, & O. Svensson, *Decision making: Cognitive models and explanations* (pp. 167–188). London: Routledge.

Gärling, T., & Romanus, J. (1997). Integration and segregation of prior outcomes in risky decisions. *Scandinavian Journal of Psychology, 38*, 289–296.

Gärling, T., Romanus, J., & Selart, M. (1994). Betting at the race track: Does risk seeking increase when losses accumulate? *Perceptual and Motor Skills, 78*, 1248–1250.

Heath, C. (1995). Escalation and de-escalation of commitment in response to sunk costs: The role of budgeting in mental accounting. *Organizational Behavior and Human Decision Processes, 62*, 38–54.

Henderson, P., & Peterson, P. (1992). Mental accounting and categorization. *Organizational Behavior and Human Decision Processes, 51*, 92–117.

Herrnstein, R. (1961). Relative and absolute strengths of response as a function of frequency of reinforcement. *Journal of Experimental Analysis of Behavior, 4*, 267–272.

Hirst, D. E., Joyce, J. J., & Schadewald, M. S. (1994). Mental accounting and outcome contiguity in consumer-borrowing decisions. *Organizational Behavior and Human Decision Processes, 58*, 136–152.

Hoch, S. J., & Loewenstein, G. F. (1991). Time-inconsistent preferences and consumer self-control. *Journal of Consumer Research, 17*, 492–507.

Kahneman, D., & Tversky, A. (1979). Prospect theory: an analysis of decision under risk. *Econometrica, 47*, 263–291.

Kahneman, D., & Tversky, A. (1984). Choices, values and frames. *The American Psychologist, 39*, 341–350.

Keren, G., & Roelofsma, P. (1995). Immediacy and certainty in intertemporal choice. *Organizational Behavior and Human Decision Processes, 63*, 287–297.

Koopmans, T. C. (1960). Stationarity ordinal utility and impatience. *Econometrica, 28*, 287–309.

Kojima, S., & Hama, Y. (1982). Aspects of the psychology of spending. *Japanese Psychological Research, 24*, 29–38.

Larrick, R. P. (1993). Motivational factors in decision theories: The role of self-protection. *Psychological Bulletin, 113*, 440–450.

Linville, P. W., & Fischer, G. W. (1991). Preferences for separating or combining events. *Journal of Personality and Social Psychology, 60*, 5–23.

Loewenstein, G. (1988). Frames of mind in intertemporal choice. *Management Science, 34*, 200–214.

Loewenstein, G. (1992). The fall and rise of psychological explanations in the economics of intertemporal choice. In G. Loewenstein and J. Elster (Eds.), *Choice over time* (pp. 3–34). New York: Russel Sage Foundation.

Loewenstein, G. (1996). Out of control: Visceral influences of behavior. *Organizational Behavior and Human Decision Processes, 65*, 272–292.

Loewenstein, G., & Prelec, D. (1992). Anomalies in intertemporal choice: Evidence and an interpretation. In G. Loewenstein and J. Elster (Eds.), *Choice over time* (pp. 119–145). New York: Russel Sage Foundation.

Loewenstein, G., & Prelec, D. (1993). Preferences for sequences of outcomes. *Psychological Review, 100*, 91–108.

Mischel, W., Cantor, N., & Feldman, S. (1997). Principles of self-regulation: The nature of willpower and self-control. In E. T. Higgins and A. W. Kruglanski (Eds.), *Social Psychology: Handbook of Basic Principles* (pp. 361–399). New York: Guilford.

Mischel, W., Shoda, Y., & Rodriguez, M. L. (1992). Delay of gratification in children. In G. Loewenstein and J. Elster (Eds.), *Choice over time* (pp. 147–164). New York: Russel Sage Foundation.

Modigliani, F., & Brumberg, R. (1954). Utility analysis and the consumption function: An interpretation of cross-section data. In K. K. Kurihara (Ed.), *Post Keynsian Economics.* New Brunswick, NJ: Rutgers University Press.

Peeters, G., & Czapinski, J. (1990). Positive-negative asymmetry in evaluations: The distinction between affective and informational negativity effects. *European Review of Social Psychology, 1,* 33–60.

Prelec, D., & Loewenstein, G. (1991). Decision making over time and under uncertainty: A common approach. *Management Science, 37,* 770–786.

Rachlin, H., & Siegel, E. (1994). Temporal patterning in probabilistic choice. *Organizational Behavior and Human Decision Processes, 59,* 161–176.

Ranyard, R. (1995, August). *Mental accounts in financial decision making: a cognitive-psychological analysis.* Paper presented at the 20th IAREP Conference, Bergen, Norway.

Romanus, J., Hassing, L., & Gärling, T. (1996). A loss-sensitivity explanation of integration of prior outcomes in risky decisions. *Acta Psychologica, 93,* 173–183.

Romanus, J., Karlsson, N., & Gärling, T. (1997). Loss sensitivity and concreteness as principles of integration of prior outcomes in risky decisions. *European Journal of Cognitive Psychology, 9,* 155–166.

Samuelson, P. (1937). A note on measurement of utility. *Review of Economic Studies, 4,* 123–132.

Savage, L. J. (1954). *The foundations of statistics.* New York: Wiley.

Selart, M., Karlsson, N., & Gärling, T. (1997). Self-control and loss aversion in intertemporal choice. *Journal of Socio-Economics, 26,* 513–524.

Shelly, M. K. (1993). Outcome signs, question frames, and discount rates. *Management Science, 39,* 805–815.

Shelly, M. K. (1994). Gain/loss assymetry in risky intertemporal choice. *Organizational Behavior and Human Decision Processes, 59,* 124–159.

Shefrin, H. M., & Thaler, R. H. (1988). The behavioral life-cycle hypothesis. *Economic Inquiry, 26,* 609–643.

Shefrin, H., & Thaler, R. (1992). Mental accounting, saving, and self-control. In G. Loewenstein and J. Elster (Eds.), *Choice over time* (pp. 287–330). New York: Russel Sage Foundation.

Stevenson, M. K. (1993). Decision making with long-term consequences: Temporal discounting for simple and multiple outcomes in the future. *Journal of Experimental Psychology: General, 122,* 3–22.

Strotz, R. H. (1956). Myopia and inconsistency in dynamic utility maximization. *Review of Economic Studies, 23,* 165–180.

Taylor, S. E. (1991). Asymmetrical effects of positive and negative events: The mobilization-minimization hypothesis. *Psychological Bulletin, 110,* 67–85.

Thaler, R. H. (1980). Towards a positive theory of consumer choice. *Journal of Economic Behavior and Organization, 1,* 39–60.

Thaler, R. H. (1981). Some empirical evidence on dynamic incinsistency. *Economics Letters, 8,* 201–207.

Thaler, R. H. (1985). Mental accounting and consumer choice. *Marketing Science, 4,* 199–214.

Thaler, R. H. (1990). Anomalies: Saving, fungibility, and mental accounts. *Journal of Economic Perspectives, 4,* 193–205.

Thaler, R. H., & Johnson, E. J. (1990). Gambling with the house money and trying to break even: The effects of prior outcomes on risky choice. *Management Science, 36,* 643–660.

Tversky, A., & Kahneman, D. (1981). The framing of decisions and the psychology of choice. *Science, 211,* 453–458.

Tversky, A., & Kahneman, D. (1991). Loss aversion in riskless choice: A reference-dependent model. *Quarterly Journal of Economics, 106*, 1039–1061.

Tversky, A., & Kahneman, D. (1992). Advances in prospect theory: Cumulative representation of uncertainty. *Journal of Risk and Uncertainty, 5*, 297–323.

von Neuman, J., & Morgenstern, O. (1947). *Theory of games and economic behavior* (2nd ed.). Princeton: Princeton University Press.

Wärneryd, K.-E. (1988). Economic psychology as a field of study. In W. F. van Raaij, G. M. van Veldhoven, & K.-E. Wärneryd (Eds.), *Handbook of economic psychology* (pp. 2–41). Dordrecht: Kluwer.

Winett, A., & Lewis, A. (1995). Household accounts, mental accounts, and savings behaviour: Some old economics rediscovered? *Journal of Economic Psychology, 16*, 431–448.

Chapter 11

Attitudes, Values, and Opinions: Models and Dynamics

Lennart Sjöberg
Stockholm School of Economics

It is commonly assumed in attitude research that attitudes are causally related to beliefs and values. In this chapter, I suggest that a different type of psychological dynamics is involved, and that the seemingly good fit often obtained by expectation models of attitude is due to the existence of a common component in attitudes, values, and beliefs: an underlying image. The image dynamics is revealed in belief–value correlations, which measure thought constraints; high belief–value correlations, often observed, show that beliefs and values are frequently not independent. Three studies will be presented. In Study 1, imagery data are shown to be related to attitude and to belief–value correlations. In Study 2, the concept of negative beliefs, called for in Fishbein scaling, is pursued and psychologically explained. In Study 3, the concept of salient beliefs is challenged. It is found that improbable properties also add importantly to the explanation of attitudes. The chapter is concluded with a discussion of consequences for attitude formation models.

Fishbein and Ajzen (1975) gave an exhaustive overview of the field of attitude measurement. They pointed out that all the traditional measurement methods could be conceptualized in the same manner in the sense that they required participants to indicate agreement or disagreement with statements about belief–value combinations of the type "Object X has the property Y." The property Y needs to have value implications, of course. Thus, all attitude measurement calls for observing to what extent people attribute value to the attitude object, to what extent they find it good or bad. Even a simple singular rating on a bipolar category scale, going from "very, very bad" to "very, very good" usually catches a large share of the attitude variance.

In their well-known model, Fishbein and Ajzen suggested that attitudes are causally related to beliefs and values as follows:

$$A_o = \Sigma bV \tag{1}$$

where b is the belief that the object has a certain property and V the value of that property. Summation is across all salient properties of the object.

Opinions, on the other hand, concern factual statements that need not have value implications, formally speaking. This formal definition is misleading, however, because people seldom make a very clear distinction between their values and their factual beliefs. In the following I propose that model (1), and similar formulations, work because there is a common underlying substrate: the image, which is responsible for attitudes, values, and opinions jointly.

Three studies will be presented in the present paper, in order to clarify the psychological dynamics between attitude models of the type exemplified by Equation 1.

STUDY 1: IMAGE AND ATTITUDE

Zajonc (1980) has argued for the noncognitive nature of affect, presumably including attitudes in the sense in which Fishbein uses the term. He gave considerable evidence in favor of his standpoint. McGuire (1985) pointed out that it has not been possible to predict attitudes from beliefs very efficiently, implying that attitudes are determined, at least partly, by factors beyond beliefs. A successful application of the Fishbein model may involve up to 40% explained variance of attitude (see Sjöberg, 1996 for examples). A more typical value would be some 25% explained variance (van den Putte, 1991). Sjöberg, Derbaix, and Jansson (1987) and Derbaix and Sjöberg (1994) provided further data in favor of Zajonc's notions of primacy of affect.

In previous work, I suggested that attitudes, beliefs, and values are all derived from a common basis, regarding the image evoked by the object (Sjöberg, 1982b; Sjöberg & Biel, 1983). The image is a set of associations evoked by the mentioning of the object. For example, if the phrase "national defense" is heard or read, various concepts and sensory images may be elicited; these constitute the mental contents that are present when the object is assessed, thought about, or talked about. This is a notion that is related to Zajonc's concept of the primacy of affect. Another possibility is that attitudes are the basis for inferences about beliefs (Feldman & Lynch, 1988; Thomas, 1975).

The reason why attitude models like Fishbein's fit to data may be that participants fail to distinguish between beliefs and values and conceive of attitudes, beliefs, and values as a common set of components used to compose messages conveying their basic affective reaction. Figures 11.1 and 11.2 illustrate the different approaches to attitudes.

In earlier papers (Sjöberg, 1982a, 1982b; Sjöberg & Biel, 1983) I made extensive use of belief–value correlations. The Fishbein model assumes that beliefs and values are independent. However, data show very clearly that they tend to be correlated to a different extent for different individuals. (Correlations for separate individuals can be computed if many properties are sampled.) A strong positive correlation is a sign of wishful thinking, given that attitude to the object is positive. In other words, a well-liked

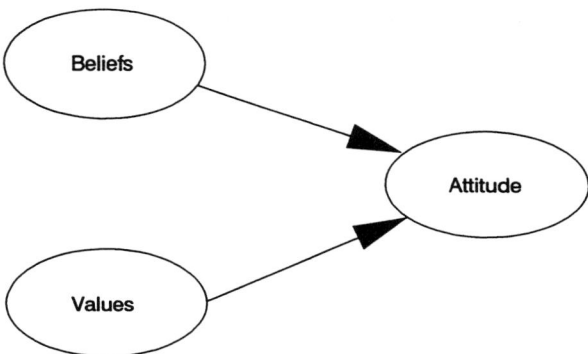

FIG. 11.1.   The expectancy-value type of model of attitudes.

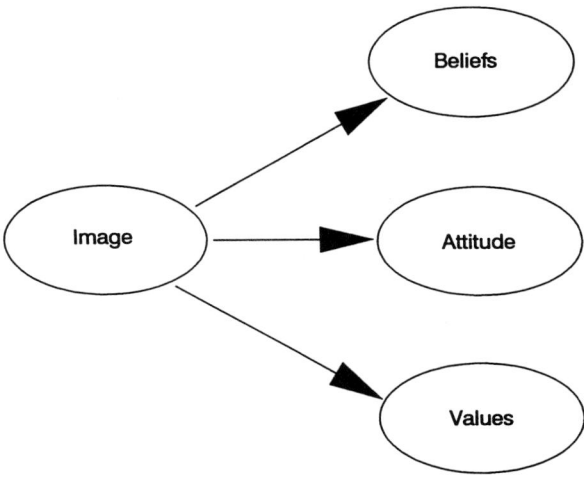

FIG. 11.2.   Image model of attitudes.

object is seen as having many of the positive properties and few of the negative ones.[1] This is indeed the typical finding, although, as noted above, the strength of the relationship varies across individuals. The belief–value correlation is suggested as a measure of constraint of thinking. Least constraint is revealed by a low correlation around 0, and highly constrained thinking is revealed by high belief–value correlations, whether they are negative or positive.

In the present study the image model of attitudes is tested by relating belief–value correlations to the imagery generated by the attitude object. Furthermore, since high belief–value correlations appear to be related to heated argumentation about an issue, an attempt was made to measure communicative intentions in the area and to relate them to belief–value correlations.

The content area was that of school marks. This was indeed a hot issue in Sweden and many people argued for a complete abolishment of marks. Several steps in that direction had been taken, but school marks still existed in the upper secondary school and they played an important role in the process of selection to postsecondary education. In the most attractive lines of study admission was highly competitive. In Sweden, use was made of relative marks; i.e., only a limited number of students in a class could receive the highest marks (at least such was the practice of the system). Students were therefore usually quite aware of intense discussions about the effects of marks, and they tended to be much concerned with their own marks, especially if they belonged to graduating classes.

Method

Participants. The participants were students in the upper secondary school, specializing in economics or social science. In all, 157 participants participated, 105 girls and 52 boys. Their mean age was 17.2 years. They were approached while in class and asked to take part in the study. None refused to do so. The data were collected in two waves ($N = 73$ and 84, respectively), with some very slight variation of procedures. Participants in the first group were about a year younger than those in the second group. The older participants were enrolled in the graduating classes, and therefore probably more concerned with their grades. Data were collected in the middle of the fall term (younger participants) and in the end of the fall term (older participants). In the following the two groups will be referred to as the "young" and the "old" group.

Questionnaire. The questionnaire asked for date of birth and sex of the respondent, but was otherwise to be answered anonymously. The participants were told that we asked them to state their opinions on the question of school marks, in particular the effects of marks, and that they should not discuss the questionnaire with other students (because everyone could not be tested at the same time).

They first judged the overall value of the system of marks on a five-category scale, from "very bad" to "very good." A second question asked them to rate how involved they were in the problem of school marks, also on a five-category scale from "very uninvolved" to "very involved."

In the next section, they were asked to rate how they typically felt when receiving their grades, on five-category scales. The scales were bipolar and defined by the following anchors:

Sad — pleasant
Nervous — calm
Tiring — stimulating
Others decide over me — I decide for myself
I am treated in an unjust manner — I am treated in a just manner
Not exciting — exciting
Uninteresting — interesting
Unimportant — important

These scales were included in order to measure the image of school marks. It was assumed that the imagery was mainly concerned with the experience of the student when he or she receives his or her marks.

In the next section participants rated the value of effects of grades. The effects were said to be possible and the participant was instructed to rate the value of each effect, should it occur, on a five-category scale from "very bad," rated as −2, to "very good," rated as +2. Based on preliminary interviews we had compiled a list of 42 possible effects.

Then the participants were instructed that they were to judge the same effects again, but this time with respect to how likely or unlikely they were, on a five-category scale from "very unlikely," rated as 1, to "very likely," rated as 5. The same 42 effects were presented again, in the same order.

In the final section of the questionnaire the participants stated their opinions about 31 attitude statements (Likert-type items) concerned with school marks. Each item was rated on a five-category scale, from "I have a completely different opinion" to "I agree completely." It took about 40 minutes to respond to the questionnaire.

Results

In order to make it possible to study attitudes to school marks in some detail, the 31 attitude questions were factor analyzed; three factors emerged. They were interpreted as (a) stressing both good and bad sides of marks and the complexity of the problem, (b) trusting what experts say about the effects of marks, and (c) stressing the need to decide definitely on the question. The three factors are denoted as (a) complexity, (b) trusting experts, and (c) decision. The factor scores were estimated by means of averages of defining items. The global attitude to grades was measured by an item asking for an overall rating of how good or bad the system of marks was.

The eight items mapping the image of receiving marks were correlated. All items except one (tension — calmness) correlated strongly and positively, so they were pooled to a composite average measuring pleasantness. Calmness was retained throughout as a separate item. Hence, imagery entered further data analyses by means of a two-dimensional representation.

Correlations between beliefs and values were computed separately for each individual and transformed to Fisher's Z. The mean correlation was 0.35, implying an overall tendency towards a positive relationship. About half of the group gave significant correlations between beliefs and values.

Fishbein's model was implemented in two ways. First, the mean product (bV) was computed with positive belief scores and bipolar (-2 to $+2$) value scores. This is termed the single bipolar model. Second, the belief scale was also transformed to the -2 – $+2$ range before computing products, yielding a double bipolar model. The two models were not linearly or otherwise functionally related; they correlated 0.91 and 0.81 for young and old participants, respectively. Their correlations with global attitude were however almost identical for young participants: 0.578 and 0.587 for the single and double bipolar models, respectively. The corresponding correlations were somewhat different for old participants: 0.461 and 0.505. There was, thus, a trend towards a better fit for the double bipolar model, especially for older participants.

The correlations between dimensions of attitude and image, belief value correlations and the two attitude models are given in Table 11.1.

It is clear that belief value correlations were related to image dimensions but not to communication attitudes. The relations among global attitude, image dimensions, and belief value correlations with Fishbein's double bipolar model constant are given in Table 11.2. Although the correlations have decreased, there are still statistically significant relations left, implying that images carry psychological meaning not contained in Fishbein's attitude model in its double bipolar version. At the same time, communication attitudes still have no explanatory power when it comes to attitudes or to belief–value correlations.

Discussion

It is striking that a few imagery items were related to global attitude quite clearly, and beyond the Fishbein model. Imagery is not explicitly accounted

TABLE 11.1
Correlations Among Belief-Value Correlations
(Transformed to Fisher's Z), Attitudes, and Image Dimensions

	1	2	3	4	5	6	7	8
1. Belief-Value Correlation	-							
2. Pleasantness	56***	-						
3. Image Calmness	26*	22	-					
4. Single Bipolar Model		79***	67***	15	-			
5. Double Bipolar Model	95***	62***	20	91***	-			
6. Complex Issue	-10	-24*	06	-12	-11	-		
7. Trusting Experts	14	-04	-08	13	12	-04	-	
8. Decision	-12	-09	03	-03	-09	12	22	-

*$p < 0.05$.
**$p < 0.01$.
***$p < 0.001$.

TABLE 11.2
Partial Correlations, Fishbein's Double Bipolar Model Held Constant

	1	2	3	4	5	6	7
1. Image Pleasantness	-	13	278	-09	-04	-15	-22
2. Image Calmness	17*	-	-14*	22*	05	-	08
3. Global Attitude	43***	07	-	-02	-07	09	-16*
4. Belief-Value Corr.[1]	16*	-18*	10	-	-11	08	03
5. Complex Issue	15*	13	19*	-04	-	-03	-19*
6. Trusting Experts	-01	-10	08	-07	-01	-	09
7. Decision Necessary	21*	-01	11	218	11	04	-

[1]In Z form.
*$p < 0.05$.
**$p < 0.01$.
***$p < 0.001$.

for in the Fishbein model; here it is argued that it is prior to, and the basis, of beliefs, values, and attitudes. The results support that assertion.

Study 1 also brings up the issue of the belief scale polarity. There were indications that the practice embraced by Fishbein, to score beliefs on a bipolar scale (implying negative beliefs) gave better fit than a unipolar scale, which is in itself more conceptually appealing. Pursuing this problem, I will relate it to the underlying psychological dynamics of attitude in the two following studies.

STUDY 2: THE POLARITY OF BELIEF WEIGHTS
IN AN EXPECTANCY-VALUE MODEL OF ATTITUDES

Fishbein's model has not escaped criticism. It has been pointed out (Schmidt, 1973) that the model assumes ratio scale measurement of beliefs and values, a requirement that is unlikely to be met. The model is multiplicative so the additive constant in the belief scale does make a difference. Different A_o's arising due to different additive constants would not be linearly related to each other. In a linear model, of course, the selection of a zero point is usually unimportant because it involves only a linear transformation of the scale. Also, the test of the model provided by Fishbein of the model has been criticized by Anderson (Anderson, 1971; Evans, 1991) as being too coarse, because important deviations from linearity are easily hidden even by very high correlation coefficients.

The belief scale should, according to Fishbein, be bipolar, yielding what has been termed, in the present paper, the double bipolar model. This is a somewhat disturbing standpoint, in that negative probabilities, whether they be subjective or "objective," are not usually regarded as a meaningful concept. In order to test the model one must, however, make a decision on this matter.

The single and double bipolar models differ with relation to the effect of varying values at a constant level of belief. For a low level of belief (below 0) there is a *decreased* contribution to global attitude if value increases within the double bipolar model. This may, at first sight, appear to be counter intuitive. Two explanations are possible.

One can speculate about psychological mechanisms whereby the bipolar belief model might be made plausible. For example, if there is a strong component of anticipated regret, as there might be in individual, decision-based evaluation situations, it could be the case that the anticipated loss of a large value is so painful that it contributes in a negative way to the overall attitude. It could also be the case that very low probabilities are associated with the belief that the event will not occur and the nonoccurrence of a very much desired event may be sufficiently negative so as to contribute in a negative manner to overall attitude. However, if an expectation framework is adhered to, as I believe was intended by Fishbein, retaining the bipolar belief model is hard to defend. An option should become more attractive if the value of the prize is increased rather than decreased, no matter how small the probabilities are. Furthermore, value change has no effect if belief is intermediate in the double bipolar model, also a counterintuitive property.

The issue can be decided empirically by trying out various placements of the zero point on the belief scale. It could, for example, be the case that regret mechanisms and beliefs in nonoccurrence of events enter at a very low level of probability and that an insertion of a zero point at a low level could be psychologically valid. The possibility can be tested by inserting zeros at various points on the belief scale and testing the correlations between the resulting sums of products and the overall attitude. As will been shown below, it is also possible to estimate empirically the position of the zero point by assuming the validity of the Fishbein model.

These matters are all somewhat elusive. Fishbein's own answer to the question of which type of belief scale to choose can be found in the 1975 book. Before proceeding any further I shall give a detailed discussion of Fishbein's argument for a bipolar belief scale, as found in that book (Fishbein & Ajzen, 1975).

Critique of Fishbein's Arguments for a Bipolar Belief Scale. The central part of Fishbein and Ajzen's argument goes as follows. Any attribute has a negation or a complement—that is, the attribute "aggressive" has the complement "not aggressive." Suppose that "aggressive" is valued −2 and "not aggressive" +2. Suppose also that the attitude object is considered to be "aggressive" with a probability of 0.2, and hence by implication "not aggressive" with probability 0.8. If the belief scale is unipolar, it is true that if only one of the two manifestations of the attribute dimension of aggressiveness is included in the scale the outcome will largely depend on which is included. If "aggressive" is included it will contribute −0.4 but "not aggressive" will contribute +1.6. However, if the unipolar probability scale is transformed to a bipolar form as

$$p' = 2p - 1 \tag{2}$$

it will no longer matter which attribute is included, both will contribute, in our example, +1.2. The reasoning assumes that values for an attribute and its negation are symmetrical around zero, a condition that may be unrealistic but it will not be under dispute in the present paper.

Fishbein's view of belief scales thus gives rise to a need for bipolarity when negations or complements are not presented separately. The underlying belief concept is still unipolar; bipolarity is really a mere trick to try to solve the problem of complementary attributes.

The reasoning assumes, of course, that negations are psychologically active, evoked by the stated attributes. This assumption has not been supported, to my knowledge. It appears more likely that salient attributes are usually positively stated attributes rather than negations, and that they dominate thinking at the expense of more or less imaginary and less clearly defined complementary events. At any rate, it is unclear why complimentary events should be at all evoked.

A sampling of studies using the Fishbein model reveals that most authors have used unipolar probability scales in spite of Fishbein's argument for bipolar scales, perhaps because negative probabilities are considered to be improper as measures of subjective probability (Oliver & Bearden, 1985; Pagel & Davidson, 1984; Park & Young, 1986). Some authors use 0 for the smallest category while others use 1. Another strategy is exemplified by Taylor and Todd (1995), Morrison, Simpson, Gillmore, Wells, and Hoppe (1996) and Elliott, Jobber, and Sharp (1995), who simply used a symmetrical bipolar scaling of beliefs without discussing the issue. Rutter, Quine, and Chesham (1995) also used bipolar scaling but justified it with reference to Hewstone and Young (1988), which may seem strange as the latter author found support for unipolar scoring. (See the General Discussion later in this chapter.)

The belief scale is not even described in some published papers (Gardner, 1985) and otherwise thorough methodological discussions fail to mention the problem of the origin of the belief scale (Mitchell & Olson, 1981; Sheppard, Hartwick, & Warshaw, 1988). It is interesting to note that Fishbein, in the original presentation of his attitude model (Fishbein, 1963), applied bipolar belief scales but without mentioning the paradoxical implications of negative beliefs and without giving any other rationale for negative beliefs.

A Model for a Ratio Scale of Probability Weights. Consider, again, the basic Fishbein model of attitude:

$$A_o = k\Sigma bV \tag{3}$$

where k is a constant needed to absorb the arbitrary units of the three scales involved. If both b and V are, at best, measured on interval scales, it is problematic how to test the model. However, if it can be assumed that the origin of the value scale is known, perhaps because it is specified in the instructions to the participants, we may first transform the V scale to a ratio level measurement by means of adding an appropriate constant that yields the value of 0 to the response category so marked:

$$V' = \alpha_1 V + \beta_1. \tag{4}$$

The next step is to assume that there is a ratio level measurement of belief, b', which is obtained by

$$b' = \alpha_2 b + \beta_2, \tag{5}$$

but so far β_2 is unknown.

The Fishbein model then becomes

$$A_o = \Sigma V'(\alpha_2 b + \beta_2), \tag{6}$$

or, allowing for A_o being measured only at the interval level,

$$A_o = \alpha_2 \Sigma V' b + \beta_2 \Sigma V' + C, \tag{7}$$

where C is an additive constant that absorbs the additive constants of the A and b scales and yields no further information. The interesting property of Equation 7 is that it demonstrates that β_2 may be estimated from data, assuming the model to be correct. Hence it is possible to investigate empirically which form of belief scale should be applied, and to estimate an additive constant that transforms the belief scale to a ratio scale.

A similar procedure was suggested by Holbrook (1977). Holbrook, however, suggested estimating simultaneously the additive constants for both evaluation and belief scales, but there seem to be few applications of his approach, for example in a paper by Ajzen (1991; cf. Bagozzi, 1984). Multicolinearity problems may be difficult to deal with in the dual constant case, and an a priori fixed origin of the value scale seems to be a reasonable condition to start from. In addition, the empirical illustrations by Holbrook and Ajzen yielded some negative belief scale values, a finding that may have deterred many researchers from further consideration of the findings, in spite of several findings that bipolar belief scales work better than unipolar ones, for example Sparks, Hedderley, and Shepherd (1991).

Method

Three data sets were analyzed: the first set, concerned with attitudes to school marks, is described in Study 1. The two additional data sets[2] concerned attitudes to the national defense and to the restriction of alcohol sales.[3]

Defense Attitudes. There were 40 participants, 21 women and 19 men. Their mean age was 39 years. They belonged to various organizations and were sampled in order to get as wide a range of attitudes to the Swedish military defense as possible.

The questionnaire first asked for three global ratings regarding attitude to the present Swedish defense, including military defense, disarmament of Swedish military defense, and involvement in questions concerning defense, disarmament, and peace. These ratings were all made on seven-category scales. The questionnaire then went on to a section including ratings of value, on a seven-category scale, of possible effects of disarmament or continued use of military defense. The scale went from −3 ("very bad") to

+3 ("very good"). The number of events was 44. In the final section, participants were instructed to rate the likelihood of the same 44 events, given continued use of a Swedish military defense and given a disarmament of the Swedish military defense. The scale had seven categories, and went from −3 ("very unlikely") to +3 ("very likely").

Restriction of Alcohol Sales. The number of participants was 40, 22 men and 18 women. Their mean age was 33 years. They belonged to various organizations and were sampled in order to get as wide a range of attitudes as possible to the policy of implementing legislation regarding the restriction of alcohol sales, implying that each person could only buy a specified amount of alcohol in a given time period. Some further details of the suggested policy were also specified.

The questionnaire opened up asking for two ratings on five-category scales, asking the participant to evaluate the policy of sales restriction and how involved he or she was in the issue. Then followed a number of open questions, to be answered by the participant in his or her own words. They will not be analyzed here. The participants were then asked to judge, on five-category bipolar scales, the values of 44 events and the probabilities of the same 44 events. Finally, they were asked some questions about alcohol habits.

Results

Model 7 was tested by regressing A_o on ΣVb and ΣV. The ratio of the two regression coefficients was used as an estimate of the additive constant β_2 in Equation 5. The regression coefficients and the goodness of fit of the equation are given in Table 11.3.

The goodness of fit is much better for alcohol and defence attitudes than for attitudes to school marks. The reason is probably that the latter attitudes varied less than the two former ones, which were collected from participants with as varying attitudes as possible.

TABLE 11.3
Goodness of Fit of Equation (8) b-Values and Estimated Values of β_2 for Three Data Sets

Data	Adjusted	b_1	b_2	β_2
School marks	0.280	0.575**	-1.295*	-2.252
Alcohol sales restriction	0.585	0.801**	-1.951*	-2.436
National defense	0.719	0.629**	-2.050	-3.262

*$p < 0.50$.
**$p < 0.001$.

TABLE 11.4
Transformed Belief Scales

	Transformed Scale Value		
Original Scale Value	School Marks	Alcohol	National Defense
1	-1.25	-1.44	-2.26
2	-0.25	-0.44	-1.26
3	0.75	0.56	-0.26
4	1.75	1.56	0.74
5	2.75	2.56	1.74
6	-	-	2.74
7	-	-	3.74

Note that all three models implied a need for a bipolar belief scale in this model. The estimates are different in the first two data sets as compared to the third. The reason may be that the third set employed seven categories while the first two sets used only five. Allowing for this fact, the transformed belief scales are remarkably similar in the three cases (see Table 11.4). Note that the zero point lies between the middle category and the category one step to the left in all three cases. Assigning the midpoint to the middle category is a reasonable approximation, although it would be better to assign it to the next lowest category, or, better still, to estimate it.

Discussion

The present study clearly supports the notion of a bipolar belief scale, although the rationale offered by Fishbein is not convincing. We are back to the puzzle: how could there be negative probabilities? What could be the meaning and psychological dynamics behind such seemingly meaningless entities?

Consider the psychological characteristics of the attitude objects that have been studied in the present paper: school marks, alcohol, and national defense. They are all examples of objects that exist in a context of threat or conflict. They may be considered either as threatening agents themselves, or as instrumental in defense against a possible threat. They may be seen, by some participants, as threats, while others regard them as rewards (e.g., alcohol).

There is a different psychological dynamics in the case of things you can own. These are objects that usually exist outside of a context of threat and conflict. Take a sum of, say, $1 million as an example. For most people, owning such a fortune is good, and the larger the chance of getting it, the better, even if the chance is small. Suppose you are offered two lotteries, each with a chance of 0.0001 to win either $1 million or $2 million. The price of a ticket is $50 in both cases. Which one would you rate as the one you like best? The second one, of course. Surely, there should be a positive correlation between attitude and value even for very small probabilities in the case where the object to be rated is the prospect of simple, straightforward ownership. Consider on the other hand two persons that both are convinced that the National Defence could not avert a foreign invasion: they both rate the probability of success in averting an invasion as very small. They differ as to how important they consider it to be to avert an invasion. It is only natural that the person giving the highest importance rating (highest value) should also have the most negative attitude to the defence, on the basis of this particular aspect, because he expects failure and failure is not a neutral but a negative state.

The hypothesis suggested by the present results, then, is that negative probability weights are called for in cases in which there is a negative consequence associated with failure, not just a lack of reward, or when that consequence looms larger than the reward. The latter may be the case because people tend to be more concerned about losses than rewards, especially certain or virtually certain losses (Kahneman & Tversky, 1979).

I end up endorsing a version of Fishbein's original argument for bipolar probability scales, but I do not assume the evocation of opposites nor do I assume that such scales are always called for. It is an empirical question, and the origin of the scale can be estimated.

Both studies 1 and 2 have relied on exhaustive property lists. The obvious objection to this kind of design is that the results may be somehow misleading because of this, and that only what Fishbein terms salient properties should be retained in the design. The argument assumes, of course, that Fishbein is right in his claim that only such properties are important. In the following study I investigate the matter.

STUDY 3: STRENGTH OF BELIEF AND PREDICTIVE POWER OF ATTRIBUTES IN EXPECTANCY-VALUE MODELS OF ATTITUDE

Fishbein's attitude model (Fishbein & Ajzen, 1975) is founded on the notion of salient attributes. Indeed, Fishbein (1963) found that the attributes most likely to be mentioned also were the ones given the highest probability ratings. In order to test and apply the model properly one therefore needs to measure salience. The selection of salient and important attributes is a difficult issue in applications of the Fishbein model. The procedure for selecting attributes at the individual level is possibly accept-

able but in practical applications one has to deal with a group of participants and it is desirable to have a sufficiently long list of attributes which
are relevant for all participants. The Fishbein procedures do not guarantee
that a list of well-functioning salient attributes is produced (see Sjöberg,
1996 for both successful and unsuccessful examples). Others have found
that nonsalient attributes often seem to function just as well as salient ones
(Hackman & Anderson, 1968; Kaplan & Fishbein, 1969).

It is proposed here that salience can be equated with Tversky and Kahneman's (1973) concept of availability. Because they claimed that subjective
probability partly reflects availability, it should be possible to use probability
as a measure of salience. The most probable attributes would then be the
salient ones.

When it comes to salient beliefs, it also is plausible to assume that salient
attributes are particularly highly loaded in value, either positively or negatively. The validity of these assumptions can be tested by selecting systematically those attributes that have high probability ratings and extreme
values for inclusion into the sum of products prescribed by Fishbein's
model.

Method

Data and Plan of Analysis. The three data sets of Studies 1 and 2 will
be analyzed as follows. The global attitude rating was correlated with ΣbV
or $\Sigma bV/n$, basing the sum on a selection of attributes only, where n is the
number of terms included in the sum. The models that arise in this way
are termed restricted models. The beliefs were throughout adjusted according to the previous results, producing some negative probabilities.
Values were scored on a bipolar scale as before.

The selection strategy was to delete attributes that were given certain
ratings of probability or value. For example, only probability ratings = 1
were included (all others treated as missing data), or only 1 and 2, and
so on. Because values seemed to be of minor importance, I exclude results
from deleting values from the present exposition. Also, choosing ΣbV or
$\Sigma bV/n$ was of little importance and I will throughout report results based
on $\Sigma bV/n$.

Results

The most important results are given by the correlations between global
attitude ratings on the one hand, the restricted models on the other. The
results are given in Tables 11.5, 11.6, and 11.7.[4] The results presented here
clearly show that both very likely and very unlikely events contribute to
the overall attitude. The very likely events may be somewhat superior, but

TABLE 11.5
Correlations Between Global Attitude and Restricted Fishbein Models for Various Strategies of
Deleting Probability Ratings, Three Sets of Data, Low Probabilities, and Up

Included Added	Correlation With Attitude		
	School Marks	*Alcohol*	*National Defense*
1	0.43	0.58	0.75
1-2	0.30	0.61	0.81
1-3	0.18	0.59	0.82
1-4	0.47	0.68	0.86
1-5	0.54	0.79	0.86
1-6			0.86
1-7			0.86

TABLE 11.6
Correlations Between Global Attitude and Restricted Fishbein Models for Various Strategies of
Deleting Probability Ratings, Three Sets of Data, High Probabilities, and Down

Included	Correlation With Attitude		
	School Marks	*Alcohol*	*National Defense*
7			0.81
-6			0.84
-5	0.51	0.66	0.85
-4	0.55	0.79	0.85
-3	0.51	0.79	0.86
-2	0.52	.79	0.85
-1	0.54	0.79	0.86
1 + 7			0.77
1 + 5	0.51	0.64	
1.2 + 6.7			0.82

not much. Adding attributes rated in the middle of the probability scale
does not add much to the fit of the model. It may even, as was true in
one case here, detract from its validity.

Note that these results were obtained with corrected probabilities; that
is, with bipolar probability scales. If the probability scales are retained in
their unipolar form the fit of the Fishbein models for low probabilities
will be clearly negative. As an example, consider the results given in Table
11.8. As can be seen from the table, there is no doubt that unlikely events

TABLE 11.7
Correlations Between Global Attitude and Restricted Fishbein Models for Various Strategies of
Deleting Probability Ratings, Three Sets of Data, Single Probabilities

Included	Correlation With Attitude		
	School Marks	Alcohol	National Defense
1	0.43	0.58	0.75
2	0.31	0.64	0.64
3	-0.22	-0.09	0.44
4	0.48	0.61	0.17
5	0.51	0.66	0.36
6			0.59
7			0.81

TABLE 11.8
Correlations Between Restricted Fishbein Models and Rated Global Attitude, Unipolar
Probability Scale

	Data Set		
Probabilities Included	School Marks	Alcohol	National Defense
1	-0.43	-0.60	-0.74
1-2	-0.30	-0.63	-0.77
1-3	-0.29	-0.59	-0.74
1-4	0.29	0.07	-0.63
1-5	0.51		-0.27
1-6			0.48
1-7			

contribute negatively to the attitude to a larger extent if they have a more positive value. This is contrary to what can be hypothesized if Fishbein models are regarded as expectation models, an assumption that is in itself tempting to make. The effect of a negative contribution of small probabilities is quite substantial and tapers off only when the very highest probability levels are added. Clearly, the use of unipolar probability scales in Fishbein scaling should be strongly discouraged.

On the other hand, the assumption that salient attributes are the ones of greatest importance is not supported here. Both likely and unlikely events or attributes contribute. In further work on his topic, individual differences in which attributes are salient should be considered (Elliott et al., 1995).

GENERAL DISCUSSION

The concept of attitude as a cognitive integration of beliefs and values is not supported by the present results. In Study 1, the image evoked by the concept was operationalized in terms of self-related associations. They were found to be strongly related to the global attitude to the concept. In Study 2, strong evidence was found for negative probability weights, quite incompatible with an expectation model of attitude. With low probabilities, higher levels of value were hence associated with decrements in contribution of the attribute to the global attitude. Furthermore, origins could be estimated and were found to be slightly asymmetrically placed, clearly implying a need for negative probability weights. In Study 3, the concept of a few salient beliefs was challenged by findings showing that also *unlikely* properties contributed to the attitude. These findings imply that whatever attitude is, it is not expectation.

When people are asked to rate attitude objects and their properties, in a typical application of an expectancy-value model of attitude, they are faced with a task that calls for either the retrieval of beliefs and values or their construction. The idea of using salient attributes presumably is there to guarantee, as it were, that retrieval occurs, not construction. But the evidence reported here points in the direction of construction, because:

- imagery data were quite strongly related to attitude
- beliefs and values were strongly correlated, exhibiting constrained thinking
- negative belief weights were strongly supported by the data and clearly showed that attitude is not an expectation
- salient attributes were not much better in accounting for attitude than nonsalient ones.

Sjöberg and Montgomery (in press) studied what they termed double denial, partly using the same data as in the present paper. In double denial, participants make subtle shifts in which belief they refer to when they rate beliefs explicitly or when they rate values (which of course must refer to beliefs to be meaningfully related to attitude [Eagley & Chaiken, 1993]). This notion further underscores the constructive nature of attitude components. However, attitudes cannot, just as the Universe cannot, be constructed out of nothing. The "something" that exists before the constructive process, and is used by it, is suggested here to be the Image.

The Image makes it possible to construct beliefs and evaluations for *anything*, including pigs with wings and little green men. Semantic cues are elicited by the words used to describe the objects, and people seemingly have no difficulty in forming opinions about many strange things they had not ever thought about, or even less seen.

Finally, let me comment on some pertinent research results. Hewstone and Young (1988) reported results in two studies that appear to be inconsistent with the present ones. They found that bipolar scaling of the probability scale was clearly inferior to unipolar scaling when evaluated for predictive power against the global attitude measure, in a multiplicative model. However, additive and multiplicative models differ only strongly for probabilities scored as negative. In that case the two models are even negatively correlated. Hewstone and Young apparently had no items with very low probability ratings; the ones that were negative, on the average, were still close to the origin.[5]

The reason why Hewstone and Young did not include beliefs eliciting very low probability ratings may have been that they used modal salient beliefs in their Study 2 and probably something similar[6] in their Study 1. If investigators use salient beliefs as a basis for Fishbein scaling of attitudes, they are unlikely to obtain data that strongly favor bipolar scoring of beliefs and a multiplicative model.

It does not appear likely that improbable events or attributes are salient. Fishbein's procedure, which aims at the elicitation of salient attributes, may therefore miss some important determinants of attitudes. Compare recognition and recall. A belief may be present and have attitude implications without being spontaneously recalled; when presented in a judgment task, it may be recognized and rated with psychological validity. It is a general observation that recall data are only weakly related to recognition data, for example in survey work where answers to open questions are compared to answers to questions with predetermined options.

The effects reported here are quite strong. The message they convey about attitude functioning would appear to be important. The picture emerging from these studies is that attitudes and opinions are related by being caused by a common factor, which may be termed the *image*.

In this context it is interesting that debates about social concerns of various kinds, as exemplified by political debates, tend to be concerned not with values but with opinions; see Guerin (1994). Values are commonly expressed in a language of beliefs. There are probably several reasons for this. First, it is hard to justify making priorities among values. Why should one good be better than another? Second, if it can be shown that a proposed policy leads to commonly valued outcomes it is clearly preferable. Third, reality judgments are typically quite elastic and it is very easy to think of reasons for embracing one set of beliefs rather than another.

Fishbein and Middlestadt (1995) rather recently initiated a discussion about the role of noncognitive factors in the formation of attitudes, in the *Journal of Consumer Psychology*. They argued that when attitudes, beliefs, and values are measured by "standard procedures" (i.e., Fishbein-type procedures), regression analyses of attitude and other analyses show that beliefs and values absorb all the predictive power. Noncognitive factors allegedly are only statistically potent when the models are inadequately specified. This argument met with a number of opponents (Haugtvedt et al., 1997; Miniard & Barone, 1997; Priester & Fleming, 1997; Schwarz, 1997) who pointed to an extensive literature in experimental social psychology demonstrating what seems to be effects of noncognitive factors, such as the effect of mere exposure. Fishbein and Middlestadt (1997) countered, however, that cognitive factors have rarely, if ever, been adequately investigated in such work and concluded that cognitive factors still must be seen as *the* determining factors of attitudes.

In my view, beliefs and values may well appear to be determiners of attitudes, when analysis is confined to simple regression analysis. But the correlations that are the basis of the regression analyses may well reflect a very different psychological dynamics, as I have demonstrated in the present chapter. Causal relations are not proven by correlations and regression analyses. Expectancy-value models are basically very misleading because they appear to fit, while not capturing the psychological processes in an adequate manner (Sjöberg & Montgomery, in press).

ACKNOWLEDGMENTS

The author is grateful to Martin Fishbein, Henry Montgomery, Norman Anderson, and Amos Tversky for discussions of some of the problems treated in this paper.

NOTES

1. Of course, some objects may be of that kind and perceived in a veridical manner. Wishful thinking is implicated when there is a large prevalence of such objects or, with one object, wishful thinking is one factor (but not the only one) behind a belief–value correlation.
2. These data were provided by Henry Montgomery.
3. It should perhaps be pointed out that Sweden has a long history of state-regulated alcohol sales, and until 1955 even a rationing system. Since then, regulation is carried out by means of price policies and restricting sales to a few state-controlled stores with restricted time for selling alcohol. Because alcohol consumption by many still is considered to be too high there is, from time to time, a discussion about introducing further restrictions, such as a new rationing system.
4. In Tables 11.5–8, I have denoted ranges of included probability ratings as follows. "1" means that only category 1 was included, all others were treated as missing. "1–2" means

that both 1 and 2 were included, all others treated as missing. "1–7" means all ratings from 1 through 7 were included, "1 + 7" that only 1 and 7 were included.

5. In Study 1, the smallest average belief rating was –0.56 and the largest 0.81. In Study 2 the corresponding values were –0.73 and 1.58. The ranges of value ratings were considerably larger. These are values on a 7 category scale going from –3 to +3.

6. They do not explain how the set of beliefs was constructed in their Study 1.

REFERENCES

Ajzen, I. (1991). The theory of planned behavior. *Organizational Behavior and Human Decision Processes, 50*, 179–211.

Anderson, N. (1971). Integration theory and attitude change. *Psychological Review, 78*, 171–206.

Bagozzi, R. P. (1984). Expectancy-value attitude models: An analysis of critical measurement issues. *International Journal of Marketing, 1*, 295–310.

Derbaix, C., & Sjöberg, L. (1994). Movie stars in space: A comparison of preference and similarity judgments. *International Journal of Marketing Research, 11*, 261–274.

Eagley, A. H., & Chaiken, S. (1993). *The psychology of attitudes*. Fort Worth, TX: Harcourt Brace Jovanovich.

Elliott, R., Jobber, D., & Sharp, J. (1995). Using the theory of reasoned action to understand organizational behaviour: The role of belief salience. *British Journal of Social Psychology, 34*, 161–172.

Evans, M. G. (1991). The problem of analyzing multiplicative composites. *American Psychologist, 46*, 6–15.

Feldman, J. M., & Lynch, J. G., Jr. (1988). Self-generated validity and other effects of measurement on belief, attitude, intention, and behavior. *Journal of Applied Psychology, 73*, 421–435.

Fishbein, M. (1963). An investigation of the relationships between beliefs about an object. *Human Relations, 16*, 233–240.

Fishbein, M., & Ajzen, I. (1975). *Belief, attitude, intention, and behavior: An introduction to theory and research*. Reading, MA: Addison-Wesley.

Fishbein, M., & Middlestadt, S. E. (1995). Noncognitive effects on attitude formation and change: Fact or artifact? *Journal of Consumer Psychology, 4*, 181–202.

Fishbein, M., & Middlestadt, S. E. (1997). Noncognitive effects on attitude formation and change: A response to five commentaries. *Journal of Consumer Psychology, 6*, 107–116.

Gardner, M. P. (1985). Does attitude toward the ad affect brand attitude under a brand evaluation set? *Journal of Marketing Research, 22*, 192–198.

Guerin, B. (1994). Attitudes and beliefs as verbal behavior. *The Behavior Analyst, 17*, 155–163.

Hackman, J. R., & Anderson, L. R. (1968). The strength, relevance, and source of beliefs about an object in Fishbein's attitude theory. *Journal of Social Psychology, 76*, 55–67.

Haugtvedt, C. P., and the Consumer Psychology Seminar. (1997). Beyond fact or artifact: An assessment of Fishbein and Middlestadt's perspective on attitude change processes. *Journal of Consumer Psychology, 6*, 99–106.

Hewstone, M., & Young, L. (1988). Expectancy-value models of attitude: Measurement and combination of evaluations and beliefs. *Journal of Applied Social Psychology, 18*, 958–971.

Holbrook, M. B. (1977). Comparing multiattribute attitude models by optimal scaling. *Journal of Consumer Research, 4*, 165–171.

Kahneman, D., & Tversky, A. (1979). Prospect theory: An analysis of decisions under risk. *Econometrica, 47*, 263–291.

Kaplan, K. J., & Fishbein, M. (1969). The source of beliefs, their saliency, and prediction of attitude. *Journal of Social Psychology, 78*, 63–74.

McGuire, W. J. (1985). Attitudes and attitude change. In G. Lindzey & E. Aronson (Eds.), *Handbook of Social Psychology* (pp. 233–346). New York: Random House.

Miniard, P. W., & Barone, M. J. (1997). The case for noncognitive determinants of attitude: A critique of Fishbein and Middlestadt. *Journal of Consumer Psychology, 6*, 77–92.

Mitchell, A. A., & Olson, J. C. (1981). Are product attribute beliefs the only mediator of advertising effects on brand attitude? *Journal of Marketing Research, 18*, 318–332.

Morrison, D. M., Simpson, E. E., Gillmore, M. R., Wells, E. A., & Hoppe, M. J. (1996). Children's decisions about substance abuse: An application and extension of the theory of reasoned action. *Journal of Applied Social Psychology, 26*, 1658–1679.

Oliver, R. L., & Bearden, W. O. (1985). Cross over effects in the theory of reasoned action: A moderating influence attempt. *Journal of Consumer Research, 12*, 324–340.

Pagel, M. D., & Davidson, A. R. (1984). A comparison of three social-psychological models of attitudes and behavioral plan: Prediction of contraceptive behavior. *Journal of Personality and Social Psychology, 47*, 517–533.

Park, C. W., & Young, S. M. (1986). Consumer response to television commercials: The impact of involvement and background music on brand attitude formation. *Journal of Marketing Research, 23*, 11–24.

Priester, J. R., & Fleming, M. A. (1997). Artifact or meaningful theoretical constructs?: Examining evidence for nonbelief- and belief-based attitude change processes. *Journal of Consumer Psychology, 6*, 67–76.

Rutter, D. R., Quine, L., & Chesham, D. J. (1995). Predicting safe riding behavior and accidents: Demography, beliefs, and behaviour in motorcycling safety. *Psychology and Health, 10*, 369–386.

Schmidt, F. L. (1973). Implications of a measurement problem for expectancy theory research. *Organizational Behavior and Human Performance, 10*, 243–251.

Schwartz, N. (1997). Moods and attitude judgments: A comment on Fishbein and Middlestadt. *Journal of Consumer Psychology, 6*, 93–98.

Sheppard, B. H., Hartwick, J., & Warshaw, P. R. (1988). The theory of reasoned action: a meta-analysis of past research with recommendations for modifications and future research. *Journal of Consumer Research, 15*, 325–343.

Sjöberg, L. (1982a). Attitude-behavior correlation, social desirability and perceived diagnostic value. *British Journal of Social Psychology, 21*, 288–292.

Sjöberg, L. (1982b). Beliefs and values as components of attitudes. In B. Wegener (Ed.), *Social psychophysics* (pp. 199–218). Hillsdale, NJ: Lawrence Erlbaum Associates.

Sjöberg, L. (1996). *Risk perceptions by politicians and the public* (RHIZIKON: Risk Research Reports No. 23). Stockholm: Center for Risk Research.

Sjöberg, L., & Biel, A. (1983). Mood and belief–value correlation. *Acta Psychologica, 53*, 253–270.

Sjöberg, L., Derbaix, C., & Jansson, B. (1987). Preference and similarity: Affective and cognitive judgment? *Scandinavian Journal of Psychology, 28*, 56–68.

Sjöberg, L., & Montgomery, H. (In press). Double denial in attitude formation. *Journal of Applied Social Psychology.*

Sparks, P., Hedderley, D., & Shepherd, R. (1991). Expectancy-value models of attitudes: A note on the relationship between theory and methodology. *European Journal of Social Psychology, 21*, 261–271.

Taylor, S., & Todd, P. (1995). Understanding household garbage reduction behavior: A test of an integrated model. *Journal of Public Policy and Marketing, 14*(2), 192–204.

Thomas, K. (1975). The relationship between attitudes and beliefs: Comments on Smith and Clark's classification of belief type and predictive value. *Journal of Personality and Social Psychology, 32*, 748–751.

Tversky, A., & Kahneman, D. (1973). Availability: A heuristic for judging frequency and probability. *Cognitive Psychology, 4*, 207–232.

van den Putte, B. (1991). *20 years of the theory of reasoned action of Fishbein and Ajzen: A meta-analysis.* Unpublished manuscript, University of Amsterdam.
Zajonc, R. B. (1980). Feeling and thinking—preferences need no inferences. *American Psychologist, 35,* 151–175.

Part III

JUDGMENT AND DECISION MAKING IN A SOCIAL CONTEXT

Chapter 12

The Importance of Fairness for Cooperation in Public-Goods Dilemmas

Anders Biel
Daniel Eek
Tommy Gärling
Göteborg University

"Thou shalt not steal." Whether or not this was news to the Israelites is unknown to us, but the fact that it has been handed down to us signifies that rules or norms are important in society. Sometimes they are handed down in order to establish a proper social behavior, other times they summarize established proper conduct. One of their functions, we guess, is to restrain egoistic incentives in favor of collective outcomes. To take but one example: tax evasion among Swedish citizens is more determined by beliefs about other citizens' inclination to evade rather than beliefs about actual possibilities to escape discovery (Laurin, 1986). In other words, citizens are guided by a norm concerning proper behavior instead of evaluating how much they can earn from tax evasion.

This chapter attempts to show that norms about distributive justice, such as equity and equality, can have an important effect when people decide whether to contribute to a common good or not. We will also suggest that preferences for justice principles vary across situations as well as between groups of members in society. We will do this based on evidence from experiments and a survey investigating the resource for child care. But before we present such evidence, we will justify why we believe that norms deserve attention in social dilemma research.

WHY NORMS MATTER

In 1944 von Neumann and Morgenstern published their expected-utility theory of decision making. Their work was a normative model specifying

245

how decisions ideally should be made. The model was also taken to be a descriptive model, referring to how typical decisions are actually made. However, it was soon discovered that people violate the principle of maximizing expected utility. Since then, attempts have been made to develop alternative models that capture how decisions are reached. It has been pointed out (Ullman-Margalit, 1977) that von Neumann and Morgenstern realized that game theory can not predict which equilibrium will predominate when several possibilities exist. However, von Neumann and Morgenstern stressed the importance of standards of behavior or social norms in order to reach such understanding.

In a stimulating article, Baron (1994) suggests that people deviate from normative standards because they overgeneralize rules or norms that are consistent with consequentialism in a limited set of cases. Consequentialism as a normative model implies that people should base their decisions on their judgments about consequences for achieving their goals rather than, for example, social norms or rules. This could be due for example to tradition, habit, or choosing in line with what led to good outcomes in the past in a similar situation. Baron also cites several own studies that illustrate possible violations of consequentialism. At the same time he points out that consequentialism may be consistent with common sense or everyday moral intuition, but this is most likely to be the case in interpersonal interaction rather than when people make judgements about major political issues. It is also clear from Baron's writing (p. 34) that the same moral intuition is involved in different situations or in decisions at various levels in society.

One example provided by Baron is taken from a social dilemma, a situation that is relevant in the present context. Participants were asked whether they should vote for or against coercive reforms such as a 100% tax on gasoline. Many participants said that they would vote against the tax. Nevertheless, they did think that a tax would do more good than harm on the whole. The explanation provided by Baron for this nonconsequentialist decision is that people erroneously applied the "do not harm" heuristic. A reason that it would do more good than harm can be expressed in terms of consequences for the environment (global warming). However, participants opposed the tax, presumably because some people would be economically worse off.

Facing a decison such as this one, people are asked several things. They should recognize that they are in a situation where rules cannot be applied as a routine matter. The situation calls for a more deliberate consideration. How to solve this "paradox" and know when you should interrupt a routine process is a problem outside the scope of this chapter. Another thing people are asked for is to more or less deliberately compare values or goals. It is quite clear that Baron had intra-individual comparisons in mind

(Baron, 1994, p. 36). Although Bentham's hedonistic calculus once seemed to solve this problem of intra-individual comparisons of values, doubts are still there (see, e.g., Montgomery, 1989). But major political issues, issues where Baron claims that people make nonconsequentialist decisions, are often serious, large-scale societal problems where solutions have to be reached based on individual decisions in interdependence situations. An aggregated solution taking into account multiple values between individuals can be traced in ethical hedonism (see Allport, 1985, for an account), but not everybody is convinced that values can be compared between people (see Simon, 1983). To rely on fairness norms in such situations could be efficient. If fairness norms are widely shared, others can realize your motives. Because others are affected by your decision, you also signal that you are doing the socially right thing. In other words, a decision in line with fairness norms is a decision to cooperate. A consequentialist decision might of course also result in a cooperative choice, but it is less clear to others concerned.

The above is spelled out only to underline that in social contexts norms do matter in decision making. Based on our own research, the present chapter seeks to give insight into how they matter in dilemmas concerning the public good.

SOCIAL DILEMMAS AND FAIRNESS

In a social dilemma, the individual outcomes are not only affected by the person's own choice but also by how other members of the group or the society choose. Interdependence constitutes the social part. The dilemma is dictated by the structure of the situation (Dawes, 1980). The individual has to choose between maximizing self-interest or collective interest. Regardless of what the other society members do, each individual is better off by maximizing self-interest. Yet if all do so, they are worse off than if everyone had maximized collective interests.

Research on social dilemmas has shown that in social contexts people do not always choose the option that promotes their own interests, but are prepared to choose an option that advances collective interests. Although people are concerned about their own private interests, they are also sensitive to distributive justice or fairness: people want to do what is right.

Most research on social dilemmas has been performed as experimental games in which people have to choose between well-defined alternatives. That the alternatives are well-defined in terms of payoffs promotes internal validity, as the properties of a true dilemma can be specified. At the same time, parallels to real-life dilemmas have been suggested (see, e.g., Dawes, 1980). One type of social dilemma—resource dilemmas, where the task is designed to simulate the shared use of a replenishable resource—has been compared to pollution due to motor vehicle traffic. Because each person's own contribution to the pollution problem is negligible, it is in the best interest of each individual to refrain from biking or walking rather than driving his or her car. Yet all are worse off driving and thereby maintaining the pollution. The other type of dilemma—public-goods dilemmas, in which members of a group have free access to a good whether they contribute to its provision or not—simulates situations such as joining a union or paying taxes. In our research reported in this chapter we seek to extend findings from choices in experimental games to choices in everyday public-good dilemmas.

It has long been recognized that fairness, along with self-interest and efficient use of resources, does matter when a group of individuals has to distribute a finite amount of resources among themselves. In line with Deutsch (1975, 1985), three categories of allocation rules represent strongly held beliefs regarding fairness: equality, equity, and need. Deutsch also specified (1975) why people hold one or the other to be fair. If a group is oriented toward economic productivity, it should embrace an allocation norm that encourages efficiency and distribute resources based on past contribution; that is, equity. When the goal of the group is to support relationships among its members, an equality norm that signals equal status among its group members is expected to be applied. Finally, when personal development and well-being is the primary goal, an allocation based on relative need should manifest itself.

At the same time, it seems unlikely that the world is so neatly divided as Deutsch seems to suggest. Rather, each motive or norm may be present simultaneously but in degrees. This is in line with suggestions made by Samuelson, Messick, Wilke, and Rutte (1986) and later expounded by Wilke (1991). Wilke proposed that three factors affect cooperation in social dilemmas: greed, efficiency, and fairness (the GEF hypothesis). In essence, the hypothesis states that greed is constrained by a desire to use a resource efficiently but also by the motive to realize fairness. Greed refers to the well-known assumption that individuals try to maximize their own benefits. However, if this leads to the depletion of a resource, individuals will constrain their greed in order to preserve the resource efficiently. Furthermore, individuals generally attempt to ensure that the distribution of benefits to themselves and to others is fair.

Laboratory research has shown that people acknowledge fairness in social dilemmas (Messick & Schell, 1992; Van Dijk, 1993). Moreover, equality seems to be a naturally applied principle (Allison & Messick, 1990). This is especially true when information about others' wealth or interest in the resource is lacking (Van Dijk & Grodzka, 1992). However, in public-goods dilemmas with asymmetric assets people tend to prefer equity

(Wilke, Liebrand, Lotgerink, & Buurma, 1986), just as people with larger assets contribute a larger share to the public good (Rapoport, 1988; Rapoport & Suleiman, 1993). In our own research we have extended previous laboratory research by means of a survey of the real-life public-goods dilemma of payment for the provision of community child care (Biel, Eek, & Gärling, 1997). The main survey results have been replicated and extended in experimental studies (Eek, Biel, & Gärling, 1997, 1998). Our aim has been twofold. On the one hand we have investigated the hypothesis that cooperation (willingness to pay) in a public-goods dilemma increases with perceived fairness of the outcome distribution. Furthermore, we have studied under what conditions different norms of outcome distributions are perceived as fair. These findings will be integrated below along with results that spell out individual differences.

FAIRNESS NORMS AND PROVISION OF A PUBLIC GOOD

All studies presented here investigate a willingness to contribute to resources for child care. In a first series of three experiments and in a survey study, the hypothesis that contributions to a common resource are related to perceived fairness was tested. The first experiment paralleled the survey study and will be commented upon together with results from the survey under the heading Survey and Experimental Control. Experiments 2 and 3 were extensions and are presented under Experimental Studies. In all these studies, child care was provided by the municipality. In a new experiment, we varied the provision holder and also included private corporations. Results from this experiment are presented under the heading Structural Changes.

Experimental Studies

In the first series of three experiments a hypothetical society paradigm (Mitchell, Tetlock, Mellers, & Ordóñez, 1993) was used. In a booklet (from which only the most common manipulations will be described here) participants were instructed to imagine that they were married and either were in need of municipality child care or not. Furthermore, there were variations in disposable household income. Participants were asked to imagine that they had an income above or below average in the municipality. For each scenario (combinations of need and income), groups of participants were asked to decide how fair they perceived three distributions of resources for the quality of the child care, one for each of the principles equality, need, and equity: "All children have equally good care," corresponding to the equality principle; "Younger children need better care and have better care than older children," corresponding to the need principle; and "If parents pay more, their children have better care than if they pay less," corresponding to the equity principle. Ratings were made on a scale from 0 (*not at all fair*) to 100 (*very fair*). Finally, participants were asked how willing they were to voluntarily and anonymously pay for the child care under the different conditions. Participants were told that due to the bad finances in the municipality, an extra monthly fee in order to maintain the quality of the child care was needed. In Experiment 2 participants were asked for their willingness to pay under the condition that if less than 50% of the households paid, considerable reductions in the quality of the child care would be unavoidable. In Experiment 3 the provision threshold (that is, the number of contributors that are needed in order to establish or maintain a good) varied from 25% through 50% to 75% of the households.

As for perceived fairness of distribution the equality principle was rated as fairest (mean = 84 and 77 in Experiments 2 and 3, respectively), followed by need (mean = 62 and 69), and equity (mean = 16 and 24). In order to investigate the effect of fairness on willingness to pay for child care, participants' willingness to pay for different principles was contrasted and used as dependent variables in separate hierarchical regression analyses. Because an equal distribution of the quality of child care was perceived as fairest, and earlier research has shown that equality is the distributive principle most often preferred in social dilemmas (e.g., Allison & Messick, 1990), in both experiments the first dependent variable contrasted partici- pants' willingness to pay when the equality principle applied with the mean of participants' willingness to pay when the equity and need principles applied. The second dependent variable contrasted participants' willingness to pay when the need principle rather than the equity principle applied.

In a first step of a hierarchical regression analysis, personal need of child care (Experiments 2 and 3) and income (Experiment 2) were en- tered. Participants with personal need of child care and participants with high incomes were more willing to contribute in order to keep the quality of the service intact. Also, the constant effect was significant in all four analyses, indicating that participants were more willing to pay when equality rather than need or equity was the applied principle for distributing re- sources, and more willing to pay under need rather than equity. This constant effect thus reflects the order of preferred principle for distributing resources for child care in the municipalities.

In a second step, ratings of perceived fairness for each comparison (equality versus need and equity and need versus equity, respectively) were entered. In all four analyses, the increase in explained variance was sig- nificant. Furthermore, perceived fairness of distribution eliminated the constant effect. Thus, the effect of distributive principle on willingness to pay could be explained by perceived fairness. In line with the GEF hypothesis, fairness mattered. People are more willing to contribute to a public or common good if they experience that the resource is distributed in a fair manner.

There are some other results worth mentioning from these experiments, which parallel findings from experimental social dilemma research where the resource has been points representing small amounts of money rather than resources for social services. As referred to above, participants with a larger interest in the resource were more willing to contribute. This has been shown in experimental social dilemmas (Van Dijk & Wilke, 1993, 1995). High income was another factor that resulted in a higher willingness to pay. Experimental studies have shown that in asymmetric public-goods dilemmas with continuous contributions, those with larger resources contribute more than those with smaller resources (Kerr, 1992; Van Dijk & Grodzka, 1992). Similarly, Rapoport (1988) and Rapoport and Suleiman (1993) reported that people with different amounts of endowments contributed the same proportion of their endowments.

Another finding is that people in public-goods dilemmas adjust their contributions according to the number of contributors that are necessary in order to reach the provision threshold (van de Kragt, Orbell, & Dawes, 1983). In the study by van de Kragt et al., cooperation can be explained by selfish motives. However, there is evidence that people are more willing to contribute if they believe that the group, as opposed to themselves, will benefit from cooperation (Kerr & Bruun, 1983). In one of our experiments (Experiment 3) we varied (as a within-subject factor) the percentage of households that had to contribute, from 25% through 50% to 75%, in order to avoid a quality reduction. The results showed that more willingness to pay was manifested when the required number of payers increased. In line with the GEF hypothesis, this is probably due to the motive to maintain the efficiency of the public good. Participants also had to estimate how many others they thought would be willing to pay the required extra monthly fee. Paralleling earlier research (Dawes, McTavish, & Shaklee, 1977; Messick et al., 1983), there was a positive correlation between one's own propensity to cooperate and the expectation that others will do the same. If a desire to "free ride" was the sole motive, the sign of this correlation would not make sense.

The results above reflect that people are sensitive to fairness when it comes to contribute to a public good. Because equality was considered to be a fairer principle than need and equity, participants were more willing to contribute to day care resources when these were distributed equally rather than according to need or in proportion to the size of parental contributions. It is promising that results are similar from studies where points representing some minor sum of money and where contributions to social services have been the dependent variables, respectively. This speaks for a more general mechanism promoting fairness.

Survey and Experimental Control

A questionnaire was sent to almost 2800 households with at least one child below school age. The households were sampled from five municipalities of varying sizes. Usable questionnaires were obtained from 66% of the households. Respondents answered, among others, questions about what they considered to be a fair distribution of quality of child care in their own municipality, how they believed that it was actually distributed, and how willing they were to pay for the child care provided by their municipality. Three distributive principles were presented in the following form corresponding to equality, need, and equity, respectively: "All children should have equally good care," "Younger children need better care and should have better care than older children," and "If parents pay more, their children should have better care than if they pay less." An additional three questions, leaving out "should" from the statements above, asked how quality of child care is actually distributed. Willingness to pay for child care in their own municipality was tapped by the following statements: "I am prepared to pay for child care even if my own child does not have to use it" (payment by taxes) and "I am only prepared to pay for the child care my child uses" (payment by fees). Each statement was rated on a five-point scale. In the analyses of willingness to pay, for each distributive principle the absolute difference between how the quality of the child care should be distributed and how it was believed to be distributed was used as a measure of perceived fairness. Thus, the smaller the difference, the fairer was the present situation considered to be.

In an experiment (Eek et al., 1998; Experiment 1), the same wordings of the fairness principles and the same two measures of willingness to pay were used. Ratings were made in the context of hypothetical societies as in the experiments described above. In these municipalities the quality of the child care was distributed according to one of the three principles. Hence, in contrast to the survey study, participants were told about the actual distribution and rated its degree of fairness.

An overwhelming majority believed equality to be the fairest principle for distributing the quality of municipality child care. This was true for the survey (mean = 4.8) as well as the experiment (mean = 4.2). The second most preferred principle was need (mean = 2.9 and 3.9 respectively) while equity was the least preferred principle (mean = 1.2 and 1.8, respectively). We interpret the strong support for an equal distribution of the outcomes as a reflection of child care being provided by the municipalities and hence a collective or public good that everyone should have equal access to.

Two separate hierarchical regression analyses on the ratings of willingness to pay by taxes and by fees, respectively, were performed on the survey data. Let us first look at the results related to the between-subjects variation in fairness ratings. The analysis showed that willingness to pay by taxes increased when the absolute difference for the need principle decreased. In the parallel analysis of willingness to pay by fees, the beta coefficient for the absolute difference for the equality principle reached significance. However, only a small percentage of the variance was accounted for. Similar results were obtained in the experiment. Thus, the explained variance in willingness to pay related to the between-subjects variance in fairness judgments was rather low.

Because different measures of willingness to pay were used in the first, as compared to the second and third experiments, and the explained between-subjects variation was the same in magnitude, this weak effect can hardly be attributed to the measure of willingness to pay. Perhaps one should anticipate a stronger effect in the survey study with its more heterogeneous sample. However, despite the rather heterogeneous sample ratings of fairness did not vary much across individuals. This is perhaps the most single important reason for the weak support for the hypothesis that willingness to pay in a public-goods dilemma increases with perceived fairness of the outcome distribution.

Across all respondents in the survey study, ratings of payment by taxes was negatively correlated with ratings of payment by fees. We take willingness to pay by taxes as an indication of how willing the respondents were to contribute to the public good. Thus, the effect of other variables (besides fairness) on willingness to pay can say something about the support for child care as a public good. As expected on the basis of experimental social dilemma research (Biel & Gärling, 1995; Van Lange, Liebrand, Messick, & Wilke, 1992), income and degree of use increased willingness to pay by taxes. Better educated parents were also more willing to pay by taxes, just as preference for the socialist or liberal parties increased willingness to pay by taxes and decreased willingness to pay by fees. The opposite pattern was true for those preferring the conservative party; that is, an increased willingness to pay by fees and decreased willingness to pay by taxes. The effect of political party preference was mediated by perceived fairness.

Structural Changes

The results show a strong support for an equal distribution of resources for child care and a strong opposition against that children to parents who pay more receive a better care. Child care as a market good is unfair business. But why? We suggest that this reflects a structural factor. Because resources provided by the government or by municipalities are regarded as public goods, there is a general opinion that such resources should be distributed equally among all citizens. Indeed, in Lane's (1986) review about market justice versus political justice, he suggests that equality and need are preferred distributive principle in the polity. At the same time he argues that equity is regarded a just distributive principle in the market. In line with Lane's proposals and the importance of different goals of a distribution, we suggest that distribution of a service provided by the municipality is perceived as fulfilling other goals than a service provided by private corporations. Whereas a municipally provided service aims at taking care of all citizens' interests equally, a privately provided service is more focused on standard economic transactions—getting what you pay for.

If this line of reasoning is valid, there should be differences in perceived fairness between child care provided by the municipalities and privately provided child care with a larger acceptance of equity distributed resources in the latter case. In order to test this assumption, a new experiment was designed where either equality or equity was the distributive principle and where the child care was provided either by private corporations or by the municipality.

One could also suspect that the degree of acceptance for an equity division of resources varies between different groups of citizens in society. This was also shown in the survey in that those preferring the conservative party to a larger extent supported payment by fees, whereas respondents who favored the liberal or the socialist parties were more willing to pay by taxes. Such a difference might also be fostered within the educational system. Thus, Frank, Gilovich, and Regan (1993) found that students of economics were less willing to cooperate than other groups of students. This was not attributable to initial differences but rather to the fact that students of economics are more confronted with market models employed in economics. In the present experiment both students of economics and students of psychology therefore served as participants.

The distributive principles were defined as in the former studies: for equality, "All children have equally good care"; for equity, "If parents pay more, their children should have better care than if parents pay less." All participants were asked to imagine that they were married and in need of child care. Participants were asked to rate how fair they perceived each distributive principle when applied in private nurseries or in municipally governed nurseries. Finally, they had to indicate how much they thought that they voluntarily and anonymously would pay each month in order that the child care would maintain its quality, which otherwise was threatened due to financial reasons.

The results for perceived fairness are depicted in Table 12.1. As can be seen, an equitable division was more accepted under private than municipal provision, while an equal division was considered somewhat fairer when

TABLE 12.1
Mean Perceived Fairness of Equality and Equity as Related to Provision Source and Group of
Students

	Provision	
Distributive Principle	*Private*	*Municipal*
Students of economics (n = 24)		
Equality	58.2	70.1
Equity	48.5	21.8
Students of psychology (n = 24)		
Equality	79.2	83.8
Equity	14.2	6.9

child care was provided by the municipality rather than privately: $F_{1,46} =$ 17.94, $p < .001$. Furthermore, an equal distribution was considered to be fairer among psychology students than among students of economics, while the opposite was true for the equity principle: $F_{1,46} = 13.97$, $p < .001$.

In the analysis of willingness to pay, the only effect that reached significance was a main effect for perceived fairness (covariate): $F_{1,45} = 9.11$, $p < .01$. Replicating the results from the previous experiments, an increased perceived fairness thus raised the willingness to voluntarily contribute. However, the results from earlier research (Frank et al., 1993), that students of economics cooperate less, were not replicated. As long as they perceived the distribution as fair, they were as willing to pay as were psychology students.

DISCUSSION

A consistent finding across our studies is that fairness matters when people decide whether or not to contribute to a common good. This is not a direct effect of the distributive principle as such, but rather which principle is considered fair in a particular situation. In the case of municipality child care in Sweden, citizens agreed that equality is a fair and equity an unfair principle. Hence, variations in willingness to pay was low. This is in line with a welfare state ideology that, among other things, emphasizes economic support for families with children and financing of child care (Svallfors, 1995) and that the government should not minister that differences in income play a role for children's welfare. For other social sectors, the results may look different. As an example, some people may support the idea that resources for education should be distributed according to need in order to achieve equal opportunities. Others might prefer that the more talented children receive a larger share, as this will promote efficiency at a societal level. Thus, people may have a common opinion about the goal for municipality child care, reflected in the agreement about fairness ratings of the distributive principles. Had the public good been resources for education or health care, the picture might have differed. In future studies it is important to recognize that the resource itself may affect which goals and distributive principles that are seen as fair.

Another factor that might shape our preferences for justice principles is which institution distributes the good. People can associate different goals with different institutions. What is fair in the market is not fair in the polity and vice versa. There were such tendencies in our manipulation of private versus municipality child care. An interesting question is how strong such links are. In Sweden privatizing of such services as child care, social insurance, medical services, and the mail service has been controversial. Many people regard these services as public goods where everyone should receive the same treatment. But once privatized, people may be prepared to accept differences in quality and regard other distributive principles than equality as fair. At the same time it may be seen as fair that people who receive a better treatment also pay more, but it is fairer that all people are treated equally well.

That those with higher incomes were more willing to pay by taxes can be seen as a concern about just contributions to the resource. It was also the case that fairness ratings of the same combination of principle and institution differed between groups of participants. This was true both in the survey study for political party preferences as well as in the last experiment for groups of students. As long as the social system is a common good for all citizens, a larger contribution from more fortunate has a redistributional effect. If there is a possibility to choose between a governmental and a private system—and those more fortunate (assuming that conservatives and economists are on average more fortunate) choose the latter as it better matches their conceptions about fairness as equity—such a redistributional effect will decrease or vanish. Our guess is that this is the reason why political parties to the left in Sweden oppose the proposal that our future pension savings will include a part that is privately invested by each citizen.

As mentioned above, the interpretation that fairness is a motive for supporting the public good is not straightforward. One has to understand why cooperation is considered fair. That those who used child care more and those with a higher education gave stronger support for a collective solution may in fact reflect greed. In the case of child care, contributions from everybody, including those who do not utilize the service, is more profitable for users than payment by fees. Also, better educated parents may stand to lose more if municipality child care is unavailable.

Thus, to cooperate in a public-goods dilemma cannot in itself be seen as a fairness decision. Batson (1994) suggested four motives for why people cooperate. One is egoism that may favor cooperation when egoistic and collective interests coincide. Another motive is collectivism with a goal to increase group welfare. Altruism promotes one or more other individuals' welfare. The final motive was principlism or to uphold moral principles, a category that fairness could belong to. In future studies, reasons for cooperation (or defection) should be illuminated (see, e.g., Gifford & Hine, 1997, for a similar plea).

To complicate matters even more, in real-life social dilemmas there is usually an uncertainty involved. When people are dividing a pie, there is no environmental uncertainty; that is, everybody knows the size of the resource. But a social uncertainty prevails in that some may take more than others. The equality norm establishes what is a fair share and may contribute to reduce unnecessary strain between group members. However, the situation is much more complicated when people have access to a resource about which there is uncertainty about the size and regeneration rate, or the necessary provision threshold for establishing a public good. In resource situations people are known to overharvest (Budescu, Rapoport, & Suleiman, 1990; Gustafsson, Biel, & Gärling, 1997a). One possible explanation is that people estimate the actual size of the resource being closer to its upper than lower limit (Gustafsson, Biel, & Gärling, 1997b). Such an estimate paired with an equality fairness rule would result in a depletion of the resource. If it is also kept in mind that people are more likely to be driven by egoistic rather than fairness considerations, on average they will probably harvest more rather than less than a fair share.

Thus, norms that regulate social uncertainty and moderate social strain may result in cooperation with regard to the harvesters but be maladaptive in terms of the resource problem that should be kept under control. As has been pointed out (Gifford & Hine, 1997), it is important to discuss the conceptual nature of cooperation, just as it is important to understand the impact of exogenous dynamics on the resource and the choices made by harvesters (Smithson, 1997).

ACKNOWLEDGMENT

This research was financially supported by a grant from the Center for Public Sector Research.

REFERENCES

Allison, S. T., & Messick, D. M. (1990). Social decision heuristics in the use of shared resources. *Journal of Behavioral Decision Making, 3,* 195–204.

Allport, G. W. (1985). The historical background of social psychology. In G. Lindzey & E. Aronson (Eds.), *The handbook of social psychology, vol. 1* (pp. 1–46). New York: Random House.

Baron, J. (1994). Nonconsequentialist decisions. *Behavioral and Brain Sciences, 17,* 1–42.

Batson, C. D. (1994). Why act for the common good? Four answers. *Personality and Social Psychology Bulletin, 20,* 603–610.

Biel, A., Eek, D., & Gärling, T. (1997). Distributive justice and willingness to pay for municipality child care. *Social Justice Research, 10,* 63–80.

Biel, A., & Gärling, T. (1995). The role of uncertainty in resource dilemmas. *Journal of Environmental Psychology, 15,* 221–233.

Budescu, D. V., Rapoport, A., & Suleiman, R. (1990). Resource dilemmas with environmental uncertainty and asymmetric players. *European Journal of Social Psychology, 20,* 475–487.

Dawes, R. M. (1980). Social dilemmas. *Annual Review of Psychology, 31,* 169–193.

Dawes, R. M., McTavish, J., & Schaklee, H. (1977). Behavior, communication, and assumptions about other people's behavior in a commons dilemma situation. *Journal of Personality and Social Psychology, 35,* 1–11.

Deutsch, M. (1975). Equity, equality, and need: What determines which value will be used as the basis for distributive justice? *Journal of Social Issues, 31,* 137–149.

Deutsch, M. (1985). *Distributive justice: A social-psychological perspective.* New Haven: Yale University Press.

Eek, D., Biel, A., & Gärling, T. (1997). *When equitable distributions of outcomes in asymmetric social dilemmas are perceived as fair: The relationship between perceived fairness and cooperation.* Unpublished manuscript, Göteborg University.

Eek, D., Biel, A., & Gärling, T. (1998). The effect of distributive justice on willingness to pay for municipality child care: An extension of the GEF hypothesis. *Social Justice Research, 11,* 121–142.

Frank, R. H., Gilovich, T., & Regan, D. T. (1993). Does studying economics inhibit cooperation? *Journal of Economic Perspectives, 7,* 159–171.

Gifford, R., & Hine, D. W. (1997). *Toward cooperation in commons dilemmas.* Unpublished manuscript, University of Victoria.

Gustafsson, M., Biel, A., & Gärling, T. (1997a). *Overharvesting resources of unknown size.* Unpublished manuscript, Göteborg University.

Gustafsson, M., Biel, A., & Gärling, T. (1997b). *Optimism and overharvesting in resource dilemmas.* Unpublished manuscript, Göteborg University.

Kerr, N. L. (1992). Efficacy as a causal and moderating variable in social dilemmas. In W. Liebrand, D. M. Messick, & H. Wilke (Eds.), *Social dilemmas: Theoretical issues and research findings* (pp. 59–80). Oxford: Pergamon.

Kerr, N. L., & Bruun, S. E. (1983). Dispensability of member effort and group motivation losses: Free rider effects. *Journal of Personality and Social Psychology, 44,* 78–94.

Lane, R. E. (1986). Market justice, political justice. *American Political Science Review, 80,* 383–402.

Laurin, U. (1986). *På heder och samvete: Skattefuskets utbredning och orsaker (Upon my honor: The extension and causes of tax evasion).* Stockholm: Nordstedt.

Messick, D. M., & Schell, T. (1992). Evidence for an equality heuristic in social decision making. *Acta Psychologica, 80,* 311–323.

Messick, D. M., Wilke, H. A. M., Brewer, M. B., Kramer, R. M., Zemke, P. E., & Lui, L. (1983). Individual adaptions and structural change as a solution to social dilemmas. *Journal of Personality and Social Psychology, 44,* 294–309.

Mitchell, G., Tetlock, P. E., Mellers, B. A., & Ordóñez, L. D. (1993). Judgments of social justice: Compromises between equality and efficiency. *Journal of Personality and Social Psychology, 65*, 629–639.

Montgomery, H. (1989). From cognition to action: The search for dominance in decision making. In H. Montgomery & O. Svenson (Eds.), *Process and structure in human decision making* (pp. 23–49). Chichester: Wiley.

Rapoport, A. (1988). Provision of step-level goods: Effects of inequality in resources. *Journal of Personality and Social Psychology, 54*, 432–440.

Rapoport, A., & Suleiman, R. (1993). Incremental contribution in step-level public goods games with asymmetric players. *Organizational Behavior and Human Decision Processes, 55*, 171–194.

Samuelson, C. S., Messick, D. M., Wilke, H. A. M., & Rutte, C. G. (1986). Individual restraint and structural change as a solution to social dilemmas. In H. Wilke, D. Messick, & C. Rutte (Eds.), *Experimental social dilemmas* (pp. 29–53). New York: Peter Lang.

Simon, H. (1983). *Reason in human affairs*. Oxford: Blackwell.

Smithson, M. (1997). *Taking exogenous dynamics seriously in public goods and resource dilemmas*. Paper presented at the Seventh International Conference on Social Dilemmas, Cairns, Australia.

Svallfors, S. (1995). The end of class politics? Structural cleavages and attitudes to Swedish welfare politics. *Acta Sociologica, 38*, 53–74.

Ullman-Margalit, E. (1977). *The emergence of norms*. Oxford: Clarendon Press.

Van de Kragt, A., Orbell, J., & Dawes, R. M. (1983). The minimal contributing set as a solution to public goods problems. *American Political Science Review, 77*, 112–122.

Van Dijk, E. (1993). *Coordination in asymmetric social dilemmas*. Ph.D. dissertation, Department of Social Psychology, University of Leiden.

Van Dijk, E., & Grodzka, M. (1992). The influence of endowments asymmetry and information level on the contribution to a public step good. *Journal of Economic Psychology, 13*, 329–342.

Van Dijk, E., & Wilke, H. A. M. (1993). Differential interests, equity, and public good provision. *Journal of Experimental Social Psychology, 29*, 1–16.

Van Dijk, E., & Wilke, H. A. M. (1995). Coordination rules in asymmetric social dilemmas: A comparison between public good dilemmas and resource dilemmas. *Journal of Experimental Social Psychology, 31*, 1–27.

Van Lange, P. A. M., Liebrand, W. B. G., Messick, D. M., & Wilke, H. A. M. (1992). Introduction and literature review. In W. Liebrand, D. M. Messick, & H. Wilke (Eds.), *Social dilemmas: Theoretical issues and research findings* (pp. 3–28). Oxford: Pergamon.

Von Neumann, J., & Morgenstern, O. (1947). *Theory of games and economic behavior*. Princeton: Princeton University Press.

Wilke, H. A. M. (1991). Greed, efficiency and fairness in resource management situations. *European Journal of Social Psychology, 2*, 165–187.

Wilke, H. A. M., Liebrand, W. B. G., Lotgerink, B., & Buurma, B. (1986). Equity and individual preferences in a MDG. *European Journal of Social Psychology, 16*, 131–148.

Chapter **13**

Contingency and Value in Social Decision Making

Marcus Selart
Daniel Eek
Göteborg University

A difference between social and nonsocial decision making is that the former is governed by a richer complexity of factors, which makes it more dynamic in many ways. A social decision typically involves a situation in which the decision outcome of an individual not only affects the individual, but also others (another person, a group of others, or society). Hence, this form of decision requires taking into account also the objectives of others in addition to your own. The perspective taken in this chapter is that social decision behavior is context dependent and that the preference is constructed in the decision situation (Payne, Bettman, & Johnson, 1993). The chapter therefore begins by unveiling that social decision behavior is contingent on several environmental factors. Moreover, it is emphasized that a central feature of social decision making is that it is also contingent on individual difference factors such as social value orientation (individualism vs. cooperation). In the following section it is suggested how this dynamic has been studied in one of the most important areas of social decision making; the distributive justice area. In the next section of the chapter the suggestion is made that contingent approaches based on extensive empirical research also must be regarded as relevant for other areas of social decision making, such as the procedural justice area. The chapter ends by discussing some theoretical and practical implications of the approach.

THE CONTEXT DEPENDENCE OF SOCIAL DECISION MAKING

The Environmental Contingencies

Human decision behavior seems to be contingent on many environmental factors, and therefore several efforts have been made to present models in which the major factors are unveiled. In a recent model suggested by Payne et al. (1993), two major environmental factors are crystallized: the problem factor and the general social factor.

First, the importance of the problem factor is underlined by Payne et al. (1993), who assume that the use of different heuristics is an adaptive response of an information processor to the demands of the decision problem. Such demands may include how complex the problem is and if uncertainty is involved. This information processor is characterized by a limited capacity. In this process two factors play a major part: accuracy and effort. Most human strategies are considered to be intelligent responses that may include several goals, for instance the desire to be accurate and the desire to conserve limited cognitive resources. Hence, it is argued that how people decide is predictable from the cost and benefit considerations they make and that they select the appropriate decision strategies based on these considerations. Many decisions are dependent on that people make explicit trade-offs and use elimination rules. From a broad range of empirical studies, it is concluded by Payne et al. (1993) that to a large extent these types of strategies are governed by the variations in the properties of the decision task. Among such properties, a more fine distinction can be made between task and context factors. The task factors are assumed to be the most influential for accuracy and effort estimations and include response mode, number of alternatives, number of outcomes or attributes, time pressure, information display mode, and agenda constraints. All these factors are characterized by a close association with the general structure of the decision problem. The context factors are less influential for accuracy and effort considerations and involve similarity of alternatives, attribute ranges, correlated attributes, quality of the option set, reference points, and framing. These factors are to a greater extent associated with the particular values of the objects in the decision situation. For instance, it has been revealed that context factors such as similarity may result in a higher degree of mental effort. Recent research reveals that both task and context variables may inform us about how the compatibility between input and output information operates in the construction of preference (Selart, 1997; Selart, Gärling, & Montgomery, 1998). Implicit in the account of Payne et al. (1993) is the suggestion that the problem factor is the most crucial for the decision process. This position to a large extent parallels the emphasis made by Simon (1990) on the salience of task and computational capabilities for our notion of rational behavior.

The importance of the problem factors has been widely discussed among researchers in social decision making. Messick (1997) concludes that there are three important problem factors in social decision making that deserve special attention: the order of presentation, the labeling of behaviors, and the causal texture behind the variables (reasons). Interestingly, all of these factors seem to be more related to context than to task, an observation that departs from findings made in nonsocial decision making.

Second, it is pointed out by Payne et al. that inferences and decisions made in social interaction seldom are content-blind, but instead rest on domain-specific concepts. Therefore, some form of general social factor also seem to be important to take into account for our decision behavior. One of the most forceful domain-specific concepts is Tetlock's (1985) motivational concept of accountability. It states that people are often socially motivated if they are made accountable to their family or work life collaborators for their decisions. It has for instance been proposed by Simonson (1989) that people in general feel a need to justify their decisions, and that this need has the potential of influencing how the decisions actually are made. Another important domain-specific concept is the suggestion that emotions such as anger may be regarded as a valid social rationality principle in the long run. Belonging to a group or a party is also an important social characteristic. From this follows that the notion of conflict is of great interest to decision research. Conflicts may arise in a decision situation when (a) there are multiple parties, (b) the actions of one person can affect the outcomes of others, (c) the parties have different preference orderings on the outcomes, and (d) the parties are aware of the situation (see MacCrimmon and Taylor, 1976, for a discussion). A central issue is to what extent rational behavior can be reduced to the laws of probability and logic. It seems plausible to assume that social objectives and motivations must be regarded as fundamental to the consideration whether a violation of an axiom or rule is reasonable or not (see Gigerenzer, in press, for a discussion).

The Individual Difference Contingency

Individual difference also constitutes a major factor in human decision behavior (Payne et al., 1993). People with different identities may respond quite differently to the same situation. Both peoples' cognitive ability and prior knowledge are central characteristics for our understanding of individual differences. For instance, it has been revealed that experts use different strategies than novices when faced by a relevant problem (Shanteau, 1988). But it is also important to note that the memory of human values also must be regarded as a constituent of our prior knowledge from this taxonomy. Other important features of individual differences that have been examined are perceptual ability, risk-taking propensity, and aspiration level (MacCrimmon & Taylor, 1976). One of the most studied individual difference factors in social decision making is the social value orientation (McClintock & Liebrand, 1988). This type of orientation implies that some people mainly attend to their own payoff (individualists), while others try to maximize the joint payoff with another person (cooperators).

The Construction of Preference

However, people's preference cannot be explained by their social values alone. Therefore it has been suggested that a construction of preference takes part in the decision situation in which both the environmental and the individual difference factors play major parts. The idea has also been forwarded that consumer reasoning to a large extent also is constructed in very much the same way (Shafir, Simonson, & Tversky, 1993).

Central to the notion of constructed preferences is also the idea that preferences are not based on algorithms like expected value calculation (Tversky, Sattah, & Slovic, 1988). An interesting discussion with a bearing on this issue has been initiated by Fischhoff (1991). In this discussion, different arguments of two philosophies, both dealing with the application of human values, are contrasted to each other. In the philosophy of basic values it is assumed that people in general only possess well-differentiated values for the most familiar evaluation tasks. Quite contrarily, it is assumed by the philosophy of articulated values that people have values for almost all evaluation tasks, but are not always motivated to reveal them. To a large extent, this process appears to be dependent on which questions are asked and under what circumstances (see also Payne et al., 1993, for a review). For instance, it has been suggested by March (1995) that people make decisions in social situations by clustering them in terms of appropriateness. Hereby, experiences are defined in terms of scripts, routines, persons, contexts, or appropriate actions. It may therefore be assumed that these categorizations also influence peoples' motivation to reveal their value orientations in social decisions (see Messick, 1997 for a review).

IMPLICATIONS FOR DISTRIBUTIVE JUSTICE

The Contingencies and Their Influence on the Application of Rules

As was addressed in the introduction, this chapter centers on how our knowledge about peoples' adaptation to decision situations may enhance our understanding about their social decision making. In particular, we focus our interest on a central problem in everyday life: justice. This area is important, as most of us assess the fairness of different acts on a continuous basis. Such acts may be individual, interpersonal, or institutional in character. We believe that the contingencies introduced in the former section and how they interplay in the construction of preference to quite a large degree may inform us about the social decision process. Our interest is mainly focused on the study of distributive justice; that is, on peoples' decisions about fair allocations of scarce resources. These decision situations often take the form of a social dilemma in which one alternative favors the individual gain (defection) whereas another favors the collective gain (cooperation). The dilemmas are characterized by the fact that the individual always receives the highest payoff if he or she chooses the option that promotes his or her own interest. However, if all people involved choose the option that promotes individual gain, everyone will be worse off than if all had chosen the option that promotes the collective interest (see Dawes, 1980, for a discussion). Hence, an important issue to discuss is to what extent decisions in social dilemmas are influenced by the ecological contingencies and the individual difference contingency.

Although there seems to be a consensus that allocations of resources should be fair, an algorithm for what signifies such a fair allocation is lacking. Nevertheless, there are at least three major distributive principles suggested by Deutsch (1975) that can be used to determine whether a social decision is fair or not. Each of them may be perceived as fair in different environments. The first principle is based on a need for equality (equal share), and assumes that people in many situations think that it is fair to distribute a resource equally between its sharetakers. This principle is widely used in situations where the cooperation and harmony of the group is the major goal. According to the second principle, the distribution should instead be guided by equity—that is, the resource should be distributed proportionally to the recipients contribution to the resource. This principle is dominating in competitive situations, and in situations for which the productivity of the group is the main goal. Finally, in many situations it seems fair to divide a resource according to need. Thus, the need principle states that the most needy should receive the most of a resource. This principle dominates in intimate relationships in which the subjective well-being is considered to be most important (Deutsch, 1975). It is believed that a fundamental aspect of social decision making is that these principles guide our judgments of appropriateness, in the sense that they inform us about what situation we are dealing with (March, 1995). The social value orientation, on the other hand, is more tied to peoples' identity—to the way we perceive ourselves. In the following section, it will be demonstrated that the perception of the situation (environmental factors) and of the identity (social value orientation) in social decision making also must be complemented with an opinion of "what is a person like me going to do in a situation like this?" It is the answer to this question that to a large degree governs the application of heuristic rules (social decision heuristics) in this area. The cost and benefit considerations prescribed by Payne et al. will also be operating on considerations such as these. Among the heuristic rules, a heuristic based on equality is considered to be the most salient (see also Messick, 1997).

The Salience of Equality

An important feature of the equality principle is that it is quite simple to use. All one needs to know is the number of individual sharetakers and then it becomes quite easy to make a division and calculate the per capita share. For this reason, people use equality heuristically; that is, they do not always think seriously and inquisitive about their decision. On the contrary, they are fast and frugal in making their decision by the use of some notion of the idea of equality (Messick, 1993, 1995). However, this form of processing sometimes leads to incoherent preferences (Messick & Schell, 1992) and in other cases to efficient and proper allocations as prescribed by Deutsch (1975). Moreover, people often prefer equal outcomes to other outcomes that are unequal but larger (McClelland & Rorbaugh, 1978), a phenomenon that may limit the total asset of the group. A distinction must therefore be made between equality and efficiency (Messick, 1991). The concept of "efficiency" is central in economics, and has its roots in Pareto's notion of optimality. Here, the key issue is whether a distribution of outcomes is optimally good in the sense that there are no perceivable ways in which it is possible to make one party better off without hurting another party. Undoubtedly, equality does not necessarily imply this and only states that all parties should receive equal or equivalent outcomes. It may be argued that although a group as a unit probably will perform as well as possible if the distribution of outcomes is efficient, the outcome of this effort is likely to be reduced if the payoffs that the individuals receive differ too much.

Despite the fact that equal division appears elusively simple, there are lots of facts that indicate that implementing the rule in decision making is far from easy. Generally, there are three types of problems tied to the use of equality as a principle of justice (Messick, 1995): First, there is the problem of determining when the equality rule is appropriate as opposed to some other principle. For instance, in some social situations there are other competing heuristics which may be used equally well, such as "first come, first served." Second, there is the problem of deciding how equality is to be made operational. For instance, in many areas of society, there seems to be an effort toward an equality of opportunity rather than toward equality. Hereby, it becomes apparent that equality is a central fundamental for societal equity principles. The construction of grading systems in most Western countries illustrates this. A drawback with the operationalization of equality is that if people are made equal in some sense, it often results in that they become unequal in some other sense. Third, there is the problem of how to implement equality. For instance, how do we achieve equality when we divide items like a valuable piece of furniture, a complicated estate consisting of many assets, or responsibility and recognition for a successful undertaking? According to Messick (1995), all these problems may arise when an individual decision maker must make up his or her mind about how the distribution of benefits and burdens should be allocated between self and others. An idea put forward by Messick (1995) is that many of these conflicts that the individual decision maker perceives may also arise, in more extreme forms, in a social group in which the members have diverging interests. This approach makes it possible to study the formal structure of conflict both intrapersonally as well as interpersonally (see also Coombs & Avrunin, 1988).

In a recent book chapter, Messick (1993) suggests that Payne's concept of contingent decision behavior (which states that different decision strategies are evoked by different task environments) to some extent governs the appropriateness of the equality rule. For instance, it has been demonstrated that whether or not the amount of a resource is divisible with the number of sharetakers is a factor that influences the application of the equality rule (Allison & Messick, 1990). Also, to what extent the experimental procedure is perceived as fair has an impact on the use of the rule (Hoffman & Spitzer, 1985). Finally, it is emphasized by Messick (1993) that a social decision heuristic must be justifiable to a higher extent than nonsocial decisions. For instance, social decisions are consequential in that they to a higher extent influence the well-being of others, which should lead to a higher degree of justifiability. However, the issue is complex, as many factors are involved in the shaping of justifiability, such as perception of procedural justice (Lind & Tyler, 1988), causal explanations for actions (e.g., Bies & Shapiro, 1987), and the accountability of the decision maker (Tetlock, 1985). Still, it may be concluded that it is difficult to imagine a principle of social decision making that is more justifiable than the principle of equality (Messick, 1993).

Nevertheless, there are other heuristics in the area of social decision making, such as *anchoring* (Markowsky, 1988), that are equally simple to apply, but that have little bearing on justice reasoning. Others, such as *tit-for-tat* (Axelrod, 1984) and *win-stay, lose change* (Kelley, Thibaut, Radloff, & Mundy, 1962) seem more reason-based and strategic, but are also less justifiable than the equality principle. It has therefore been pointed out that strategic thinking must be complemented with ethical obligation in order to maintain justifiability in situations where reciprocity is at stake (Cialdini, 1993; Morris, Sim, & Girotto, 1994).

The Importance of Social Value Orientation in Social Decision Making: Empirical Examples

As was mentioned earlier, individual differences constitute a major factor in decision behavior. When we are involved in making social decisions, our cognitive ability, prior knowledge, and values all influence our choice, just like in other forms of decision making. However, because social justice is at stake, the value factor has been assumed to be more influential than in other decisions. In the following the importance of social value orientation in the construction of preference will be described through the presentation of some empirical studies.

In a recent study, the assessment of social value orientation was combined with a manipulation of scenarios that would appeal to the equality and equity principles (Eek, Biel, & Gärling, 1997). The attempt was to explain why inequalities sometimes are perceived as fair in real-life social dilemmas. In two experiments, social dilemma scenarios were created in the sense that characteristics of different child care centers (private/public) and type of framing (qualitative/quantitative differences) were manipulated in a way that triggered different justice principles. The results revealed that social value orientation was connected to differences in perceived fairness and willingness to pay. Individualists as compared to cooperators to a larger extent favored the equity principle, whereas the cooperators were more keen to support equality. It was also found that equity was perceived as fairer in privately owned child care centers, whereas equality was preferred in public child care. This effect was most pronounced when differences in quality was at hand.

Using a multifactorial approach, Samuelson (1986) investigated how dimensional importance vary both with the decision environment and with individual differences. As a starting point, the criteria used in the evaluation of allocation had to be established. Thus, four criteria were assumed to be important: (1) the efficiency of the system—that is, the capacity of the system to allocate the resource effectively and cheaply; (2) the fairness of the system; (3) the degree of freedom given to the people by the system, promoting their own choices; and (4) the degree of promotion of one's own self-interest by the system. In line with Thibaut and Kelley (1959), it was assumed by Samuelson (1986) that people would collapse the evaluations of all these four attributes into a general evaluation of the system.

Subsequently, participants also rated the attractiveness of four different allocation systems, which were described by the attributes presented above. They included (1) a free access system; (2) the election of a leader to perform a group harvest; (3) the division of a common resource into private pools; and (4) the imposing of a harvest cap—that is, a lowering of a maximum amount that a person could take from the pool. Taking into account the social value orientation of his participants, Samuelson found that cooperators ranked fairness significantly higher and self-interest as significantly lower in importance than noncooperators. He also gained support for the hypothesis that the environment influenced the evaluations. Thus, many interactions between social value orientation and structural differences tied to the different types of allocation systems were revealed (see Messick, 1991, for a review).

In another study, McClintock and Liebrand (1988) investigated how social value orientation, the problem structure of the decision environment, and expectations about another person's choice behavior simultaneously may inform us about social choice behavior. They argued that such a complex analysis is necessary to carry out, because social decisions are reached in surroundings in which both one's own and another person's choices to a large extent are dependent on these factors. The decision environment that they focused upon consisted of different decision matrices. It was assumed that a given decision matrix undergoes a series of transformations and eventually becomes an effective decision matrix—that is, a matrix that determines the social decisions made by outcome-interdependent individuals (see also Kelley & Thibaut, 1978). Hence, they stated that insights in this development are of great importance for the construction and testing of models in the area. Therefore, they selected a couple of distinct self–other outcome structures that depict differing forms of interdependence. They also defined and assessed three social value orientations. Finally, they manipulated the choices of the other according to a strategy that has been observed to influence decision making in outcome-interdependent situations. It was found that participants' distributive preferences were to a quite large degree influenced by their social value orientation and by their expectations concerning the other person's choice behavior. Moreover, structure interacted with value and with the other's strategy. These results clearly indicate that in order to understand the behavior of decision makers in outcome-interdependent scenarios, one should take into account the structure of the task, the values of the individual decision makers, and the other's likely choice strategies as perceived by the decision makers.

Finally, attempts recently have been made to achieve some insights into how both task and context factors may interact with social value orientation and justice principle (Selart & Eek, 1997). A research method invented by Slovic (1975) was used in which participants state their (distributive) preferences for alternatives that previously have been matched to be equally attractive. This procedure normally results in an overweighting of the prominent attribute. The attributes that were used are "own gain" and "others' gain." In several experiments it was found that factors like value range, framing, discounting, and uncertainty interact with social value orientation in the construction of social preference. It was also shown that these effects are dependent of the application of justice principle. Hence, a connection is made to the "philosophy of articulated values," which states that people have values for almost all evaluation tasks, but are not always motivated to reveal them (Fischhoff, 1991). It was therefore assumed that this process appears to be dependent on which questions are asked and under what circumstances (see also Payne et al., 1993, for a review).

IMPLICATIONS FOR PROCEDURAL JUSTICE

As may be concluded from the previous section, a number of scholars have examined the factors that influence decision making concerning distributive justice, revealing that the principles of equality, equity, and need often govern perceptions that the outcomes are fair. However, questions of fairness may also be attributed to the procedures by which a decision is reached. From this perspective, it becomes interesting to explore the basis of people's judgments about the fairness of procedures designed to settle disputes. It has been demonstrated that even if people are faced with objectively unfair or poor outcomes, their judgments of fairness and satisfaction are to a large extent influenced by concerns about the process (Thibaut & Walker, 1975). This seems particularly to be the case among individuals who, measured by some form of objective standard, have lost a dispute. Hence, also peoples' preferences for dispute resolution mechanisms can be traced to the concern for process. This concern is rooted in the fact that substantive justice requires that we administer justice with a set of procedures that are in themselves fair, and that fair procedures should lead to fair outcomes.

A good deal of research made in this area has been conducted in the laboratory. This has resulted in that many studies have been criticized for narrowness, legal naiveté, and overreliance on experimental method. However, in a recent review article, Lind and Tyler (1988) demonstrate that many field studies in real-world disputing corroborate some of the most important laboratory findings. Moreover, these authors conclude that nearly two decades of research in the area support the influence of process control on judgments of procedural judgment. An increased satisfaction with objective outcomes and authorities is also reported when process is judged to have been fair. While some theorists have argued that the aim of process control is to increase the chances of a correct or an approving outcome, a central contribution of Lind and Tyler's work is to show that process control has value-indicative functions that add to purely instrumental motives. Although some of the value indication may be linked to the specific argument itself, it may also assist in affirming the disputant's roles in the extensive groups and social system to which they belong. People seem to follow the law not only due to fear of correction or other self-interested motives.

Based on this knowledge, it may be argued that the "construction of preference" view (e.g., Payne et al., 1993) may be helpful for the creation of a lay system as well as ethical standards. Decades of research on adaptive decision behavior suggest that there are both "good" and "bad" procedures, and it must therefore be claimed that the application of the good ones probably will lead to more optimal justice decisions. However, the application of the "construction of preference" view to procedural justice raises fundamental questions, such as which weights should be assigned to different attitudes, values, and opinions in society. Another important issue is that if procedural justice becomes more salient than distributive justice, then the authorities may create fair procedures and provide unfair outcomes, but still keep the support and satisfaction of their subordinates (see Valerie, 1992, for a review).

CONCLUSION

This chapter has discussed the fact that social decision making is contingent upon the interplay between environmental factors (such as problem formulation and appropriateness considerations) and individual difference factors (such as social value orientation). It has furthermore been emphasized that the questions used in decision situations and how those are framed have an impact on the extent to which the decision process will be driven by social values. Also, it was argued that environmental and identity factors both influence the selection of social decision heuristics in the construction of preference. In this process, cost and benefit considerations are in operation, as prescribed by Payne et al. (1993) in their adaptive decision making concept. It was moreover established that the value factor plays an important role in how preferences are constructed in social decisions. Examples of studies revealing this were provided from the domain of distributive justice, which constitutes a major area of social decision making. It was argued that the contingency approach to decision behavior suggested by Payne et al. may also be of use to the area of procedural justice. We believe that more research in this area of social decision making is needed that systematically focuses on the interaction of different contingencies. Such a development will be of great support for many areas in society, for instance governmental policy making and legislation.

ACKNOWLEDGMENTS

This study was financially supported by a grant to the first author from the Swedish Council for Research in the Humanities and Social Sciences. It was intellectually supported by workshop discussions chaired by John Payne at the SPUDM-16 conference, Leeds, August 1997. The authors are also grateful to Kazuhisa Takemura and Shun Watanabe for helpful comments on a previous draft of the chapter.

REFERENCES

Allison, S. T., & Messick, D. M. (1990). Social decision heuristics and the use of shared resources. *Journal of Behavioral Decision Making, 3*, 195–204.

Axelrod, R. (1984). *The Evolution of Cooperation.* New York: Basic Books.

Bies, R. J., & Shapiro, D. L. (1987). Interactional fairness judgments: The influence of causal accounts. *Social Justice Research, 1*, 199–218.

Cialdini, R. B. (1993). *Influence: science and practice* (3rd ed.). New York: HarperCollins.

Coombs, C. H., & Avrunin, G. S. (1988). *The Structure of conflict.* Hillsdale, NJ: Lawrence Erlbaum Associates.

Dawes, R. M. (1980). Social dilemmas. *Annual Review of Psychology, 31*, 169–193.

Deutsch, M. (1975). Equity, equality, and need: What determines which value will be used as the basis for distributive justice? *Journal of Social Issues, 31*, 137–149.

Eek, D., Biel, A., & Gärling, T. (1997). When unequal distributions of benefits in asymmetric social dilemmas are perceived as fair. Unpublished manuscript.

Fischhoff, B. (1991). Value elicitation: Is there anything in there? *American Psychologist, 46*, 835–847.

Gigerenzer, G. (in press). The modularity of social intelligence. In A. Whiten & R. W. Byrne (Eds.), *Machiavellian intelligence II.* Cambridge: Cambridge University Press.

Hoffman, E., & Spitzer, M. (1982). The Coase theorem: Some experimental tests. *Journal of Law and Economics, 25*, 73–98.

Kelley, H. H., & Thibaut, J. W. (1978). *Interpersonal relations.* New York: Wiley.

Kelley, H. H., Thibaut, J. W., Radloff, R., & Mundy, D. (1962). The development of cooperation in the "minimal social situation." *Psychological Monographs, 76*, No. 19.

Lind, E. A., & Tyler, T. R. (1988). *The social psychology of procedural justice.* New York: Plenum.

McClelland, G., & Rohrbaugh, (1978). Who accepts the Pareto axiom? The role of utility and equity in arbitration decisions. *Behavioral Science, 23*, 446–456.

McClintock, C. G., & Liebrand, W. B. G. (1988). The role of interdependence structure, individual value orientation and another's strategy in social decision making: A transformational analysis. *Journal of Personality and Social Psychology, 55*, 396–409.

MacCrimmon, K. R., & Taylor, R. N. (1976). Decision making and problem solving. In M. D. Dunnette (Ed.), *Handbook of industrial and organizational psychology.* Rand McNally.

March, J. G. (1995). *A primer on decision making.* New York: Free Press.

Markowsky, B. (1988). Anchoring justice. *Social Psychology Quarterly, 51*, 213–224.

Messick, D. M. (1991). Social dilemmas, shared resources, and social justice. In H. Steensma & R. Vermunt (Eds.), *Social justice in human relations, vol. 2* (pp. 49–69). New York: Plenum.

Messick, D. M. (1993). Equality as a decision heuristic. In B. A. Mellers, & J. Baron (Eds.), *Psychological perspectives on justice* (pp. 11–32). Cambridge: Cambridge University Press.

Messick, D. M. (1995). Equality, fairness, and social conflict. *Social Justice Research, 8*, 153–173.

Messick, D. M. (1997). Alternative logics for decision making in social settings. Unpublished manuscript.

Messick, D. M., & Schell, T. (1992). Evidence for an equality heuristic in social decision making. *Acta Psychologica, 80*, 311–323.

Morris, M. W., Sim, D. L. H., & Girotto, V. (1994). Time of decision, ethical obligation, and causal illusion. In R. M. Kramer & D. M. Messick (Eds.), *Negotiation as a social process.* London: Sage.

Payne, J. W., Bettman, J. R., & Johnson, E. J. (1993). *The adaptive decision maker.* Cambridge: Cambridge University Press.

Samuelson, C. D. (1986). *Determinants of preference for structural change in social dilemmas.* Ph.D. dissertation, University of California, Santa Barbara.

Selart, M. (1997). Aspects of compatibility and the construction of preference. In R. Ranyard, R. Crozier, & O. Svenson (Eds.), *Decision making: Cognitive models and explanations.* London: Routledge.

Selart, M., & Eek, D. (1997). Decision structure, social value orientation, and justice reasoning as determinants in social decision making. Unpublished manuscript.

Selart, M., Gärling, T., & Montgomery, H. (1998). Compatibility and the use of information processing strategies. *Journal of Behavioral Decision Making, 11*, 59–72.

Shafir, E., Simonson, I., & Tversky, A. (1993). Reason-based choice. *Cognition, 49*, 11–36.

Shanteau, J. (1988). Psychological characteristics and strategies of expert decision makers. *Acta Psychologica, 68*, 203–215.

Simon, H. A. (1990). Invariants of human behavior. *Annual Review of Psychology, 41*, 1–19.

Simonson, I. (1989). Choice based on reasons: The case of attraction and compromise effects. *Journal of Consumer Research, 16*, 158–174.

Slovic, P. (1975). Choice between equally valued alternatives. *Journal of Experimental Psychology: Human Perception and Performance, 1*, 280–287.

Tetlock, P. E. (1985). Accountability: the neglected social context of judgment and choice. *Research in Organizational Behavior, 7*, 297–332.

Thibaut, J., & Kelley, H. H. (1959). *The social psychology of groups.* New York: Wiley.

Thibaut, J., & Walker, L. (1975). *Procedural justice: A psychological analysis.* Hillsdale, NJ: Lawrence Erlbaum Associates.

Tversky, A., Sattah, S., & Slovic, P. (1988). Contingent weighting in judgment and choice. *Psychological Review, 95*, 371–384.

Valerie, H. P. (1992). Judgments of justice. *Psychological Science, 3*, 218–221.

Van Lange, P. A. M., & Liebrand, W. B. G. (1991). The influence of others' morality and own social value orientation on cooperation in the Netherlands and the USA. *International Journal of Psychology, 26*, 429–449.

Chapter 14

(Dis)Agreement in Peer Review

Sven Hemlin
Göteborg University

This chapter is concerned with the cognitive and social psychological aspects of the peer review process in science. More specifically, it focuses on judgments and decisions made by individuals in groups that result in disagreements about a scientific matter. The analysis encompasses various kinds of peer review conflicts, whether about a manuscript, a grant proposal, a university department's research, or something else. This research is completed by reviewing relevant literature on peer reviews, group conflicts, group decisions and scientific controversies; and analyzing a peer conflict on a Ph.D. examination committee. The chapter results in a framework for studies of peer review disagreements.

Peer disagreement is a common phenomenon in science. To some it is the gist of scientific development, or at least a fruitful event (Fuller, 1996; Hackett, 1992; Harnad, 1985; Nowotny [cited in Mendelsohn, 1987]; Popper, 1972). To others a dispute among peers is seen as a weakness in the scientific community (Cicchetti, 1991; Cole, Cole, & Simon, 1981; Merton [cited in Mendelsohn, 1987]). This ambiguity has been discussed mainly by sociologists and philosophers. Two main reasons for disputes can be found in the literature. Disagreements can arise because scientists hold opposing but rational beliefs (in the sense used by Giere, 1987, for example) about two theories or findings in science. Both theories and findings may be supported by empirical evidence. On the other hand, disagreements can also have their roots in less rational causes. Such causes may influence a decision to support one kind of research before another.

For instance, nepotism and sexism (Wennerås & Wold, 1997) or judgment errors (Hogarth, 1987) may distort decision processes. Furthermore, according to some authors the two reasons may be intertwined and inseparable (Bloor, 1976). Bloor (1976) argued that all arguments for a scientific claim, both correct and incorrect ones, are socially based, which make it difficult and perhaps impossible to resolve a peer disagreement on purely epistemic grounds. Related to this tradition in the sociology of knowledge are studies of scientific controversies. In such studies, researchers have analyzed opposing knowledge claims in terms of epistemic and non-epistemic factors in attempts to explain a scientific controversy (Engelhardt & Caplan, 1987). A less elaborated but interesting idea by Harnad (1985) stresses the dynamic aspects of scientific development, in which ideas and data interact in a process he called "creative disagreement."

One way to approach disagreements in science is by means of psychological theories of decision making and group processes, both of which are relevant to peer review. According to Kerr, McCoun, and Cramer (1996) relatively few studies have been performed on group judgments and decision making and even fewer on disagreements. The psychological focus on group decisions also highlights the routine to trust group decisions without full knowledge of how well these decisions perform. The knowledge of group-decision biases also is not very impressive. Moreover, there are few studies of psychological decision making aspects of peer reviews. La-Follette (1994) asked for such studies in a recent report of peer review deficiencies and Kassirer and Campion (1994) particularly stressed the cognitive aspects of the review process to be investigated.

Specific Questions

The main purpose of this chapter is to create a framework for studies of peer disagreement in science by means of an analysis of the relevant literature and a group decision case. Moreover, the chapter intends to shed light on the following questions: How do individuals make a decision about a scientific product in peer reviews? How do peer group processes influence this decision? How is a peer review disagreement explained? Which individual and group reasons can be traced in a disagreement? If both social and cognitive aspects can be traced, how do they affect peer reviews and decisions?

A SYNTHESIZING REVIEW

The literature reviewed is collected mainly from the three fields pertinent to the problem of peer review disagreements in science. First, peer review studies are covered and especially those focusing on conflicting peer evaluations. Secondly, I draw on the rather large body of psychological literature concerning individual and group decision making. Also, in this field I focused on group processes resulting in conflicts. Thirdly, sociological studies of scientific controversies have raised interesting questions related to peer disagreement.

Peer Review

As a background it is important to note that in the 18th century peer reviews started as a means for editors to select manuscripts for scientific journals. Interestingly, the evaluation of grant proposals developed quite independently of the former peer review tradition (Burnham, 1992). For a historical review of the peer review system, see also Burnham (1990).

In more recent years, a growing concern has arisen about the functioning of the peer review system, especially to prevent fraud, deception, and misconduct in science (Cicchetti, 1991; Chubin & Hackett, 1990; Hargens, 1988; Hemlin, 1996; Judson, 1994; Wennerås & Wold, 1996). The most striking finding of peer review biases is probably the Peters and Ceci study (1982), which found that when 12 articles were resubmitted to the psychology journals that had already published them, 8 were rejected on methodological grounds (with high inter-referee agreement) and 3 were detected as already published (Harnad, 1982). The findings awoke a heated debate (Harnad, 1982). A conclusion drawn by Millman (1982) from this debate is notable. He claimed that ". . . allegedly expert reviewers are not expert" (p. 226), which points to the problem of choosing the right peer. And, as is probably correctly argued, the outcome of a review is foremost a question of peer choice (Fuller, 1995). However, judgment biases by individuals as well as by groups must not be overlooked as a problem even for the most expert reviewers.

LaFollette (1994) summarized the problems found in an investigation of American research councils, for example NSF and NIH by the General Accounting Office. It was pointed out that they lacked in the following respects: there was a bias against younger applicants, women, and minorities, not articulated judgment criteria such as expectation of results, Matthew effect, and halo effects.

Judgments Before or After Research Is Carried Out. Montgomery and Hemlin (1990) distinguished between ex ante judgments such as peer reviews of grant proposals and ex post judgments such as peer reviews of manuscripts. This coincides with the historical process of peer review provided by Burnham (1990, 1992). Contradictory results from studies concerning the degree of agreement between peers on both ex ante and ex post judgments were reviewed by Montgomery and Hemlin (1990) and Cicchetti

(1991). Some of the studies reviewed showed a low to moderately high inter-referee agreement (e.g., correlations of .19–.54 for manuscript reviews) and others demonstrated consistently low figures (e.g., .18–.37 for grant reviews). It is probably important to divide peer disagreement along this line—that is, if the peer conflict concerns research that is not yet carried out or finished research. For instance, it might be a problem to grasp the potential of a proposed research project, while a completed task is more easy to put into a research context in terms of success or not. Judgments in the first case are more risky than the second one.

The Rejection of Innovative Research. A drastic outcome of peer review deficiencies is the rejection of innovations in research. This problem is illustrated in Ruderfer's (1980) case study concerning an erroneous rejection of a valuable manuscript in physics. He proposed the hypothesis that the probability of rejection increases with the degree of innovation in a publishable manuscript to be tested in peer review studies. Ruderfer also found that there is a lack of adequate raw data for a scientific study of peer review (also notified by Kassirer and Campion, 1994).

In the same vein, a list of 18 rejections of manuscripts and grant proposals of innovative research mainly in medicine was highlighted by Horrobin (1990), who stressed that peer review aims at not only quality control, but tracing innovations in science. An analysis of the 400 most cited articles in *Current Contents* was performed by Campanario (1996) to identify problems in publishing innovative research articles. He found that 10.7% of these had been severely criticized or rejected, but were eventually published. He concluded that scientific journals should publish bolder (if riskier) science, and not only science that is correct and familiar. The three papers referred to above focus on the difficult balance between quality control and encouragement of new ideas in science. It is a problem if peers focus more on the former task than on the latter. One reason is that the decision to support a new idea is more difficult than the decision as to whether research is acceptable to scientific standards or not.

Reliability and Validity in Reviews. Empirical investigations of peer reviews of papers submitted for publication have over the years shown a remarkable lack of reliability and validity of refereeing. A tentative explanation of this fact was proposed by Burnham (1992): that the standards against which manuscripts were judged varied to a high degree between disciplines and journals. Moreover, it is found that social science journals have very high rejection rates (for instance, 87% in sociology according to Hargens, 1988) as compared to hard science journals with considerably lower rates: 19% for nuclear physics and 22% for condensed matter (although more general fields in hard sciences have higher rejection rates—for example, 30% for general physics; Cicchetti, 1991). Studies by

Hargens (1988, 1990) showed that disciplinary differences in consensus on research priorities and procedures contribute to variations in the journal peer review systems. For instance, it was found that astrophysics accepted 91%, physiological zoology 59%, and sociology 13% of submitted manuscripts in leading journals. This could mean that there is generally a higher degree of consensus on trustworthy research in hard sciences, whereas the disagreement is high in the social sciences and the humanities. This gives rise to questions about peer disagreement in several ways. Is the prevailing peer agreement in mainly the natural sciences as mirrored in reviewer reports fruitful or not? How are the corresponding disagreements often found in the social sciences interpreted?

Different criteria have been proposed in an attempt to explain differences in acceptance and rejection decisions, respectively in peer reviews (Cicchetti, 1991; Van Lange, 1996). Generally, it is found that between 60–70% of peer reviews are in agreement of an overall acceptance and rejection decision for grant proposals and manuscripts in the investigated disciplines (physics, psychology, medical sciences, and economics). More specifically, Cicchetti found that reviewers of manuscripts for scientific journals agreed about accepted manuscripts in specific and focused disciplines or subfields (e.g., nuclear physics and behavioral neuroscience) and disagreed about submissions in general and diffuse disciplines (or subfields), for example general fields of medicine, cultural anthropology, and social psychology. Studies on grant proposals showed that reviewers were unanimous about rejected proposals in general. Cicchetti concluded that there is reason to believe that the criteria for rejection are more reliable because of the greater agreement. This could also mean that the characteristics of a proposal to be rejected are more distinctive than the other kinds, leaving some proposals in a neither reject nor accept category during an initial phase of the decision making process. Conversely, Van Lange (1996) found that there was greater agreement about acceptance than rejection of manuscripts in social psychology. Furthermore, social psychologists believed their own manuscripts to be superior to others in quality, when acting as reviewers. However, his study was in contrast to Cicchetti's conclusion based on a manuscript review, restricted in sample size (48 participants) and using a simple method (ratings of quality of imagined manuscripts). In conclusion, the distinction between manuscript and grant proposal review must be taken seriously when studying the decision process in peer review. In addition, the former is often an individual decision (made by the editor) and the latter is foremost a group decision (made by scientists). However, this distinction is not clear from the studies referred to above. Niemenmaa, Montgomery, and Hemlin (1995) have found support for the claim that acceptance and rejection decisions about grant proposals in psychology differ.

Cognitive Particularism. It has been shown that "school thinking" is prevalent in judgments of grant proposals, that is that one subfield is favored to another (e.g., cognitive psychology to personality psychology). This was shown in two empirical studies, one based on research council protocols in the Swedish Research Council for the Humanities and Social Sciences (HSFR) group for psychology during the years 1988–1993 (Hemlin, Niemenmaa, & Montgomery, 1995; Niemenmaa, Montgomery, & Hemlin, 1995). The other one, by Travis and Collins (1991), was based on observations and tape recordings of discussions at 10 meetings with the Science and Engineering Research Council (SERC), UK. Results showed that granted applications were of the same cognitive field as the peers who evaluated them. The authors called this effect cognitive particularism. It appears from these two studies that the cognitive similarity of applicants to its peers is an important factor in explaining success in grant applications. However, the empirical data are few and the delimiting of a scientific field is not clearly defined.

Summarizing Peer Review Studies. Empirical studies of peer review judgments show that there is (a) consensus on manuscripts in certain hard sciences (special physics) and disagreement in other (general physics, medicine) and behavioral sciences, and (b) consensus on grant proposals of rejections and disagreement of approvals (according to Cicchetti; Van Lange found higher agreement regarding approvals of manuscripts in social psychology). It might be suggested from these studies that the understanding of judgments and decision making in peer review is scarce. Three parameters appears to be important in peer review results so far: decision about acceptance or rejection, disciplinary (hard–soft) or subfield direction (general–special), and grant proposal or manuscript peer review (see Table 14.1).

TABLE 14.1
Summary of Studies Concerning Peer Evaluations of Grant Proposals and Manuscripts to Scientific Journals

	Acceptance	*Rejection*
Grant proposal	Disagreement (S)	Agreement (H/S)
Manuscript	Agreement (specific & focused H/S) Disagreement (general & diffuse H/S)	Agreement (general & diffuse H/S)

Note. H = hard sciences, S = soft sciences.

Decision Making and Conflicts in Groups

In a review of the literature concerning the social psychology of decision making, Ajzen (1996) described intrapsychic decision making conflicts. Although I am mainly concerned with conflicts between decision makers, I cannot omit decision conflicts within an individual. Furthermore, conflicts do not show up at one delimited moment of the judgment and decision making process. It is common to view a decision as a process through various stages—that is, assessing the need for a decision, reviewing the available alternatives, weighing the alternatives, choosing an alternative, and adhering to the choice, in which conflicts can emerge at any stage (see Hogarth, 1987).

Brehmer (1976) was an early proponent of studying cognitive aspects of interpersonal conflicts as opposed to conflicts of interest. He found that cognitive conflicts about a task might lead to conflicts that are difficult to resolve. They may even be the basis for emotional and motivational conflicts. This suggests that cognitive conflicts among individuals are as important to study as interest conflicts (cf. Hemlin et al., 1995; Travis & Collins, 1991).

Group Decisions. Perhaps the most well known studies of group decisions have been conducted by Janis (1982), resulting in the model concerning *groupthink*. In sum, the model predicts that the quality of the decision is reduced when groupthink phenomena are prevalent. Janis specified three situations when this occurs. First, a situation in which there is strong group cohesiveness among the decision makers is typical for groupthink. Second, there is a risk for groupthink in situations where there are structural weaknesses in the organization (i.e., the group is isolated, leadership is strong, biased decision making procedures are prevalent, and the group is largely homogeneous). Third, groupthink is characterized by provoking situations in which there is strong stress and low self-esteem among group members because of previous mistakes, and where difficult decision problems and moral dilemmas are treated. Groupthink can result in the omission of a number of valid decision alternatives, that new information is not treated and that consequences of a decision (i.e., risks, weaknesses) are not penetrated.

Aldag and Riggs Fuller (1993) concluded from a review of experimental studies, field research, and theoretical analysis that the empirical support for Janis's groupthink model is weak. The authors suggest a more comprehensive and descriptive model ("general group problem-solving model") as a starting point for studies of group processes in problem solving. The model assumes that four types of factors are crucial for this research. First, there are three antecedents for the group process: decision characteristics (importance, time pressure, task features), group structure (homogeneity, power of the leader, group history), and decision making context (organizational policies and norms, goal definition, previous treatment of the subject). Second, there are two types of emergent group characteristics: group perceptions of vulnerability, moral, unity, and oppositions, and group processes concerning responses to negative feedback, treatment of deviants, censorship, and limits for freedom of thinking. Third, the model treats the three main features of the decision making process: problem identification, generation of alternatives, and evaluation and choice. Fourth, the model is concerned with the outcome of the group processes about the decision, policy, and affective group components. In sum, the four types of factors create a promising structure for studying group decisions, which entail both rational and political (or cognitive–social) factors. The authors criticize previous research on group decisions being much too experimental and lacking in problem treatment and external validity. There needs to be more studies of real and ongoing decision making situations supported by methodological approaches, which are better at catching the richness and complexity of group problem solving.

Moscovici and Doise (1994) discussed the distinction between judgment and decision—that is, the choices that always accompany a decision. The latter mental process involves feelings of regret and responsibility, which might lead to conflict according to Moscovici and Doise. They also make an interesting distinction between "compromise consensus" and "polarized consensus" in group discussions. The former result of a group's negotiations "preserves a certain autonomy as regards individual representations" (p. 182), while "polarized consensus around a dominant value tends to integrate points of view and to root them firmly in group representation" (p. 182). A group representation, according to Moscovici and Doise, is a transformation of individual representations into a social representation or framework that each individual internalizes and shares with others to adjust her/his attitudes and judgments (cf. Allwood, 1995; Wegner, 1987). A group decision has the consequence that individuals remain loyal to it and feel committed. The consensus seeking theory of group decision making is probably applicable also in peer review contexts. However, as is pointed out by the authors, the differing judgments of individuals may lead to group conflicts, which raises the question what circumstances contribute to conflicts rather than consensus.

Jury decision making is the most researched area in group decision. A successful explanation of group decision outcomes is given by the Social Decision Scheme (SDS), which predicts that an initial two-thirds majority agreement determines the verdict in juries (Davis, 1973). Investigating the SDS, Kerr, MacCoun, and Kramer (1996) compared individual and group judgment. They concluded that six factors identify if a group is or isn't likely to make a biased judgment: 1) the size of the group, 2) the magnitude of individual bias, 3) the location of the bias, 4) the definition of the bias, 5) the normative ideal, and, 6) the nature of the group process. Group processes should be studied more intensely to find out the contribution of the six factors in judgments.

Worchel, Wood, and Simpson (1991) described research about group processes in decision making. Studies showed that dissidents and heterogeneous members of groups appear to contribute to a better quality of group decisions. Also, disagreement between group members proved to be important for a high decision making quality in a review of group decision making under uncertainty (Sniezek, 1992).

Decision rules in groups may also influence the quality of the decision. Miller (1989) reviewed the literature in this field and concluded that stricter rules—rules leading to compromises and adjustments of individual preferences—are better than lenient ones. Stricter decision rules suggest greater agreement among group members.

Finally, I draw on ideas described in empirical studies by Shafir, Simonson, and Tversky (1994), which views and analyses choice as reason-based. This means that the tracing of sociocognitive reasons for a certain judgment may lead to an understanding of why a disagreement arose in a peer review context. Furthermore, Pennington and Hastie (1986) used arguments and reasoning by individuals in jurors to explain complex decision making.

In conclusion, I have selected literature mainly in group decision making and group conflicts that will contribute to the analysis of peer disagreement. More specifically, it appears sensible to use naturalistic approaches along the lines proposed by Aldag and Riggs Fuller because peer review disagreement studies are new, still few, restricted in fields and encompass both social and cognitive reasons; and also to follow the analysis of decision making in groups as conflict or consensus processes.

Group Conflicts. Group conflicts about information may be responded to in three ways, according to a review by Levine and Thompson (1996): conflict avoidance, conflict reduction, and conflict creation. Avoidance is suggested by the literature to be accomplished in five ways by groups, namely by (1) trying to control their own or others' thoughts so that disagreeing opinions cease to exist, (2) trying to control their own or others' behaviors so that disagreeing opinions are not publicly expressed, (3) developing or importing shared rules, or norms, that reduce the likelihood that disagreements will lead to open conflict, (4) (mis)interpreting disagreements in ways that reduce its importance, and (5) shifting their public positions to a mutually acceptable compromise position. There are probably ingredients from all five in a peer group conflict. The first way, "thought-control," may be achieved by identification with another person to establish or maintain a relation (Kelman, cited in Levine and Thompson, 1996). Perhaps this is especially common in hierarchical systems, of which Academia is one. The second way, "behavior control," is likely to happen when certain topics cannot be discussed because of their conflict provoking character. This phenomenon was referred to by Janis (1982) as "mindguards"—that is, group members keep silent to reach consensus in group decisions because of conformity pressures. Also, this is probably found in peer review settings. The third way, "decision rules," are applied and specified in advance to resolve disagreements. For instance, in an examining committee of a Ph.D. thesis, the decision rule is the majority rule (cf. Miller, 1989). The fourth way, "(mis) interpretation of disagreement," might be accomplished by reducing the importance of the disagreeing person or that the view is not really representative of that person (e.g., s/he may be indoctrinated by some perceived stereotypical opinion). This might be prevalent in science by diminishing a minority opinion by referring to its inferior prestige in the academic society. The fifth way suggested by the authors, "compromise," implies avoidance of a conflict among group members who disagree by shifting their opinions to a moderate position acceptable by all. This resolution among disagreeing individuals is explained by Sherif (cited in Levine & Thompson, 1996) as mutual social influence originating from the uncertainty produced by stimulus ambiguity. Another explanation, "normalization," was offered by Moscovici (see Moscovici & Doise, 1994), who suggested that interpersonal conflict produced intrapersonal conflict or uncertainty about one's own position. To reduce both conflicts reciprocal influence is emitted aiming at finding a reasonable middle position that can be acceptable by all members in consensus. The former (Sherif's) explanation involves stimulus ambiguity and uncertainty while the latter (Moscovici's) focuses on individual motivations to avoid conflict. Whatever the explanation is for consensus seeking in disagreeing groups it is a hardly surprising phenomenon in peer review groups, for instance examining committees which appears to end up very often in full agreement to accept or (less often) reject a Ph.D. thesis. Conflict creation is regarded as a term for techniques aiming at an improvement of group decisions according to Levine and Thompson (1996). A number of such instruments were found: for instance, dialectical inquiry, devil's advocacy, group polarization, minority influence, and measures to reduce groupthink (e.g., bringing in outsiders) of which group polarization and groupthink have been referred to previously. The overall purpose of these techniques appears to be conflict resolution at a higher level of group functioning by inducing antagonists. This is certainly an important purpose for peer groups. However, it remains for the group to reach a decision and not end up in endless controversy terminated by other means than sound arguments. In sum, the social psychology literature reviewed by Levine and Thompson indicated that the three main mechanisms for group resolution of conflicts might be active in the same group over time. For the purpose of this chapter it is suggested that conflict avoidance, conflict reduction, and conflict creation mechanisms be studied in peer review contexts.

Scientific Controversy Studies

The sociological study of scientific controversies gained interest foremost in the 1970s and 1980s, as documented in a volume edited by Engelhardt and Caplan (1987). This book aims at answering two main questions. First, it is asked whether controversies in science are internal or external (that is, cognitive or social). Second, it is questioned how scientific controversies are closed or terminated. The first question is answered in different ways by the contributing authors of the book. Generally, McMullin (1987) and Giere (1987) argue that it is possible to distinguish between internal and external scientific conflicts. The former author uses a dichotomy between epistemic and nonepistemic factors to differentiate knowledge-based claims from social, political, ethical, and other claims in a controversy. Giere argues that science possesses the best procedures to answer questions about the empirical world. He (as well as McMullin) also distinguished between factual, methodological, and theoretical scientific controversies (see a similar analysis by Laudan, 1984). Mendelsohn (1987) and Nelkin (1987) take a more relativistic standpoint. Both stress social forces in scientific disputes—Mendelsohn giving examples from the history of science and Nelkin from more up-to-date events—in which science's traditional authority is questioned. In particular, Nelkin emphasizes the value-ladenness and political choices embedded in science and technology (see also Szanto, 1993). It appears that Mendelsohn and Nelkin do not want to exclude that nonepistemic factors play an important role in internal scientific controversies, whereas McMullin and Giere are more reluctant to support this claim. Conversely, they argue that scientific controversies may be purely epistemic and internal. A Swedish sociologist, Tomas Brante, has argued for the former position, namely that internal scientific controversies may be both cognitive and social (Brante, 1993).

The second question of Engelhardt and Caplan's book, concerning the termination of scientific conflicts, is less clearly answered. However, the editors suggest five ways that resolve conflicts. First, closure occurs through loss of interest, which of course is not a rational solution. Second, closure results through force, which equally is no rational solution. Third, closure through consensus, which denotes that members of a group unite by means of nonepistemic influences to a common belief, which may be more or less rational. Fourth, closure through sound argument, that is, "a generally justifiable system of arguments is used to deliver a solution" (Engelhardt & Caplan, 1987, p. 14). At this point a further two level dichotomy is proposed: (a) sound argument closure in the strict sense, and, (b) sound argument closure in the broad sense. The latter closure is relative to the historic and cultural context, while the former is not. Moreover, the authors suggest that there are two modes of the sound argument closures in the broad sense: a simple and a complex closure. The former denotes controversies within a scientific community and the second between scientific communities. Fifth, there is a final form of closure through negotiation in which there is neither a consensus nor a sound argument closure is suggested.

A general conclusion of the book is that scientific controversies are complex, involving social and cognitive factors of a great variety and on several levels. This implies that studies of scientific controversies initially should attempt to take all aspects and levels of the analysis into account (cf. Aldag & Riggs Fuller, 1993).

A program related to the studies of scientific controversies is Fuller's (1996) research program called social epistemology, which advocates naturalistic studies of research. He proposes four social ecologies in which to study scientific practice, namely the research production (at the department or elsewhere), investigations of peer review, university libraries ("the marketplace"), and the reading functions—for example, understanding, persuasion, self-serving ("the consumer perspective").

In sum, there is an agreement among scholars studying science to focus their research on disagreements in science in order to answer questions on how science relates to people and cultures and how controversies are resolved (if they are resolved). What is missing in these studies are the cognitive and social psychology mechanisms in scientific controversies and their resolution. For instance, I have not found any studies using knowledge from the study of group processes, group decision making, and social influence and very few empirical studies on peer review in the science studies field.

In the next section I will make an attempt to apply the knowledge from the review just presented to a case study. It concerns a disagreement between peers examining a Ph.D. thesis. The case is presented along the following lines: decision maker characteristics, decision task and context, group (dis)agreement, decision processes, and decision consequences. This structure is inspired by the group problem-solving model in Aldag and Riggs Fuller (1993) and studies in naturalistic decision making (Orosanu & Connolly, 1993).

A CASE STUDY OF A DISAGREEING EXAMINING COMMITTEE

To explore a disagreeing group in a peer review context, a case was chosen that concerned a disagreeing Ph.D. examination committee. The disagreement criterion demanded that one of the three members of the committee deviated—that is, voted against the other two when the decision for acceptance or rejection was made. In this particular Ph.D. committee, two peers voted for acceptance and one for rejection, which resulted (and probably always will result) in an accepted thesis. If two were against and only one pro, a Ph.D. degree is not obtained. The case study approach (see Stake, 1994) is intended to investigate a large number of aspects of a group decision conflict in a peer review. The information of the case was collected by means of interviews with the six persons involved. The documents connected with the case were the faculty protocol, the Ph.D. thesis, and a critical review of the thesis. This information was studied as a background for the case.[1]

Interview

Six persons were interviewed: the author of the thesis (A), his supervisor (S), the opponent (O), and the three members of the examining committee (X, Y, Z), who made up the peer group. A semi-structured interview concerning three themes was performed. First, questions were asked to gather data about the crucial persons who influenced and made the decision (the interviewees). These data were about their own research and its resemblance to the Ph.D. thesis being defended, as well as the favored scientific ideal. Secondly, questions were posed about the individual and collective judgment and decision making processes. Each respondent was asked to describe how his judgment was made before the public event, his impressions from the public dispute of the thesis and its impact, and how the group decision was reached when the committee members met after the public defense. Thirdly, there were questions concerning the thesis. These questions regarded individual as well as collective judgments of the scientific value of the thesis and the public defense by the author.

Interviews were conducted in a rather free manner, giving the respondent an opportunity to extend his answers on certain topics that seemed to be important for him. However, all themes of the interview guide were treated in the interview. The interviewer, here the author, sometimes and when needed for a clarification or else, followed up the respondent's answer with further questions. Interviews were conducted at the interviewee's office, but for one, which was made at the author's office and

lasted between approximately 40–75 minutes. Interviews were tape re-
corded and transcribed.

Procedure

The analysis was done in six main steps. First, all transcribed interview
texts were read through to get a full picture of the group decision. Second,
notes about important observations in the texts were taken. Third, each
answer referring to a theme was described in a summary sheet for each
respondent and, when particularly elucidating, followed by a citation from
the interviewee. At this stage the full interview of each respondent was
reread in order to find further information on the focused theme in other
parts of the text. Fourth, the summary and eventual citations for each
respondent on each theme were set up in a matrix for an analysis of
common and distinguishing factors influencing the three group member's
individual judgments and the group decision. Fifth, a comparison of answers across themes for each individual was performed to trace the individual and group decision processes (alternatives' attractiveness, reasons
for final choice—social and cognitive—and inconsistencies in reasoning).
Sixth, the analytical procedure for interpreting data roughly followed the
group problem solving model proposed by Aldag and Riggs Fuller (1993)
by including the components of the model in the analysis as a way to catch
a comprehensive picture of the decision making.

RESULTS

Decision Maker Characteristics

Roles and Relations. The Ph.D. committee consisted of two professors
from the home university—one from the same discipline (Y) and one from
a different discipline as the candidate (Z)—and a third member (X) from
another university but the same discipline. The opponent was selected
from the same discipline at another university abroad. The two members
from outside had met the author and seen portions of his work before
the defense of the thesis. The third peer was selected as a member of the
faculty at the thesis author's department. The opponent was known to one
of the committee members before the public defense and was selected
after two other candidates were dismissed by the departmental chair. The
thesis supervisor was one of the few professors at the department interested
in the author's research topic. The doctoral student and his supervisor
had, according to the tradition at this department, influenced the selection
of examining committee members.

Scientific View. Two of the three committee members (X and Z) did research in the same field as the doctoral student, characterized themselves as methodologists, and applied qualitative approaches. Another pair (Y and Z) was pronounced empirical, while X showed a less dedicatedly empirical view. Also, the supervisor declared that he was more empirically than theoretically oriented. The opponent expressed a less clear view on his scientific ideal. However, he was convinced that the thesis was below the academic standard because of the incorrect empirical analysis and conclusions, implying a lack of methodological rigor. In contrast, the author claimed the thesis to be close to a Kuhnian "exemplar" of disciplinary research uniting theory and empirical data in a hypothetical-deductive way.

Decision Task and Context

Evaluated Objects: Ph.D. Thesis and Author. Two committee members (X and Z) appreciated the research problem of the thesis, while a third member and the opponent did not. Overall, the committee judged the thesis as scientifically weak, particularly the empirical analysis (interviews and interpretations were not trustworthy). The author had not applied the "academic method" (an expression used by one of the peers). Hence, he did not show the variation in respondents' answers, and he relied too much on his theory rather than of the data in conclusions. The committee members as well as the opponent expressed this in different ways, but the author and his supervisor rejected the criticism and/or did not, in their own words, "understand it." However, the supervisor criticized the polemic style of the thesis. All interviewees claimed the thesis to be theoretically well above average and well written, and even "close to the research forefront." Two committee members had previously met the thesis author in an academic setting and a third had heard about his reputation, which announced a brisk, ambitious, and creative doctoral student. The opponent had no previews of the person before the public defense. In retrospect the author viewed himself as an academic failure.

The Public Defense of the Doctoral Thesis. The opponent was well prepared and performed a very critical, exhaustive, and thorough examination of the thesis. The criticism concerned the methodology and conclusions. Peer X criticized the opponent for not creating a dialogue with the thesis author. It was also obvious that the doctoral student did not respond convincingly to the opponent's questions. Z noticed a discrepancy between the tough-minded attitude he had seen before and the speechless person during the defense. The supervisor remarked that a milder opponent and a tougher respondent would have lead to another decision. The respondent had felt completely unprepared to the critical questions (although we know that

the opponent had warned the supervisor in advance about shortcomings).
Both the opponent and the respondent described the event as very unpleasant. The opponent had anticipated a strong defense and got the
impression that the audience perceived his critical examination as an attack
against the thesis' subject. The opponent was convinced that the examining
committee would accept the thesis (interpreted as three acceptance votes
and none against). The reasons for this conviction was that routinely a
doctoral thesis is previewed and accepted by a departmental committee
before it is defended in public (this was also the case here).

Decision Making Context Factors. The opponent had enough time to
review the thesis. He had asked the supervisor for instructions for the
review, because he was uncertain about Swedish Ph.D. standards, but none
were given. There were no contacts between the three committee members
during the time period from their selection to the defense.

Decision (Dis)Agreement

Surprisingly, the examining committee members agreed rather than disagreed about the group decision. The three members answered that the
thesis had weak methods. Therefore it should be discredited by a disagreeing vote, on which all members agreed. "Basically, we were rather united
in that there was a very serious criticism against the thesis" (an expression
by one of the committee members). The opponent's opinion was that the
board members should have rejected the thesis, but that they did not for
social reasons. The implication of this argument was that you can't reject
a thesis that is accepted by previewers. This is the informal rule of the
group decision. The two defenders of the thesis (author and supervisor)
mainly attributed the decision outcome to the controversial subject of the
thesis and the author, not the methodological weaknesses of the thesis,
which they both claimed they did not understand.

Decision Processes

Individual Decisions. Peer X (same discipline, another university) was
appointed to be an external reviewer about a year before the defense and
had criticized the empirical analysis, suggesting corrections. He was shocked
when seeing the final thesis not changed as expected, but his decision to
reject the thesis was impossible because of political reasons. This meant that
he was committed to new ways of viewing science and to the thesis field.
However, he was well aware of the methodological weaknesses and acknowledged the thesis could be rejected on this ground by another person. This
was experienced as a conflict by the professor. In retrospect, he regretted

the collective decision to criticize the thesis by two accept and one rejection votes. The main reason proposed was that the author could not pursue his academic career in this field the professor found so important—or any other academic field. He expressed a deep concern that the thesis was used as a textbook in university courses. His view was that the book could be used politically but not in academia. In conclusion, it was obvious that this peer experienced a decision making conflict between academic and political interests, which he solved by not being able to reject the thesis individually, but in the group decision he took part in a collective decision that marked the thesis as not fully acceptable.

Peer Y (same discipline and university) had considered a rejection, but had no real intention to make it. He accepted the opponent's remarks, but expressed a relativistic view regarding the criteria for acceptance/rejection. It was clear that also this peer had ambivalent feelings toward the group decision in retrospect. He remarked that if he had been able to read the thesis before he was asked to participate in the examining committee, he might have rejected to participate in the committee at all. A crucial argument for him to accept the thesis was the department's positive thesis preview. In conclusion, this peer's decision indicated that a negative decision for him demanded stronger criteria than a positive in this context.

Peer Z (different discipline, same university) accepted the thesis by weighing the pros and cons to a ratio of 60 to 40. During the public defense his ambivalence increased as a consequence of the opponent's strong criticism, the author's weak arguments, and the author's attitude, which differed from his picture of a tough-minded and clever doctoral student. In the committee meeting he found X at least as critical as himself, whereas Y appeared less engaged. X argued for a collective decision of two acceptance and one rejection votes, in which individual votes were anonymous. When this group decision alternative was found illegitimate, Z decided to take the responsibility of making the rejection decision, although he expressed concern over this by referring to negative colleague reactions. Z defended the acceptance group decision because of the excellent theoretical parts and the writing style of the thesis. In sum, this peer solved his individual decision conflict by viewing it as a collective responsibility. This is an indication of a decision transformation from the individual to the group.

Group Decision: The Decision Making of the Examining Committee. In all, the group had four decision alternatives. There were two decision alternatives for agreement. First, the choice of acceptance (all three peers vote yes). Second, the choice of rejection (all three peers vote no). Furthermore, there were two alternatives if the group disagreed. First, the choice of acceptance by two peers voting yes and one no. Second, the choice of rejection by two peers voting no and one yes. A decision alternative in which the doctoral thesis was accepted but not without further notice emerged after discussion. As is apparent from the decision alternatives, the first one of the disagreement alternatives was chosen: two yes and one no. The chosen alternative showed that the group tried to reach consensus in an agreement that the thesis was weak but accepted. A rejection decision was never "a real alternative" and no one was initially ready to vote for rejection. Two peers were bound by standards preventing them to act differently than to vote for acceptance. One standard was the preview decision with peer Y. The other one was peer X's critical stance toward traditional science. Peer Z, less bound by standards in this context, expressed the most critical remarks against the thesis and accepted to vote for rejection. The reason suggested for this choice was the unanimous agreement in the peer group to accept the thesis, but with a clear signal (the one rejection vote) that it had serious drawbacks. The opponent and the supervisor participated in the examining committee's meeting but were not involved formally in the decision. The opponent told the committee, at an early stage of the meeting, that he thought the thesis should be rejected. It was told that the supervisor made a few unsuccessful attempts to defend the author and the thesis during the meeting. The supervisor confirmed the overall information of the meeting as they were told by the peers. It was communicated to the doctoral student that the thesis was accepted immediately after the meeting. It was assumed by doctoral students at the department that the number of disagreeing (at least at face value) committees was a sign of setting higher standards for doctoral theses.

Decision Consequences

All three committee members agreed that it was a sound decision for science to discredit the thesis by two votes for and one against. This referred to a cognitive argument meaning that the empirical description, analysis, and conclusions of the thesis were inadequate. By means of this decision, the peers claimed that a warning was issued to the doctoral student, the supervisor, and the department that scientific methods must be followed. In addition, one peer argued that it was a bad decision for political or social reasons: a Ph.D. committee disagreement is a mechanism for exclusion from the academic society (and, in fact, the author did not pursue his or her research career). To the opponent, it was a negative decision, because it was detrimental to epistemological development. However, he appreciated the warning that the peer disagreement implied. In contrast, the author considered the outcome as a personal defeat, but was less prone to use epistemological arguments as support. To the supervisor it was a negative decision for epistemological reasons, mainly because he was convinced that the conclusions of the doctoral thesis were true.

TABLE 14.2
Reasons for Individual and Group Decisions in the Examining Committee

	Individual Decision		Group Decision
2 decision alternatives: Accept, Reject			4 decision alternatives: 3 Accept, 0 Reject 2 Accept, 1 Reject 1 Accept, 2 Reject 0 Accept, 3 Reject
Peer X	Peer Y	Peer Z	Group X-Y-Z
Accept (Reject impossible)	Accept (Reject impossible)	Accept (Reject possible)	2 Accept (X, Y), 1 Reject (Z) (Rejection impossible)
Reasons:	Reasons:	Reasons:	Reasons:
Pro accept + critical to "normal science" (c)	Pro accept + thesis writing style (c)	Pro accept + thesis theory and writing style (c)	consensus based on a mixture of sociocognitive reasons
+ clever student (s/c)	+ clever student (s/c)		
Con reject	Con reject	Con reject	
+ colleagues in the thesis field (s)	+ home departments acceptance (s/c)	+ colleagues at university (s)	
+ exclusion from academia (s)	+ social reasons (student) (s)		
	+ different criteria for rejection (c)		
	+ not field expert (c)		
Pro reject - thesis method (c)	Pro reject - thesis method ("not academic") (c)	Pro reject - thesis method ("not scientific") (c)	
- opponent right (c)	- opponent right (c)	- opponent right (c)	
Con accept	Con accept	Con accept	
- weak defense (c)	- weak defense (c)	- mismatch student before and after defense (s)	

Note. c = cognitive reason, s = social reason, s/c = mixed sociocognitive reason.

DISCUSSION

Disagreements, controversies, or conflicts in peer reviews provide us with
knowledge regarding decision making in the academic society, the peer
review process, and about researcher's thinking and behavior. The following discussion focuses on some of the most important issues found in the
reviewed literature illustrated by findings in the case study.

The Group Decision as a Social Representation

The formal decision made in the group of examining committee members
was a consensus decision in accordance with the Moscovici and Doise
collective consensus theory (1994). This was clearly a decision searched
for in group consensus, though the formal voting showed a disagreeing
group. The decision alternative favored by the group could be described
as a decision of acceptance with severe remarks. As Moscovici and Doise
puts it with reference to Solomon Asch:

> It is no mere play on words that the decision has the effect of transforming
> the representation of each individual into a social representation, which is
> the common base sought after. . . . If, after having taken a decision together,
> individuals remain loyal to it and feel themselves committed, it is most
> certainly in order not to disrupt the harmony once it has been reached.
> (Moscovici & Doise, 1994, p. 173)

But how was this decision made? The three individual choices (or rather,
prejudgments) of the decision object were acceptance. However, the group
decision alternatives made it possible to choose between two acceptance
alternatives: (a) and (b). So, the one and only alternative for an individual
if he chose acceptance was turned into two alternatives of acceptance for the
group as a collective mind (accept by 3–0 or accept by 2–1 votes). Peer Z,
who explicitly responded that he solved the conflict between acceptance and
rejection by transferring his decision to the group, gives an example of the
transformation. The (b) alternative appeared early on in the group's
discussions as a promising alternative for a decision because of the inade-
quacies of the thesis. The thesis was considered clearly weak by two of the
three peers before the defense. As is known from several studies of jury
decisions (Ajzen, 1996; Davis, 1973; Kerr, MacCoun, & Kramer, 1996), a
two-thirds majority nearly always prevails. This was also the case here.
Furthermore, the weakness was enhanced by the opponent's strong arguments and the defendant's equally weak arguments during the public
defense.

The De-emphasizing of Group Conflict

Social influence and group interactions were of course playing an important role for decisions in this case. First, there were influential social processes during the public defense of the thesis, reducing the probabilities for a total agreement of an acceptance alternative. Second, the peer meeting in which the opponent and the supervisor also took part made up a group of conflicting interests and views, which enhanced a future compromise solution.

The potential conflict between acceptance and rejection of the thesis in this case was quickly avoided or reduced by using a decision making rule acceptable to all parties. But there were other factors in the game.

It is a "well-kept secret," to quote Moscovici and Doise (1991, p. 175), that servitude plays an important part in most of the published research possesses. With reference to Knorr-Cetina (cited in Moscovici & Doise, 1991) it is suggested that researchers must take into consideration what is trendy in research, what one can or cannot do, who one can criticize and who one can associate with. This was typically part of the decision processes in this case. Peer X was committed to his research community, thereby supporting the thesis. Peer Z expressed negative feelings regarding his colleagues' reactions to the rejection alternative, though these feelings did not stop his choice. Finally, peer Y was strongly committed to his colleagues' acceptance decision at the home department, making the only decision alternative possible. The informal rule of the group decision was that you couldn't reject a thesis that was accepted by previewers.

It is clear that the mainly socially based factors influenced the peer review decisions as much as the cognitive (or epistemological) factors. In this case it appeared that the former factors overruled the latter according to the weight these factors were attributed. Two questions become important here: Is this case an exception or are social factors as strong in other cases? Are social factors also found as strong in other parts of the peer review system, for example grant proposal decisions? It can also be added that one or perhaps two of these social reasons never were openly expressed acting as "mindguards" and preventing an open conflict to take place in the group.

Accept and Rejection Criteria

Peer Y claimed that he applied different criteria for acceptance and rejection alternatives. Furthermore, the two other peers also did this, as was apparent from the analysis of reasons. This result supports previous findings that there are different criteria for accept and reject decisions in peer review of manuscripts and grant proposals especially in general or diffuse disciplinary fields, which is typical of the case studied here (Cicchetti, 1991; Hargens, 1988).

A Methodological Note

It is common to criticize retrospective data collected by interviews, as in this case for hindsight bias. This means that people's memory of judgments and decision processes are distorted by justifications made afterwards. However, as was argued by Lipshitz and Bar Ilan (1996), it is important to use such data because they also reflect the contents of the problem-solving schema the interviewed person applies in the investigated and similar situations. This does not mean that we should abandon real ongoing group decisions in further research on peer disagreement, although it is difficult to get access to these situations.

GENERAL CONCLUSIONS REGARDING A CONCEPTUAL FRAMEWORK ON PEER REVIEW DISAGREEMENT

The theoretical part of this chapter led to the conclusion that peer review studies could benefit from three fields of research. Such knowledge is found in the group decision making literature. Furthermore, group processes in conflicting groups are relevant for the study of peer review disagreement. Finally, studies of scientific controversies provide us with knowledge of the social and cognitive arguments, which have been used by scientists but also ideas about the termination of scientific disputes. The case study show us in turn that it is possible and fruitful to draw on this knowledge in an analysis of peer disagreement. Two important findings emerged in this case study: (a) that there is a difference between individual and group decisions in peer review because of different decision alternatives involving both social and cognitive reasons (group decision alternatives could be described in terms of a social representation); and b) that decision conflicts were de-emphasized by means of "mindguards," the informal rules in science that you don't express openly.

To study disagreement in peer review, it is suggested that the following framework consisting of nine points be applied.

1. The preferable designs at this stage of the research program are naturalistic studies of peer review decisions in retrospect or in ongoing group decision making before and after group meetings.

2. There are three key concepts in peer review studies to be analyzed: (i) the persons who perform the peer review (evaluators), (ii) the process by which the evaluators judge the research (evaluation process), (iii) the research which is evaluated (evaluation object). This is a distinction resembling the ones in naturalistic decision making of groups and individuals. Evaluator and evaluation object correspond to decision maker and decision making task.

3. The disagreement is investigated from a distinction between social and cognitive factors, though one should be aware that these factors may be intertwined and connected to each other in scientific disputes. However, it is a useful conceptual tool found in research in decision making and sociological studies of scientific controversies. In decision making, an analysis of the consequences is suggested to elucidate the distinction between choice on social and/or cognitive grounds in peer review (cf. Zakay, 1997).

4. The analysis of social and cognitive reasons for individual acceptance and rejection judgments should be carried out before and after group meetings, if possible, to prevent from hindsight bias. However, also data from retrospective interviews might be used.

5. It is important to distinguish between evaluators who make judgments and decisions individually and those who also meet to make group decisions as part of a peer review. In the latter case also group interactions and other social influences contribute to the evaluation results.

6. Disagreements in peer reviews may involve different number of peers—at least two, but often three or more. A conflict between two peers, who take opposite stands is different from a three- or four-group conflict in important ways in terms of group dynamic effects (e.g., more relations and interactions, the possibility of coalitions, homogeneity or heterogeneity among group members).

7. The separation of acceptance and rejection choices is preferred due to previous research findings suggesting different criteria for the two choices.

8. The analysis of group meeting processes and especially conflict resolution strategies and consensus seeking is crucial to explain the outcome of the meeting.

9. The distinction between individual and group decision alternatives (individual representations versus group or social representations) explains in part the group meeting outcome.

ACKNOWLEDGMENTS

This research was supported by a grant from FRN (Swedish Council for Planning and Coordination of Research). Portions of this paper were presented to the European Group for Process Tracing Studies in Decision Making (EGPROC) meeting, 14–16 August 1997 in Leeds, UK. I wish to thank Ingemar Bohlin and the editors for valuable comments on a previous version of the manuscript.

NOTE

1. Due to the delicate matter of the decision, the revealing facts are disguised or omitted as far as possible without making the study uninteresting. This includes the omission of the documents referred to above in the reference list.

REFERENCES

Abelson, R. P., & Levi, A. (1996). Decision making and decision theory. In G. Lindzey & E. Aronson (Eds.), *Handbook of social psychology, volume 1: Theory and method* (pp. 231–309). New York: Random House.

Ajzen, I. (1996). The social psychology of decision-making. In E. T. Higgins & A. W. Kruglanski (Eds.), *Social psychology: Handbook of basic principles.* New York: Guilford.

Aldag, R. J., & Riggs Fuller, S. (1993). Beyond fiasco: A reappraisal of the groupthink phenomenon and a new model of group decision processes. *Psychological Bulletin, 113,* 533–552.

Allwood, J. (1995). Dialog as collective thinking. In P. Pylkkänen & P. Pylkkö (Eds.), *New directions in cognitive science* (pp. 1–8). Publications of the Finnish Artificial Intelligence Society. International conferences—no. 2, Helsinki.

Bloor, D. (1976). *Knowledge and social imagery.* Chicago: University of Chicago Press.

Brante, T. (1993). Reasons for studying scientific controversies and science-based controversies. In T. Brante, S. Fuller, & W. Lynch (Eds.), *Controversial science: From content to contention* (pp. 177–191). Albany: State University of New York Press.

Brehmer, B. (1976). Social judgment theory and the analysis of interpersonal conflict. *Psychological Bulletin, 83,* (6), 985–1003.

Burnham, J. C. (1990). The evolution of editorial peer review. *Journal of American Medical Association, 263,* 1323–1329.

Burnham, J. C. (1992). How journal editors came to develop and critique peer review procedures. In *Research ethics, manuscript review, and journal quality* (pp. 55–61). Soil Science Society of America, Crop Science Society of America, and American Society of Agronomy, Madison, WI: ACS Miscellaneous Publication.

Campanario, J. M. (1996). Have referees rejected some of the most-cited articles of all times? *Journal of the American Society for Information Science, 47,* 302–310.

Chubin, D. E., & Hackett, E. J. (1990). *Peerless science: Peer review and U.S. science policy.* Albany: State University of New York.

Cicchetti, D. V. (1991). The reliability of peer review for manuscript and grant submissions: A cross-disciplinary investigation. *Behavioral and Brain Sciences, 14,* 119–186.

Cole, S., Cole, J. R., & Simon, G. A. (1981). Chance and consensus in peer review. *Science, 214,* 881–885.

Cole, S., Rubin, L., & Cole, J. R. (1977). Peer review and the support of science. *Scientific American, 237,* 34–41.

Davis, J. H. (1973). Social decision schemes. *Psychological Review, 80,* 97–125.

Engelhardt, H. T., & Caplan, A. L. (1987). Patterns of controversy and closure: The interplay of knowledge, values, and political forces. In H. T. Engelhardt, Jr., & A. L. Caplan (Eds.), *Scientific controversies* (pp. 1–25). New York: Cambridge University Press.

Fuller, S. (1995). Cyberplatonism: An inadequate constitution for the republic of science. *The Information Society, 11,* 293–303.

Fuller, S. (1996). Social epistemology and psychology. In W. O'Donohue & R. F. Kitchener (Eds.), *The philosophy of psychology* (pp. 33–49). London: Sage.

Giere, R. N. (1987). Controversy involving science and technology: A theoretical perspective. In H. T. Engelhardt, Jr., & A. L. Caplan (Eds.), *Scientific controversies* (pp. 125–149). New York: Cambridge University Press

Hackett, E. J. (1992). *More to do about peer review.* Paper presented to the annual meeting of the Society for Social Studies of Science, Gothenburg, Sweden.

Hargens, L. L. (1988). Scholarly consensus and journal rejection rates. *American Sociological Review, 53,* 139–151.

Hargens, L. L. (1990). Variation in journal peer review systems: Possible causes and consequences. *Journal of the American Medical Association, 263,* 1348–1352.

Harnad, S. (1982). Peer commentary on peer review. *The Behavioral and Brain Sciences, 5,* 185–186.

Harnad, S. (1985). Rational disagreement in peer review. *Science, Technology and Human Values, 19,* (3), 55–62.

Hemlin, S. (1991). *Quality in science: Researchers' conceptions and judgments.* Ph.D. dissertation, Department of Psychology, Göteborg University.

Hemlin, S. (1993). In the eyes of the scientist: A questionnaire study. *Scientometrics, 27,* 3–18.

Hemlin, S. (1994). [Review of Chubin, D. E., & Hackett, E. J. (1990). *Peerless science: Peer review and U.S. science policy.* Albany: State University of New York)]. *VEST Tidskrift för Vetenskapsstudier (VEST Journal for Science Studies), 7,* 111–115.

Hemlin, S. (1996). Research on research evaluation. *Social Epistemology, 10,* (2), 209–250.

Hemlin, S., Niemenmaa, P., & Montgomery, H. (1995). Quality criteria in evaluations: Peer reviews of grant applications in psychology. *Science Studies, 8,* 44–52.

Hogarth, R. M. (1987). *Judgment and choice: The psychology of decision.* Chichester: Wiley.

Horrobin, D. F. (1990). The philosophical basis of peer review and the suppression of innovation. *Journal of the American Medical Association, 263,* 1438–1441.

Janis, I. (1982). *Groupthink* (2nd rev. ed.). Boston: Houghton Mifflin.

Judson, H. F. (1994). *Structural transformations of the sciences and the end of peer review.* Invited paper presented at the International Congress on Biomedical Peer Review and Global Communications, July 13, 1994, USA.

Kassirer, J. P., & Campion, E. W. (1994). *Peer review: Crude and understudied, but indispensable.* Invited paper presented at the International Congress on Biomedical Peer Review and Global Communications, July 13, 1994, USA.

Kerr, N. L., MacCoun, R. J., & Kramer, G. P. (1996). Bias in judgment: Comparing individuals and groups. *Psychological Review, 103,* (4), 687–719.

LaFollette, M. (1994). Measuring equity. The U.S. General Accounting office study of peer review. *Science Communication, 16,* 211–220.

Laudan, L. (1984). *Science and values. The aims of science and their role in scientific debate.* Berkeley: University of California Press.

Levine, J. M., & Thompson, L. (1996). Conflict in groups. In G. Lindzey & E. Aronson (Eds.), *Handbook of social psychology, volume 1: Theory and method* (pp. 745–776). New York: Random House.

Lipshitz, R., & Bar Ilan, O. (1996). How problems are solved: Reconsidering the phase theorem. *Organizational Behavior and Human Decision Processes, 65,* 48–60.

McMullin, E. (1987). Scientific controversy and its termination. In H. T. Engelhardt, Jr., & A. L. Caplan (Eds.), *Scientific controversies* (pp. 49–91). New York: Cambridge University Press.

Mendelsohn, E. (1987). The political anatomy of controversy in the sciences. In H. T. Engelhardt, Jr., & A. L. Caplan (Eds.), *Scientific controversies* (pp. 93–124). New York: Cambridge University Press.

Miller, C. E. (1989). The social psychological effects of group decision rules. In P. B. Paulus (Ed.), *Psychology of group influence* (pp. 327–355). Hillsdale, NJ: Lawrence Erlbaum Associates.

Millman, J. (1982). Making the plausible implausible: A favorable review of Peters and Ceci's target article. *The Behavioral and Brain Sciences, 5*, 225–226.

Montgomery, H., & Hemlin, S. (1990). Cognitive studies of scientific quality judgments. *Studies of Higher Education and Research* (newsletter from the council for studies of higher education), *3*, 15–21.

Moscovici, S. (1985). Social influence and conformity. In G. Lindzey & E. Aronson (Eds.), *Handbook of social psychology, volume 1: Theory and method* (pp. 347–412). New York: Random House.

Moscovici, S., & Doise, W. (1994). *Conflict or consensus. A theory of collective decisions.* London: Sage.

Nelkin, D. (1987). Controversies and the authority of science. In H. T. Engelhardt, Jr., & A. L. Caplan (Eds.), *Scientific controversies* (pp. 283–293). New York: Cambridge University Press.

Niemenmaa, P., Montgomery, H., & Hemlin, S. (1995, March). *Peer review protocols of research applications in psychology II: The applicants' background and the decisions.* Reports from the Department of Psychology, Stockholm University, No. 794.

Orasanu, J., & Connolly, T. (1993). The reinvention of decision making. In G. A. Klein, J. Orasanu, R. Calderwood, & C. E. Zsambok (Eds.), *Decision making in action: models and methods* (pp. 3–20). Norwood, NJ: Ablex.

Pennington, N., & Hastie, R. (1986). Cognitive and social processes in decision making. In L. B. Resnick & J. M. Levine (Eds.), *Perspectives on socially shared cognition* (pp. 308–327). Washington, DC: American Psychological Association.

Peters, D. P., & Ceci, S. J. (1982). Peer-review practices of psychological journals: The fate of published articles, submitted again. *The Behavioral and Brain Sciences, 5*, 187–195.

Popper, K. (1972). *Objective knowledge: An evolutionary approach.* Oxford: Clarendon Press.

Ruderfer, M. (1980). The fallacy of peer review—Judgment without science and a case history. *Speculations in Science and Technology, 3*, 533–562.

Shafir, E., Simonson, I., & Tversky, A. (1994). Reason-based choice. In P. N. Johnson-Laird & E. Shafir (Eds.), *Reasoning and decision making* (pp. 11–36). Cambridge: Blackwell.

Sniezek, J. A. (1992). Groups under uncertainty: An examination of confidence in group decision making. *Organizational Behavior and Human Decision Processes, 52*, 124–155.

Stake, R. E. (1994). Case studies. In N. K. Denzin & Y. S. Lincoln (Eds.), *Handbook of qualitative research* (pp. 236–247). London: Sage.

Szanto, T. (1993). Value communities in science: The recombinant DNA case. In T. Brante, S. Fuller, & W. Lynch (Eds.), *Controversial science: From content to contention* (pp. 241–263). Albany: State University of New York Press.

Travis, G. D. L., & Collins, H. M. (1991). New light on old boys: cognitive and institutional particularism in the peer review system. *Science, Technology and Human Values, 16*, 322–341.

Van Lange, P. A. M. (1996). *Why reviewers are (believed to be) overly critical: A study of peer review.* Unpublished manuscript, Free University, Amsterdam.

Wegner, D. M. (1987). Transactive memory: A contemporary analysis of the group mind. In B. Mullen & G. R. Goethals (Eds.), *Theories of group behavior* (pp. 185–208). New York: Springer Verlag.

Wennerås, C., & Wold, A. (1997, May 22). *Nepotism and sexism in peer review. Nature, 387,* 341–343.
Worchel, S., Wood, W., & Simpson, J. A. (Eds.). (1991). *Group process and productivity.* London: Sage.
Zakay, D. (1997). *Deciding and implementing are two different decisions.* Abstract for the SPUDM conference, 17–20 August, 1997, Leeds, UK.

Part IV

COMMENTARIES

Chapter 15

Mats Björkman and Swedish Studies of Judgment and Decision Making

Kenneth R. Hammond
University of Colorado

MEETING MATS

Meeting Mats Björkman in Stockholm in 1965 was not what I expected. Instead of a stately, formal Swedish professor immersed in the intricacies of long-forgotten psychophysics, the first thing I saw when I was ushered into Mats's office was a wire and glass model of Brunswik's Lens Model! Mats knew I would be astounded and he greeted my astonishment with a big grin and then a hearty laugh; Mats likes a good joke. So then we sat down and had a good talk about Brunswik. It may be fair to say that he was the lone Brunswikian in Europe, I the lone Brunswikian in the U.S.; iconoclasts who discover one another always have much to talk about. I soon discovered that I had a valuable ally: a determined, independent thinker who not only held strong views but had a great deal of technical competence, and very high standards of research and scholarship. He was a good man to know.

In many ways Mats and Swedish psychology resemble one another. Both are strong, independent, and clear-headed; somehow, Swedish psychologists have a knack for coming straight to the point, for using direct, plain language. A few years ago I stumbled upon the following example from a little-known article by Mats that makes a devastating argument against the overwrought Bayesian view in the field of judgment and decision making. Because Mats is a scholar, he is well acquainted with the work of Karl Popper. And he brought his knowledge to bear on the claims made by the advocates of the "heuristics and biases" point of view by evoking Popper's distinction between "three worlds": As he put it, "World 1 is the world of physical objects and states, World 2 is the subjective world (perception, thinking, dispositions to act), and World 3 is the world of scientific concepts, problems and theories" (Björkman, 1984, p. 399). Mats pointed out that as a result of overlooking this distinction, those researchers devoted to Bayesian explanations of human judgment vastly over generalized their conclusions from World 3 to World 1. For example, he quotes M. Bar-Hillel as follows: "In the typical Bayesian reasoning contexts which people encounter in daily life, there is every reason to expect the fallacy to operate" (Bar-Hillel, 1980, p. 232). And he also quotes D. Lyon and P. Slovic: "Since the world operates according to Bayes' Theorem, experience should confirm the importance of base rates" (Lyon & Slovic, 1976, pp. 296–297). But Mats pointed out "World 1 is not in itself Bayesian, it is the Bayesian's representation of it that is Bayesian. What 'people encounter in daily life' are not 'Bayesian reasoning contexts.' They encounter objects, events, other people, all entities of World 1" (Björkman, 1984, p. 409). He further criticizes A. Tversky for being surprised at the "failure of people to infer from lifelong experience such fundamental statistical rules as regression toward the mean" (Tversky & Kahneman, 1974, p. 1130) and other statistical principles: "Discovery of statistical and other principles of World 3, e.g., the Pythagorean theorem, the law of the inclined plane, regression toward the mean, by pure induction is quite impossible. Had everybody's induction been sufficient it would not have required a Pythagoras, a Galileo, a Galton to make the discoveries" (Björkman, 1984, p. 412).

I was so impressed by this straightforward argument that I immediately quoted it in the book I was writing at the time (Hammond, 1996, pp. 219-222). I thought: "Why can't I get to the point like that?" My answer was that Mats has a talent that I don't have. But I can say this: the idea that Mats was expressing so well centers on the question of how are we to describe those "objects, events, other people" that we encounter in daily life? And it is this discussion that will provide the theme for my comments. For it is this discussion the brings out very clearly the need for a theory of the environment, or more specifically, the need for a theory of tasks. Note how the Bayesians simply and confidently assert that people encounter Bayesian reasoning contexts in daily life, and therefore "there is every reason to expect the fallacy to operate" and that "the world operates according to Bayes' Theorem" without offering the slightest justification for such a theory, or even a hint that they have uttered a theory. Yet, as Mats showed, such assertions are, to say the least, misguided. But although he drew a valuable distinction that helps us, Mats didn't offer a theory of tasks either, although he came close in his early, and brilliant, papers (Björkman, 1962, 1965). So in my comments on the following chapters I will come back to this topic—the need for a theory of tasks in our efforts to understand human judgment under uncertainty.

The several chapters that have been assigned to me can be grouped into two categories, those that expand Brunswikian psychology into broader ecological areas than have previously been considered, and those that do the opposite: namely, narrow the focus of Brunswik psychology. In the first category are those by Brehmer, Jansson, and Rigas; in the second are those by Juslin, Olsson, and possibly, Allwood and Granhag. Both categories contain innovative efforts that are impressive in their thoughtfulness and professional competence; all a credit to Swedish psychology.

EXPANDING BRUNSWIKIAN PSYCHOLOGY: ELABORATION OF REPRESENTATIVE DESIGN

No one can doubt that Berndt Brehmer was Mats Björkman's student; no one better exhibits Mats's characteristic combination of bluntness in speech and writing with depth of analysis. And both these characteristics have been put to work in Brehmer's use of the method of "microworlds" to expand Brunswikian psychology in the study of judgment and decision making. He believes "microworlds" will provide a method for just what the Brunswikians need in their effort to fulfill their demands for the representative design of experiments, and thus the meaningfulness of their work. Requirements for the representative design of experiments as put forward by Egon Brunswik (1956) are not only difficult to satisfy, but difficult to understand, at least for those who have been indoctrinated in the conventional design of experiments. But Swedish independence of thought meant that such indoctrination was absent from Mats Björkman's laboratory, and there is no doubt that Brehmer has a deep understanding of Brunswik's intent. Independence of thought provided the perfect context for the even-handed examination of Brunswikian methodological iconoclasm, and thus provided no difficulties for Björkman and his students. And it is just that spirit of independence and clearheadedness that characterizes Swedish psychology, and it is these characteristics that led Mats Björkman and his students to become advocates—and expanders—of Brunswik's unorthodox views.

Brehmer had plenty of experience with Brunswikian ideas and with the development of experiments that would approximate the requirements of Brunswik's representative design—he was a prolific researcher—so when he encountered Dörner's use of microworlds he knew immediately that he had come upon a method he could use. He also was familiar with the "heuristics and biases" approach that never tired of demonstrating that people are irrational decision makers, and admonishing us that there was no way to remove that irrationality. But Brehmer has a broader view. In his chapter in this book he asserts that "the focus on comparisons between normative theories and actual decision behavior has had two unfortunate consequences." First, it has narrowed and thus distorted "psychologists' conception of what a decision is" and "has limited the study of decision making to situations which confront the decision maker with a choice dilemma." Second, "it has turned psychologists' attention away from what should be their special task, that of studying what people *do* when confronted with decision problems." This situation, Brehmer claims, has left us with very little knowledge "about what people actually do when making decisions." That is a strong indictment of research in the field of judgment and decision making. But proclaiming the king to be naked is just what might be expected of Swedish psychologists, or at least, of Mats Björkman and his students. I agree that the focus on expected utility theory and the endless attacks on it as a descriptive model have had unfortunate consequences in that they have narrowed psychologists' views of decision making, but I find Brehmer's description of the remedy to be inadequate. He has been seduced by the realism of the microworld.

Brehmer intends to improve matters by turning his attention to the matter of dynamic decision tasks that "require a series of interdependent decisions" and in which "the state of the task changes, both autonomously and as a consequence of the decision maker's actions" and in which "the decisions have to be made in real time." He does so because he believes that these task conditions will require dynamic decision making, and that in turn will represent conditions that will teach us about "what people actually do when making decisions." He then presents us with "NEWFIRE: A microworld for studying dynamic decision making," which offers a computer program that provides the conditions of interest as well as recording the participant's response to these conditions. Now the question is: should we be satisfied with this? Before answering, we need to take a closer look at what Brehmer wants to achieve and what he has achieved.

It is clear that Brehmer wants to achieve a set of task conditions that will evoke what is, in his words, "what people actually do when making decisions." Few will quarrel very much with this goal, though many will stand on the ground that there are better ways to learn about judgment and decision making. With the enormously successful model of physical science in mind, they will find Brehmer's argument to be absurd, and will take a stand in favor of precisely defined conditions carefully established to test specific hypotheses about rationality, exactly the circumstances Brehmer finds to be nearly worthless after 50 years of application. Will we find Brehmer's work with NEWFIRE so productive of new insights into decision behavior that the argument will be settled in his favor? Maybe, but I have doubts.

To begin with, Brehmer uses the dangerous word "actually," a word that is a trap. It is a trap because using it implies that the user, in this case Brehmer, already knows the truth; that is, he knows what the decision maker "actually" does, otherwise how would Brehmer know when he has achieved his goal of discovering what people actually do? But if he does know, then the research would be unnecessary, for he already knows what the decision maker "actually" does. It turns out, however, that the word "do" is ambiguous. By "do" one might expect Brehmer to be referring to the cognitive activity of judgment and decision making. But he may not be referring to the judgment and decision making process; he may be referring to the overt behavior of the participant, the choices she or he makes (to deploy resources in a certain way, for example). But, of course, that is what the targets of his criticism also do; they examine this choice of action against that one. Thus, one might conclude that Brehmer's criticism of those researchers who focus on rationality is without merit; his research model is not different from theirs.

That criticism may be too harsh, however; after all, he does specify the conditions—and these are very different ones from those whom he criticizes—that he believes will evoke the cognitive activity that he believes to be—somehow—important, and therefore exactly that which he wants to observe; perhaps that is all we can demand of him. And perhaps he deserves praise for this, for it is true that few other researchers specify and justify their choice of conditions in terms of their representativeness of the complex judgment tasks in the human ecology. Here is where Brehmer's commitment to Brunswik's representative design of experiments remains steadfast. Indeed, he has extended Brunswik's conception of task properties to include changing task properties (that's what makes his decision making tasks dynamic). He certainly deserves praise for this because the construction of these tasks was exceedingly demanding of time and ingenuity. (I have personal knowledge of this; I tried the same and failed.) Not only that, but Brehmer had the courage to take this path when he was almost alone. He deserves credit for that as well.

Nevertheless, Brehmer falls short of meeting his own goals, and that is because his choice of conditions is arbitrary, that is to say, atheoretical. He makes no appeal to a theory of tasks; he chooses task conditions that simply appear to him to be important for reasons he does not disclose other than that they seem important to the participants whose cognitive competence he is studying, or that they somehow seem to be "real." He seems to have forgotten his own advocacy of the principles derived from Brunswik (curiously, he does not reference Brunswik). As a result, his description of the fire-fighting task is very long on the details of fire-fighting but very short on psychology; the only psychological concept that is mentioned in relation to the task is "frequency matching." That is interesting, but after several pages of fire-fighting description in nonpsychological terms, there simply isn't much there, as Brehmer seems to realize in his acknowledgment of the "triviality" of his results. In short, after all this, we don't learn very much about judgment and decision making.

I think I know the reason that Brehmer's work took this turn. The omission of a reference to Brunswik (and other work that follows from his) is no accident. Brehmer has fallen victim to the "naturalistic" approach advocated by Klein and his associates, whose work he does reference. Although I have high regard for the work of Dörner, and his painstaking construction of microworlds, I regard Klein's work—and his use of the term "naturalistic" decision making—to have created a false and misleading path to the goal outlined by Brunswik; that is to say, results that will generalize over conditions. I have high regard for Dörner's work because he has taken seriously the entanglement of the ecological conditions that are met by human judgment, and has done the hard work required to simulate these conditions. That is certainly praiseworthy. But once this work is done, those of us who study judgment and decision making from a psychological point of view need to translate (or better, interpret) those simulated conditions in terms of a psychological theory of task conditions; we cannot just accept task conditions as described by various professionals, economists, political scientists and others *in their terms*. As Stewart, Roebber, and Bosart (1997) put it: "Task properties are important both because they can facilitate or limit judgmental accuracy and because they describe the environment in which the judgment process was learned" (p. 206). And that is what is conspicuously missing from Klein, and now from Brehmer, as he becomes immersed in fire-fighting details; there is no interpretation of all those details in psychological terms.

That interpretation was not missing from earlier work by Brehmer, in which he painstakingly described the task in terms of uncertainty, cue intercorrelations, and the like. He may have found that task theory inadequate for several reasons, and would be justified if he did; there can be no doubt that we need better task theory. But he didn't replace that putatively inadequate task theory; he simply followed the (Klein) procedure of describing the task as a professional firefighter sees it, which meant no psychological theory at all.

To sum up: Brehmer was right to see that Dörner's work could lead to new knowledge that is not likely to be obtained by the traditional work in the judgment and decision making field (including my own). Dörner's work is gradually getting the recognition it deserves (see Sunstein, 1998, for an important review of Scott, 1998). And as Brehmer and his colleagues pursue their psychological experiments with microworlds they are providing world leadership in building a knowledge base that will be of use to those who study human judgment and the making of social policy. They

will expand our knowledge of human judgment and social policy making—provided that he and his colleagues free themselves from task descriptions by those who create the simulations and engage the more demanding work of creating a psychological theory of judgment tasks.

In a highly ambitious (another feature of Swedish psychology) effort,
Jansson brings us to a real challenge: assume you are a consultant to a
group that wants to make life better for its society-client. We will give you
the task, he says, and we will see what you can do with it. This approach
is a demonstration of the use of microworlds at its best. As the reader will
by now anticipate, however, I have some questions about the productivity
of this procedure. Will it really inform us about the psychology of judgment
and decision making in a manner that will allow generalization over similar
situations? Or will we find ourselves embedded so deeply in the task (as I
think Brehmer was) that we fail to improve our knowledge of judgment
and decision making?

But Brehmer and now Jansson may retort: "*You* may be interested in
improving psychological knowledge, but we are good Swedish pragmatists;
we want to know what people do—or as Brehmer put it, 'actually do'—when
they try to manage a complex and opaque system, and we want to know
how well they do it. What could be more important than that?" And
Brehmer and Jansson would further assert that they want to know that
because that is what people have to do in this world, and as anyone can
see, as Scott (1998) points out in detail, they are very poor at this task,
and the people of the world are paying a high price for that. What better
place for psychologists to place their efforts? Moreover, psychological theory and research have become mired in petty details about petty problems,
and we have lost our patience with them. So Brehmer and Jansson want
to leave behind the customary ways of studying judgment and decision
making and they want to expand Brunswikian psychology by moving on
to studying the behavior of people trying to cope with those critically
important judgment tasks so well simulated by microworlds.

That seems to me to be a pretty good argument; we need to see how
it works out.

We can begin with Jansson's introduction in which he makes a good
distinction: "Observability and action possibilities are properties of the task
to be performed, whereas goals and models are properties of the decision
maker." That's a good distinction, so it is too bad that Jansson moves away
from it so quickly, which he does a few sentences later when he says, "It
is not important whether [microworlds] approximate a certain decision
task or not, as long as the behaviors of the microworlds are congruent
with the participants' expectations." Thus, after making a good and proper
distinction between the properties of subject and object, he obliterates
that distinction by indicating that "participants' expectations" will deter-

mine the acceptability of the task properties. Perhaps we should be grateful for that stumble, for it makes very clear the need for a theory of tasks that is independent of the participant, just as Jansson put it before he ignored his message.

An even better argument for the need of a psychological theory of tasks can be seen in Fig. 3.1 (p. 27), in which the structure of the MORO system is presented; here is a dynamic—and daunting—system indeed! Where did it come from? Is this the careful computer representation of an actual tribal system? Or is it a creation of some imaginative sociologist/political scientist/economist/geographer? Jansson should tell us which it is, for that is a critical distinction. If it is the former, we have the satisfaction of knowing that someone was able to collect the data that would enable some genius to write a program that simulates a real economy that is highly complex. If the latter, we must ask why *this* program? For if the program simulates an actual tribal system, then it provides its own justification; it represents a slice—a very good slice—of reality. But if it is a creation of someone's imagination, someone who merely wanted to create a complex, opaque, and dynamic system, then we need more justification; why *these* arrangements? To test the participants' ability to cope with extraordinary complexity? It hardly seems necessary to learn that few, if any, can cope with this system under any circumstances. Without some anchor for this task, all we can say is that some strategies were better than others. That may be important in Jansson's eyes, and indeed, he may be right; this task may be a touchstone; behavior here may be predictive of behavior everywhere. But it may not. So those hard-headed Swedish psychologists will soon be testing that proposition.

It may appear that I am overly critical of the research that employs microworlds, and that appearance may be correct; I may indeed be *overly* critical. So to avoid being overly wrong, let me say again that I think Swedish psychology deserves credit for providing world leadership in taking advantage of the opportunities offered by microworld simulation. Mats Björkman's independence of thought and farsightedness in understanding that the fundamental ideas of Brunswikian psychology carried the seeds of investigations that would lead to the use of microworlds when others ignored them. I completely agree with that turn in research and theory, and I agree with Brehmer and Jansson that this could be a productive and stimulating effort, and I congratulate them for having the courage and stamina to carry out the work. My wish is that they will be true to themselves and to the Brunswikian psychology that they stand on, and go on to develop theories of these complex microworlds.

Rigas and Brehmer are to be congratulated for putting their fingers on one of the most important and yet most neglected topics in psychology—the theoretical underpinnings of intelligence testing, and the relation of measured intelligence to performance in settings that (apparently) demand intelligence, of some kind. The authors consider the question of whether performance in microworlds provides a proper testing ground for the validity of intelligence tests, and suggest that they might well do so. But they reject that hypothesis in view of the fact that they do not find correlations between the two types of performance. As a result, they conclude that "we need new forms of tests aimed at the more complex processes that we find in the every day tasks that are simulated by microworlds." That is, performance in microworlds is taken to be the criterion for establishing the validity of the intelligence test because microworlds simulate "everyday tasks," and, in their view, intelligence tests do not. Therefore, if there is no correlation between these two domains, then it is the intelligence test that is at fault, and it is these, not the microworlds, that should be revised. That, of course, is a profound conclusion; is it justified? I do not think so.

Space does not permit me to address this problem in the detail it deserves; let me just say that my position is that *both* efforts need revision, and that the revision should be based on Brunswikian methodology that calls for a theory of tasks.

Consider first the Advanced Progressive Matrices that these authors used to measure intelligence. Rigas and Brehmer are right to note the importance of denoting and specifying the cognitive processes involved in coping with the problems in the Raven test, and they are right to contrast and compare these to the cognitive processes involved in coping with the demands of a microworld. And their treatment of these relationships seem to me, not an expert in this field, to be admirable, and quite in line with traditional psychology. But I am not a traditionalist; traditionalists always look inside the organism for their explanations, as do these authors, but iconoclastic Brunswikians like me look outside the organism. Therefore my objection is that nowhere is there a consideration or justification of the origin and selection of the Raven *problems.* What theory of intelligence insisted that these problems should be used as markers of intelligence? In short, why *these* problems? What theory of tasks led to the selection of these problems?

Thanks to the success of Carpenter, Just, and Schell (1990) in modeling the cognitive processes of persons taking the test, we now know that the test demands the successful discovery and use of five different rules. What determined the choice of these rules and the problems that exemplify them in the test? Fortunately, Carpenter et al. provide us with a rare event; they give us a clear answer, and show us how casual the traditionalists are with respect to matters outside the organism.

> John Raven constructed problems that focused on each of six different problem characteristics, which approximately correspond to the different types of rules that we describe later. He used his intuition and clinical experience to rank order the difficulty of the six problem types. Many years

later, normative data from Forbes (1964) . . . became the basis for selecting problems for retention in newer versions of the test and for arranging the problems in order of increasing difficulty, without regard to any underlying processing theory. Thus, the version of the test [examined here] . . . is an amalgam of Raven's *implicit* theory of the components of reasoning ability and subsequent item selection and ordering done on an actuarial basis. (Carpenter et al., 1990, p. 408; italics added)

This is a fascinating account of the development of a test that has been used thousands of times, not only to measure the intelligence of a wide variety of people, but as a marker for other tests. This account indicates that the original basis for the choice of the discovery of rules is defenseless; what should have been a coherent presentation of a series of ideas or concepts that provides the justification for why the discovery of rules is important is missing. Raven may well have had such a theory—and he may not—but it has never been available. Nor has a such theory been presented. The defense for the use of the test lies within the correspondence metatheory—that is, "it works." The "actuarial basis" for item ordering and the various psychometric explorations of its relations with other tests (all equally like to have dubious theoretical origins) provide the justification for its use for making decisions about the intelligence of people. And the modeling provided by Carpenter et al. of the cognitive activity induced by the problems affords, long after its development and wide application, further empirical evidence of the nature of the test. Thus we see how a test that demands "analytical intelligence" from its participants did not demand "analytical intelligence"—that is, coherence competence—from its originator, or at least did not demand that he make it explicit, nor from its developers, but did demand from them empirical competence, and thus correspondence competence. Ironically then, the test makers demand coherence competence from their participants, but correspondence competence from themselves.

Thinking about how this might have been otherwise helps to see the importance of coherence competence and the need for a theory of tasks. Instead of relying on "intuition" (whatever this may mean to Carpenter et al.) and "clinical experience" (whatever this may mean to anyone) Raven might have decided that he was interested in analytical competence, and then decided to discover what the logicians had to say about this, since analytical competence has generally been their field of interest. That might have led him, for example, to consult a book similar to R. Jeffrey's (1981) *Formal Logic*, where a perusal of the table of contents would have shown him seven chapters, with the following headings: Truth-Functional Inference; Truth Trees; Truth-Functional Equivalence; Conditionals; First-Order Logic; Undecidability; Completeness. That discovery might then have led him to decide that this book covered a reasonable variety of types of analytical challenges, and that he would be on safe ground if he were to include in his test of "analytical intelligence" a number of problems from each of these chapters. The content of his test then at least could be defended by pointing to his method of selection, rather than by an appeal to his "intuition" and "clinical experience." In the empirical investigations that would follow, the investigators would then have the benefit of knowing what they were investigating, namely the main subjects of formal logic.

Thus, we see that the choice of these problems was a happenstance of undocumented "intuition and clinical experience," both doubtful justifications for drawing conclusions about the intelligence of other persons. But, you will say, the Raven test has been empirically tested many times by comparing it with other intelligence tests, and it has passed this test many times, and has come to be one of the most widely used measures of intelligence. So who cares what its origins may be? Anyone taking this position has declared their allegiance to the correspondence theory of truth; if an idea corresponds to a fact, it is true (or at least, useful), never mind that the idea lacks coherence. Now, however, we need to ask about the justification that rests on this correspondence; where did the problems in those *other* tests come from? Through item selection procedures well known to test makers. These, too, are based on the correspondence theory of truth; if it correlates, keep it; if it doesn't, drop it; never mind any questions of coherence.

Of course, these brief sentences are oversimplifications, but I believe they speak to the question of why performance on the Raven problems should or should not be expected to be related to performance in a microworld with its emphasis on "everyday tasks." Performance on the Raven means performance in relation to a set of tasks—arbitrarily chosen—that lack theoretical justification. And although it is true that Carpenter et al. do a heroic job in explicating the nature of performance on the Raven problems, it remains performance on arbitrarily chosen tasks, tasks that lack theoretical justification.

Which brings us to the justification of the specific choice of the problems of the microworlds. How are these to be justified? These authors think that they are justified by virtue of the fact that they demand "the more complex processes that we find in the everyday tasks that are simulated by microworlds." But if the reader will glance at their Figure 2, which represents the causal structure of the central variables in the MORO simulation, my guess is that he or she will be surprised, perhaps astounded, to find that this is an "everyday task." Surprise or not, how do Rigas and Brehmer support that claim? Certainly not by the correspondence theory of truth; there are no empirical correlations with performance on "everyday tasks," or at least none are offered here. And if correspondence is lacking, where is the justification that comes from coherence? It, too, is nonexistent. This is one of the consequences of failing to be guided by a specific theory of tasks; one just makes careless generalizations. But justification for this specific microworld must come from two sources; either a microworld is a reasonable representation of a tribal situation that exists, or it is a construction of one based on some unspecified notion of what might exist. In either case, it is a useful task for a study of social policy making, and as I indicated above, I applaud this research approach. That does not mean, however, that research that links these two sets of tasks—those in the intelligence test and those in the microworld—is likely to be fruitful. Why should anyone anticipate or require that two arbitrarily selected tasks produce correlated responses? To avoid having to answer questions like that we need a defensible and defended theory of tasks. And that theory should be applied to both tests of intelligence and tests of judgment.

NARROWING THE FOCUS: EXAMINATION
OF CALIBRATION

Rather than comment on each of the chapters that consider the thorny problem of calibration, I will discuss them in general. That is because I lack the technical competence to examine the many details that are involved in this complex and carefully studied topic, and because my comments address the problem of calibration itself.

The several authors offer a sophisticated, technical account of the overconfidence phenomena that seems to me to be an impressive but dangerous scholarly effort. It is certainly scholarly; combining the probabilistic theories of Brunswik and Thurstone is no task for the timid. Nor will that task permit a shallow approach; one has to be master of the field to be convincing. Are the authors convincing? Not entirely. I am primarily worried about the lack of robustness of the overconfidence phenomena. It doesn't seem to take much tinkering with the task conditions to make overconfidence disappear, and indeed, small changes can produce underconfidence. That is worth knowing. And in addition, the authors seem to be leading to a constructive convergence of what formerly seemed to be separate approaches.

But I worry about work that is narrowly focused and apparently requires extensive reductionism in order to bring about closure (even though I admire the excellence and ingenuity of the closure attained). For situations of this kind I offer a solution, and that is the Campbell and Fiske (1959) multitrait multimethod approach (see also Hammond, Hamm, & Grassia, 1986, for an example of its application to judgment and decision research). I suggest this approach because it eliminates the danger attached to a too close wedding of method and concept, and that is the danger that I see here; too many experiments attached to the use of too few methods (the use of almanac, or general knowledge questions). That is exactly the situation that has led to the demise of seemingly robust findings in psychology (recall the "risky shift" fiasco). Moreover, I am uneasy with the application of the Brunswikian "cues" to such questions.

Juslin and his colleagues point to the Brunswikian cast of the their research that addresses the relation of subjective probabilities to ecological probabilities. That means that they have turned the topic from a consideration of the *coherence* of subjective probabilities (e.g., do they add up to 1.00?) to the question of the extent to which subjective probabilities *correspond* to ecological probabilities. (Does my subjective probability of *xx* that rain occurs on this date correspond with the ecological facts that rain occurs with a relative frequency of *yy* on this date?) That may appear to be a simple idea, but in fact it represents a profound change in the field of psychology, which Juslin recognizes (although the originators of the calibration problem did not). Indeed, in a long-forgotten contribution to what was once a very important symposium in 1941 involving Clark Hull and Egon Brunswik, Kurt Lewin, himself now nearly forgotten, took aim at Brunswik's conception of probability. Lewin denied a legitimate place for calibration studies in psychology; Brunswik's position gives them a central place.

Here is Lewin separating himself from Brunswik: Brunswik "wishes to include in the psychological field those parts of the physical and sociological world which, to my mind, have to be excluded. These parts, he states, have to be studied in a statistical way, and the probability of the occurrence of events calculated" (Lewin, 1943, p. 308). He became more explicit: "To my mind, the main issue is what the term 'probability' refers to. Does Brunswik want to study the ideas of the driver of a car about the probability of being killed or does he want to study the accident statistics which tell the 'objective probability' of such an event. If an individual sits in a room trusting that the ceiling will not come down, should only his 'subjective probability' be taken into account for predicting behavior or should we also consider the 'objective probability' of the ceiling's coming down as determined by the engineers. To my mind, only the first has to be taken into account, but to my inquiry, Brunswik answered that he meant also the latter" (p. 308). These remarks neatly divide two of the most important theorists of the twentieth century.

It is ironic that a half-century later Brunswik's view is the basis for establishing research programs, such as Juslin's, in psychology, while Lewin's view, which denies calibration research a place in psychology, is hardly considered. Curiously, Lewin is seldom read today, yet is far better known than Brunswik. Even so, although no one today would accept Lewin's *explicit* argument that "the physical and sociological world . . . have to be excluded" from psychology, we must be alert to the *implicit* acceptance of his argument. For we can find it in those overbearing assumptions of the "heuristics and biases" Bayesians about the nature of the world, assumptions identified and corrected by Mats Björkman. Their work is focused on the interior dynamics of judgment and decision making—is it rational?—to such an extent that they could blithely declare—without defense—that the world is structured according to their statistical theory of those dynamics.

Lewin (1943) thought we had no need for a theory of environmental tasks, because their was no room for consideration of the ecology in psychology. Although we see that the research on calibration defies Lewin's view, that research unfortunately retreats from the development of a theory of its questions. For example, research on calibration (and thus overconfidence) starts with "general knowledge" questions, and then proceeds to disentangle various aspects of participants' responses to these questions. But I wonder what these researchers had in mind when they chose general knowledge questions as the basis of their research paradigm; what kind of cognitive activity are these task/questions intended to evoke? Better, what sort of cognitive *competence* are they supposed to evoke, or test? Are such questions supposed to test the coherence of their participants' cognitive work? That is, do they test their ability to raise a series of answers and then test their consistency? Lewin would approve of this. Or do they test the participants' ability to think of empirical facts and apply them accurately to the case at hand? That would be closer to what Brunswik had in mind.

Juslin and Olsson (in Chapter 5) offer their thoughts about this in an example: ". . . a participant may recall that Indonesia lies in Asia while Sudan lies in Africa, and use these facts as a probabilistic cue to which country has a higher mean life expectancy. The participant may believe that Asian countries tend to have higher mean life expectancy than African countries and thus that within Asian–African pairs of countries the Asian country most often has the higher mean life expectancy. The continent cue thus suggests that Indonesia probably is the correct answer. This illustrates how limited knowledge of a natural environment can be used to make probabilistic inferences."

Well, maybe. But I see this as farfetched (even if this process can be simulated). I interpret this circumstance as one that presents the participant with a nearly impossible task in that it offers almost no information other than what the participant can bring to it through his or her general knowledge, which, in all likelihood, is empirically minimal as well as incoherent. (The fact that experts generally perform better than novices offers some support for my judgment, which I acknowledge to be based largely on ignorance.)

Under these circumstances (if I have them right), what results are to be expected? The opposite of robustness; that is, results highly contingent upon task, and or method, conditions, which certainly seems to be the case. Indeed, Juslin and Olsson report that the change from half-range to full-range formats produces the astounding result that "there can be simultaneous over- and underconfidence depending on the assessment format"(!). Therefore I am troubled by the sensitivity of the results to what Juslin and Olsson call the "idiosyncrasies in the methods and scales used for the overt response elicitation."

Of course, I may be wrong to be troubled about this; after all, the authors present a strong case for the soundness of their conclusions. Juslin and his colleagues have an explanation for this, and it lies in what I regard as an heroic combination of Brunswikian and Thurstonian views of probability. But I believe they went in the wrong direction; that is, they went inside the organism rather than outside. Indeed, their entire approach seems to favor interior explanations rather than exterior ones, as a Brunswikian effort would require. Going inside always seems to result in a plethora of explanations piled on top of one another. The collapse of learning theory derived from running rats in mazes, as well as well as Lewinian theory, offer examples.

SUMMARY

Sweden should be proud of its psychologists and their accomplishments. The chapters that I have reviewed demonstrate clearly that their psychologists are in the forefront of the research community; indeed, they may well be ahead of their time. I have done my best to be critical, for the reason that first-rate work deserves first-rate criticism. I have tried to follow Karl Popper's dictum that one should direct criticism at an author's *strongest* points. That is why I have addressed the central issue in these papers, the question of the theory of the tasks they have employed, for it is in this area I believe they lead the world.

REFERENCES

Bar-Hillel, M. (1980). The base-rate fallacy in probability judgments. *Acta Psychologica, 44,* 211–233.

Björkman, M. (1962). On learning to predict events. *Scandinavian Journal of Psychology, 3,* 233–240.

Björkman, M. (1965). Studies in predictive behavior: Explorations into predictive judgments based on functional learning and defined by estimation, categorization, and choice. *Scandinavian Journal of Psychology, 6,* 129–156.

Björkman, M. (1984). From dualism to pluralism: The third world in judgment under uncertainty. In K. M. J. Lagerspetz & P. Niemi (Eds.), *Psychology in the 1990s* (pp. 399–424). Amsterdam: Elsevier.

Brunswik, E. (1956). *Perception and the representative design of psychological experiments* (2nd ed.). Berkeley: University of California Press.

Campbell, D. T., & Fiske, D. W. (1959). Convergent and discriminant validation by the multitrait-multimethod matrix. *Psychological Bulletin, 56,* 81–105.

Carpenter, P. A., Just, M. A., & Shell, P. (1990). What one intelligence test measures: A theoretical account of the processing in the Raven Progressive Matrices Test. *Psychological Review, 97,* 404–431.

Forbes, A. R. (1964). An item analysis of the advanced matrices. *British Journal of Educational Psychology, 34,* 1–14.

Hammond, K. R. (1996). *Human judgment and social policy: Irreducible uncertainty, inevitable error, unavoidable injustice.* New York: Oxford University Press.

Hammond, K. R., Hamm, R. M., & Grassia, J. (1986). Generalizing over conditions by combining the multitrait-multimethod matrix and the representative design of experiments. *Psychological Bulletin, 100,* 257–269.

Jeffrey, R. (1981). *Formal logic: Its scope and limits* (2nd ed.). New York: McGraw-Hill.

Lewin, K. (1943). Defining the "field at a given time." *Psychological Review, 50,* 292–310.

Lyon, D., & Slovic, P. (1976). Dominance of accuracy information and neglect of base rates in probability estimation. *Acta Psychologica, 40,* 287–298.

Scott, J. (1998). *Seeing like a state: How certain schemes to improve the human condition have failed.* New Haven: Yale University Press.

Stewart, T. R., Roebber, P. J., & Bosart, L. F. (1997). The importance of the task in analyzing expert judgment. *Organizational Behavioral and Human Decision Processes, 69,* 205–219.

Sunstein, C. (1998, May 18). More is less. *New Republic,* 32–37.

Tversky, A., & Kahneman, D. (1974). Judgment under uncertainty: Heuristics and biases. *Science, 185,* 1124–1131.

Chapter 16

Well-Calibrated Claims
About Difficult Questions

Baruch Fischhoff
Carnegie-Mellon University

When I went back to school to get a PhD., I had the extraordinary good fortune to stumble into Amos Tversky and Danny Kahneman's research group, at the time that they were creating their "heuristics and biases" approach to judgment under uncertainty. It was an exciting time, seeing important science created before your very eyes, with a remarkable cast of fellow students, some of whom will be known well to readers of this volume: Maya Bar Hillel, Ruth Beyth-Marom, Zur Shapira, Ruma Falk, Gershon Ben-Shakhar, and David Navon, among others.

As we struggled to master what was already "out there" in the field of decision making, it quickly became clear that the action was disproportionately in a few academic centers. Most were in likely places—namely, major American research universities, with the intellectual resources needed to feed an emerging interdisciplinary field. The University of Michigan was one, the University of Colorado another, the Oregon Research Institute a third (which made more sense once we realized that this anomalous organization was mostly ex-Michiganders, a long stone's throw from the University of Oregon).

Then there were the Swedes. They had exotic names, like Mats Björkman (how did you pronounce it?) and Ola Svenson (man or woman?) and Henry Montgomery (exotic in the Swedish context, at least). More important for us students, they were doing significant work (defined, in part, by our advisors' insistence that we read it) in a small country, remote from the American centers of power. We didn't know exactly how they did it, but it gave us some confidence that we might do the same. Moreover, their work was stimulating and insightful.

Studying my assigned chapters (8–14) in this excellent volume made me reflect on our old question, "How do the Swedes do it?" With 25 years of additional perspective, I realize that they were less isolated than it seemed, even back then, before the Internet (or even, sometimes, reliable international phones). I also realize that we were less isolated than it seemed. Faculty traveled, got training elsewhere, had their invisible colleges, and so on. And we were the beneficiaries.

Still, I think that there were some common elements in the Swedish experience and our own, which turned geography to some advantage—and gave their work a particular resonance. And, judging by these chapters, they are still doing it. If I may be allowed, let me use these fine papers as an opportunity to speculate on some of the processes that may make Swedish decision making so rewarding to the reader. These are not ruminations about how Swedish "national character" reflects itself in research (which, to me, would be an offensive question), but thoughts about how local conditions affect the pursuit of knowledge that will be universally recognized. A word like "seems," "my guess is," "perhaps," or "possibly" should go in every sentence. It would take a historian to do the task justice. Even then, we would be limited by the fact that, in life, we are always in the experimental group, without a control group, showing what would have happened had any element been changed (the current research interest in counterfactuals notwithstanding).

One essential element in the success of Swedish decision making research was leadership, from Mats and a few others who said, in effect, "We can do this and we're going to do it right." Central to the definition of "right" was dealing with problems that mattered. Thus, Gärling, Karlsson, and Selart wonder how ordinary people manage to make potentially complex economic decisions, limited by time and attention. Svenson, Montgomery, and Willén wrestle with how people impose (or extract) structure in everyday situations lacking the tidiness of laboratory experiments. Sjöberg asks how citizens' attitudes, values, and opinions fit together when evaluating national defense policies. Selart, Eek, Biel, and Gärling examine coordination and conflict in social decision making. Hemlin places scientists themselves under the microscope, examining the intellectual discipline in the peer-review processes that determine the character of scientific disciplines.

Other features follow from the decision to look hard at people's real problems. One is that the commitment to the people and the problems militates against methodological and ideological rigidity. It makes one more likely to do whatever it takes to figure out what is really happening—and not be bound to the endogenously generated issues that arise within a research paradigm. For example, beginning with Svenson's pioneering work, Swedish investigators have been in the forefront of process-tracing research. Their innovations have adapted a technique that had proven itself with highly structured tasks to the more complex world of decision making. Then, having done so, they succeeded in making the case for the approach to other disciplines, still entrenched in experimental methods as the sole path to knowledge.

Svenson, Hemlin, Montgomery, and Willén show the productivity of the process-tracing approach, with results and theory that would be unthinkable without it. Their approach embodies standards of evidence that make their results more than just interesting collections of people's reflections about their encounters with natural settings. Rather, their research poses testable hypotheses about recurrent patterns of behavior, whose prevalence (or absence) can be examined in diverse settings. These investigators' narratives are distinguished by their readiness to allow that behavior is complicated, with different determinants in different circumstances—but drawn from a well-characterized set of possibilities. It is heartening to see investigators describe the progress in their own thinking, free of any self-imposed compulsion to show that the world is cut of a single cloth. Although not represented in this volume, the phenomenological approach of Gunnar Karlsson involves a further extension of disciplined attempts to get at what is on people's minds.

The same complexity can be seen in chapters using other methodologies. Gärling, Karlsson, and Selart integrate research on mental accounting and behavioral life cycles, in order to accommodate the range of results on temporal perspective. They also feel obligated to reconcile results in economics and cognitive psychology, then conclude with a research agenda that involves grappling with the wrinkles induced by greater monetary and affective stakes. Similarly, Hemlin casts a wide net in his account of the controversies that can arise in scientific peer review. He uses results from sociology, philosophy, cognitive and social psychology, both to provide insight and to ensure the robustness of his interpretations. Selart, Eek, Biel, and Gärling also cross disciplines, thereby reducing the risks of "definitiveness through exclusivity," in the sense of narrowing one's field of view to one in which a predicted behavior pattern is disproportionately likely (or even obligatory).

Indeed, rather than claiming to have studied behavior in (self-defined) ideal surroundings, these authors typically bend over backward to characterize the strengths and weaknesses of their research settings. That, combined with the diversity of those settings, provides a rich account for the reader. In most cases, the interpretations are very judicious, freed of any feeling that the authors are advancing some agenda through their research. Instead, the reader is left with clear pictures of complex phenomena. For example, by acknowledging that people take different degrees of initiative in structuring their tasks, Svenson, Selart, Gärling, Karlsson, Eek, and others avoid aggregating data that might be produced by different processes (hence, would defy a common account). In other cases (e.g., Hemlin, Biel, Eek, and Gärling), authors remind us of individuals' social and political identities, providing a context that is often missing in psychology, with its individualistic focus—yet might be essential to individuals, as they project themselves into decision-making tasks.

The result of all this care and context is often a highly nuanced account, which leaves the reader with a good feeling for the robustness and generalizability of research results. The claims are well-calibrated, in the sense that one can afford them the credibility that the authors do. This is all the more remarkable, considering the difficulty of the topics that are tackled. Or perhaps it is to be expected; given the importance of the topics, it would be a social disservice to claim any more or less than the data warrant.

What, in Swedish conditions, might have fostered this dedicated, nonsectarian approach to research? One possibility is that, in small countries, scientists from diverse disciplines are more likely to know one another. They are, for example, more likely to have common friends or experiences, such as public school, avocations, or military service—through which they can gain mutual credibility. Psychologists who know sociologists may take sociology seriously, just as experimentalists may take think-aloud protocols more seriously if they dine with researchers who collect them. Of course, familiarity can also breed contempt and petty rivalries. However, by and large, that is absent from these chapters. The authors seem to respect one another, and to feel an obligation to accommodate the results that emerge from the diverse realities created by their different methods.

A second, and related, possibility is that people from small countries travel abroad. If they go in different directions, then they may bring back different ideas, the merit of which they can then evaluate, relatively free of the group pressures arising from the battles between competing schools in larger countries. Consistent with this possibility, the authors in this volume sometimes draw upon competing paradigms, whose proponents rarely cite one another (except, perhaps, as targets of approbation). They also have a noteworthy willingness to reach back in time, tracing the historical roots of ideas that tend to be overwritten by contemporary versions (although this may reflect a scholarly tradition, quite independent of country size).

A less-related possibility is that remoteness can foster a taste for problems that can be pursued at one's own pace. Freed of the pressure to follow (and respond to) the latest breaking results in congested areas, one can afford to focus on problems, and not paradigms. Although the world is shrinking, these tastes might remain, even after no one in the scientific community is really that remote. That reflective character might be sharpest in fields where Swedish researchers take the lead. However, that speculation, like all the other explanations offered here, is but a speculation, attempting to understand "how the Swedes do it," producing such interesting and thoughtful work. It is altogether possible that the explanation is not structural at all, but a product of the personal commitments of the individuals who founded this research tradition as well as those who, today, are sharing the load. Whatever the explanation, I hope that they keep it up.

Author Index

Subject Index